Owners of the Sidewalk

GLOBAL INSECURITIES

A series edited by Catherine Besteman and Daniel M. Goldstein

Duke University Press   Durham and London   2016

# Owners of the Sidewalk

Security and Survival in the Informal City

Daniel M. Goldstein

Printed in the United States of America on acid-free paper ∞
Designed by Natalie F. Smith
Typeset in Quadraat by Westchester Publishing Services

Library of Congress Cataloging-in-Publication Data
Goldstein, Daniel M., [date] author.
Owners of the sidewalk : security and survival in the informal
city / Daniel M. Goldstein.
pages  cm—(Global insecurities)
Includes bibliographical references and index.

ISBN 978-0-8223-6028-5 (hardcover : alk. paper)
ISBN 978-0-8223-6045-2 (pbk. : alk. paper)
ISBN 978-0-8223-7471-8 (e-book)

1. Street vendors—Political activity—Bolivia—Cochabamba.
2. Markets—Government policy—Bolivia—Cochabamba.
3. Informal sector (Economics)—Political aspects—
Bolivia—Cochabamba.  4. Cochabamba (Bolivia)—History.
I. Title.  II. Series: Global insecurities.
HF5459.B5G65 2016
381'.18098423—dc23
2015027536

Cover art:
Photograph by the author.

Frontis: F.1  Part of the Cancha, looking east. Photograph
by the author.

For my boys, Ben and Eli

# Contents

# Prologue

Don Silvio and I sit across from each other at a small wooden table in my office above the call center. The table, scarred with rings of Nescafé, has one short leg and tilts when either of us leans in. Nacho sits in a chair to my left; Don Silvio's associate, a dark unsmiling man whose name I didn't catch, sits to his right. Traffic noise and the cries of vendors slip through the open window overlooking Avenida Honduras. Diesel exhaust mixes with the smell of toasting wheat and wafts up from the sidewalk below.

The man across the table, Silvio Mamani, is the president of the trade federation representing the street vendors of Cochabamba. He wears a beaten brown fedora bearing the stains of many years selling juice on the streets of the city. Beneath it his hair is receding and wiry, not straight, full, and shiny black like that of most Bolivians. It is a contrast to his face, which is a caricature of the classically Andean: rich brown skin, sharply angled brow, hooked nose, protruding chin. Don Silvio speaks through clenched teeth, his lower jaw deviating from the line of his face, as though it had once been broken and never properly reset. He wears a blue denim shirt, black pleated pants, and battered black half-boots with a zipper down the side. Don Silvio walks with a limp, dragging his bad leg behind him as he pushes his little juice cart through the market. He looks like a man with deep damage, like a case of fruit tossed from the back of a delivery truck. But there must be iron in Don Silvio as well for him to have attained the position he now holds.

I have invited Don Silvio here to my little office to talk about the possibility of doing ethnographic research with his organization, the *federación* of ambulant street vendors, or *ambulantes*. My work as a cultural anthropologist is based on establishing close, trusting relationships with the people whose lives I study, to understand their perspectives and experiences. I hope to discuss my research plan with Don Silvio, to get his blessing on the project, and to ask for his help in meeting his constituents.

The ambulantes who sell in Cochabamba's enormous outdoor market, the Cancha, are notoriously reluctant to talk to outsiders (figure F.1). This is not surprising. Ambulantes like Don Silvio can count themselves among the poorest people in Bolivia, Latin America's poorest country. The ambulantes of Cochabamba's sidewalks earn even less than the average Bolivian, who brings home a meager $500 a year. As street vendors, the ambulantes work in daily violation of municipal law, which prohibits selling on the street. So they are constantly harassed—chased from sidewalk to street corner by the police, insulted and abused by motorists and pedestrians, preyed on by shoplifters and muggers, and threatened with violence by other vendors who have established, legal venues. Yet with no better way to make a living in Bolivia's perpetually weak economy, they continue to work on the streets. If the ambulantes are mistrustful and closed, they have good reason to be.

I hope to study how market vendors survive amid the many perils they face on the city's streets, through work in what is often called the "informal" economy—the underground system of buying and selling that parallels the official economy. I am especially interested in the relationship between informality and illegality and with the ways in which informality and insecurity correlate in the marginal spaces of the Latin American city. In a post-9/11 world obsessed with security and with controlling threats to it, how do the urban poor, facing unrelenting insecurity, create and maintain personal safety and economic stability through informality? What is the relationship of the state to the informal economy and to the people whose livelihoods depend on it? What role does informality play in the operations of the state itself? These questions frame my research plan.

I explain to Don Silvio that I want to write a book about the lives of the ambulantes, and he eyes me, calculating, across the rickety wooden table. Don Silvio is no fool: he is a market vendor, a shrewd capitalist who understands the value of commodities, including information. He is also, without contradiction, a committed socialist who knows that struggles for social justice are best accomplished through solidarity, a concern for the common good, and the strategic deployment of collective resources. Don Silvio knows that he can grant me access to the ambulantes, and he has something to ask of me in return.

Don Silvio leans in closer, causing the table to tilt in his direction, and tells me his dream: to build a market for the ambulantes. His stony countenance softens as he talks, his flat black eyes kindled by an inner light. The market will be the ambulantes' to administer, he says, and stalls within it will be distributed equitably to members of the ambulantes' federation. "We will run the market ourselves," Don Silvio says. "It will be our market."[1] The market will have two stories—"It has to have two stories, carajo!"—with cement floors and a good roof to block the punishing sun and the seasonal downpours. The entrances and exits will be gated, to control access and to ensure that any delinquent who wanders in will have a hard time getting out again with stolen property. In that market, Don Silvio believes, the ambulantes will be transformed from roving street vendors, poor, dirty, and despised, into citizens with rights, able to earn a decent, reliable living. It will be like alchemy.

The other man, Don Silvio's brooding associate, offers some context. He says that Don Silvio and his colleagues in the federation's leadership have only just begun talking about a market. For years they and their constituents have been selling on the streets of Cochabamba, and a market of their own has never seemed an idea worth entertaining. Too remote, too impossible. But now they are getting organized. For the first time, the ambulantes have formed their own federation, with their own elected leaders. For the first time they are out from under the control of the comerciantes de puesto fijo, the vendors with fixed market stalls who are their direct competitors in the Cancha but who historically have controlled the federations to which they, the ambulantes, have always belonged. With their own federation, and with Don Silvio as their president, the ambulantes can set their own agenda. People are beginning to think big. "A market of our own," the brooding man says, smiling now. "Just imagine!"

We are silent, Nacho and I and our visitors, all of us contemplating the enormity of this fantasy. I, for one, am skeptical. The likelihood of the ambulantes' getting their own market is infinitesimal. The costs would be too high, the real estate too scarce, the political pressures against it too great for such a thing ever to come to pass. But in the faces of Don Silvio and his *compañero* I can see the light of true believers. They clutch at this idea with the ferocity of men clinging to a life raft, and they are not going to let go of it easily.

"*Bueno*," Don Silvio says to me, returning to the business at hand. "How can you help?"

# Acknowledgments

The research on which this book is based began in 2005 and continued through 2012, the bulk of it conducted between June 2006 and August 2007, although I continued to make six- to eight-week return visits during each of the subsequent summers. For their assistance with this project, I thank Rose Marie Achá, Eric Hinojosa, and Ruth Ordoñez, as well as the pseudonymous Nacho Antezana. I am, of course, eternally grateful to the men and women of the Cancha who allowed me to work with them and to write about their lives. In particular, I am thankful for the collaboration of the men I call Don Rafo and Don Silvio, whose help and assistance, while not disinterested, was fundamental to the success of my project.

The material contained herein is based on work supported by the National Science Foundation under Grant No. 0540702. Any opinions, findings, and conclusions or recommendations expressed in this material are mine and do not necessarily reflect the views of the National Science Foundation. Portions of chapters 16, 22, and 29 previously appeared in the article "Color-Coded Sovereignty and the Men in Black: Private Security in a Bolivian Marketplace," *Conflict and Society* (2015). Some of the data from Chapter 32 was also used in a chapter titled, "Aspiration: Dreaming of a Public Policing in Bolivia," in *Ethnography of Policing*, ed. Didier Fassin (Chicago: University of Chicago Press, forthcoming).

I appreciate the collaboration and support of my colleagues at Rutgers University and the Department of Anthropology. Thanks to friends, colleagues, and students who have read and commented on parts of this book, especially Catherine Besteman, Asher Ghertner, Assaf Harel, David McDermott Hughes, and Ieva Jusionyte. In Bolivia, I extend my gratitude to Alberto Rivera, Humberto Vargas, Kathryn Ledebur, Lee Cridland, and Carlos and Anna Aliaga. I also thank the people who made it possible for me to present portions of this work in progress, provided comments, and otherwise supported me and my work on this project: Asad Ahmed, Carolina Alonso, Philippe Bourbeau, Pamela Calla, Diane Davis, Tessa Diphoorn, Susana Durão, Didier Fassin, Catarina Frois, Erella Grassiani, Carol Greenhouse, Michael Herzfeld, Rivke Jaffe, Gareth Jones, Don Kalb, Kees Koonings, Mark Maguire, Sally Engle Merry, Martijn Oosterbaan, Wil Pansters, Dennis Rodgers, Ton Salman, and Nils Zurawski. Gisela Fosado and the staff at Duke University Press have been great to work with on all of my books. Bill Nelson drew the maps, and Margie Towery provided the index. I thank my cousin, Lisa Berg, who provided many of the photos in the book. I appreciate the comments and feedback of the three anonymous reviewers, which were very helpful in shaping the final version of this text. Love to my family for all their support.

# 1. The Fire

The air in the Cancha is always brown and heavy with diesel fumes and the smoke of cooking fires, but this morning it smells like the whole place is burning. A dark cloud rises from Avenida Pulacayo, at the southern edge of the market sector called "La Pampa." Stepping out of the taxi, Nacho and I immediately head in that direction. Vendors in their stalls crane their necks to see what is happening; street vendors and their customers stop in their tracks, everyone frozen in mid-transaction by this unusual sight.

As we approach, the situation becomes clear: A section of the market is on fire. The furniture dealers—*comerciantes* who sell beds, chests, tables, and chairs, inexpensive stuff made from rough-hewn pine and eucalyptus—stand watching as an entire block of market stalls burns. Thick black smoke billows high into the morning air. The fire softens the metal stanchions that support the stalls' tin roofs, and they come down in a crash. Some people cry softly; others yell in fury and frustration, helpless to intervene. There are no emergency vehicles to be seen, just masses of vendors crowding Pulacayo and the adjacent streets and sidewalks, observing with curious empathy from their own places of business. Nacho and I stand transfixed alongside the other spectators, watching as people's livelihoods are consumed by the flames.

Finally, having destroyed everything combustible, the fire subsides, leaving behind an expanse of charred and twisted metal. Where once a hundred small businesses thrived, there is now a black, steaming field of debris. Vendors pick through the ashes, singeing their fingers on the still hot metal, looking for something to salvage. But little remains. The fire that originated in La Pampa's furniture section has spilled over into neighboring stalls, scorching the wares of other comerciantes: shoe peddlers, food sellers, clothing vendors. Amid the rubble the devastated comerciantes find a few worthless items—melted rubber sandals, charred signs, blackened metal racks on which they once displayed their merchandise—but nothing of value, nothing that might mitigate their staggering losses.

Hours later, municipal workers arrive: men in khaki jumpsuits wearing floppy khaki hats and women in rubber orange aprons and the white, broad-brimmed sombreros typical of Cochabamba valley women. They bring with them wheelbarrows and shovels; some have small hoses that they connect to local hookups and use to douse the hot spots remaining from the fire. They shovel ashes and debris into the wheelbarrows. Many of the vendors pitch in, already working to reestablish some kind of normalcy amid the ruins. The effort will continue for months.

In the aftermath of this calamity, comerciantes with stalls in La Pampa market look to assign blame. One culprit they identify is the municipal government, the Alcaldía of Cochabamba city.[1] The fire, it is eventually determined, began with a short in one of the electrical wires that bring light and power to the furniture sector of the market. As is the case everywhere in La Pampa, these wires have been strung haphazardly by the vendors themselves: self-help electrification to supply their businesses with the needed utility. The entire market, in fact, is powered this way, with one cable grafted onto another onto another onto another, a cat's cradle of electrical lines tenuously intertwined above the huge expanse of La Pampa. When one of these precarious connections sparks a conflagration in perhaps the most flammable section of the market, vendors throughout La Pampa attribute responsibility to the municipal government, whose refusal to provide infrastructure and services to the market has led to this disastrous, if predictable, outcome (figure 1.1).

Fire destroys, but its destructive power can also cleanse exposing layers of accumulated history. In La Pampa, this history includes the conflict between two groups of market vendors—the comerciantes de puesto fijo, who have fixed market stalls, and the comerciantes ambulantes, who do not—engaged in a life-or-death struggle for control of the commercial spaces of Cochabamba's Cancha marketplace. Comerciantes fijos blame the fire

1.1 The aftermath of the fire in La Pampa. Photograph by the author.

on the comerciantes ambulantes, and on those vendors who illegally purchased the right to sell on the street from the municipality. There are thousands of roving vendors selling an infinite number of wares on the streets and sidewalks of Cochabamba. These ambulantes have become an ever more frequent presence in the city in recent years. Most of them are concentrated in the interstitial spaces of the Cancha, Cochabamba's principal marketplace and the largest of its kind in the country. Ambulantes now clog the streets and sidewalks, the alleys and passageways of Cochabamba's Cancha, making movement difficult for shoppers and vendors alike. Usually the police chase them away, keeping them constantly on the move; but sometimes, as in this case, the municipality sells parcels of land to comerciantes who lack a fixed stall, often on the sidewalk or in the street itself, and allows them to set up shop. At the time of the fire, as many of the vendors with fixed stalls inside La Pampa are quick to point out, ambulantes and street stalls blocked Avenida Pulacayo, obstructing the timely arrival of emergency services that might have contained the fire before it completed its rampage through the furniture section. La Pampa comerciantes blame the street vendors for blocking access to the market and the Alcaldía for having allowed—indeed, for having profited from—the proliferation of street vendors on the market's fringes.

The conflict between fijos and ambulantes is an expression of the challenges facing people everywhere—not just in Bolivia but around the world—as they struggle to survive in today's globalized economy. In the second decade of the twenty-first century, good jobs are few, and the state provides no kind of safety net. As other forms of employment have disappeared amid a global economic transformation that has further contributed to the historic poverty of the world's poorest countries, more and more people across the Majority World (what is often referred to as the "global South" or "Third World" and includes Latin America, Africa, and parts of Asia) have moved to the cities and turned to small-scale commercial activity as a survival strategy.[2] Amid mounting poverty and diminishing alternatives, "informal" commerce proliferates worldwide, in many countries becoming the largest economic sector, employing the majority of the nation's workers.[3] Informal work enables the survival of those denied the prosperity generated by the restructuring of global capitalism and its flows of goods and finance—people who now constitute the majority of the global population.[4]

The rise of informal commerce has implications not only for individual vendors and their families but for entire cities and societies. As more people

1.2 Selling on the sidewalk. Photograph by the author.

become retail sellers, traditional urban marketplaces become overcrowded. The competition for livelihood spills out onto sidewalks, street corners, median strips, parks, doorsteps—vendors convert any open area into a place of business, stripping urban public spaces of their intended purposes and colonizing them for buying and selling (figure 1.2). Vendors compete for these spaces as they do for customers: urban public space becomes a private commodity to be bought and sold, with transactions governed by commercial syndicates, local politicians, and public officials. Markets like Cochabamba's Cancha—bright and colorful, so dynamic and lively and attractive to tourists—are in fact sites of furious contestation, battlegrounds where people war against the poverty that gnaws at them, and against each other as they fight for resources and control within an increasingly competitive commercial environment.

The La Pampa fire, and the subsequent conflict over where to lay the blame for it, also reveals the complex political contestations between citizens and the state—conflicts that can be found worldwide, wherever governments have labeled particular locations or populations "informal" or "marginal" or "illegal." Many observers regard places like the Cancha, locus of Bolivia's informal economy, as being outside state control, as though the government, the police, and the law were completely absent.

Informal spaces and the activities within them are often characterized as chaotic, disorderly, criminal, and dangerous, as lacking a state authority to regulate them. It is true that in marginal and informal contexts, the state provides little in the way of services or support to citizens—a condition that has proliferated in urban areas of the Majority World under regimes of neoliberal democracy and that contributes to their pervasive insecurity.[5] This fact is very clear to the comerciantes of La Pampa, who accuse the state of neglecting their needs to such an extent that the disastrous fire in the market became an inevitability. On this basis, it may be assumed that the state has simply abandoned the Cancha, that the market lacks any state presence whatsoever, and that disorder and devastation are the result.

Such assumptions fail on two counts. For one, they ignore the fact that the state is present in the Cancha in a variety of ways. The municipal government has long been involved in managing urban commerce and to the present day is active in determining who can sell what, when, and where. The Municipal Police (comisarios) are a daily presence in the market, regulating the activities of comerciantes and collecting payments and fines for any violations of municipal law. More fundamentally, the municipality itself is the owner of the Cancha—the government owns the land on which the market stands, and comerciantes must pay, day after day and year after year, for the right to sell there. In fact, the municipality has on many occasions attempted to privatize the Cancha, to generate more revenue for itself at the expense of those who depend on it for their livelihoods (see chapter 23). Comerciantes feel the weight of official presence and law in their daily affairs and fear what might happen to them if the authorities gained even greater control over what vendors consider "their" market. At the same time, however, the state does nothing to provide security for market vendors. The National Police are not present in the market (the result of a historical process described in chapter 22), leaving comerciantes entirely on their own to confront the threats to their livelihoods and personal safety that the precarity of market life presents. Rather than absent, then, in the Cancha, as in other informal urban spaces, the state is partially but not helpfully present. Elsewhere, I have called this phenomenon the "absent presence" of the state, a form of sovereign rule that imposes certain kinds of legal regulation but neglects others, making the state into a phantom, at once there and not there, a ghostly presence that generates more insecurity than it prevents.[6]

The second failure of the assumption that the state's absence leads to chaos lies in the origins of chaos itself. A subsidiary assumption here is that the state is a rational, formal institution governed by law. Rather than the spontaneous result of state neglect, the market's chaos (like that of other neglected spaces, including poor urban neighborhoods) is to a large extent engineered, an *organized disorder* that is the result of the state's presence rather than its absence. There are rules and laws, but they are inherently discriminatory, applying differently to people or categories of people. What is more, these rules and laws are enforced inconsistently and arbitrarily. In the process of enforcement, state actors themselves behave irregularly; they demand money from comerciantes, particularly from ambulantes, in a manner that goes well beyond their formal authority, or sell public spaces and allow them to be converted into private commercial spaces (as noted earlier; see also chapter 26). The rules themselves are often so vague that they permit a range of interpretations, allowing for the proliferation of irregularities that depend on the whim of the individual officer or, at a higher level, the political commitments of government authorities rather than a rule of law that applies equally to all.[7] The government will at one moment decry "illegal" selling in the streets, but at another moment it will sell the rights to set up market stalls on the sidewalk to a group of comerciantes willing to pay. For the urbanist Ananya Roy, this is the essence of informality, a condition in which "the law itself is rendered open-ended and subject to multiple interpretations and interests" so that the law becomes "as idiosyncratic and arbitrary as that which is illegal."[8] Roy calls this a condition of "deregulation," though I prefer to call it *disregulation*—the former term suggests a prior state of regulation that has since become undone. The informal, "chaotic" space of Cochabamba's Cancha marketplace is not unregulated. It was never regulated to begin with. It is, instead, disregulated— the state administers its own preferred forms of regulation while ignoring others, privileging a system of discretionary surveillance and enforcement. The government allowed the Cancha to emerge as a space of informal activity because informality was an expedient way both to manage the city's rapidly growing population and to satisfy its various needs while enabling administrations and officials to profit at the same time. This arrangement permitted the growth and evolution of informal marketing, and over time has produced the disorder that we find today (see chapters 8, 13, and 17). Not surprisingly, these areas of urban disregulation—what others have colorfully termed "red zones" or "brown zones" or "gray spaces" on the "margins of the state"—are also the city's most violent and insecure.[9]

This is important to understand, both for observers of cities and for those who run them. For one thing, chaos and criminality are not unique to the informal world. The journalist Katherine Boo, for example, whose book about urban informality in India, *Behind the Beautiful Forevers*, won a Pulitzer Prize, describes India's informal economy as "unorganized," implying that it lacks an order that characterizes the regular world and the formal economy.[10] As my brief description earlier demonstrates, however—and this point is reinforced throughout the chapters that follow—this overstates both the disorganization of the informal world and the organization of the formal one. States can act criminally and obey an informal logic, just as informal actors and institutions can be deeply rule-governed and formal in their operations. Furthermore, it is important to recognize that the intersection of insecurity and informality in the cities of the Majority World is not coincidental. As I will explore in more detail (see, e.g., chapter 16), the production of informality by the state has also led to the proliferation of insecurity in those same spaces, producing conditions of violence, uncertainty, and criminality that make life there so difficult.[11] Awareness of this calls attention to the insecurity of informal spaces as a historically produced, structural phenomenon that depends not on the nature of the "informals" who live or work there or on their propensity for illegal activities but on how these spaces have been configured over long periods of urban growth and state formation. It also alerts us to the many ways in which the urban poor—those who live and work informally and often illegally on the fringes of the global economy—are engaged in daily struggles to make their worlds more secure, bringing their own forms of order and security making to their lives and livelihoods.

One consequence of the informalization of urban life is the expansion of spaces only loosely controlled by the state. Here—in spaces like the Cancha marketplace or the peri-urban, "marginal" neighborhoods where I previously worked[12]—new forms of authority emerge, alternatives to state sovereignty that create their own kinds of order and security. But these new authorities also create insecurity, especially for the ambulantes, the poorest and most vulnerable workers in the market (chapter 22). Similarly, the informal spaces of the Cancha provide opportunities for people to challenge the rules that do exist, to push against them in ways that are both subtle and extreme, with the goal of expanding their commercial and political power.

In the Cancha, people work as individual agents but also as organized commercial guilds or syndicates (*sindicatos*) to make order within the market and to enhance their own security (points I return to in chapter 37).

Despite its insecurity, the Cancha allows people room to create for themselves a precarious economic and political security that otherwise is unavailable to them. The informal nature of the market permits people to organize and to make a living the only way they can: through street commerce. The work is dangerous, and people feel constantly insecure, but for some of them it provides opportunities that the formal economy simply does not.[13] For the occupants of the Cancha's market stalls—the comerciantes de puesto fijo—the market is their second home, and selling there is a tradition inherited from their parents, a passport to the middle class. For the city's poorest people, meanwhile, the Cancha's sidewalks and streets are places to establish some basic minimum of economic stability and family maintenance. The Cancha is a place to work when all other opportunities have been foreclosed, affording them the chance to earn just enough to feed their children for another day. For these people, the comerciantes ambulantes of the city's sidewalks, the Cancha is all about survival.

# 2. Writing, Reality, Truth

Anthropologists, jokes a friend of mine—herself a member of that strange and poorly understood tribe—are people who can make the most interesting subjects sound boring. Although they—we—study the world's most critical problems, work in all parts of the world with some of the most amazing people on the planet, when it comes to writing about our work anthropologists can be astonishingly dull.

There are, of course, some excellent anthropological writers, people who combine the insights of skilled observation with a talent for expressive communication. But anthropological writing often speaks to an audience— other anthropologists—that prides itself on complexity and theoretical ingenuity. Anthropological writers typically speak not to a general readership, but to other professionals like themselves. Like academics of any discipline or specialists in other fields, anthropologists use jargon, a professional language that serves as a shorthand for complex ideas, both well established and innovative, employing terms that cannot be operationally defined every time they appear. Of course, jargon can also be used simply to show off or to cover the fact that the writer does not really know what he or she is talking about. Whatever the motive, in academia, the complexity of the idea is sometimes believed to correlate with the complexity of the sentence. Some academics seem to regard good, clear writing as insufficiently complicated to be worthy of their consideration.

This book is an attempt to move beyond some of the limitations that academic conventions impose on ethnographic writing. It speaks to a broad audience without trying to oversimplify the conditions it describes. Indeed, writing accessibly does not mean we must sacrifice complexity or rigor in our analyses—we should not insult our readers with a priori assumptions about "dumbing down." But accessibility requires us to write above and beyond what Alfred Kroeber once called the "smog of jargon," to write in a way that reflects how people actually think and speak.[1] That can make anthropology a voice whose insights are heard outside the narrow realm of our discipline. Didier Fassin quotes the work of the French anthropologists Alban Bensa and François Pouillon, who contrast the writing of great novelists with that of anthropologists; they remark on "the unreal impression and tremendous boredom so often felt with anthropological and learned works," as if "the conventions and concepts of anthropology produced a smoke screen masking our relation to the world."[2] Who among us is not familiar with such sensations? In this book I have tried to write my way past the smog and smoke screens of academic conventions without losing the theory, the core ideas and analytics that distinguish ethnography as a genre.

This book is further motivated by an effort to represent the Cancha and the people who make their living there in all of their rich complexity, to present as far as possible both the *reality* and the *truth* of market life. By this I mean (borrowing from Fassin) that I seek to represent both the details of what exists and has actually happened (what Fassin calls the horizontal dimension of the "real") and a deeper, more vertical "truth" hidden beneath what is believed and generally accepted and that requires excavation.[3] The real includes empirical fact, whereas the true refers to the buried meanings and submerged histories that make the real meaningful. This is where anthropology has the edge over fiction. Novelists and other artists, Fassin points out, are masters of representing truth, albeit through an invention of the real that no ethnography would employ. Anthropology, by contrast, grounds its authority in its access to the real. This book, based entirely on fact, is an example: it is through extended field research that I have come to know and am able to report on what really happens in the Cancha and can offer interpretations of its truth that carry the weight of that experience. It is through attention to both of these cross-cutting dimensions of life— the real and the true, the horizontal and the vertical—that ethnography can make its unique contributions to knowledge.[4]

Nevertheless, there is much that we can learn from other kinds of writers, from other literary genres. In writing this book I have tried to pay attention to narrative and characterization, two features of novelistic writing that are often absent from books by anthropologists and other academics. Many of the chapters of this book are based on narrative descriptions of the fieldwork process, particularly with an eye to collaborative research and activist anthropology and the ways in which I tried to ground my work in those paradigms. I feature in the book as a character and narrator, leading the reader through the process of discovery that characterizes anthropological investigation. In doing so, I mean neither to celebrate myself as a conquering hero—my work was marked as much by stumbling inadequacy as by anything resembling heroics—nor to hold up my approach as a model for how anthropological fieldwork ought to be done (although I do have my biases, I admit). Nor do I attempt to make my personal experience the central object of study, as reflexive, first-person ethnographies are sometimes accused of doing. Rather, I use a first-person recounting of my experience doing research in the Cancha as an instrument to capture the reader's attention, to bring him or her into the frame of experience to make the Cancha, and my fieldwork there, feel both real and true. In doing so, I also try to say something about the Cancha itself and about the nature of field research under difficult political and social conditions.

There are, of course, many other important characters in this book. The story is structured around the activities and interactions of four individuals: Don Silvio, leader of the comerciantes ambulantes; Don Rafo, leader of the comerciantes fijos; Nacho, my field assistant and collaborator; and me. The key characters in this story, therefore, are all men. I attribute this to several factors. As a man, first of all, it was simply easier for me to get to know other men, to establish close personal relationships with them in a way that was harder with women. I did have many friendships with women in the market, especially with Doña Tahlia and Doña Rosa, and their perspectives feature prominently in the chapters that follow. I also include a gendered analysis of Cancha life and history—and particularly of Cancha politics—throughout the text. My emphasis on men's experience, however, also reflects the central fact that, since the days in which a previous generation of anthropologists were writing about Andean market women, far more men have entered the business of market selling (a fact I discuss in chapter 27). By writing about men's experience in the Cancha marketplace, I aim to explore a phenomenon about which very little anthropological work has been done. Overall, my hope is that, by rendering all of these individuals with empathy, humor, and an eye to truth, I have been able to portray them as real people with lives and concerns with which readers can identify, more than merely the producers of handy quips, ciphers meant to typify some aspect of Bolivian or market "culture."

Throughout the book, I have relied on direct quotations from interviews and fieldnotes to illustrate the points I make and to enliven the text by weaving natural dialogue into my descriptions. In nearly every case, quoted material is translated directly from recordings or my written notes. While all of the dialogue and events related in the text are real, in some places I have taken liberties with sequence, reordering some events in relation to others to provide a more coherent narrative flow. In other places, I have withdrawn my editorial hand entirely, presenting long sequences of actual speech, transcribed and translated directly from field recordings, allowing the voices of my counterparts in the Cancha to be heard (see especially chapter 32). Elsewhere I have included direct excerpts from fieldnotes, both mine and those of my collaborators. All of these techniques advance the narrative and provide an experience of the Cancha that is less mediated by the author's interposing his interpretive voice over that experience. Citations and more specialized discussions are in the endnotes so as not to interrupt the flow of the story.

The greatest challenge in writing this book has been to balance and present its diverse goals or themes. It offers a thick description of the daily reality of life and work in the Cancha; its historical formation, contemporary organization, and place within the broader urban environment of Cochabamba. In addition, it aims to provide insight into the direct experience of fieldwork, particularly collaborative, engaged fieldwork, through a narrative account of my research process. The book is also grounded in a theoretical reflection on the nature of informality and security/insecurity in the Cancha and comments critically about life on the fringes of the global economy. These different themes demand different approaches and different writing styles and required me to structure the book in a particular way. Instead of the long chapters typical of ethnographies, I divided the book into shorter chapters, each focusing on a particular theme or goal of the book. There were, perhaps, other ways to organize the text, but this seemed to be the most accessible and enabled me to provide the rich historical and structural context needed to understand contemporary Cancha life while maintaining the narrative arc of my experience. For readers who do not like a particular chapter or theme, I offer the same advice Mark Twain supposedly gave about the weather in New England: wait five minutes and it will change.

Anthropologists lead many lives. We are scholars and teachers, researchers and writers, concerned citizens and professional strangers.[5] To the people we study, we are threats and opportunities, freaks and friends. All of this cannot be contained in a single text, and this book does not try to be all things to all people. It does not look like a traditional ethnography; nor does it read like one. It cannot—nor does it attempt to—reproduce the insights generated by the important ethnographies of market life and informality in South America that have preceded it, although books such as Florence Babb's *Between Field and Cooking Pot*, Linda Seligmann's *Peruvian Street Lives*, and Daniella Gandolfo's *The City at Its Limits* are important influences. It does not provide complete coverage of the multistranded debates pertaining to markets and street economies in the urban global South or document the histories of those debates (although I discuss them in chapter 4). It does not claim to solve the "riddle" of the Cancha or to lay to rest the question of the formal and the informal that continues to trouble market researchers. It does provide a glimpse into one anthropologist's experience doing fieldwork in an urban market, where the fault lines dividing formal and informal, secure and insecure, legal and illegal are never abundantly clear. In the end, I hope this book inspires more questions than it attempts to answer.

# 3. Don Rafo

At the beginning of fieldwork, so much is yet to come. My meeting with Don Silvio of the ambulantes, the fire in the Cancha, the commitments and compromises of the activist research process—all of these are in the future. Now I have to make arrangements, make contacts, establish rapport. I have to get things going.

As I develop my plans to conduct research on insecurity in the informal spaces of the Cancha marketplace, I decide to focus my attention on the market's oldest and largest sector, La Pampa. Nacho and I understand that we have to target one market section to study it effectively and, given La Pampa's reputation for insecurity, it is the clear choice. For a few weeks Nacho and I (assisted by other members of my research team) have been doing informal reconnaissance in the Cancha,[1] exploring the different sections of the market, talking with vendors whom Nacho knows, with Padre Abelardo of the local Catholic church, trying to figure out how to begin our research. Now, having decided to focus our energy on La Pampa, we have arranged a meeting with Rafael ("Rafo") Punto, president of the Federación de Comerciantes de La Pampa (FCP), one of the market's largest organizations of comerciantes fijos. To do the kind of work we envision, we will need Don Rafo's permission and help in getting started: we need the blessings of the leader of the federation if we hope to talk to his constituents. I wipe my hands nervously on my pants as Nacho and I wend our way through the market's alleys to the *plataneros'* (banana sellers') section, on the far side of La Pampa, almost to the market's eastern border at Avenida República, and the stall of Don Rafo.

Rafo Punto owns a banana stall, but he is no platanero. For more than ten years, he has run the FCP as his own personal fiefdom. A classic *caudillo*, Don Rafo is a charismatic bulldog of a man.[2] His charisma derives not merely from his personal qualities, as I will discover with time and observation, but also from his ability to command the world of the Cancha, to harness its resources and put them to work in the service of his various projects.[3] With graying hair, a winning smile, and a face as smooth and uncreased as his sharply pressed slacks, Don Rafo looks more like an executive than a market vendor and spends his days like one. While various relatives tend to his shops (he owns a couple of hardware stores in addition to the banana stall), Rafo does politics. He solves problems. Rafo visits his constituents throughout La Pampa, promising solutions to their problems and accepting their gratitude for problems already resolved. Rafo talks to the media, communicating the problems of the market to a wider public. He hustles politicians, trying to bring the resources of the municipality to bear in resolving the market's problems. This is not easy work, and it explains his interest in talking to me, an outsider who may offer much needed resources in dealing with market insecurity.

Don Rafo is a man with political connections and political ambitions. To begin our meeting, he boasts of his many contacts in the municipal government, the media, the police force, and the *Intendencia* (the municipal department that supervises urban commerce). He has the cell phone number of the mayor and speaks of President Evo Morales as though he were a personal friend. "Everyone asks me," Don Rafo says, "'Why don't you run for office? You could be Mayor of Cochabamba!'"[4] But Rafo is biding his time, waiting for the right moment to make his move. With Morales campaigning for reelection, Rafo wants to see how the political situation shakes out. In the meantime, he cultivates his reputation as the president of the FCP, his springboard to bigger things.

Even before I can explain our purposes, Don Rafo knows who we are and why we are there. He is frank about his ambitions and the potential role of my research in them. Our research project, he tells us, is of tremendous importance to him, as security is one of the greatest problems facing comerciantes in La Pampa. A study of the causes and possible responses to market insecurity will be of great value to him and his constituents as they organize to improve the situation. Beyond that, Rafo confesses, this research on security will serve to show his constituents that he is someone who follows through on things, a man who can address their most troubling issues. Our success in this project, Don Rafo tells us, will be his success. "I will rise and fall with you," he says and shakes our hands with feeling.

Nacho and I are skeptical. Rafael Punto is too skilled a politician to place his reputation in the hands of a *gringo* researcher and his oddball Bolivian colleague. Nevertheless, his statement is a welcome one for our project. It expresses a personal investment in the success of our research and a promise that he will do all he can to help us move the project forward. Plus, we know that while the issue of security is politically charged, it nevertheless remains a critical matter to the men and women who work in the Cancha each day. Whatever political hay Don Rafo might make of our work, security is a topic of great concern to ordinary folks, as well, and we expect that our research will be of great interest to the comerciantes of the market.

But Don Rafo wants concrete results. Doing a study and publishing a book in English will not help him reach his political goals; nor will it help his constituents deal better with problems of insecurity in the market. The comerciantes could not care less about being "given a voice" in a U.S. classroom. No, what Don Rafo wants is a book, in Spanish, based on what he calls "a scientific study" that documents the problems of insecurity in La Pampa. This book will give him the evidence he needs, something he can present to the authorities as proof that they are not doing enough to provide security for the market. He emphasizes this point repeatedly—it has to be a *scientific* study. I am skeptical generally about the notion of anthropology as a science, and Rafo's insistence that objective science be somehow deployed to support his predetermined political ends strikes me as both amusing and problematic. Nevertheless, I understand what Rafo means. This project is to be more than simply a statement of opinion, something that he could do himself; it is to be a solid piece of research based on data that support its claims, written by an outsider with no stake in the outcome. If I promise to write that book, Rafo will introduce me to his constituents, who can serve as the subjects of my research.

The arrangement suits me fine, and I tell him so. Rafo suggests we come back the following Tuesday, when the comerciantes of La Pampa will be celebrating Carnaval, so he can introduce us around.

# 4. The Informal Economy

Despite economists' continuing attempts to define and inventory the informal economy, reliable measures of it are scarce. In an economy in which everything is illegal, disreputable, or simply unfathomable, firm numbers are hard to come by. How many glasses of quinoa juice does a Cochabamba quinoa juice vendor sell in a day? All the quinoa juice vendors taken together? When even the quinoa juice vendors do not know and are not the least bit interested in talking to anyone who might be trying to find out? Informality, by definition, eludes measurement.

But the extent of Cochabamba's informal economy is readily on display for anyone who spends even five minutes in that city's enormous Cancha marketplace. The market is an explosion of sounds, colors, and smells, packed from sidewalk to sidewalk with vendors selling everything imaginable. Especially on market days—Wednesdays and Saturdays in Cochabamba—the streets and sidewalks are impassable, clogged with the carts, wares, and bodies of street vendors. Between the stores and fixed market stalls, the ambulantes set up shop wherever they can find space. Sellers of food and drink park their carts at every available curb and street corner. Women sit right on the sidewalk, spreading their merchandise on blankets, the folds of their multilayered skirts, called *polleras*, splayed on the ground beneath them. Men walk through the crowd, holding out watches, radios, DVDs, or packages of men's briefs, trying to entice buyers. Others push wheelbar-

4.1  A young ambulante sells bread out of a wheelbarrow. Photograph by Lisa Berg.

rows full of small things—hardware, soap, cosmetics, bananas, bags of rice—and pedestrians somehow have to make space to let them through or risk being run down. "La Cancha tiene de todo," says my friend Nacho, "y todo el mundo viene." The Cancha has everything, and everybody comes to the Cancha.[1]

Amid the noise and crush of this carnival of commerce, very little that is bought or sold is formally registered or recorded, and many of the people doing the selling have no formal right to be there. This trade constitutes the informal economy of Cochabamba, mainstay of national economic life (figure 4.1). But what does informality actually mean in this setting? In many ways, the concept obscures more than it reveals.

.............................

Since the early 1970s, scholars have used the idea of the "informal economy" or the "informal sector" to describe the work done by rural migrants to African and Latin American cities.[2] As opposed to those who hold a job and earn a regular wage, migrants and the urban poor more often base their livelihoods on self-employment and petty capitalism. Unlike jobs that are steady, well paying, and skilled, work in the informal sector is identified as generally unskilled, easy to get, low paying, and done largely by an immigrant workforce.[3] With the "discovery" of the informal economy, many scholars began to conceptualize these distinctions within a dual framework that posed the formal and the informal as separate, bounded socioeconomic domains.[4] In 1972, the International Labor Organization popularized the notion of dual sectors, identifying the informal sector as including the activities of "petty-traders, street hawkers, shoeshine boys and other groups of 'underemployed' on the streets of the big towns."[5] In addition, scholars understood informal economic activity as occurring outside the awareness and control of the state.[6] In a subsequent turn that focused on the "extralegal" nature of this kind of work, Manuel Castells and Alejandro Portes defined the informal as being that which is "unregulated by the institutions of society, in a legal and social environment in which similar activities are regulated."[7] For some analysts, the informal and the illegal were one and the same.[8] The Peruvian economist Hernando de Soto, for example, in a well-known study of the informal economy in Lima, defined informality as "illegality . . . designed to achieve such essentially legal objectives as building a house, providing a service, or developing a business."[9] People become informal to escape legal regulation, de Soto suggested, setting themselves up outside the law because the law and the legal bureaucracy are so onerous that they discourage people from operating legally. This argument had significant real-world consequences: it was taken up by promoters of neoliberal policies, who argued that a minimalist state would erect fewer hurdles to capitalist development, resulting in more robust economic efficiency, capital creation, and poverty reduction, thereby reducing the number of informal/illegal workers.[10]

"Informality" also came to be a familiar buzzword in discussions of urban housing. The shantytowns, slums, and squatter settlements created by rural-to-urban migrants—sometimes through invasions of public land and the "autoconstruction" of housing by the residents themselves, in other places through the unregulated purchase of land from private vendors—were understood as part of the informal system of housing in the Latin American city.[11] As with employment, scholars often described the informal housing market as though it were separate and distinct from the formal market, with the latter regulated by state law while the former supposedly operated in its absence—that is, illegally.[12]

Anthropologists, economists, and sociologists have long debated the precise meaning of the term "informal" and what, exactly, constitutes the informal economy.[13] Clearly, large numbers of people in Latin America—as much as 50 percent of the region's population, according to some estimates[14]—work in jobs that require neither white nor blue collars. These people work without contracts, guaranteed wages, pensions, social security, environmental safeguards, or legal guarantees of workers' safety and health—all measures of employment informality.[15]

Yet as many scholars have observed, to say that informality exists does not mean that we can easily identify a coherent "informal sector."[16] Many people, for instance, simultaneously hold both formal and informal jobs, sometimes switching between them in the course of a single day. Under neoliberalism (see chapter 6), increasing job "casualization"—the reduction of employers' guarantees to workers, with permanent jobs becoming subcontracted or temporary employment—means that many people work formal jobs but lack the benefits that such jobs once promised. Many formal-sector workers live in informal housing that they have illegally constructed. Families and households have some members who work formally while others work informally.[17] And many people with formal jobs either manage and employ informal workers, buy things from informal sellers, or have other routine contacts with people doing informal work. In terms of housing, many neighborhoods dismissed as "illegal" slums in fact consist of a heterogeneous mix of homes, purchased, built, and regularized in a variety of different ways on land that is both legally and illegally occupied.[18] Drawing a line around the formal and the informal, the legal and the illegal, as though they constituted distinct and bounded sectors is thus deeply problematic.

The blurring of the lines between "sectors"—what the anthropologist Daniella Gandolfo calls informality's "radical fluidity"—can be illustrated by looking at the two kinds of vendors who sell in the Cancha marketplace.[19] Cochabamba's comerciantes ambulantes represent a population that survives off work that in most senses can be understood as informal. The work the ambulantes do is officially prohibited—city ordinances ban street vending, and the ambulantes are constantly in violation of codes that forbid vendors from setting up shop on street corners, from blocking vehicular and pedestrian traffic, from selling without a license, or from being a public nuisance. Many ambulantes sell contraband, items brought into the country illegally for sale in the market at reduced prices. All of the ambulantes' transactions go unrecorded, and they pay no taxes on anything they sell. Their very existence is unrecog-

4.2 A comerciante de puesto fijo. Photograph by Lisa Berg.

nized and unregistered by any official agency, and they receive no benefits through their work, such as health care, disability insurance, or retirement. By any of these measures, the ambulantes are informal workers in the national economy.

But the comerciantes ambulantes are not the only informal workers in the Cancha. The vendors who sell from fixed market stalls—the comerciantes de puesto fijo—are economically better off than the ambulantes and officially recognized by the municipality (figure 4.2). These vendors have legal permission to sell and established locations from which to conduct their business. Fijos are vehement, sometimes violent opponents of the ambulantes, whom they view as illegal interlopers who poach their clientele and deprive them of profits that rightly belong to them. Although some fijos regard the ambulantes with quiet tolerance, many others would like to see them forcibly driven from the streets and consider the Alcaldía criminally responsible for their presence in the market. The response to the fire in the La Pampa market (see chapter 1) is an illustration of this sentiment. For their part, many ambulantes consider the fijos brutal, selfish villains, people with resources who cannot bear to share the wealth with their poorer brethren. The animosity between these groups is a palpable presence on the Cancha's sidewalks.

But the fijos, though part of Bolivia's formal economy, are simultaneously part of its informal economy, as well. Although they enjoy the legal right to sell from their puestos, much of what the fijos sell is contraband. Like the ambulantes, the fijos report little to the state, give no receipts, pay little to nothing in the way of taxes, and receive no social benefits for their work.[20] In addition, many fijos employ ambulantes to sell their goods in the street, or they work as ambulantes doing the same thing. Although openly antagonistic to the street vendors, people with fixed stalls commonly take up selling in the streets as a way to supplement their income (see chapter 25).[21]

Perhaps even more surprising, the physical structure of the Cancha is itself informal and illegal. As the incident of the fire among the furniture stalls makes clear, the municipality invests little in the marketplace, the existing infrastructure put there by the vendors themselves (the wires in which the fire began are an example). Although on paper the Cancha is publicly owned—the municipal government is the official owner of the market puestos—in practice everything is privately held, sold, and traded. This has produced a huge secondary market for real estate that operates in the Cancha entirely without official sanction, and many market vendors are involved in the illegal transfer of puestos or the rights to sell from them (see chapter 31). Comerciantes fijos invest huge sums of money in these transactions, and the market stalls, illegally owned and acquired, are the repositories of vast quantities of unmeasured capital.[22] Again, no records of any kind track these exchanges and investments, no measures of their magnitude are taken, and state authorities are not involved in the transactions.

Like the dual sectors model, which assumes that the informal exists as a bounded domain set apart from the formal, this example demonstrates that calling the informal economy a zone of illegality and unregulation mischaracterizes what is in fact a domain of constant flux, of perpetual slippage between the legal and the illegal.[23] Indeed, as other scholars have noted, the existence of the formal depends on having an informal counterpart against which it can be contrasted. Without the illegal, in other words, there is no legal. And these distinctions are heavily value-laden: to classify one thing as formal and another as informal is to praise and reward the one and to marginalize, condemn, and "illegalize" the other. For some local actors, something can be seen as licit or "legitimate" even though it might technically be illegal, while other things—taxes, for example—can seem illegitimate to local people even if they are formally licit.[24] The anthropologist Alexander Dent has noted something similar regarding piracy—the unauthorized reproduction and circulation of goods and services—which is an important dimension of the global informal economy. By labeling some things pirated or illegal, powerful institutions can determine who can and cannot participate in the formal, mainstream economy, relegating others to the informal realm.[25] Yet in practice the pirated and the "legitimate" are not separable and distinct: indeed, they are intimately linked, much as the formal is to the informal and the legal is to the illegal. As Dent says, "Without piracy, there is no 'legitimate' circulation."[26]

The same thing can be said of informal selling in the Cochabamba market: the formal requires the informal for its very survival. What we consider formal and legal may in fact be shot through with informality and illegality, and vice versa. These are themes that will reappear, in different ways and in the discussion of different practices and institutions, as the story that follows unfolds.

# 5. Nacho

Nacho stands at the corner of Lanza and Honduras, just outside our office, and counts his change. He has just bought a glass of orange juice from a street vendor and rests the glass carefully atop her little cart while he examines the coins in his palm. Suddenly there is a shout, and someone runs by him on the sidewalk, full speed, a blur at the edge of his vision. "He took my money!" a woman screams. "For God's sake, somebody stop him!" She is struggling to chase someone, but the sidewalk is crowded, and her long skirts and petticoats make it difficult to run. Nacho looks around. Isn't anyone going to help this poor woman? No, everyone else is watching curiously, backing away from the running thief. Nacho sighs, glances wistfully at his glass of orange juice, freshly squeezed and dewed with perspiration, and takes off after the guy. Within a block he has caught him—Nacho is strong and fast, and the thief is a skinny nothing of a guy, probably eighteen or so, with dirty clothes and dirty face, his greasy hair flecked with dandruff and soot. He is lying on the sidewalk now, collapsing as Nacho grabs him from behind. Nacho demands the return of the stolen money, but the guy pulls out a knife instead. Again Nacho sighs. He is a black belt in more than one martial art and has no desire to hurt anyone, but now he has no choice. He quickly disarms the guy with a swift kick that snaps his wrist and retrieves the black leather purse that the thief has dropped on the sidewalk. The thief takes off running, cradling his broken wrist, but Nacho lets him go, concentrating instead on what he has in his hands. In the purse is an enormous wad of cash, probably $10,000 in $20 and $100 notes. The woman who was robbed comes trotting up, one hand pressing her bowler hat to her head, out of breath but beaming. "God bless you," she says, over and over. "God bless you." Sobbing and panting, she hugs Nacho, who hands back the stolen purse.

Nacho laughs as he tells this story. The poor *cholita* with the layered skirts and the bowler hat is actually a money changer, carrying thousands of dollars in her wallet. But that money is not hers—she has it on credit from a rich moneylender, and had it been stolen, she would not in a lifetime have been able to pay it back. Seeing that much money all in one place has left Nacho bemused. This is one of the Cancha's many secrets—the wealth concealed amid the appalling poverty. The story is funny because it reveals what is supposed to remain hidden, a sudden glimpse of a different truth at the heart of the marketplace.

If anyone was prepared to discover that truth it was Nacho. My closest friend and constant companion in Cochabamba, Nacho (short for Ignacio) can be almost supernaturally perceptive, and as the story shows, he is always ready to thrust himself into new and unexpected situations, leaping into action while others remain apart. As guide, consultant, collaborator, and confidant, Nacho helped me toward many of the insights contained in these pages. Our work together led to understandings of the sort that only collaborative ethnographic fieldwork can produce.[1]

Nacho does not fit easily into any familiar category. In a country in which racial and ethnic divisions have long provided the basic organizing framework of social and political life, Nacho defies easy labeling (figure 5.1). He is a native speaker of Quechua (in addition to Spanish) but is not what you would call "indigenous" and does not think of himself in those terms. His upbringing was split between the countryside and the city, and he feels equally at home in both. He dresses however he wants, sometimes in the stained woolen sweater of a Cancha laborer and at other times in a track suit and sneakers. Nacho rejects Catholicism and Christianity—the religions of his family and his wife, as they are of the majority of Bolivians—and embraces his own peculiar blend of Eastern philosophies, including Taoism, Zen, and a vague sort of New Age spirituality. He is light-skinned and freckled, a few gray hairs beginning to appear among the black. He is tall and muscular, but he does not lift weights or take artificial supplements. Instead, he uses herbal remedies to treat what ails him. He likes to

5.1 "Nacho." Photographer unknown.

drink *yerba mate* as the Argentines do, sucking the warm, grassy beverage through a straw from a metal cup that he carries around in his ubiquitous yellow backpack. Nacho eats like a horse but does not gain weight, and he drinks like a fish, to the dismay of his wife, Veronica, who calls me when she does not know where to find him. On his iPod is a mix of contemporary pop, classic Bolivian folk music, and the droning chants of Chinese Buddhist monks. Nacho dances the traditional Bolivian folkloric dances of the Morenada and the Diablada, and in his youth he led a high-stepping Caporales dance troupe in Bolivia's national Carnaval celebration. He plays the charango, and when he was a teenager he won international competitions on the instrument. Nacho takes every opportunity to meditate—he will close his eyes on a crowded city bus, earbuds in, and you will think he has gone to sleep, but he jolts to attention when the bus reaches his stop and clambers off refreshed. Nacho can talk to anyone and make anyone laugh, although he is his own best audience. He is at ease with the roughest street thug and the meanest cop, speaks Quechua to all of the old market ladies, and dances at every fiesta. He is consistently voted "most charismatic instructor" at the *tecnológico* where he teaches classes in electronics. Although he has no training in the social sciences, his odd combination of qualities and talents make him an excellent fieldworker and ethnographer. I often tell him that he is a born anthropologist.

When he was a very young boy, Nacho lived with his family in a village called Santa Rosa, on the frontier between the states of Cochabamba and Potosí. His father, a journalist by trade and a native of the Beni, one of Bolivia's tropical lowland departments, had come to Santa Rosa in the early 1970s to report on some long-forgotten matter. But he met Nacho's mother, fell in love, and never went back to the tropics. The couple bought land and turned to farming while raising Nacho and his two older siblings.

But Nacho was a sickly boy, weak and short of breath, and no local doctor could diagnose the problem. So when Nacho was eight years old, his father took him to the Hospital Viedma, Cochabamba's oldest and most established medical center, to try to find out what was wrong. The doctors diagnosed some sort of cardiac defect—Nacho's heart was not pumping enough blood to sustain him, they said, and his life was in danger. Without money to pay for a major operation, there was nothing they could do for the boy. They prescribed bed rest.

Nacho's father returned to his other responsibilities in Santa Rosa, leaving Nacho in the care of his grandmother, who lived in Cochabamba on a small plazuela in the city's historic downtown. For nearly a year Nacho was confined to his bedroom, forbidden by the doctors to exert himself for fear of inviting heart failure. Nacho's room had one small window that looked out on the plazuela and the busy Avenida Tumusla below. Lonely, bored, and depressed, Nacho spent hours staring out the window, watching the life of the plazuela: children playing, old men on benches chatting and watching passersby, the ubiquitous street vendors selling their wares, traffic going to and fro.

On a visit to his son in Cochabamba, Nacho's father happened to meet Justino, an Argentine teacher of martial arts who lived on the same plazuela as Nacho's grandmother. Justino was living in Cochabamba where he had opened a dojo, training students in his own idiosyncratic mix of kung fu and Zen Buddhism, some of it with roots in the ancient Shaolin teachings of China, some of it straight out of Southern California. Justino believed that inactivity was harming Nacho's chances of a recovery, a belief that Nacho's father shared, and the two men came to an agreement: Nacho would live in the dojo and study with Justino, with the idea that rigorous physical and spiritual training would cure what Western medicine could not. Nacho moved his few possessions from his grandmother's apartment to a small, windowless closet at the back of the dojo. It would be his bedroom for the next nine years.

Under Justino's tutelage, Nacho flourished. He went to the local school in the mornings and spent the rest of the day studying martial arts—jiujitsu, tai chi, but mostly kung fu, what Nacho would later call his *arte madre*, the principal discipline of his training.[2] Justino also taught Nacho how to eat (a lot of protein and grains, but also vegetables and fruit) and how to use herbs to treat infirmities. Nacho was fascinated and quickly became an expert in the rich Bolivian herbal pharmacopeia, making frequent trips to the Cancha to buy various plants and herbs, from which he would fashion *mates*, poultices, and vapors for himself, his grandmother, and his friends at the dojo. As Nacho grew stronger, his heart ailment—which the doctors said could not be cured without surgery that his family could not afford—simply disappeared. A year after Nacho moved in with Justino, his doctor could find no sign of what had seemed a permanent disability.

The years of living in Justino's dojo transformed Nacho from a skinny, fragile boy into a strong and flexible young man. But Nacho was a young man being raised without parental supervision, and although Justino did his best to monitor the boy, Nacho had a tendency to wander off on his own. As a teenager, Nacho began to explore the city, particularly the Cancha and some of its darker corners. Nacho developed a taste for *chicha*, the sweet, yellow corn beer served in bars throughout the city, and began to spend his evenings running with a different crowd from the kids at the dojo. Some of them were homeless kids, glue sniffers and petty thieves, filthy from living on the street—kids much like the purse snatcher Nacho would later waylay sprinting down Avenida Honduras. Others were burglars and car thieves, guys who stole from people elsewhere in the city and brought their stuff to sell in the Cancha's notorious Barrio Chino. Nacho was wholesome and naïve compared with these men, but he was fit and could defend himself, and they found him amusing and let him hang around. It was from them that Nacho learned to speak the rich slang of *el hampa*, the criminal underground, and explored the demimonde of Cochabamba's informal nightlife. But Nacho was always a tourist in these shadier districts, his running with the bad guys a kind of personal exploration of his own limits and possibilities. Always, his grounding in martial arts and the broader questions of health and healing pulled him back from whatever edge he might have fallen over. But he never cut ties with some of his old buddies, and when he disappears of an evening, alarming his wife and turning up sodden and smelly the next morning, it is with these friends that he has passed the night.

Nacho finished high school and enrolled in a technical college, where he studied electronics and electrical repair. This was not such a departure, it turns out: Nacho, always fascinated by flows—the channeling of energy through the body in tai chi, the liquid movements of the martial artist, of the saber and the nunchucks—was drawn to the flows of energy in electrical systems, the circuits and wires that make up the nervous systems of electronic devices, and the movement of electricity through their components. On his own time he studied computers and engineering and learned how to control the flow of his bodily energy through Reiki, which he learned from a local teacher.

Like most Bolivians, Nacho had to piece together a living for himself using his array of talents to generate an income. Nacho dreamed of opening a holistic healing center where he would deploy his knowledge of herbs, physical training, and energy flow to work with patients, but until such a time came he needed to survive. So Nacho found work. He did electrical repairs and installations in homes and businesses, built computers from the ground up, and taught electronics courses at a technical college in the city. In the evenings, he gave classes in martial arts—tai chi, especially, but also kung fu and sometimes judo—at the public gymnasium downtown and at the fancier *Formas* gym on the north side, where the children of the wealthy go to lift weights and do aerobics. When Justino decided to return to Argentina, Nacho began training in a dojo that belonged to a German expatriate named Georg. It was through Georg that I met Nacho.

I was doing research on crime and insecurity in the barrios of Cochabamba's south side, assisted by a team of four researchers: Eric, Ruth, Rose Marie, and Georg.[3] As part of our project, we offered free martial arts classes to children in the barrio, a service that local parents—always worried about the safety of their children in a violent city—received with enthusiasm. When the classes began to conflict with Georg's other responsibilities, he suggested that we hire Nacho to lead them. This was a stroke of genius. Nacho proved to be a wonderful teacher, able to coax even the shyest girl out onto the mat, to convince the toughest boy in the group to do the crab walk, and to motivate a group of barrio kids to bow to the teacher while murmuring polite phrases in Chinese. Nacho's class combined intense physical exercise with martial arts, so by the end of the hour everyone was exhausted. Most important, Nacho's class was never about violence. Martial arts for him is about self-control, learning to use your body deliberately in the world, to prevent violations of your integrity and to restrain yourself from violating that of others. Under Nacho's instruction, the barrio children became so expert they went on to win citywide competitions in judo and jiujitsu, competing against kids from much wealthier communities on the city's north side.

Nacho soon proved capable of much more than martial arts instruction. As we began to spend time together, talking about the topics and methods of my research, I found that he had an almost instinctive knack for anthropology. His fundamental confidence, intelligence, and charm made him a gifted fieldworker, and his ambiguous social position (light-skinned, Quechua-speaking, educated but of indeterminate socioeconomic class) enabled him to talk to anybody, about anything. From the lowliest shoeshine boy to the mayor of Cochabamba, no one could refuse Nacho, making him an invaluable research assistant. Plus, I enjoyed his company. Always laughing, always chattering about whatever came into his head, Nacho was an engaging companion as I navigated the trials of fieldwork.

And fieldwork suited Nacho. He liked earning a living from his brain instead of his body, and the work paid well. He enjoyed the research, enjoyed being outside talking with people and learning about their lives. For our other colleagues on the research team, Nacho had a cool contempt: they were office workers, in his opinion, more comfortable behind a desk or at a computer than out working in the field, engaging with the world. But he felt a kinship with me, that despite our very different backgrounds we shared an appreciation for the stories that people could tell about their lives.

When I decided to begin a research project on insecurity and daily life in the Cancha—a spinoff of the work I was doing in the barrios—I asked Nacho to be my principal research assistant and collaborator. He was happy to accept. Nacho was the ideal counterpart for the project. He had a deep personal knowledge of the Cancha, having spent a good part of his youth there, buying herbs for his therapeutic remedies and running with the less reputable characters of the market's underworld. Nacho taught me how to find my way around the vast, winding, ever changing expanse of the marketplace; to identify the many unfamiliar items being sold and understand their uses. He was my colleague as well as my guide, helping to set up and conduct interviews, record observations, propose interpretations of our experiences, and suggest new avenues of investigation. It also did not hurt that Nacho was streetwise and could handle himself in a fight. As we walked through the crowded marketplace, Nacho would position himself behind me, one hand resting gently against my back, eyes scanning for pickpockets and muggers. I felt very secure in Nacho's company, as he literally had my back in many potentially dangerous situations. We joked that he was my *guardaespaldas*, my bodyguard, but it was not far from the truth.

# 6. The Bolivian Experiment

The informal economy, as chapter 4 suggests, is not as separate and distinct from the formal economy as those concepts would lead one to believe. Nevertheless, it is almost impossible to talk about economic life without employing the distinction. For all of its limitations, "informality" remains a useful descriptor of the kinds of work that many people worldwide do daily.[1] Whether through various forms of unregulated commerce or in more obviously illicit activities such as drug dealing, smuggling, and prostitution, people everywhere and at all times have earned their living in ways that are not officially sanctioned by the state, without paying the proper tributes mandated by the state, and without receiving benefits from the state. Even little Susie who earns unreported income by babysitting and operates an (unlicensed!) lemonade stand in her driveway is part of the great informal economy that thrives the world over. A United Nations study reports the astonishing news that 85 percent of all new employment opportunities in the world today are in the informal economy.[2]

But nowhere is the informal economy as widespread and robust as it is in Bolivia. Although informality is notoriously difficult to define and measure, all available data show Bolivia to be the worldwide leader in this dubious statistic. Bolivia has the largest "informal sector" of any country in Latin America, with nearly 80 percent of employment in both rural and urban areas being in the informal economy.[3] As a share of gross national product

(GNP), Bolivia's informal sector is responsible for 67 percent of the nation's productivity—the highest percentage of any country in the world. (The U.S. informal economy, by comparison, accounted for 8.8 percent of GNP in 2002 and a study conducted in 2011 put it at 18–19 percent.[4]) About 70 percent of Bolivian workers are not registered in the nation's pension system—another indicator that the majority of workers have no official employment, and receive no kind of social benefits through their work. We need to regard such numbers with caution—it is ironic that the informal economy is widely reckoned to be unmeasurable owing to the very fact of its informality, yet at the same time entities such as the World Bank and the United Nations confidently state precise numerical measures of it. Nevertheless, these numbers do give a sense of the world-leading scale of Bolivia's informal economy. Understanding why this is the case requires a bit of historical excavation and is linked to the country's neoliberal political-economic transformation and accelerated urbanization during the past forty years.

Bolivia is a landlocked country in the heart of South America and, like most poor countries in the Majority World, it exists outside the awareness of most northerners (see map 6.1).[5] But the economic struggles that U.S. residents have faced since the start of the "Great Recession" reflect what Bolivians have been experiencing for decades: huge and widening gaps between rich and poor, with the nation's wealth increasingly concentrated in the hands of a small elite; the disappearance of steady, well-paying jobs with benefits; the rise of temporary, insecure forms of employment with dwindling options for health care and retirement; mounting debt and difficulty getting credit; higher education, with its promise of a better life, increasingly beyond the reach of the working poor and even the middle class; and a shrinking social safety net that heightens individual vulnerability.[6] All of these have characterized life in Bolivia since at least the mid-1980s, persisting in spite of the reforms initiated under the government of president Evo Morales.[7]

Bolivia is the second-poorest country in the Western Hemisphere (after Haiti) and has one of the highest levels of income inequality in the world. In Bolivia, as in the United States, a very small segment of the population controls the vast majority of the wealth. This distribution follows racial patterns in place since the colonial era: white people have the money while indigenous people and people of African descent largely do not, even though nonwhites make up the majority of the Bolivian population. Until relatively recently, these distributions of wealth and race could be mapped ideologi-

Map 6.1 Bolivia. Map drawn by Bill Nelson.

cally onto the Bolivian landscape: white people were in control of the nation's cities, while racial others, despite having an urban presence, were understood as properly belonging to the countryside.[8]

Not long ago, Bolivia was a predominantly rural society, with the majority of its people living in the villages and hamlets of the countryside and working as small-scale farmers or agricultural laborers. A significant percentage of the workforce was employed in the state-controlled mining industry, which produced the mineral wealth that had once inspired the Spanish to conquer the region. Some people worked in the country's lowland tropical zones—the Chapare of Cochabamba or the Yungas of La Paz—cultivating the coca leaf for both traditional uses—as tea, medicine, or an ingredient for indigenous rituals—or for the international cocaine trade.[9] Bolivia's cities, even into the 1970s, were small, somnolent affairs, maintaining much of their colonial character, evident in both their architecture and their social relations. Despite a predominance of poor indigenous and *mestizo* (mixed-race) residents, Bolivian cities were controlled by middle- and upper-class whites, who could still imagine their urban worlds as bastions of colonial society and privilege.

But things were soon to change, in Bolivia and throughout the world. Encouraged by global lending agencies such as the International Monetary Fund (IMF) and the World Bank and by the foreign governments that control these institutions (especially the United States), governments of poor countries in the 1970s began borrowing from Western banks to support large-scale development projects. Under the military dictatorship of President Hugo Banzer Suarez, Bolivia ran up a huge debt to these international lenders in an effort to spark internal development and to maintain the stability of the state. Loans financed expensive and ill-advised investments in mining and petroleum development and private loans to wealthy, large-scale cotton-growers in lowland Santa Cruz, Banzer's home region. These projects were largely unsuccessful, dependent as they were on falling world commodity prices, and produced little return on investment. Meanwhile, officials in the Banzer administration siphoned off large amounts of the borrowed funds, further impoverishing the country. Inflation skyrocketed; currency became overvalued; foreign borrowing continued; and in 1978, Banzer was deposed by the military, though none of the short-lived successor administrations could address the nation's financial crisis, either.

With the country buried under debt and caught in an intractable cycle of hyperinflation, the center-right government of Victor Paz Estenssoro came to power in 1985 and, under the guidance of Minister of Planning Gonzalo Sanchez de Lozada, immediately established a plan to "stabilize" the Bolivian economy.[10] Called the New Economic Policy (NEP), the plan was based on a blueprint for economic restructuring being promoted worldwide as a strategy for debtor nations to remake their struggling economies. In a departure from earlier proposals focused on state management of and investment in national development, the IMF and the World Bank by the 1980s were advocating a neoliberal policy prescription: allowing the free market to operate without state interference, they contended, would generate revenue and facilitate debt repayment. Neoliberalism also entailed deep cuts in social services that the state provided to its citizens in areas such as education, health care, and retirement. The international institutions—again with U.S. support—contended that the wealth produced under neoliberalism would ultimately benefit all in society: a rising tide, they claimed, raises all boats. (This approach was also a key rationale of "Reaganomics," then being rolled out in the United States, and "Thatcherism" in the United Kingdom, both premised on the hope of a "trickle down" effect, which never arrived but even today is invoked to justify free-market policies.) Threatened with the cutoff of additional foreign loans, Bolivia had no choice but to take up this basket of policies as part of an overall strategy of "structural adjustment." This wholesale adoption of externally imposed, neoliberal policies would come to be known internationally as the "Bolivian Experiment."[11]

Hailed for its economic restructuring, Bolivia became a model of austerity and the supposedly successful implementation of neoliberal economic "shock therapy."[12] Under the NEP, the Bolivian government instituted a strict monetary policy that quickly brought hyperinflation under control. Barriers to trade were lowered, and foreign investment was encouraged. In a move that would reverberate for decades, the state began to withdraw from direct involvement in the economy, privatizing publicly owned enterprises and sharply reducing the number of workers under its employ. Neoliberal policies were deepened and extended with the election to the presidency of former Planning Minister Gonzalo Sanchez de Lozada (known as "Goni") in 1993.

Neoliberal reforms had profound effects on rural people and communities.[13] In agriculture, for example, the state eliminated subsidies to farmers while cutting tariff rates and ending restrictions on the amount of foreign agricultural produce that could be brought in from other countries. As a result, imported food (grown in neighboring countries that still subsidized their farmers) poured into Bolivia, making it nearly impossible for Bolivian farmers to compete in local markets.[14] In the mining sector, largely state-run since the national revolution of 1952, private investment soared while national mines closed; some 25,000 unionized miners lost their jobs. Some displaced miners formed workers' cooperatives, but the state granted the rights to the better mines to private firms, leaving cooperatives with nearly depleted mines and little money to invest in new equipment or technology. The hydrocarbon sector was similarly privatized in 1993. Under an investment strategy called the Plan de Todos, the state gave private companies long-term leases that allowed them to extract subterranean oil and gas resources while it auctioned off the assets of the national oil company to private bidders. Transnational corporations became major players in the Bolivian hydrocarbon industry, but they made little investment in Bolivia itself, extracting the resources for export and processing elsewhere. Thousands of rural Bolivian workers lost their jobs in this "capitalization" of the oil and gas industry.[15]

If in 1985 Bolivia was a "poster child for neoliberalism's successes," by the mid-1990s it had become an exemplar of that philosophy's failures.[16] As in other countries where they were adopted, free-market policies enriched a small elite of capitalists and landowners, but overall economic growth slowed, and wealth inequalities worsened. The foretold trickle down never materialized, while wealth shifted from the public to private investors in a process the geographer David Harvey has termed "accumulation by dispossession."[17] The poor got poorer, in other words, as the rich got richer. State investment in basic services reached a nadir, augmenting the vulnerability of an already precarious population. Urban workers suffered, as the so-called flexibilization of labor—another hallmark of neoliberal philosophy—gave Bolivian employers the ability to replace long-term contractual and often unionized workers with short-term hires who were not guaranteed the benefits or pensions of traditional employment models. Tens of thousands of Bolivians found themselves unable to make a living from the occupations on which they, their parents, and their grandparents had always relied.

The neoliberal era in Bolivia fundamentally altered residential and work patterns in the country. Unable to depend on their traditional means of making a living, displaced miners, workers, and highland peasant farmers relocated to other parts of the country in search of economic opportunity. Movement—typically seasonal migration from the highlands to the lowlands and back again—had always been part of the family livelihood system on the Bolivian altiplano.[18] And, as I discuss in chapter 17, rural farmers from the Cochabamba valley had increasingly become reliant on a seasonal strategy of urban migration following the national agrarian reform of 1953. But from the 1980s on, the migrations of highlanders became more permanent than seasonal, as people abandoned their natal towns and villages to seek work elsewhere.[19] Some people displaced by neoliberal reforms—

especially tin miners, but also peasants and laborers—moved to the lowland Chapare region and began planting coca.[20] Many more relocated to the cities, and the urban centers of La Paz, El Alto, Santa Cruz, and Cochabamba experienced unprecedented population growth.[21]

For its entire history a predominantly rural society and economy, Bolivia became, in the course of a just a few decades, predominantly urban. This is revealed in national census figures. In 1950, only 34 percent of Bolivians lived in cities; today, the country is 67 percent urban, and that percentage is expected to climb to 75 percent by 2020.[22] Small towns have been transformed into big urban centers, their populations swollen by the arrival of migrants fleeing the poverty of the countryside. This reflects a pattern common throughout Latin America and the rest of the Majority World, where economic restructuring has produced similarly rapid urban growth. Whereas in 1900 only about 14 percent of the world's people lived in urban areas, today 51 percent of the world's population is urban.[23] This is expected to reach 70 percent by 2025.[24]

Around the world, people urbanize for a variety of reasons, but most go to the city in search of employment. The city for many symbolizes opportunity, possibility, and hope—for steady work, education for their children, home ownership, a chance for a better life. People are undeterred by the overcrowding, poverty, and filth that characterize many of the world's cities. They have seen the desolation, poverty, and filth of rural life in the neoliberal era and believe that they can do better, that their children can do better, in the city. Recall, though, that the decision to urbanize is not merely a matter of "rational choice," as the World Bank and other prophets of neoliberalism would like to suggest.[25] Poor, rural people do not simply weigh their options and choose the one that is most likely to yield the most rewards. The movement of people to the cities of Bolivia is often a last resort: dispossessed of their land, resources, and jobs, farm families often have no choice but to go elsewhere in search of opportunity.

But in the cities, too, opportunity is hard to find. Urban jobs are scarce, and without capital to invest or skills to trade on, most rural-to-urban migrants take whatever kinds of work they can find. Skilled workers take jobs as plumbers, electricians, carpenters, and mechanics, while the unskilled work as laborers, taxi drivers, or restaurant workers. Some men find work in construction, building the residential, commercial, and professional spaces of the expanding city. Some women take jobs as domestics, working for wealthier families in the better parts of town.[26]

6.1 An ambulante finds a place to rest on the street. Photograph by the author.

Many other people, men and women alike, turn to street vending as an economic survival strategy in the city (figure 6.1). Selling on the streets is a common practice today in cities around the world, as people unable to find other ways to make a living create their own work in an industry that seems to offer limitless possibilities.[27] In the city, widespread demand for cheap stuff means that if you can get your hands on something to sell, no matter how small and insignificant, you stand a chance of making a living. The fact that street vending is not obviously regulated also means that selling is open to virtually anyone. Street vending is often illegal, as it breaks the rules about who is allowed to sell, and where. It is also usually untaxed and unmeasured by the state. All of these facts makes street vending part of the informal economy.

Nowhere on earth does the informal economy play such a significant role in the survival of the national population as it does in Bolivia. Driven by need and the absence of alternatives, Bolivians have had to find new modes of economic survival. Even under the regime of Evo Morales—hailed by many as the harbinger of "post-neoliberalism," and marked by a series of reforms intended to address the nation's historical social and economic inequalities[28]—the promise of a sound economy with good jobs remains elusive amid an unrelenting neoliberal hangover. Bolivia, once the model of neoliberal development, is now the model of its desperate consequences for workers and their families.

This broader national and transnational context—of neoliberal transformation, rural dispossession, and urban migration—helps us to understand the local realities that unfold every day in the Cancha marketplace. The quotidian practices of workers in the informal economy are conditioned by these structural and historical processes, which are difficult to observe in the hustle and flow of daily life but are nonetheless necessary for making sense of the choices and behavior of individuals in their personal and professional lives.

# 7. Meet the Press

Even though Rafael Punto and the comerciantes fijos he leads are deeply antagonistic to the comerciantes ambulantes, I might never have met the ambulantes had it not been for Don Rafo.

It is the Friday before Carnaval, and the thumping baseline of my Bolivian ringtone jars me out of bed. It is Don Rafo calling. "Daniel," he says, "meet me in the Plaza Principal at 10." Before I can reply or ask any questions, he hangs up the phone. I look at the clock: 6 AM.

I call Nacho, and we arrange to meet in the plaza a little before 10. Eric, another assistant on my research team, accompanies us. We seat ourselves on a park bench across from the Prefectura, the colonial-era building that houses the administrative offices of Cochabamba Department, but we do not have long to wait. From across the park strides Don Rafo. He hails us with a greeting considered polite among acquaintances and friends, male and female alike: a handshake, followed by a half hug—a sort of pat on the back with both hands, arms embracing but bodies not touching—followed by a second handshake. Rafo then seats himself on the bench beside us and immediately flips open his phone and punches some numbers. "Are you coming?" he says into the phone. "Hurry up." He snaps the phone shut, then jumps to his feet and paces for a minute, before sitting back down on the bench and flipping the phone open again. "Are you almost here? Well, hurry up!" He snaps the phone shut again.[1]

Finally we meet the object of Don Rafo's anxious calling. A neatly groomed man in a dark suit steps out of a taxi in front of the Prefectura, waves to some people standing on the sidewalk across the way, then turns and heads in our direction. Don Rafo emits an angry sigh and gets to his feet to shake the man's hand. He then introduces us to Melvin Gutierrez, who, Rafo explains, is his lawyer. Melvin greets us with the same handshake-hug-handshake combination, smiling brightly through gold-capped teeth. His hair is shiny and black, and although we are outdoors I can smell his cologne. While Rafo exudes nervous energy, Melvin is cool as a *pepino*.

Rafo cuts short any small talk. "Daniel," he says, "what we need to get things started on the project is a big meeting of all the leaders of the different *sindicatos* in La Pampa, where we can talk about the issues of insecurity."

"A seminar," says Melvin, supplying the missing term.

"Yes, a seminar," echoes Rafo. "We'll invite all the sindicato leaders and have a big meeting. And then a lunch."

"A lunch?" I ask.

"Yes," says Melvin, "a lunch."

"Yes," says Rafo, "a lunch. You know, to thank everybody for their participation. You can pay for that, right?"

"Well," I begin, "that sounds . . ."

"Let's go," Rafo says, and with Melvin at his side he bulls his way across the street from the plaza to the Prefectura, heedless of the oncoming traffic. Nacho and I exchange glances but follow them.

A crowd of people is gathered outside the Prefectura, holding microphones, video cameras, and audio recorders, and they descend on Rafo and Melvin like piranhas on fresh meat. They are reporters, and I will learn later that this is a common way for journalists in Cochabamba to collect news. Every morning they gather in front of the Prefectura, and anyone with news to report can come and try to interest them in covering his or her story. This seems like a democratic system on the face of it, but in reality the journalists are interested in talking only to established newsmakers like Don Rafo.

I listen in as Rafo talks with the reporters and learn the reason for this urgent appearance at the Prefectura. Rafo wants to publicize our research project, using the occasion to talk about problems of insecurity in La Pampa and to rail against the authorities who fail to do anything about it. But, he tells the assembled journalists, we are not waiting for the authorities; we are going to solve this problem of insecurity ourselves. He then introduces me, describing me as a foreign researcher who has come to help the comerciantes of La Pampa with their security problems and who is organizing a major seminar on the issue. I am as surprised as anyone by this announcement, but now the cameras are pointing at me.

Over the years I have gained a certain facility in speaking on my feet, adopting the Bolivian style of formal speechmaking, which includes a lot of ceremonious language but says very little of substance. So when the microphones point in my direction I am able to prattle on a bit about the seminar, making it up as I go. I talk in general terms about insecurity, the aims of my research, and my hopes for a successful collaboration with the leaders and vendors of La Pampa. Don Rafo cuts in to talk about our plan to write a book about insecurity in the market—"a scientific study, with data," he says—and notes that this seminar will be an important step in producing that document.

When we have concluded these interviews, Don Rafo invites Melvin, Nacho, Eric, and me to eat a *salteña* at a nearby restaurant. Salteñas are meat pies, like empanadas but juicy inside, that Bolivians regularly consume as a mid-morning snack. We eat in a dark little place just a block off the Plaza Principal, and Rafo talks more about the seminar. He will leave it up to Nacho and me to organize the details, but he and Melvin will help to recruit participants and will introduce me to the comerciantes of La Pampa during Carnaval. Salteñas finished, Rafo signals to the waiter for the check, then passes it to me. He and Melvin rise, and with another round of handshake-hug-handshakes, they depart.

Nacho is red-faced and furious. "He invited *you!*" he exclaims. "He should have paid the bill. Why did you agree to pay it?" I try to calm him down. I am so delighted to have this kind of cooperation from the leaders of La Pampa—direct access to the comerciantes fijos, people who would never speak to me without this kind of introduction—that the cost of a few salteñas is insignificant in comparison. I explain this to Nacho, but he just shakes his head, still angry at this violation of the scared Bolivian rules of hospitality.

When he has calmed down, Nacho gives me encouraging news. While Rafo and I were talking to the reporters, Nacho and Eric struck up a conversation with a man called Don Silvio, a representative of another group that had also come to the Prefectura hoping to publicize their cause. Silvio and his colleagues are the leaders of a group of comerciantes ambulantes, upset about a decision recently taken by the Alcaldía to impose "order" on the streets of Cochabamba—code for a plan to remove the ambulant vendors from the city's streets and sidewalks. The municipality has passed an ordinance (number 3615, according to these ambulantes) that will prohibit them from selling in the streets, and the ambulantes are organizing against the measure. They had come to the Prefectura hoping to put their case before the public via the media representatives gathered there. Those representatives, though, were much more interested in what Don Rafo and a gringo anthropologist had to say than in the problems of a bunch of street vendors. Don Silvio and the ambulantes are interested in talking more to us: if the journalists will not publicize their case, perhaps an anthropologist can. Nacho has arranged for us to meet with them in our little office over the call center.

# 8. The Colonial City
## Cochabamba, 1574–1900

Cochabamba, Bolivia, ranks pretty far down on the list of great world cities. It is not what demographers would call a "megacity," like São Paulo (population 20,186,000 in 2012) or Mexico City (19,463,000) or Mumbai (16,910,000).[1] Even Bolivia's capital city, La Paz, has more than a million inhabitants. Cochabamba has a mere 632,000.[2] But during the past half-century, Cochabamba has experienced growth (as a percentage of population) on par with any world city. In 1952, at the time of the Bolivian national revolution, Cochabamba was a sleepy market town of about 50,000 people. By the start of the twenty-first century, its population had surpassed 500,000. And the numbers keep growing.

Although today only the fourth-largest city in Bolivia, Cochabamba is the heart of the nation's informal economy, just as it has always been the backbone of its official one. From its very inception, Cochabamba was a market town.[3] The streets and plazas of the historic city center (the *casco viejo*) date to the late 1500s, when the city was founded by the Spanish amid the fertile, stream-fed fields of Cochabamba's lower valley. Spanish colonialism in what was then known as Alto Peru focused on the extraction of mineral wealth from the heart of the Andes mountains, much of it centered in the mines of Potosí and its Cerro Rico (Rich Hill), from which vast quantities of precious metals were exported to fill the coffers of the Spanish rulers in Europe. The city of La Paz was founded in 1548, in part to protect the transport of minerals from Potosí to the Pacific; the Villa de Oropesa, later renamed Cochabamba, was established in 1574 as an exporter of agricultural products to feed the workers and administrators of the highland mines.[4]

Cochabamba's history is characterized by contentious social relations surrounding the meanings and uses of public space—conflicts that persist in the Cancha today. Like every other Spanish colonial city of the era, Cochabamba was founded around a central plaza containing the principal administrative, religious, and economic buildings and institutions of colonial rule. The Spanish urban aesthetic was premised on an ideal of geometric order, with rectilinear streets dividing square blocks of neatly constructed houses and shops (the "checkerboard" pattern of colonial urban design), a physical reflection of the orderly "civilization" that the colonial city was meant to both symbolize and bring into being.[5] This was especially true of Cochabamba's Plaza Principal, called the Plaza de Armas and, later, the Plaza 14 de Septiembre, around which were situated the offices of government and church, the two main institutions of the Spanish civilizing mission. Humberto Solares Serrano, a chronicler of Cochabamba's urban development, describes the plaza as "the space where the power of the colonial State was made material, the seat of its authority, the place from which law was exercised and from which radiated the sense of social and economic order that the conqueror imposed over its vassals."[6]

The space of the plaza had racial significance, as well. The Plaza Principal, with its aura of power and order, was the seat of whiteness in the colonial city, with nonwhite (mainly indigenous and mestizo) peoples relegated to its more peripheral zones.[7] The former group included *forasteros*, indigenous people who had abandoned their natal communities to avoid the tributary demands and labor drafts imposed by the colonizers.[8] Many of these people entered into small-scale artisanal and manufacturing work, producing textiles and other goods required both in the highland mines and by the growing population of Cochabamba itself. Like later generations of rural-to-urban migrants, the forasteros established their homes and workshops in the peripheral zones, mostly to the south of the city's central plaza and its adjacent streets.

For centuries after its initial founding, Cochabamba's Plaza Principal was also the locus of urban commerce. During the seventeenth and eighteenth centuries, the sidewalks surrounding the plaza were regularly the sites of buying and selling as small-scale artisans and vendors hawked the basic necessities of life to urban consumers. Although formally excluded from the city center, indigenous vendors and artisans nevertheless claimed the space of the sidewalks, their presence tolerated because of the vital function they served as purveyors of staples—food, clothing, and other essentials—to the urban populace. Solares Serrano conjures this market scene, so different from the austere and official purposes for which the plaza was intended:

> One can imagine the hustle and bustle of the buyers and sellers: here are the venerable Hispanic matrons or *patronas* accompanied by their cooks carrying their heavy wicker baskets over their shoulders, searching frantically for the best meat for their roasts or their *puchero*, the fattest chicken for the stew or the most succulent *chicharrón* to accompany the *mote* and the *quesillo*. . . . It was not unusual, this constant spectacle, the coming and going of mules and [other beasts of burden bearing] various goods amid the shouts and urgings of the animal herders, of artisans offering a variety of leather goods, weavings and an infinity of other objects. The grand plaza of Cochabamba probably was more colorful on these occasions and gained more life from these ordinary persons, than from the severe processions and displays of the royal military.[9]

This description hints at a tension—the idealized city space of the white colonial imagination versus the reality of daily urban life for people of all races (white, indigenous, and mestizo) who actually lived in the city—that would continue to characterize the growth and development of Cochabamba. Especially as the urban population increased, the streets, sidewalks, and plazas became the sites of endless contestation over the nature and identity of the greater city.

During the eighteenth and nineteenth centuries, the municipal government struggled to control and regulate urban growth and complexification through official ordinances, guided by a persistent colonial imagination but forced to accommodate a contemporary urban reality. For example, in 1895 the Alcaldía of Cochabamba issued the first ordinance to regulate vehicular and pedestrian traffic in the city, prohibiting large animals and carts from entering the Plaza Principal and mandating that houses fronting the city's main plazas conform to a particular "architectural" (i.e., Spanish) aesthetic.[10] This was followed in 1896 by another ordinance that defined the minimum width of city streets based on their distance from the

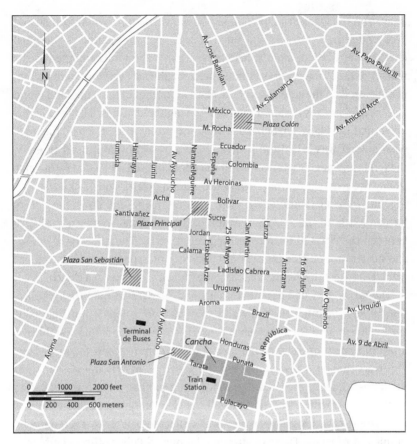

Map 8.1 Downtown Cochabamba today. Map drawn by Bill Nelson.

Plaza Principal, with the greatest concern given to streets adjacent to or intersecting the plaza and more flexibility allowed for streets more distant from the city center.[11] These ordinances suggest the effort by the authorities of the day to preserve the colonial ideal while acknowledging the reality of the growing city, maintaining the centrality of the Plaza Principal and the colonial checkerboard while widening the streets to make room for the large numbers of people, including commercial vendors, who were then using them. It also suggests the city's willingness to allow growth on its periphery in exchange for preserving the colonial order and aesthetic of its central core (map 8.1).

In the first decades of the nineteenth century, thriving markets, patronized largely by mestizos and indigenous people, developed in Cochabamba's southern zone.[12] On the margins of the city, only a few blocks but a world away from the Plaza Principal, these popular markets, or *ferias*, formed and proliferated in the streets and small plazas, open areas amid the colonial checkerboard called, simply, *canchas* (spaces).[13] The ferias emerged as the market of the Plaza Principal diminished: small-scale vendors were no longer tolerated on the sidewalks of the plaza or in front of the banks and grand commercial houses that now supplied the highland mines. The ferias grew up around the Plaza San Sebastián south of the city center, where the principal market was called the Pampa Grande.[14] As they continued to grow, the ferias extended east, occupying the edges of the Pampa de las Carreras (today the Avenida Aroma), where the working classes enjoyed horse racing, bull fighting, and other popular entertainment, and down the streets farther south, to the Plaza San Antonio, the unofficial southern boundary between the city and its surrounding countryside. The ferias grew denser and busier around this plaza and the streets and spaces that radiated out from it, and as they did the area became known simply as "La Cancha."

The ferias provided essential goods and services to the urban population while remaining relatively autonomous from official municipal control.[15] Throughout the nineteenth century, the Alcaldía did not establish a uniform system of weights and measures for commerce in the ferias; nor did it tax market transactions. But the government was not absent from the ferias. Indeed, the Alcaldía imposed an annual licensing fee, called a *patente*, on operators of market stalls. It also charged a payment for site occupancy, called a *sentaje*, which was collected weekly or even daily by municipal officials. These comisarios, Municipal Police officers employed by the Alcaldía, regularly patrolled the market, charged with ensuring that only authorized people set up stalls and that the goods provided met certain standards of quality. These agents and their activities constituted a state presence even in the supposedly "unregulated" spaces of the market. To this day, the comisarios perform the same functions in the Cancha (figure 8.1).

Meanwhile, the old city center was increasingly the object of regulation and policing. This was particularly the case after 1878, when a typhus epidemic ravaged the city, providing a justification for authorities to "clean up" (*limpiar*) the old downtown.[16] Commerce was more strictly limited than before, and the raising of animals (mainly pigs and chickens, used to make chicharrón, a popular dish of the lower classes) was prohibited. Most significant, the municipality introduced ordinances to gradually remove the popular bars, known as *chicherías*, from the Plaza Principal. The bars, sites of

8.1 Comisarios of La Pampa. Photograph by the author.

cross-class and interethnic mixing and revelry, were deemed incompatible with the clean, orderly, European sensibility to which local elites and municipal leaders aspired.[17] The removal of the chicherías was accomplished through regulation: bar owners had to buy patentes to operate their establishments, with those situated closer to the Plaza Principal required to pay much higher fees than those located farther to the south. This graduated fee scale encouraged movement to the periphery, especially to the area around the Plaza San Antonio, where the Cancha was now located.

By this time in the city's evolution, according to Solares Serrano, two distinct ways of "thinking the city" had become evident.[18] For those who saw themselves as the "owners" of the city, the members of the white upper class who historically had held dominion, the urban continued to signify Europeanness and civilization. The city was to be characterized by order, law, and health, reflected in the architecture of their homes, the layout of their streets and plazas, the kinds of goods and services sold there, and, most particularly, the kinds of people who resided and worked in those spaces. For this group, the burgeoning markets of the southern zone, and the growing indigenous and mestizo populations that frequented them, were not only a violation of the long-standing hegemonic vision of colonial urban society and privilege but an emerging chaos that threatened the values and virtues of the city center.[19]

This vision of the city as a sort of "urban *latifundio*" contrasted fundamentally with that of the lower classes, including the small-scale comerciantes and artisans who represented the forces of growth in the city.[20] To them, the urban meant a dynamic commercial market based around the large concentration of consumers who inhabited the city and could potentially buy their wares. For these people, the "chaos" of the southern markets was something to be welcomed, a kind of business model that perfectly served their interests. For them, urban disorder represented a distinct relationship to urban space, one that deliberately "anarchized" the regulatory order of the checkerboard, "giving expression to a freedom and an informality that were not possible in other, institutional or ideological spheres."[21] From this perspective, the proliferation of urban commerce was a means of contesting the colonial order and, later, its enduring postcolonial manifestations. Urban "chaos" was a product of a deliberate effort by market vendors to transform the contemporary city, wresting it away from the elites who historically had controlled it.

But the state also had an investment in the intentional anarchization of these urban market spaces—a recognition that challenges any simple notion of the market-as-resistance perspective. As mentioned earlier, throughout the city's history the municipal government had to balance the competing demands of different groups and interests; the colonial ideals of urban life, held by the city's ruling class, were in constant tension with the practical demands of its more ordinary inhabitants, who required space for the basic needs of daily life, which increasingly included small-scale commercial activities. By allowing the development of market spaces according to the requirements of commerce, the municipality was able to preserve the "ordered" and regulated spaces of the city center, within which the colonial ideal could continue to find expression. This exchange allowed the center and its northern suburbs to develop as orderly, Europhile, and (in the coming decades) "modern" spaces wherein the established elites and the oligarchy could raise their children, run their businesses, and make their laws while marginalizing the "others" who had no place in that society.

But this was more than a mere devil's bargain, a trade-off of chaos in one quarter of the city for order in another. Rather, city officials profited immensely from the chaos of the market, taxing its users both to support the municipality and to line their own pockets while providing little in the way of costly services, investment, or oversight. The municipal government continued to demand that both large wholesalers and small retailers purchase annual patentes and pay daily sentajes authorizing them to conduct business in the markets. The commerce of the market, seemingly anarchic and anachronistic, was both regulated and taxed but otherwise ignored, enabling the orderly stateliness of the modern city to develop and providing the state with the revenue needed to run it.

The two visions of the city—the urban as order versus the urban as chaos—were not distinct and separate, therefore, but conjoined, the former vision dependent for its very existence on the latter. Like the interpenetration of the formal and the informal, discussed in chapter 4 and again in what follows, the chaos of the markets from the very outset was an essential part of the city, an instrument of its development and prosperity, despite official attempts to deny and marginalize it. The same can be said of the many people who would later become workers in this informal economy, a point to which I return in later chapters.

# 9. Conflicts of Interest

"Bueno," says Don Silvio, president of the ambulantes' federation. "How can you help?"[1]

Uncertain how to respond, I ask Don Silvio to explain what kind of help he needs. Don Silvio places his hands on the rickety table, which tilts in his direction. His fingers, I notice, are bent and twisted. He interlaces them on the table before him and tells us about his organization. The El Paso federation—La Federación Integral de Comerciantes Minoristas "El Paso" is its full name—has 1,500 members, all of them ambulantes who sell on the streets of Cochabamba. Unlike other groups of ambulantes, which belong to the larger federations that are run by comerciantes fijos (such as Don Rafo's Federación de Comerciantes de La Pampa), the El Paso federation is independent. It was formed just two years earlier, when Don Silvio and other ambulantes grew tired of belonging to federations controlled by the same people who were their direct competitors and who had very different and conflicting interests from those of the ambulantes. So they created their own federation and in a short period of time gained official recognition from the state, being granted the *personería jurídica*, the all-important foundational document that gives their federation the right to exist (i.e., legal personhood). El Paso, Don Silvio emphasizes, is an *asociación integral*, an integrated association consisting of twelve smaller sindicatos of street vendors who have joined together to work collectively to resolve their issues.

Despite this enhanced political organization, the ambulantes have yet to make strides in improving their working conditions. To the contrary, the Alcaldía has recently adopted a more intransigent posture, expressed in Ordinance 3615, which threatens to force the ambulantes from the streets.

"Look," says Don Silvio's associate, the dark man whose name I did not catch, "we don't want to be on the streets, either. Can you imagine? We are on the street from six in the morning until ten at night, in the rain, in the sun. Sometimes we come home with only ten or fifteen bolivianos [about $2] in our pockets from a whole day of work. And the poor *señoras*, they then have to cook and clean. Imagine what it's like. We can't be selling on the streets until we are old and worn out. We need roofs over our heads. We need a place of our own."

"In other words," Don Silvio says, "we need a market that we ourselves control." In a market, he explains, the ambulantes would have a permanent location from which to sell. And it cannot be somewhere really remote, on the edge of town someplace. The ambulantes' market has to be centrally located in the Cancha so that its occupants can actually make a living by selling where the crowds are. "This," says Don Silvio, "is what the El Paso federation is trying to achieve."

It is my turn now, and the table tilts in my direction as I lean in to speak. I explain to these men who I am and what I am doing in Cochabamba, emphasizing the academic nature of my work. I am there, I tell them, to study insecurity and how it affects the lives of people who work in the Cancha. Don Silvio immediately understands, and expresses a keen recognition of the breadth of "security" (*seguridad*) as a concept: it is not limited to problems of crime or terrorism, for example, as it typically appears in the academy, the media, or the mouths of politicians. He readily connects "insecurity" to problems of daily survival and a lack of basic rights.

"We ambulantes," Don Silvio says, "are deeply insecure. We have no place to go, nowhere to rest. We are poor. And we are constantly harassed, by the police and by the delinquents in the streets. We have rights, but they are not respected by the authorities. We have the right to work, above all, a right guaranteed by the constitution. But the authorities don't permit us this right." Furthermore, he says, the ambulantes have been abandoned by the Alcaldía. Though they have invited representatives of the state to come and speak at their meetings, no one has ever appeared, and they cannot get the municipality to listen to their grievances. The journalists' lack of interest the other day was just another example of the ambulantes' invisibility.

I have an idea now of how I can help the ambulantes, at least in the short term. Given their lack of publicity, I suggest, what if I were to write an article about them and pay for it to be published in the newspaper? In this way, they could communicate their concerns to a wider audience in the city. The ambulantes are taken with this idea and accept the suggestion with enthusiasm. Pressing my luck, I borrow a line from Don Rafo. I would also be interested, I tell them, in writing a book about the ambulantes—a "scientific study," I say, that would tell the real story of the ambulantes' insecurity, something they could use to present their grievances to the authorities. They respond warmly to this idea, as well. To be the subject of a book, one that would present their needs directly to a broader readership, would give them the kind of publicity they cannot get any other way. It will surely help them, Don Silvio says, in their quest for a market of their own.

We arrange another meeting for later in the week, this time with additional leaders of their federation, to talk in more detail about the newspaper article I am going to write and to coordinate a research strategy. Don Silvio asks whether I can give them an audio recorder so they can record their own meetings, and I agree to this request. The men leave with broad smiles and handshake-hug-handshakes all around.

When they are gone, and I am flushed with the excitement of the moment, Nacho turns to me with a frown. "How will we explain this to Don Rafo?" he asks. I stare back at him, not understanding, but then it dawns on me. I have now agreed to work with two mutually antagonistic, rival groups. How will the leaders of one group react if they learn I am working with the other group? Nacho says that if Silvio finds out I am working with Rafo, he will never speak to me again. Rafo, likewise, already sees himself as the owner of our project; his reaction, should he discover I am working with the ambulantes, would not be pretty. What will Rafo say if he reads an article in the paper about the ambulantes, published under my name? Plus, I realize, I am now committed to writing two separate books with two very different sets of protagonists and to paying for the publication of those books out of my own pocket.

More important, is it a betrayal of one group to work with and for the other, even if my work for the one does not have direct effects on the other? Although I approached each group independently and with the best intentions, is it politically and ethically possible to work with both groups at the same time? However, would it have been possible to do things any differently? With these competing commitments, I now have access to both of the principal sets of actors in the drama that is daily life in the Cancha. Access of this kind does not come easily, or cheaply.

I suddenly feel very much in over my head and wonder at my own naïve enthusiasm. The promises I have made seem overwhelming, and I am filled with doubt about the ethical dilemma in which I now find myself.

The resolution to this problem is not immediately evident. Nacho and I decide to keep things quiet for now, to work separately with each group and to resolve our conflict of interest later on. We hope it will not blow up in our faces before we do.

# 10. Decolonizing Ethnographic Research

This book tells the stories of two competing groups: the comerciantes ambulantes and the comerciantes de puesto fijo of Cochabamba's Cancha marketplace. In researching the book, I established close working relationships with the leaders and members of each group to understand these stories from the perspectives of those who live them. This is the basic approach of cultural anthropology, whose methodology includes long-term interaction and close, personal engagement with the subjects of our research. But the price of these relationships—the entry fee, as it were, to the lives I wished to document—was a political commitment that required me to go beyond the usual role of academic researcher. As the previous chapters suggest, in exchange for their stories, the people with whom I worked required from me a solidarity with their struggles and a willingness to put my research and writing at the service of resolving their problems. This was as true of the fijos as it was of the ambulantes. But doing so required me to scrutinize closely my own political, ethical, and intellectual commitments and to explore the limits of what a collaborative, activist anthropology can achieve.

Given the centrality of the Cancha to the cultural, economic, and political life of Cochabamba—not to mention its compelling energy and charm—it is surprising how little has been written about the place. But after spending time in the Cancha doing research myself, it is easy to understand why. Journalists offer the promise of publicity, of quickly bringing the concerns of those interviewed to the attention of the general public; academic researchers traditionally offer no such guarantees. Instead, the standard social-science research model is extractive. It is based on a dyadic but non-reciprocal relationship between researcher and research subject, in which the former asks questions and the latter answers them. In this model, information flows one way—from subject to researcher—and the benefits of that research obtain solely to the person asking the questions, not to the person answering them. Such a model reflects the colonial regimes of power that have long framed the relationships between researcher and researched, and rather than offering a critique of social inequality, the model tends to reproduce it in the very process of conducting research.[1] It is no wonder, then, that some people would be skeptical about sharing information with an outsider asking questions.[2]

The research relationship can be even more complicated in the Cancha, where the local culture of market exchange dominates the framing of any personal interaction. In the Cancha, potential research subjects are also adept capitalists and salespeople. They perceive the value of their knowledge and experience and are not willing to give it away for free. The research interaction, from their perspective, is a commercial exchange like any other and must include some kind of return for their participation. "How can you help?"—Don Silvio's challenge to me in the book's prologue—and Don Rafo's request for a scientific study of market insecurity can be understood in these terms. For many of the urban poor, it is all too obvious that their poverty and marginality relate in part to their lack of education, and to their lack of access to information and modern technology, all of which limits their opportunities and keeps them stuck where they are. These people recognize that an outsider coming to study their lives is going to take from them the one thing of value that they possess: their stories. What would motivate these people to share these stories freely with an anthropologist? This is particularly problematic when working with indigenous peoples, who have long endured colonial and postcolonial exploitation and inequality. Given that history, as the indigenous intellectual Linda Tuhiwai Smith puts it, "'Research' is probably one of the dirtiest words in the indigenous world's vocabulary."[3] In such a context, traditional researchers operating with the one-way model of knowledge transmission typically encounter a stony refusal. They may misrecognize this as an expression of the stereotypically "closed" nature of the highland Indian or the "tough" character of the *chola* market woman.[4] But whatever their explanation, this resistance remains intractable, and they gain little insight for their efforts.

Another element of the traditional research model that proves problematic in the contemporary fieldwork setting is the commitment to scientific objectivity. When teaching introductory classes in anthropology, I often encounter students who insist that, to truly understand another culture, one must be objective—that is, neutral, detached from the political and emotional lives of one's research subjects, and unclouded by bias or personal connection to them.[5] But objectivity in these terms is impossible to achieve, a point that is widely accepted by now within anthropology. More often, anthropologists opt for an awareness of our own social positioning, paying explicit attention to how we are situated vis-à-vis our research subjects and how that situatedness influences the kinds of questions we ask and the kinds of knowledge we produce.[6] This explicit attention to positionality brings into focus important questions of race, class, gender, sexuality, and other elements of social and personal identity that influence the encounter between researcher and researched. Nevertheless, some professional anthropologists still assume that political neutrality and personal disengagement are necessary for successful fieldwork.[7]

What's more, a stance of neutrality or objective distance can be alienating to people in a contemporary research setting. The people with whom many anthropologists work today demand our engagement—they will not tolerate distance. In the Cancha, my research was successful because I was open to recognizing the political potential of my activities and willing to align myself and my work with the people whose struggles I studied. Unconcerned with objectivity in the classic sense, I put my work at the service of my research subjects and their political projects. This kind of "engaged" or "activist" anthropology opened doors that otherwise would have remained closed, providing insights that a distanced, detached kind of social science never could have achieved.[8] I engaged my research subjects as collaborators, people with as much investment in the project as I had. This sense of collaboration became the overall framework of the project, the guiding ethos by which I conducted my work in the Cancha, both with ambulantes and with fijos.[9] Through this approach, I learned much more than I ever would have had I adopted a stance of distanced neutrality. People who are invested in a project share more than those who are not.

Key to my ability to engage Cancha market people in my research, to enlist their collaboration, was the fact that my research interests were in perfect alignment with the deepest concerns of comerciantes themselves. My work has long focused on questions of security and insecurity in Latin America, with a particular interest in the ways in which the law, the police, and the judicial system operate (or fail to operate) in marginal urban neighborhoods. In turning to the Cancha, I was interested in extending my research to look at how questions of security and insecurity were shaped and expressed in the heart of the city's informal economy. I came to the Cancha with the goal of exploring the kinds of insecurity that existed in the market and especially how being regarded as "informal" or "illegal" shape one's sense of security and ability to survive as a commercial vendor.

As it turned out, the issue of personal security topped the market vendors' list of concerns, as well. Both fijos and ambulantes suffer from crime, losing inventory and proceeds to thieves and enduring a sense of physical threat from potentially violent criminals who are ubiquitous in the market zone. Both groups lose business as shoppers' fears of Cancha insecurity mount, making criminality a threat not only to one's person and property but to the entire basis of one's economic livelihood. Neither fijos nor ambulantes trust the police nor rely on them for protection from crime, and the members of both groups feel that they are left to their own devices in trying to create security in the market (chapter 16). Although their vulnerabilities differ in important ways (chapter 26), fijos and ambulantes both rank insecurity as among the most critical, frustrating, and apparently irresolvable problems with which they must regularly contend.

It was this mutual concern with insecurity and my expressed intent of sharing my findings with them, of allowing them to use those findings in ways that contributed to their ongoing projects to enhance their security, that enabled me to befriend the various comerciantes whose contributions were so central to this project. One key element of collaborative research is that the research subjects themselves identify and drive the goals of the project rather than those goals' being dictated from the "top down."[10] That was the case in my Cancha research. Although I came to the project with my goals well in mind, I was able to adapt them to reflect the goals of the comerciantes, agreeing, for example, to organize a seminar and write a book on behalf of the comerciantes fijos. Had I chosen any other topic, I surely would have had much more trouble enlisting local collaboration, as shown by the attempts of other scholars to do research in the Cancha. Where others encountered resistance, Nacho and I were welcomed with smiles and warm greetings most everywhere we went. Though I would like to think that this was due to our sunny personalities, it probably had more to do with the comerciantes' perceptions of us as people working with them toward shared objectives.

Although the collaborative, activist approach was clearly productive, adopting a "decolonizing" stance—one that explicitly aims to invert the power dynamics characteristic of traditional research practice[11]—required a certain amount of ongoing negotiation with my collaborators and imposed burdens on me that a more "colonial" approach might not have.[12] For one thing, rather than being able to dictate the course of the project, I had to respond to the instructions, requests, and demands of my collaborators, usually research-related things like the kinds of questions I should include in my interviews or the timeframe of my production. While generally a concern in collaborative research, in my case this was complicated by the fact that the collaboration was of a different sort from that often discussed in the literature, when, for example, a North American anthropologist collaborates with South American intellectuals, academics, or activists.[13] In my case, my collaborators were merchants, not intellectuals, keen to profit from the presence of a gringo anthropologist and always willing to test the limits of our relationship. Thus, their collaboration not only entailed their input into the project; at times, it also included requests for resources that went beyond the scope of collaboration, sometimes verging on abuse. I also had to adjust the goals and output of my project to suit local interests. In addition to writing an academic book about the market, I was, by the terms of our collaboration, committed to writing on behalf of the comerciantes, a project that would require additional effort and resources and by definition would not overlap with my more academic goals. I thus had to work in such a way that the project had multiple outcomes, some of which could benefit my collaborators in their diverse, ongoing political projects, and others of which could benefit me in my goals as writer and anthropologist. All of this consumed a lot of my time in the field and sometimes provoked tensions with Nacho, who appointed himself watchdog over the excesses of the comerciantes.

A decolonizing approach to research also helped me deal with problems of representation. Anthropology with an activist bent can sometimes portray its subjects as passive and downtrodden, dependent on the intervention of an enlightened foreign researcher to rescue them and help them to achieve their goals.[14] In that model, the anthropologist "gives voice" to those who have been silenced, as though the anthropologist's writing is somehow a form of service to others—even if those others cannot read, cannot read English, or are likely never to see a copy of the book in print. I try to avoid this trope of anthropologist-as-hero, acknowledging up front that my work was as much self-serving as it was in the service of my collaborators. Here, the market context of the work made things easier. My research was frankly transactional from the outset, part of a balanced kind of reciprocity, in which my research subjects acknowledged the value that my presence among them could have for them and in exchange allowed me to learn about, and subsequently write about, their worlds. My commitment to the political projects of my research subjects was based on an explicit relationship of mutual engagement, in which each party to the research exchange contributed something, and from which each party could benefit. For the comerciantes of the Cancha, this transactional relationship made perfect sense and made me comprehensible to them, much more so than if I had presented myself as a disinterested do-gooder, a stance that would only have invited deep skepticism.

In the end, both Nacho and I had to confront our personal biases in collaborating with two very different groups of comerciantes. It was difficult at times not to feel a greater loyalty to the comerciantes ambulantes, even as we also collaborated with the comerciantes fijos. For Nacho, the lines were clear: he saw the ambulantes as victims and the fijos as victimizers, and he felt a much stronger commitment to our collaboration with the ambulantes than he ever did for the fijos. For my part, I tried to view both groups with understanding, to identify with their perspectives, and to work to support them in their initiatives. This at times produced conflicts of interest, and I am not sure I ever successfully mediated them. But I did my best to live up to my commitments to both groups and to my own academic goals. This book is the product of those relationships.

# 11. A Visit to the Cancha

Nacho and I visit the Cancha on a cold Saturday morning. All the mornings in Cochabamba are cold, summer and winter, and all the afternoons are hot and sunny. The cold returns at night, when the sun takes with it all memory of warmth as it sets behind the mountains of the *cordillera*. As we sometimes do, we take a taxi to the bus terminal on Avenida Ayacucho, below Avenida Aroma south of the *casco viejo*, Cochabamba's historic downtown. It is not much to look at, with its clots of buses, trucks, and taxis, but Ayacucho gives the pedestrian the most direct access to the Cancha. A few vendors have stalls on Ayacucho itself, but the main reason to shop there is to buy a barbecue grill. These are made by the enterprising inmates of the San Antonio prison, a forbidding concrete structure set right there on Ayacucho, and sold on the sidewalk outside the main gate. The quality of these grills is good, and the prices are better than anywhere else in town, I guess because the overhead is low in jail.

Right across from the bus depot and perpendicular to Ayacucho is a wide street called Avenida Tarata (see map 11.1). Filled with shoppers and vendors of various kinds, Tarata runs a short couple of blocks into the heart of the market. It is lined with small sidewalk eateries where many Cancha-goers have their breakfasts, and on an early morning visit the benches are crowded with people leaning over hot cups of *mate* (herbal tea) or *api* (a thick, purple beverage made from corn and spiced with cinnamon and sugar),

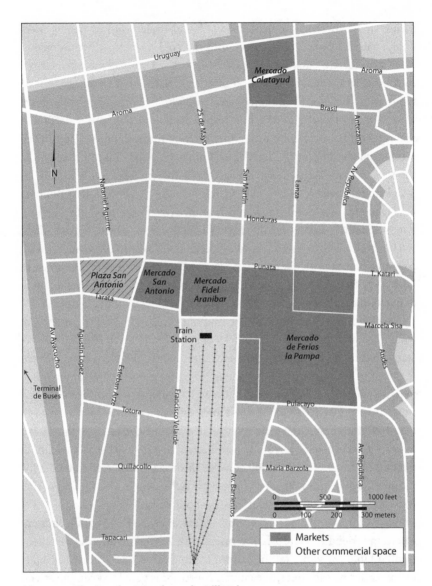

Map 11.1 The Cancha. Map drawn by Bill Nelson.

eating small, football-shaped loaves of bread (*maraquetas*) or freshly fried dough called *buñuelos*. Steam rises into the cold morning air from enameled Chinese army cups and escapes the mouths of the vendors who call out to passersby to come sample their offerings. Nacho and I walk past these temptations but stop by the cart of an elderly cholita, an indigenous woman whom Nacho knows, selling hot herbal drinks on the corner of Tarata and Agustín Lopez. Nacho orders in Quechua for both of us. The vendor mixes some herbal concoction drawn from a selection of jars stacked atop the tiny cart and ladles in steaming hot water from a central kettle, all of which she decants into two tall glasses that she presents with a flourish to Nacho and me. The drink smells foul, but Nacho promises it will clean out my kidneys—not something I knew I needed—so I down it, grimacing. Nacho smiles with pleasure, handing the glasses back to the vendor, and I pay three bolivianos—about 45 U.S. cents—for the two drinks. My sinuses, I discover, have suddenly drained, and I can breathe easier amid the hubbub of the market.

Pushing through the crowds, we find ourselves in Plaza San Antonio, a wide open area about two city blocks in size. Vendors sell from carts and stalls around the perimeter of the plaza, but not in the plaza itself, which is closed to the public by a black metal fence, its gates chained shut with a massive padlock. At one time the plaza was a principal locus of the Cancha, a place to sit and chat amid the noise and confusion of the market. But with the proliferation of street vendors, the Alcaldía decided to close the plaza, to keep it from being overrun by commerce. Now it sits absurdly vacant, a huge emptiness amid the stifling crowds. The plaza is preserved forever, a fly in amber, by the gates that keep the people out—people who might put the space to some sort of "improper" use (see chapter 14).[1]

Across from the plaza, on the south side, stands the San Antonio church, where my friend Abelardo is the priest. San Antonio church is a cream-colored building with a tall bell tower fronted by an open courtyard. Like the plaza across the street, the church courtyard is gated to keep the street vendors from setting up shop, although this gate is usually left open, as one would expect from the house of God. The present building is about eighty years old, but there has been a Catholic church on the site for hundreds of years, dating back to before independence. During the renovation of the church a few years ago, workers discovered human remains buried beneath the old stone floor. Padre Abelardo, an amateur archaeologist with a passion for Bolivian history, decided that the bones were the remains of the "heroines of the Coronilla," a group of women who famously gave their lives in defense of Cochabamba during a revolt against Spanish rule in 1812. A monument to these *heroinas* stands on a hill that overlooks San Antonio, though few people visit it because it is a very good place to get mugged. Abelardo constructed a small crypt behind the main altar of the church, where he interred the remains—human skulls, pelves and femurs, ulnae and radii—behind glass, under an eerie red light. He hopes that this will attract visits by tourists, history buffs, and the faithful. Although my specialty is not archaeology or human osteology, I gave Abelardo's interpretation of the remains my official anthropological imprimatur in the form of a letter on university stationery, for which the padre was extremely grateful. A framed copy of my letter adorns the crypt, standing watch over the bones of the (possibly) ancient dead.

Ignoring the appeals of the money changers—who are excited to see a gringo, perhaps with dollars to change—Nacho and I pause at the corner of the locked-up plaza to take our bearings. We stand now at the corner of Tarata and Esteban Arze, a street that runs through the heart of downtown to the Cancha. Were we to turn left, to the north, after about a dozen blocks we would find ourselves in the Plaza 14 de Septiembre, also known as the Plaza Principal of Cochabamba, where the government buildings and the city's main cathedral are located. To the south, our right, Esteban Arze runs alongside numerous small stores, many selling electronics and computer equipment. On the sidewalks in front of these shops, vendors have set up small, curtained booths from which they sell any manner of object, from hardware and domestic items (light bulbs and extension cords, drain plugs, blenders, hand tools, and towels) to clothing and vegetables and cooked food. Other vendors walk or push wheelbarrows and carts loaded with merchandise through the crowded streets.

Ahead of us lies a large section of the Cancha, maybe two city blocks in size, called the San Antonio market. The southernmost row of vendors consists entirely of people selling *artesania*, the folkloric handicrafts that attract tourists to the market. Here, stall after stall sells Bolivian tchotchkes: woven items such as scarves and mittens; tin and ceramic renderings of llamas, *diablos*, saints, and virgins; wall hangings made from alpaca or sheep's wool; T-shirts bearing coca leaves or llamas or witty, if baffling, sayings ("Does this shirt make me look Bolivian?"; "Buy me a [picture of a beer mug], I'm Bolivian"). Among the tourist items you can also find some real treasures, such as antique weavings and hand-thrown pots. Pickpockets and purse snatchers, rampant everywhere in the Cancha, are a particular threat in the aisle where tourists gather: distracted by the wonders on sale, they are easy marks.

Nacho and I detour briefly into the artesania section to greet our friend Doña Giovana, a lovely, soft-spoken Quechua woman with long silver braids and a big smile studded with gold-capped teeth. She asks after my wife and tries to sell me something. Bolivians have a particular way of speaking when they really want something, a tone of voice that to a North American ear sounds like a whine. In situations where North Americans might get insistent and raise their voices to get their way, Bolivians wheedle. Doña Giovana does that now. "Don Daniel," she whines, "take home a little something for your wife. A blanket, maybe?" This is a long-standing ritual between us, and we pretend to haggle before I agree to buy the blanket, for what seems like a good price but probably is not. "This is why you're the best saleslady in the Cancha," I tell her, and Doña Giovana laughs, admitting that it is true without losing her disarming humility.

Just beyond the San Antonio market lies the somewhat larger Fidel Aranibar market. It is a quiet oasis amid the surrounding mayhem. One of the newer sections of the market, the sector is laid out in neat rows, each row lined with individual stalls. The vendors in Fidel Aranibar are grouped according to trade—an ideal to which vendors in other sections of the market aspire but rarely achieve. In Fidel Aranibar, all is orderly: one long row of men's tailor shops, one long row of shoe stalls, one long row of dressmakers, one long row of toy sellers, one long row of cake vendors. The tranquility of this section of the market is perhaps due to this orderly layout—shoppers seek out the exact service they require, avoiding the crush of the surrounding streets (figure 11.1).

The Fidel Aranibar market is bounded by Avenida Francisco Velarde on the west, Tarata on the south, the busy Avenida Barrientos on the east, and the narrower Calle Punata to the north. Although Punata marks the more-or-less official northern limit of the Cancha, shops and street vendors of all kinds continue several blocks beyond it, lining the sidewalks of the avenues Nataniel Aguirre, Esteban Arze, 25 de Mayo, San Martín, Lanza, and Antezana. A few blocks farther north lies the Calatayud market, one of the oldest markets in the city, though much smaller than the Cancha. To the south of Fidel Aranibar, below Avenida Tarata, lies the old railway station, out of use ever since railroad service to the towns and villages of Cochabamba's high valley was discontinued in the 1970s.[2] Now it stands

11.1 Part of a series of photos that I call "Insane Cancha Mannequins"; the mutilated heads and bright blue eyes are deeply unnerving. Photograph by the author.

deserted, although a few vendors with no better option sell on its disused patio, and some homeless men make beds there on its cold pavement. All around the outside of the old station, vendors sell from every possible perch. These vendors mostly sell clothing, their stalls crowding the sidewalks right to the curb. More and more vendors choke the narrow alleys south of the station. Clothing stalls eventually give way to shops selling electronics, housewares, and appliances. Amid the semipermanent stalls of the sidewalk vendors are occasional mini-malls, clusters of shops around open courtyards, selling higher-end electrodomestics, computers, stereos, and large appliances. Even farther south, larger stores sell construction supplies, paint, and furniture, car parts, tires, and glass. These streets extend for several kilometers, ending at last at another major street, the Avenida 6 de Agosto, beyond which lie the airport, the algae-choked Laguna Alalay, and the residential neighborhoods of Cochabamba's southern zone.

Heading back out to Tarata, Nacho and I pass between the vendors of school supplies who line Fidel Aranibar's southern fringe and the clothing vendors outside the train station. The street here is insanely congested—it is Saturday, the busiest day of the week, and the place is packed with sweaty, impatient shoppers. Nacho says that Aymara people believe that you pick up someone's bad energy when you bump into him or her in public and have to cleanse yourself with a special herb. Being in the Cancha on a Saturday, one can easily appreciate this belief.

In addition to the many shoppers, the street is blocked by a long line of cars, buses, taxis, and trucks. Despite the throngs of pedestrians, the municipality permits unregulated vehicular traffic through the heart of the market, and virtually every bus and trufi (minibus) line in the city passes through the Cancha on its way to and from someplace else. On Tarata, foot traffic moves more quickly than the line of vehicles, although one has to be careful of a sudden surge: the large, protruding side mirror of a bus nearly decapitates me as I navigate through the press.

At last, the congested thoroughfare opens into a wide intersection. Here, Avenida Tarata ends at Avenida Barrientos, a busy one-way street that changes its name to San Martín after it crosses Punata and leaves the Cancha heading north. Named for General René Barrientos Ortuño—a Bolivian president of the mid-1960s who is most famous for having captured and executed Che Guevara[3]—the avenue is a popular transit route for buses and taxis from the southern zone. Nacho puts a hand on my shoulder and carefully surveys the oncoming traffic before deeming it safe to cross.

As we are about to cross the street, a young woman leading a little girl by the hand approaches us. "Excuse me," she asks, "do you know where I can buy an oso hormiguero (an anteater)?" I am stunned silent by this bizarre question, but Nacho immediately responds, explaining to the woman exactly and in detail where in the market she can go to acquire such a beast. I stare at him with astonishment and admiration. "What?" he says, as though this sort of thing happens all the time.[4]

Directly across Avenida Barrientos from Fidel Aranibar lies the Cancha's easternmost section, La Pampa, the largest section of the Cancha.[5] La Pampa is the antithesis of Fidel Aranibar. Whereas the latter is sedate and neatly organized, La Pampa is a vortex of frenetic activity, with no apparent order or plan. La Pampa, like other markets, is divided into distinct sectors—vendors of cosmetics, for example, occupy two neat rows in the northern part of La Pampa; vendors of candy, plasticware, shoes, and tools have their own sections, as well (figure 11.2). But in other parts of the market, vendors mix together, creating a sense of disorder, of randomness. Meat is sold next to shoes, which are sold next to clothes, next to hardware.

11.2 The candy sellers have one of the more orderly and brightly lit sections of La Pampa. Photograph by the author.

Some of La Pampa's alleys are laid out geometrically, forming neat blocks like those elsewhere in the Cancha and in the historic city center. But much of La Pampa consists of short lanes that curve, angle, abruptly come to an end, or head off in new and unexpected directions. Finding one's way in La Pampa takes experience and alertness. Even after years in the market, Nacho still sometimes loses himself, and we quarrel about the proper direction in which to search for a particular vendor's stall.

The oldest section of the Cancha and the busiest, La Pampa is also the most "popular"—it is where you can get the cheapest prices on anything you might need, and all manner of *cochabambinos* shop there, from the richest *jailona* housewife to the poorest cholita from the barrios. In recent years, though, La Pampa has also come to be known as one of the most dangerous sections of the Cancha. This is due partly to the general sense of chaos and disorder in this section of the market: its internal disorganization, its crowds, and its dirt all seem to suggest a lurking criminality that the clean, well-lighted passages of Fidel Aranibar do not.

La Pampa is also well known as the place to go to buy and sell stolen property. In the southeastern corner of La Pampa lies a small subsection called the Barrio Chino. Here, vendors known as *albertos* resell goods that are brought to them from all over the city, no questions asked. There are many dealers in electronics here, in books, jewelry, bicycles—anything portable can be found for purchase at reduced prices in the Barrio Chino. A whole set of dealers specializes in auto parts—rearview mirrors, hubcaps, license plates, the electronic *cerebros* (brains) that control the workings of modern cars—and victims of theft know to come here to buy back their stolen items. One alley of the Barrio Chino is a veritable rogues' gallery: grimy men line both sides of the little passageway, offering wristwatches, iPods, bracelets, and cell phones, whispering prices to all who walk by.

La Pampa's location on the eastern edge of the market adds to its seedy reputation. Beyond Avenida República, La Pampa's eastern boundary and the end of what is generally understood to be the Cancha, the streets turn sharply uphill. Here lie more established vendors of stolen goods. These albertos sell larger items than do the vendors in the Barrio Chino, including household appliances, tools and construction equipment, lumber, paint, bags of cement—all stolen or illegally purchased, probably from building sites or smugglers. These men will also lend you money at unfavorable rates if more reputable lenders turn you away. Alongside the albertos' shops are *telos*, unlicensed flophouses where young men gather to drink and sniff glue, watch violent and pornographic videos, and sleep away the day, waiting for night to fall so they can go on the prowl, looking for unsuspecting passersby to beat up and rob. It is to these neighboring hillsides and the darkness of the telos that pickpockets and thieves will flee to avoid pursuit following a robbery. The sense of danger associated with this unsavory section of town attaches itself to the nearby La Pampa market.

Nacho and I pass through La Pampa and the Barrio Chino and emerge into traffic on Avenida República. This is a good place to catch a bus heading north, where I have an apartment. It is also not far to our office at Lanza and Honduras. We head there now, to write our fieldnotes and share our impressions of the market.

# 12. The Informal State

I push through the crowd of street vendors who have set up shop on the sidewalks bordering Avenida Sucre, trying to make my way to Cochabamba's municipal administrative offices. These vendors are selling an array of wares—school supplies, souvenirs, books, clothing, food and drink—some from established wooden stalls and others spread out on blankets on the ground. The crush of vendors, shoppers, and pedestrians is intense and persists right to the doorway of the municipal offices. Escaping from the crowd, I step into the limestone hush of the municipal building and climb the marble stairs to the second floor. There, at the top of the stairs for all to see, hangs a large, colorful poster bearing the seal of the Honorable Alcaldía Municipal—the Mayoralty of Cochabamba city—announcing Municipal Ordinance 4242, dated April 5, 2011. The ordinance declares, without a trace of irony, "No private individual, institution or organization of any kind . . . may use the public way as a space for sale, exposition, storage, display or protection of any type of product, food, articles, goods or general merchandise."

Much as the formal and the informal are not clear and distinct economic sectors (the subject of chapter 4), in the realm of politics "the state" cannot be understood as a purely legal and rational entity to which the disorder and illegality of "the streets" can be opposed. The state—not a monolithic institution but a heterogeneous set of actors and entities, ranging from the local to the national levels[1]—consists of offices, officials, procedures, and codes that regulate the use of space, manage the environment, and control commerce, among other things, within a designated territory. The state promises rule-governed order and equity and publicly condemns informal and illegal behavior. But in practice the state itself often operates informally, its enforcement of its own rules selective and its functioning organized by unofficial and sometimes illegal relations and procedures.[2] As any comerciante can attest, formality is no guarantee of legality, just as the informal does not necessarily equate with the illegal. Or, as the anthropologist Carolyn Nordstrom puts it, "Legality is a fluid concept."[3]

"The important analytical (and political) question," says Ananya Roy, "is why some forms of informality are criminalized and thus rendered illegal while others enjoy state sanction or are even practices of the state."[4] Roy suggests that we understand informality as a ruling logic of contemporary urban life, "a system of norms that governs the process of urban transformation itself."[5] From this perspective, informality can be understood as produced by the state, the result of what the state chooses to regulate and what it chooses to ignore. While the state has laws and procedures that supposedly govern its practices and those of its functionaries, in daily life these principles of ordering are embedded within larger frames of ambiguity that tolerate—that may, in fact, depend on—a wide range of interpretations and behavior. This ambiguity allows certain norms to be enforced while others are not, certain people to be punished for doing things—selling in the street, for example—that others can do with impunity. It is a process that appears to derive from the corruption of individual officers but in fact extends from categorical definitions of people and practices that provide the structural pillars of state power.[6] An ambulante, in other words, is an object of legal regulation, whereas a fijo engaged in identical work is not. Authorities continually obstruct the work of the ambulantes, even as they turn a blind eye to the informality of the fijos and, what's more, to the informal activities of the authorities themselves.

Various ethnographic examples illustrate this apparent contradiction. The geographer Asher Ghertner, for example, has explored the question in Delhi, India, where practically the entire built environment violates some law of zoning and construction, yet only in some areas are these laws actually enforced.[7] Ghertner shows that the residences and workplaces of the wealthy are identified by the state as exemplars of "modernity" and good taste and so are granted legal exemptions, while the slums of the poor are labeled "nuisances" and targeted for demolition.[8] Similarly, the anthropologist James Holston, writing about struggles over land claims and other legal matters in Brazil, describes the ways in which the legal system operates not impartially but in a manner so complex and arcane that ordinary people are discouraged from using it. The result is what Holston calls a "misrule of law," in which the elites who control the state can "legalize the illegal," maintaining their privilege and an inequitable distribution of power and resources while employing a conception of citizenship that recognizes some Brazilians as having rights under the law while others do not.[9] The same is true in Cochabamba, where the informal nature of state law is abundantly evident in matters of construction and land claims. As in Delhi, in Cochabamba new, "modern" high rises stab relentlessly into the sky, most of them constructed in violation of zoning and building codes (and in many cases financed by laundered drug money), while the residents of poor neighborhoods are deemed illegal occupants of their own, irregularly purchased land and face the threat of eviction. Meanwhile, the state itself routinely violates its own land laws: even the giant statue of Jesus Christ, dominating the skyline from its perch on a hill overlooking downtown, is known to be illegal, constructed by the Bolivian government on land to which it did not hold clear title.

In its regulation of economic transactions, the municipal government of Cochabamba has also demonstrated selectivity in its willingness to tolerate the informal, producing the urban *disregulation* I identified in chapter 1. On different occasions, the Alcaldía has cut deals with various factions in the city to permit their informal commercial activity in exchange for peace and quiet in the streets. The proliferation of street vendors on the very doorstep of the Alcaldía, described earlier, is one example of this, but there are others. To settle a recent conflict over land with the neighboring town of Tiquipaya, the Alcaldía of Cochabamba agreed to allow flower vendors from that town to sell on certain street corners during specific hours of the morning, in direct violation of municipal law.[10] In 2000, the Alcaldía agreed to allow vendors to sell on Avenida Totora—a street included in the city's master plan of 1961 but never developed due to lack of funds—if the vendors themselves paid to pave the street. Elsewhere, street vendors have purchased the right to sell on the streets and sidewalks directly from the Alcaldía itself—having failed at various times to privatize the market (a process discussed in chapter 23), the municipality routinely sells portions of public space to generate its own operating revenue. The comerciantes who blocked Avenida Pulacayo and who were in part to blame for the fire in La Pampa (chapter 1) acquired their market stalls through this kind of arrangement. Deals of this sort are extremely common and represent calculated exchanges orchestrated by the municipal authorities, often at the expense of the city and its inhabitants. The congestion and "chaos" of the streets today are due as much to such quasi-formal arrangements as to the spontaneous character of informal commerce.

Politics is one motive for official acceptance of informality; economics is another.[11] In the Cancha, the authorities with whom market vendors have the most frequent interactions are the comisarios, the officers of the Municipal Police. The comisarios are tasked with protecting consumer health and safety by "decommissioning" questionable or illegal products sold to the public and enforcing other municipal ordinances pertaining to market transactions. But the comisarios do not necessarily function in terms of the rational hierarchies of Weberian political order. Some comisarios selectively target ambulantes, those vendors who bear a priori the label of informal and illegal. The comisarios confiscate their goods—regardless of the quality of the merchandise and whether or not it poses a risk to consumer safety—and charge them money to get it back. Not only do they seize their wares, the comisarios confiscate the ambulantes' equipment, personal property used in the production and sale of their merchandise, seizures that go well beyond the officers' legal purview. But the ambulantes have to pay to recuperate these confiscated items, without which they cannot make a living. Some of the money they pay goes to the state, and some goes into the pockets of individual state operatives. The hierarchy of authorities raises no objection to these illegal seizures and payments: the comisarios' municipal employer is itself an impoverished institution and tolerates the rent-seeking (i.e., informal) behavior of individual agents, tacitly authorizing them to supplement their low salaries with the proceeds they bring in through confiscations. These practices can be dismissed as simply illegal acts of individual corruption, but they are better understood as fundamental to the operating structure of the state itself.[12]

Contrary to expectations, then, the state is actively involved in regulating the work of the ambulantes, denizens of the informal sector that supposedly exists outside state regulation. It is, in fact, their purported externality to the state that makes the ambulantes an object of state concern— the category of "informal," produced by academics and applied to one kind of commercial actor, colors the law and practices of legal enforcement.

Identified as informal sellers, the ambulantes are harassed and pursued by the Municipal Police and other authorities who keep them constantly on the move—the ambulatory nature of the ambulantes is as much an effort to avoid police abuse as it is due to a lack of a fixed place from which to sell. As illegal vendors, the ambulantes are at the mercy of these officials, the comisarios who confiscate their goods and equipment and demand a steady flow of unrecorded, informal payments. The ambulantes lack the right of an appeal to any neutral authority or the protection of the law— they are by definition outside the law's domain.[13] These facts render the ambulantes highly vulnerable and poorly positioned to achieve any kind of upward mobility: it is virtually impossible for them, as illegal sellers, to accumulate enough resources to gain access to the fixed stalls of the market, the legitimate, formal sector of the Cancha wherein the wealth resides and from which they might legally sell and so, perhaps, advance.[14] The poorest are excluded from control of the real wealth in the market—much of it contained in the market stalls themselves, which constitute the enormous secondary market for real estate in the Cancha—while elites can reap its benefits.[15]

..........................

One of the ways in which the state justifies its selective enforcement of the law is through claims to maintaining order. As discussed throughout this book, street vendors have taken over much of the open space in and around the Cancha marketplace, an occupation that city officials and residents typically describe as an "invasion." Informal vendors are considered an obstacle and an eyesore. They block the flow of vehicular and pedestrian traffic, as a car's right to move apparently outweighs a vendor's right to make a living. They are described as dirty and unattractive, a blight on the cityscape, by those who lay claim to formal urban occupations and roles. Their very presence on the streets is considered a drag on the modernity of the city, something retrograde and primitive, antagonistic to the progressive vision of a clean and neatly ordered modern city.[16] The impulse to modernize, to gentrify and "clean up" particular neighborhoods where the poor live and work is part of an effort to eradicate the taint of backwardness that informality seems to convey.[17] "Chaos" is retrograde, whereas "order" is modern, and the disorder of the streets is used to justify state surveillance and intervention, even as that disorder is itself a product of state practices, as the Alcaldía's willingness to sell public space to vendors makes clear.

But state sovereignty is in many ways dependent on the maintenance of the informal economy as a workplace for the urban poor. Selling on the streets provides the poor with income while generating resources for the state. This is most demonstrated by the fact that the Alcaldía, though decrying "chaos" in the city's public spaces, never really tries to remove the ambulantes permanently from the streets, to impose a real and lasting "order" that would prohibit street vending entirely. Instead, it preserves a situation in which a fundamentally exploitable population is held indefinitely in suspended animation, frozen in a condition of perpetual disorder and irresolvable informality. The ambulantes are located within an ambiguous and insecure space, what Oren Yiftachel has described as "'gray space'—positioned between the 'whiteness' of legality/approval/safety, and the 'blackness' of eviction/destruction/death."[18] Neither fully included nor entirely excluded from the market, the ambulantes and others among the criminally informal occupy a middle ground of "permanent temporariness," both tolerated and despised, always on the fringes but never fully recognized as belonging.[19] The "chaos" of the market provides the state with a convenient rationale for an ongoing, incomplete repression, an always ready justification for occasional campaigns to "clean up" the city, one that can be selectively ignored as circumstances require. The state never really removes the ambulantes—it does not kill or jail or relocate them, because to do so would eliminate this rationale of governance and deprive the state of the resources the ambulantes contribute, the payments and payoffs that constitute important sources of state revenue. Full-scale repression might also lead to the political radicalization of an as yet quiescent underclass. Instead, the ambulantes are assigned to the gray spaces of permanent informality, without pushing them into open warfare with the powers that be.

Rather than a fixed position inhabited by permanently "informal" actors, then, informality is a condition, a pervasive and fluctuating status that may characterize the operations of any given actor or institution at any given moment. State authorities selectively adopt informal behavior when it suits their needs, and at other times they rail against the informal activities of the criminal underclass. This understanding helps us to better grasp the history of Cochabamba over the past five hundred years as the city has grown to become the heart of Bolivia's informal economy—a history that the next chapter explores.

# 13. The Modern City
## Cochabamba, 1900–1953

Although the formal-informal distinction persists as a key element in how scholars conceptualize Latin American cities' organization and governance, more recent approaches to informal street economies and housing settlements speak of the "informal city," recognizing that the domains labeled "formal" and "informal" are in fact deeply interconnected.[1] In Latin America the formal and informal cities and their inhabitants have always been part of one single city. Informal housing for the urban poor, for example, was present in the colonial period, and was so ubiquitous that it typically lacked any labeling term to distinguish it from the formal housing of the elites.[2] Vendors and workers in the informal economy have long been found in these cities, since colonial times working to satisfy the needs of urban residents and providing vital services, resources, and labor that keep the entire city functioning.[3] The culture of the urban poor, far from being "marginal" to mainstream society, is in fact highly creative and characteristic of urban life more generally.[4] Nevertheless, the ideology of formal-informal and center-margins has been critical to the formation of Latin American cities, indexing distinct racial and class divisions that have persisted since colonial times.[5]

Throughout Latin America, the marginalization of non-European peoples and cultures that began during colonialism intensified in the postcolony as urban planning emerged as a discipline for remaking the city and dividing the formal and the legal from the informal and illegal. In tracing the historical emergence of *favelas* and *mocambos*, the informal neighborhoods and shacks that for centuries have housed Brazil's urban poor, the historian Brodwyn Fischer describes the entire notion of the informal as an invention of urban elites.[6] In the late nineteenth century and early twentieth century, Latin American governments, planners, and ruling classes got caught up in a global modernist obsession, a preoccupation with remaking society according to European ideals of race and culture.[7] Modernist urban planning—which aimed to make the city a locus of progress, order, and rationality, framed by an aesthetic featuring clean lines and the use of new materials such as steel and concrete—insisted on spatial segregation, with the residences, workplaces, and recreational sites of the city's poorer and darker-skinned populations marked off from those of the "modern," Europe-oriented city and nation.[8] In many cities, this included the labeling of spaces that had long existed but had gone unremarked. In Rio de Janeiro, for example, the hillside shantytowns became "favelas," a distinct socioeconomic type that contrasted explicitly with the city below, which was seen to embody "European standards of civilization, culture, hygiene, and race."[9] Similar patterns could be found elsewhere in the region, where "premodern" or "backward" forms of living and working were pushed to the urban margins and where informal political, economic, and cultural activities were allowed to proliferate.[10] As the urban sociologist Diane Davis puts it, these patterns of urbanization "not only set the basis for social and spatial separation rather than integration, they reinforced the view that those who lived in the informal city/marginal neighborhoods were second class citizens not morally worthy of inclusion or recognition, whose urban lifestyles and practices both stained and challenged the larger modernist project."[11]

As part of this project—which lasted throughout the twentieth century and in many ways continues to the present day—the social spaces at "the margins of the state" were imagined as extreme contrasts to the elite neighborhoods and workplaces of the city center, spaces of disease, barbarous lifestyles, and moral degradation.[12] These neighborhoods and zones—which included not only the poor residential neighborhoods that have been the object of much scholarly attention,[13] but also popular workplaces and markets such as Cochabamba's Cancha—became sites of burgeoning informality, where practices excluded from other parts of the city were tolerated. But, again, to describe them as spaces of informality is not to suggest that they were immune to state regulation. As this history of Cochabamba and the Cancha demonstrate, the state has always had a tenuous relationship with these marginalized, informal locations of the city, at once permitting their informal activities while simultaneously attempting to maintain state authority over them.

By the dawn of the twentieth century, when the drive toward "modernization" began to take hold, Cochabamba had emerged as a major Bolivian city, the second largest in the nation at the time. The city's population was divided into geographical sectors, with the majority of wealthy administrators, businesspeople, and landed elites residing in the north and the families of laborers, artisans, and small-scale comerciantes residing in the south. The popular markets, or ferias (which, like today, were busiest on Wednesdays and Saturdays, the días de feria), flourished in the peripheral spaces, serving not only to provision the city but to join it to its rural hinterland. Many of the patrons of the ferias were rural peasants and small-scale producers attracted to the city as a site to sell or barter their wares; itinerant vendors also frequented the Cancha as part of a regular round between the markets of the city and those of the various towns of the Cochabamba valley. Rural people were also drawn to the Cancha by the availability of cooked food and chicha and came to celebrate and drink the proceeds of their sales. Thousands of vendors could be found each week in these markets, perhaps the majority of them women, many of them wives of small farmers who sold the produce while their husbands worked the fields.[14] Women gained a measure of autonomy in these commercial spaces, and some of them established urban residences apart from their rural partners and families so they could enjoy their independence and further develop their commercial enterprises.[15]

The modernist impulse that swept across Latin America—indeed, the world—in the early twentieth century came relatively late to Cochabamba, but it came, and it transformed the city. The dreams of modernist urban planners took shape through official regulations pertaining to the development of the city center.[16] In the 1910s and 1920s, streets were widened to make room for automobiles and motorized public transport. These served to link far-flung districts into a single "urban fabric," allowing elites to work

13.1 Cochabamba, the "garden city" of Bolivia. Photograph by the author.

in the city center and live in bucolic suburban districts such as Cala Cala and Queru Queru north of town, consolidating Cochabamba's status as the "garden city" (*ciudad-jardín*) of Bolivia (figure 13.1).[17] Other infrastructural developments included electrification of homes and businesses, public lighting, running water, and sewer systems—improvements concentrated in the finer neighborhoods of the suburbs and the old downtown. In the name of "progress," planners divided the city into zones, the "separation of functions" being a fundamental feature of modernist urban design,[18] although this was more a theoretical than an actual reorganization of urban space. The area around the Plaza Principal was reimagined as the "modern commercial center" of the city, to be used exclusively by "respectable" retailers such as import-export houses, firms dealing in overseas goods, banks, foreign companies, and established family businesses.[19] The long-standing colonial hierarchies and divisions in the city were maintained yet rearticulated in a modernist idiom, the pseudoscientific dogma of racialized modernity providing elites and municipal authorities with a new way to conceptualize human difference in the city. The benefits of modern civilization, it was determined, were to be available to members of the deserving, superior "races," while the indigenous, the mestizos, and the poor maintained their "traditions" and "barbarous customs" on the urban periphery.[20] There, in the Cancha, they practiced what Gustavo Rodríguez Ostria and Humberto Solares Serrano call the "other commerce" (el otro comercio) of the city, a commerce distinct from the international businesses of the city center. It was intended to satisfy the needs and desires of the "popular" sectors of the urban population—artisans, small traders and vendors, domestic servants, and the like, all of them ethnically indigenous or mestizo.[21] Like the chicherías, this "other commerce" was considered a poor fit with the "new urban values" that accompanied modernization and was pushed to the edges of the city.[22]

Ironically, much of the "progress" toward modernity in Cochabamba was underwritten by these same "barbarous" indigenous practices, in particular the consumption of chicha. Despite the formal banishment of the chicherías from the city center, the municipality increasingly came to rely on the taxes paid on the manufacture and sale of chicha to fund urban development. Many of the streets from which the chicherías were evicted in the 1880s were subsequently paved using tax proceeds generated by patentes paid by the owners of taverns now located in the Cancha and by taxes on the sale of chicha to a largely indigenous and mestizo clientele. In 1920, the Alcaldía used these monies to acquire large parcels of land east of the city center for development of elite and middle-class housing, and in 1926 it installed running water and plumbing—infrastructural hallmarks of modernity—in the city center. Even into the 1950s, tax proceeds from chicha paid for the construction of schools and hospitals, the installation of electrical systems, and the planting of trees in the city's plazas. This form of modernization has been called "dependent urbanization," based as it is on the extraction of resources from the poor to support the modern urban façade enjoyed mostly by the wealthy.[23] Nevertheless, the gente decente (the "decent people," as the oligarchy called itself) continued to regard chicha and the people who made and consumed it as a major urban "problem" and relegated them to the margins of the city where their barbarous practices might not contaminate the rest of the population. Even today, chicha retains the stigma of the antimodern and antisocial. As Solares Serrano grumbles, "Chicha created progress for the city, but now is considered a drink for delinquents and the popular classes."[24]

Although small-scale ambulant vendors were part of Cochabamba's market scene during the nineteenth century, they first appear in the historical records in 1917. In that year, the category of "itinerant vendors" (*vendedores ambulantes*) is listed for the first time in the record of patentes paid by comerciantes to the state.[25] These records are incomplete, of course, given that most ambulantes would have been paying not the annual patente but the more informal sentaje, which was paid daily or weekly and granted them license to sell. Nevertheless, it is clear that by this time the ambulantes were enough of a presence on the city streets to begin attracting official attention. At the same time, they began provoking public discontent. In 1918, complaints about the presence of "*comerciantes minoristas ambulantes*" on the streets of Cochabamba began to appear in newspapers. Writers protested against vendors "who don't pay the *patente municipal* or any other kind of tax" and so gain an unfair competitive advantage over other comerciantes.[26] Although this claim is obviously belied by the fact that some ambulantes are listed in the aforementioned tax records, from this early date street vendors were being portrayed as undeserving interlopers, taking unfair advantage of the municipality's largesse by failing to contribute to the public coffers. The same complaint is made about ambulantes today (see chapter 26).

Beginning in 1910 and continuing into the 1980s, the municipality of Cochabamba attempted to regulate its growth and development through a series of strategic master plans.[27] The plans aimed to transform the "village" of Cochabamba into a modern city of broad, tree-lined avenues, stately parks, and monumental architecture on par with any great European city.[28] They never came to fruition, however, much beyond the central plaza and its surrounding streets. Instead, Cochabamba grew according to a different logic dictated not by modernist delusions but by a demand for housing and work that could be satisfied only on the urban periphery. The Cancha, not the city center, became the locus of urban economic and social life, the hub of urban transportation, and the object of migrants' fantasies. During the first half of the twentieth century, Cochabamba became the destination of choice for people seeking employment for themselves and education for their children.[29] Key moments included the influx of former combatants following the end of the Chaco War with Paraguay in 1935 and the "invasion" of the city by the so-called Indian hordes (*la indiada*) in the wake of the national revolution of 1952 and agrarian reform of 1953.[30] Much of this in-migration was due to the market culture of the city and the promise it held of work to be found in and around the Cancha. The ferias of Cochabamba were "an irresistible magnet" for poor migrants, who came in search of their dreams but more frequently encountered "crude reality: the stable job for which they yearned did not exist, everything—work, housing, education, health—had to come from their own effort and creativity, amidst no small amount of frustration, adversity, manifest injustice, and racial discrimination."[31]

Facing increased urbanization and expanding mercantile activity in the nation's cities, the Bolivian state in 1940 issued a law to regulate informal commerce. Announced in April of that year, the law created the Registry of Ambulant Commerce, which authorized municipalities to issue licenses permitting vendors to sell in the streets.[32] These licenses were valid for periods of six months, and their cost was based on the value of the vendors' goods. Ambulantes who failed to register under this law faced fines of up to three times the cost of the license. The registry endured until the end of the 1960s, by which time street vendors were so numerous that the law had become unenforceable. This situation would become even more overwhelming from the 1970s on, as informal commerce in the city continued to expand.

As the space of marketing grew beyond the traditional markets of the Cancha, it expanded into the streets and sidewalks of the surrounding neighborhoods. Occupancy of these commercial spaces would be the source of future conflicts between different groups of comerciantes, and between comerciantes and city authorities, as the next chapter explores.

# 14. Market Space, Market Time

Nacho is walking through the Cancha when he spies a very old woman (an *ancianita*), bent nearly in two, using an old broom handle for a cane and carrying an enormous bundle on her misshapen back. On the sidewalk in front of a closed puesto fijo she stops and lays out her hand-woven *aguayo*, on which she spreads small bundles of herbs. Nacho is about to walk on when he notices that these are not ordinary herbs. Among them is *chinchircoma*, a flower as red as fire that grows only in the highest, most mountainous parts of the Andes, places inaccessible even to goats. Nacho figures that this woman has some special, even mystical knowledge (only true mystics use chinchircoma) and heads over to speak with her.

Just then, the owner of the puesto arrives. "Get out of here!" she yells at the ancianita crouched on the sidewalk.[1] "You can't sell here, this place already has an owner!" The puesto vendor is joined by another woman, the occupant of an adjacent stall. "Who told you that you could sell here?" she demands of the ancianita. "Get moving!"

The old woman seems unfazed by this combined assault. She stares at the two women without expression and states simply that she is tired and needs a place to sit. "Just let me sell here for a couple of hours, and I'll move on," she says.

But the two fijas are having none of it. They shout insults and provocations at the ancianita, who stares fixedly off into space. This infuriates the fijas even more. One of them grabs the old woman by the arm and tries to dislodge her from her spot on the sidewalk, but the ancianita is stronger than she looks and will not budge. She tells the fijas that she has a bad back and is tired of walking with such a heavy bundle; can they not at least let her rest here for a few minutes? "One day you, too, will get old," she says, "and life will treat you as you are now treating me."

This sends the fijas over the edge. They must sense the same mystical power in the old ambulante that Nacho detected, because now their anger is mixed with fear. One of them, shrieking, declares that the old lady is a witch and accuses her of placing a curse on them ("¡Seguro que me está maldiciendo!"). The other one fetches a bucket of water from her puesto and dumps it over the head of the seated ancianita, drenching her. "India kuru (Quechua: hunchbacked Indian)," she sneers, "why don't you cure yourself if you know so much about herbs?" The old woman lashes out with her makeshift cane, sending the bucket flying.

At this point, Nacho moves to intervene, putting himself between the women to protect the ancianita from further retaliation. The fijas glare at him, shouting and cursing. But other people step in, as well, including passersby and even some neighboring comerciantes fijos, all in defense of the old ambulante. Seeing that the old woman now has adequate support, Nacho slips away, concerned about making enemies in the space of our fieldwork.

........................

The philosopher Michel de Certeau famously distinguished "place" from "space," identifying the latter as dynamic and unstable, a geography brought into being by the uses to which it is actually put.[2] The city street, for example, is a *place* defined by urban planners to serve a designated or "proper" purpose, but the street is made a *space* by the pedestrians who walk it (or, I would add, the vendors who sell in it), transforming place into space and opening new possibilities for what that space can mean and how it can be used. Places can be represented on maps, but spaces must be described through tours, constructed representations of the actual experience of being in them.[3] Chapter 11 provided such a tour of the Cancha.

The Cancha is typically thought of as a place. It can be found on maps, a big irregular splotch on the city's near-south side. The Cancha is a destination—for shoppers, for tourists, for thieves and runaways and gov-

14.1 Women selling herbs in front of a closed puesto. Photograph by Lisa Berg.

ernment officials and social scientists. Bus lines run to it, through it, from it. All of this makes it very place-like.

But one can never be too sure of oneself in the Cancha. It is not a place in the strict sense of the term, for the Cancha is not a fixed location. It moves. It changes. It has changed over the course of its history, as what began as many small markets fused into one giant one and then expanded to incorporate neighboring plazas and adjacent streets.

The Cancha changes in the course of a single day, too. Whole aisles of stalls appear on certain days of the week and disappear on others. Vendors will manifest in one place for a time, filling a sidewalk with their wares, and then vanish as the clock strikes a certain hour (figure 14.1). The space that individual vendors occupy changes from day to night as they slowly, imperceptibly advance their stalls out into the aisles, taking space from the public walkways and transforming it into their private retail space by occupying it. Where today someone is selling apples, tomorrow someone else might be selling pencils. Some days the market is so intensely crowded that one can barely squeeze through its passageways. Other days it is like a ghost town, and vendors sit idly chatting with each other, with the comisarios, with the odd customer passing by. The Cancha, in de Certeau's terms, is much more of a space than a place. The Cancha may appear on maps, but no two maps can agree on its actual frontiers, its limits and extent. Any map, any inscription, can only be a snapshot of the Cancha at a particular moment in its development, to which it never again actually corresponds.[4]

Space is the diacritic of survival in the Cancha and the subject of a great deal of ethnographic reflection on informality and market life.[5] Access to space determines who can sell, and who can survive, in the market. But market space is also about market time. The market's movement, its growth, occurs over both the long term and the short term. In the course of its history, the market has expanded, incorporating new areas, transforming streets and parks into market space. What we call the Cancha is an agglomeration of spaces, various ferias that over time have merged into a singular sprawling mass on the southern edge of the old downtown.

The Cancha has its seasons. February's Carnaval is one of them. During the weeks preceding Carnaval, new kinds of merchandise appear throughout the market: misas to burn as part of the purification ritual of the q'owa, water balloons and pistols, foam and Silly String, special food served only during the pre-Lenten festivities. The same is true for Todos Santos (All Saints Day), which falls on November 1, and the accompanying Día de los Difuntos (Day of the Dead). In the time leading up to Todos Santos, Cancha vendors sell all kinds of items for the traditional celebration of the holiday—candles, liquor, fruit, candies, mystical objects, and the ubiquitous thantha wawas (sugary bread baked in the shape of children)—that are given as offerings to the recently departed. But also available are the familiar trappings of a transnational Halloween, including masks, costumes, treats, and decorations, all of which can be found for sale at this time of year.[6]

The biggest seasonal change in the Cancha occurs at Christmas time (la Navidad). New sounds fill the air—the tinkling of bells, bands playing seasonal songs—and new vendors take to the streets. A contingent of Christmas vendors (comerciantes de ferias navideñas) suddenly materializes in early December, setting up new stalls in areas previously uncolonized by commerce, usually in the streets and roundabouts that border La Pampa. The appearance of these vendors often generates new conflicts in the market, with the introduction of new competitors for space and clientele into the already conflictive mix. Padre Abelardo at the San Antonio church has fought an ongoing battle with these Christmas vendors, who every year try to invade his church patio to set up stalls. Nevertheless, the general spirit of the time is festive as people prepare to celebrate the Christmas holiday. Vendors joke and tease one another in a lighthearted and friendly way, enlivened not only by the pending holiday but by the seasonal increase in prices. Formal workers in Bolivia customarily receive an *aguinaldo* at the year's end, a holiday bonus worth the equivalent of a month's pay.[7] In the Cancha, where everyone is "self-employed," prices on everything—not just Christmas paraphernalia but ordinary items, too—rise by a few bolivianos. Vendors call this their *aguinaldito*, and it is generally paid with good humor by the shoppers. The bribes paid to municipal authorities also increase with the season, as public employees seek aguinaldos of their own. The good-will of the period ends abruptly, though, for any Christmas vendors who try to remain in their seasonal puestos: after the new year, the comisarios are quick to drive them away.

The space of the market grows and changes in more microscopic ways, as well, shifting throughout the year but also during the course of a single day. From morning to night, the market goes through various transformations, with the use and distribution of space keyed to the time of day. In the early morning hours, before the sun even begins to rise, Nacho and I walk through the market, entranced by its tranquility (figure 14.2). The market is asleep. Puestos, covered with heavy tarps, loom ghostlike out of the darkness. Piles of trash, the refuse of the previous day, adorn the street corners, awaiting the brooms of the trash collectors. Packs of dogs roam the quiet streets, and one can spy an occasional delinquent lurking in the shadows of a street lamp. A lone *carratillero* pushes a wheelbarrow. Otherwise, stillness.

By 5 AM, the market is beginning to awaken. The trucks of the *mayoristas* roll in, bringing goods directly from the countryside or via the *mercado campesino*, a wholesale market far to the city's south. They park on Los Andes street, a block above Avenida República to the east of La Pampa, and distribute their wares to a small army of women and men, *comerciantes minoristas* who, bundled against the morning cold, are waiting to receive them. They elbow one another out of the way as they try to get the best produce from the mayoristas, shattering the morning calm with their squabbling. Many of these vendors are accompanied by carratilleros, waiting patiently in the wings for their employers, to help them wheel their goods back to their puestos. Carrots from Oruro and Parotani, onions from Mizque, tomatoes from Saipina, green beans from Pojo, bananas and lemons from the Chapare—all manner of produce comes off the trucks in red bags from the highlands and blue bags from the Cochabamba valley.

There is a notable mixing of classes at this hour, as people gather at breakfast stalls and carts to take their morning refresher. Nacho, waxing

14.2 The Cancha at night. Photograph by the author.

poetic, describes in his fieldnotes how "the first rays of the sun revive a tradition of yesteryear, in which nobles and plebeians alike come to the markets to drink a glass of linaza (flax seed) or gelatina de pata (boiled hoof), to clean out the liver and cure what ails them, to give them an easy and healthy day. There is a great demand for these traditional products, like linaza, gelatina de pata, jugo de alfalfa (alfalfa juice), mate de diente de léon (lion's tooth tea), and others."[8]

As the morning wears on, the market comes to life. Soon traffic is circulating—taxis, buses, bicycles—and people begin to fill the streets and sidewalks. In the market, the puestos are opening. The carniceros are at work, the air filled with the smell of fresh blood and the buzz of electric band saws cutting haunches of beef into marketable portions. The puestos by the train station are still closed, but the sidewalks in front of them are filled with vendors, hawkers of clothing—shirts, blouses, pants, caps, and so on— selling from the places that are currently unoccupied but later will be taken by their rightful owners. This is how space in the Cancha is used—if you are not in your regular spot, others will come along and use it, claiming usufruct rights until you show up and kick them out. The owner of space in the Cancha is the person who can occupy that space and keep others out, from one moment to the next. Livelihoods depend on people's ongoing ability to control these contested spaces through the course of days and seasons.

Similar kinds of temporally contingent marketing appear throughout the day. Later in the afternoon I am walking down Avenida Punata, one of the busiest streets in the Cancha, when a truck suddenly pulls up to the curb and discharges an enormous pile of shoes onto the sidewalk in front of me. I step back reflexively, but a mass of pedestrians surges in, picking through the shoe piles, trying to find matching pairs in their size. From the truck, a man on a bullhorn barks out an announcement: "incredible limited-time offer." I term this the "guerrilla sale," and it happens frequently in and around the Cancha. Unused (i.e., public) space suddenly is transformed into a space of marketing, and just as quickly changes back. The guerrilla shoe sale lasts about fifteen minutes, after which time some men get down from the truck, gather up the remaining shoes, and drive off.

The Cancha continues to morph throughout the day. As afternoon passes and evening begins, the market's rhythm and mood change once more. Avenida San Martín is one of the major downtown thoroughfares connecting the Cancha to the city's Plaza Principal, and by day it is filled with businesspeople hurrying to and fro. But in the evening, San Martín becomes the

Cancha. Vendors of every variety occupy spaces up and down the sidewalks, their wares spread on blankets or stacked on low stands. Tons of stuff is being sold, most of it the usual small wares, plus plenty of used clothing. Vendors of food, too, are out, selling the night food: fried tripe, hamburgers and *salchichas*, even pizza being cooked in a small sidewalk oven. Lots of beggars. The whole thing is like a fair, with not a cop in sight, though one spots many dirty, frazzled young men who could easily be delinquents or *cleferos* (glue addicts). The fair stretches from Punata all the way to Calle Jordan, an incredible eight blocks of spontaneous nocturnal commerce.

The absence of police at particular times of day is a key correlate of market temporality. The explosion of nocturnal sidewalk commerce on Avenida San Martín is not surprising when one considers that the market police go home at 5 PM. With no comisarios out to chase them away, the ambulantes can finally settle down in a spot and sell without fear of harassment. New, evening sellers also appear, including some comerciantes fijos who take advantage of these times, coming out of the market to sell on the street. Sundays, though generally slower than other days, are also good days for street selling: the comisarios do not work on Sundays, either.

The delinquents are also attuned to the timing of the police, both public and private. The private police of the market do not work at night, making that the preferred time of day for the thieves and muggers to go to work (see chapter 32). The Cancha grows exponentially more dangerous after dark, and shoppers tend to avoid it—another reason, perhaps, for the eruption of nocturnal commerce elsewhere in the downtown area.

Another night settles over the Cancha. The stragglers lock up their stalls and the remaining ambulantes stow their carts in a nearby garage, all of them heading to catch their buses home. Tomorrow will be another busy day in the market, and if they are lucky, the comerciantes might catch a few hours of sleep before heading back to work.

Soon it will be Carnaval, and the market will change its rhythms once again. I have been looking forward to the holiday, for it is then that Don Rafo has promised to introduce me to the comerciantes fijos of La Pampa.

# 15. Carnaval in the Cancha

Carnaval is celebrated in Bolivia, as it is throughout the Catholic world, on the Tuesday before the start of Lent. The official celebrations of Carnaval are held in the downtowns of the nation's cities, and Bolivia is especially famous for its Carnaval in the highland mining town of Oruro. Bands play folkloric tunes while troupes of elaborately costumed dancers parade through the streets. Historically, Carnaval has been a celebration marked by inversion, a time for the poor and marginalized to take over public space, sometimes openly ridiculing the wealthy and powerful in their dance performances.[1] In the big public shows, however, the wealthy and powerful long ago took control of the performances, with the poor serving mostly as spectators.

Far from the broad avenues and the costumed displays of downtown, Bolivian people celebrate Carnaval in humbler ways. People party in their homes and businesses, asking the deities for blessings and ritually purifying their residences. Carnaval is an occasion for people to get very drunk and eat gigantic meals before they begin their Lenten sacrifices. It is also a time to play with water, and Bolivians like to soak one another with water balloons, water guns, and buckets of water (and sometimes chicha), as well as with shaving cream, ink, paint, and whatever else is at hand. The entire month preceding Carnaval is water balloon season in Cochabamba, and gringos walking on the street are favorite targets.

On the morning of Carnaval, Nacho, Eric, and I meet at our office to prepare ourselves for our visit to La Pampa. Nacho has warned me about what to expect, and I arrive in old clothes and a cheap pair of sandals, which will be ruined by the end of the day. Uncertain of what to expect, I am nervous as we head out into the market.

All seems normal as we enter La Pampa, except for an inordinate amount of sweet-smelling smoke that fills the air—people are preparing fires for the q'owa, the purification ritual that accompanies the celebrations. In each market stall, comerciantes burn offerings consisting of herbs, llama wool, grains and seeds, and small figurines symbolizing desired objects—money, cars, houses, diplomas—to ask for health, good fortune, and success in their businesses. But the fires are intense: it is almost as though a dark fog has settled over the alleys of the market, and it is difficult to breathe. (The next day my lungs feel burned, my throat hurts, and I am coughing up large quantities of gray mucus.) Ritual purifications of this kind are conducted in the Cancha on the first Friday of every month, but the Carnaval q'owa is the most widespread and elaborate and, therefore, the most pungent.

We find our way to the puesto of Don Rafo, and he introduces us to his wife—a quiet woman in the apron and kerchief of a Cancha market vendor—before leading us out on a tour of La Pampa. Rafo walks slowly, like royalty, inspecting his subjects. People on all sides greet him as we process through the market. He points out the different sectors of La Pampa as we pass. "Here are the *comedoras* (lunch ladies)," he says. "Here they sell *telas* (cloth); here is the sector for *chiflería* (small hardware and housewares)," and so on.[2] Frequently he stops before a puesto to chat with the vendor and to introduce us, presenting us as "a project that is going to help us with security." He also explains about the seminar that we are going to have, insisting that each sector of the market send two representatives so that we can understand their experiences in dealing with security problems.

People respond to this introduction in different ways. Although everyone greets us with handshakes, some people include a hug in the salutation, offering us chicha and inviting us to come back and chat with them some time. Others are more guarded and, despite the introduction by the president of the federation, refuse to make eye contact or offer more than a perfunctory greeting. Still, most people seem happy to meet us. I take some photos, promising to return to deliver copies, and repeat Rafo's invitation that they attend the seminar.

In a quiet alley where people sell a variety of dry goods from oversize stalls, the vendors give us a particularly warm welcome. The leader of this sector is a woman, Doña Tahlia, and her second in command is Doña Irena, who runs a small breakfast shop, selling hot chocolate, herbal tea, and buñuelos. Don Rafo whispers to me that these women are likely to be two excellent collaborators in my research, and indeed, Doña Tahlia is already telling me stories about insecurity in La Pampa. For example, she says, today is Carnaval, a day on which the vendors especially need the help of the private security guards employed by the market to keep an eye on things while they are celebrating. But, she says, these security guards have decided instead to dress up as women and dance in the streets, leaving the stalls unprotected. She offers this observation with a sour smile. Tahlia complains that the market's reputation for insecurity costs her money: housewives are afraid to come to La Pampa, she says, so they go elsewhere to do their shopping.

In Tahlia and Irena's sector there is a *virgencita*—a little plaster figure of the Virgin Mary, elaborately dressed and housed in a glass box in the center aisle of the sector. On Carnaval, the women of the sector offer blessings to their little Virgin, the deity who watches over them and ensures their prosperity. I take photos of Tahlia, Irena, Rafo, and other comerciantes posing with the Virgin and promise to return with copies of the photos for the women. The vendors invite Nacho, Eric, and me to drink beer and chicha with them, then, in the friendliest way imaginable, they dump buckets of cold water over our heads. They wind streamers around our necks, and rub handfuls of confetti into our hair, laughing all the while (figure 15.1).

Before we leave, I tell Tahlia and Irena that I am delighted to have met them. And I am—in addition to being interesting and lively company, they are female leaders of a major sector of La Pampa. They will be important collaborators as I try to understand the roles of women and men as gendered actors in the market.

We move on. Don Rafo continues to point out the sights: the *sastres* (tailors), the *carniceros* (butchers), the *cristileros* (sellers of glassware), the *dulceros* (candy sellers). Soon we are passing a sector where all of the stalls sell colorful plastic kitchenware: red plastic plates, blue plastic cups, green plastic utensils, and the like. No one is celebrating in this sector—there is no alcohol to be seen, no reverie in the aisles. Rafo explains that this sector is controlled by evangelical Christians, people who do not drink, or dance, or celebrate "pagan" holidays such as Carnaval. The Carnaval celebration has

15.1 Nacho, the author, and some new friends celebrate Carnaval in La Pampa. Photographer unknown.

diminished somewhat in recent years, Rafo says, as the presence of evangelical comerciantes in La Pampa has increased.

We return to Rafo's stall for a rest, and his wife serves lunch, bringing out enormous plates of *puchero*, a stew of chicken and vegetables considered a "typical" food of Carnaval. She also serves copious amounts of alcohol, especially beer and chicha. While we eat and drink, Rafo talks, but the music from a nearby party is so loud I cannot make out anything he says. I try to look intelligent and nod at the appropriate times, but Rafo does not seem to notice.

After we eat, I offer to buy beer, and Rafo points me to a nearby shop. Nacho and I head off to get the beer, but we find ourselves continually way-laid by exuberant comerciantes who invite us to have a drink and then douse us with water. There are no shoppers to be seen amid the festivities, only drunk comerciantes and we two anthropologists. At one stall, an ancient cholita teaches me the proper way to drink. I know, of course, that before drinking I have to *ch'allar*—pour some of my drink on the ground as an of-fering to the Pachamama, the principal goddess of the earth. In La Pampa, though, you have to ch'allar in each corner and at the entrance to the stall, to provide the appropriate blessing for business success, health, and long life. There is also a style to the *ch'alla*. You can't just dump your drink uncer-emoniously on the ground, the ancient cholita says. "You have to ch'allar gently" to show respect for the Pachamama. She demonstrates with her own cup. Nacho, meanwhile, tries to show me how to ch'allar so as not to get too drunk, pouring about half of his cup on the ground. But the ancient cholita is nobody's fool: she sees what Nacho is up to, slaps his hand, and pours him another cup, which she obliges him to drink in its entirety. Nacho com-plies, chastened.

Eventually, we get the beer and return to Rafo's stall. We share the bottles among us, Rafo continuing to hold forth amid the noise of the party. We then head out for another tour around La Pampa. Rafo has a lot of people to visit. Many of the comerciantes in his sector are also his *compadres*, rit-ual kinsmen for whose children Rafo is godfather. As he passes, his com-padres call him in to their stalls, press him (and his guests—Nacho, Eric, and me) with food and drink, soak us with water and cheap alcohol, and rub confetti in our hair. In some places beer is served; in others, chicha. Some of the chicha is delicious, like a dry wine, while some is sickeningly sweet and probably adulterated with grain alcohol to increase its potency. Other people serve us sweet wine mixed with Coca-Cola, which I find revolting.

In another out-of-the way corner of the market we meet Doña Rosa, who sells clay pots and cookware. Rosa is a short, robust woman with a pageboy haircut and a large, distracting mole on the left side of her nose. I find my-self staring at the mole impolitely and realize that all of the alcohol I have consumed is starting to take effect. Rosa hugs me anyway, laughs at my dis-orientation, and invites me back, any time, for a chat. Like Tahlia and Irena, Rosa promises to be an important contact in my research.

It is about 4 PM, and the intensity of the fiesta has increased noticeably. Everywhere people are visibly drunk, dancing in the aisles, throwing water. In the cosmetics section, a girl tries to tag me with shoe polish, but I dodge and she hits Nacho next to me, smearing his forehead with black grease. We cannot walk three feet through the press without being stopped and required to drink, sometimes two or three cups. We are a special target for water, a gringo in the company of the president of the federation. I am soaked through to my underwear.

At last, realizing that I am cold, tired, and drunk, I suggest to Nacho and Eric that we make our exit. We have successfully made contact with the comerciantes fijos of La Pampa and should be able to return to converse with them, if any of us can remember anything from this afternoon of celebration. On our way back to the office and dry clothes, we pass aisles and streets closed to traffic. Water and trash are everywhere; people are dancing on the street corners. The market does not look anything like the market of yesterday, or of tomorrow. It is like another world.

............................

The next day and the Cancha is back to normal. The streets once again are filled with sellers and buyers, with no sign of the previous day's revelry but for the heaps of sodden trash still piled at every corner. The comerciantes seem less energetic than usual, but this could be my own hangover talking.

Nacho and I are exploring the fringes of La Pampa when my cell phone rings. It is Rafo's lawyer, Melvin Gutierrez. "Daniel," he says to me, "I have something very important to tell you. Can I meet you somewhere?" I give him my location, puzzled and alarmed by his urgency, and he rings off.[3]

A few minutes later, Melvin is walking toward me on Avenida Aroma, dressed in a clean white shirt and red silk tie. As he was the other day, he is neatly combed and manicured. Melvin, I realize, was not present for the Carnaval revelry—he is an evangelical Christian, it turns out. "I need 100 bolivianos," he says to me now, "50 for Rafo, and 50 for me. We need to buy phone cards, to tell people in La Pampa about the seminar." This is a small though not insignificant amount of money (about $12), but I hand it over without questioning. Melvin thanks me, saying that this will help ensure that the seminar is a success, and heads back down Aroma the way he came.

Nacho is apoplectic. "Why did you give him that money?" he demands, and I tell him that, again, I did not want to jeopardize our relationship over such a small sum. "But this is a sign!" Nacho replies, irritated by my lack of concern. "They are testing you, Daniel, to see how far they can push you, how much they can get out of you." I tell him he is exaggerating.

"No," Nacho says, quite certain about this. "Men like these are zorros (foxes), Daniel, lobos (wolves), delincuentes de cuello blanco (white-collar criminals). You have to be extremely careful with them." He pauses, thoughtful. "If we are going to give these people gifts," Nacho says, "let's make sure that they are for the benefit of everybody in the market, and not just a couple of melvin-cuentes!"

We both laugh at this neologism, which seems an apt description of our new friends.[4] But Nacho is deadly serious and, I realize, quite correct. We need to figure out some sort of benefit that we can deliver to the comerciantes fijos in the short run, to thank them for their cooperation and to secure their support for our project until the book is ready. Nacho regards me, less red now, his anger at this blatant manipulation softened by his pity for my naïveté. Nacho worries that I am a sheep who will be devoured by the wolves of La Pampa.

# 16. Security and Chaos

La Cancha, centerpiece of Bolivia's informal economy, is immense, larger than anything comparable in the United States. The Cancha is big: in the area it occupies (many square kilometers); the number of people it employs (official estimates put it at 100,000, so the real number is probably far greater); the number of shops it holds (15,000–20,000 by some counts); and the diversity of commodities and services it provides (beyond imagining). But the Cancha, like most of the Majority World's big markets, is an outdoor affair, unconstrained by law or geography to any particular place or size. It cannot be pinned down and measured, like a butterfly tacked to a corkboard. So it is impossible to say how big, exactly, the Cancha is.

Perhaps this is why one gets a sense of the Cancha as being unfathomably huge and energetic. Consider the adjectives that writers use to describe some of the so-called mega-markets around the world: "frenzied," "vast," "chaotic," "amazing," "crazy."[1] Popular street markets like the Cancha seem incomprehensible, wild, disorganized, spontaneous. They are loci of sensory overload, where sights, sounds, and smells can seem limitless, simultaneous, disorienting. Humans cannot perceive beyond the reach of our own senses, so the market seems to go on forever in every direction, the way the ocean seems endless as it bends over the horizon. Plus, the external boundaries of the Cancha are impossible to map accurately, and its internal composition is even more confounding. No cartographer has been brave enough to attempt an anatomical sketch of the Cancha's innards.[2] Even the intrepid *Lonely Planet* guidebook avoids mapping it, though it calls the Cancha "one of the most crowded, chaotic, claustrophobic and exhilarating spots in the country."[3]

But people also experience the market's perceived chaos as deeply unsettling because of the pervasive fear of crime that characterizes daily urban life.[4] Latin America has the highest homicide rate of any world region, with death rates being particularly high among women and children.[5] Rates of violent crime are similarly high, especially in cities.[6] This can be attributed to an array of factors that include enduring poverty, globally high rates of income inequality, ineffective police and justice systems, and the rise of gangs and organized crime.[7] Latin Americans feel increasingly fearful of leaving their homes and venturing into public spaces and in polls list crime as their biggest concern.[8] In Bolivia, recent survey data show that people consider crime and insecurity the single greatest problem facing Bolivian society, with poverty and the economy a distant second.[9] Moreover, people do not trust the police as effective agents of crime control, viewing them instead as corrupt and inefficient. In Bolivia, nearly 90 percent of the people surveyed expressed mistrust of the Bolivian National Police,[10] results that accord with my own, more qualitative assessments. Even when suffering as victims, many Bolivians are reluctant to report crime to the police for fear of wasting time or being re-victimized by police officials seeking bribes.[11]

Latin America is said to be experiencing a crisis of "citizen security," a discourse that emerged across the region in the late 1990s as a way to conceptualize the vulnerability to which ordinary people are exposed by criminal threat and to coordinate efforts to counter it.[12] Promoted by a variety of governments and nongovernmental organizations, citizen security is understood as a break from the authoritarian past, when "security" was largely understood to mean "national security" in the face of a presumed communist threat.[13] Citizen security, in contrast, was meant to encompass "a movement away from security debates whose primary concern was threats to the state or regime toward a concern with threats to public, social and political order posed by rising common crime and public fear of crime."[14] Although the enhancement of citizen security has become a major development goal in Latin America, particularly since the terrorist attacks of September 11, 2001,[15] little has changed in terms of improved policing or administration of justice. Rather, citizen security as a discourse of contemporary life reproduces a narrowing of the security concept, to focus now on crime and criminality as fundamental threats to the very existence of people, society, and the nation.[16] As such, "citizen security" demonizes criminals and potential criminals, often young, poor and working-class black or indigenous men, who emerge as the new "internal enemies" of the "good" people of society. Criminals, like communists and terrorists before them, are made to embody the insecurity that people feel as a general condition of their lives and become the targets of repressive police campaigns; in official statements, the media, and popular talk, they are made to bear full responsibility for pervasive insecurity. Citizen security discourse, which had promised a movement away from equations of security with state stability, trends back to older meanings in the context of criminality and fear, so that it now comes to stand once again for the maintenance of public order and permits the state to suspend rights and use force in creating security.[17]

The insistence on order becomes particularly significant in informal settings, where "disorder" and chaos are presumed to reign. In this context, the Cancha is locally perceived as especially dangerous, largely due to the sense of disorder that infuses and surrounds it. This is compounded by regular reports of crime in the market, the lack of a reliable police force, and the flourishing of informal commerce, all of which contribute to the Cancha's reputation as a place of criminality, lawlessness, and danger. Most Bolivians, in fact, perceive markets like the Cancha to be the most dangerous and insecure spaces in the country, second only to their own neighborhoods.[18] The Cancha is seen as especially productive of "delinquency" (delincuencia, in local parlance), in large part due to its supposed disorder. As stagnant water breeds the malarial mosquito, "chaos" is understood to be criminogenic, spontaneously giving rise to insecurity.

But far from being a natural phenomenon, the violence and insecurity of these spaces can be understood as a direct consequence of neoliberal disregulation (chapter 1). In Bolivian cities, as elsewhere in urban Latin America, the areas in which crime and violence are most strongly experienced are precisely those that the state deems informal and illegal. In these zones—residential spaces like the peripheral neighborhoods (barrios marginales) and areas of informal commerce like the Cancha—the state performs certain regulatory activities that serve to maintain the segregation of the informal and the formal without providing local security. To the extent that they are present in these zones, the police perform surveillance functions (often justified as being in the interest of citizen security) to monitor the "moral disorder" supposed to be present in these areas and to insure that the "pathologies" believed to prevail in informal areas do not contaminate the rest of the (supposedly formal) city.[19] At the same time, those who most clearly are engaged in informal activities represent the principal targets of police repression and extortion. So-called delinquents are the most obvious of these targets, and those suspected of being criminals (street children make the easiest marks) can be abused, removed, or even killed with impunity.[20]

But ambulantes are similarly targeted for abuse. Identified as prime contributors to the market's criminogenic disorder, street vendors, like delinquents, can be denied civil and human rights on the basis of the threat they are believed to pose to urban security. Ambulantes, the most vulnerable and economically insecure of anybody in the Cancha, suffer police raids, extortion, confiscation, and harassment, and are the victims of petty crime by thieves who take advantage of their precariousness. The most insecure are, ironically, those who are viewed as the generators of public insecurity. It is on this basis that repressive campaigns aimed at ambulantes are occasionally initiated by the state in attempts to impose "order" and, by extension, create security in the city. The city's Ordinance 3615, which would target ambulantes for removal from the streets, is an example of this ideology at work.

While they themselves are blamed for causing insecurity, ambulantes generally agree with fijos that the primary threat to security in the market are "delinquents." Many of these delinquents are juveniles who inhabit the dark corners and side streets of the Cancha and lie in wait for the comerciantes and their customers. Additional insecurity comes from the National Police and Municipal Police, who are widely perceived as corrupt and ineffective. Behind the police and their lack of efficacy are the laws and the state, which many comerciantes regard as weak, favoring the perpetrator more than the victim of crime. Here they condemn laws such as the so-called Blattman Law of 1994, which extended basic rights to criminal suspects (e.g., habeas corpus) and eliminated "preventive detention," by which the police could hold suspects indefinitely without filing charges.[21] Many people are also highly critical of the entire notion of "human rights," which they regard as a transnational ideal unsuited to Bolivian reality, and of the nongovernmental organizations that advocate for human rights in Bolivia.[22]

............................

The more time I spend in the Cancha, the more I come to learn about these problems and perspectives. Much of my information comes through informal conversations with comerciantes, a necessary prelude to conducting more formal individual and group interviews (see chapter 20). As I set out on doing fieldwork in La Pampa I begin to explore local people's understandings of security and insecurity, and their feelings about the police, the justice system, and the law.

Don Rómulo and his wife sell candy from a narrow stall in La Pampa. He tells me that "the law has ruined our [justice] system."[23] I ask which law he means. "The Blattman Law, of course." Rómulo says that what Bolivia needs is the death penalty. "Many times, the same polillas [street children, but literally moths] have come back," he says. "If there was the death penalty, it wouldn't be like that." Rómulo is a friendly, handsome, middle-class father of three children; he is well dressed, polite, and clean—what one might call an upstanding citizen. The death penalty, he says, is "the only way to stop the abuse we suffer." He also speaks in favor of death squads, saying that years ago (presumably under the dictatorships of the 1970s) the death squads would go around "liquidating gangsters." They should bring back those death squads, Rómulo says.

The risks to both comerciantes and shoppers in the Cancha are many. Comerciantes fear shoplifters; shoppers fear pickpockets, muggers, and con artists (see chapter 29). Women may have their earrings torn from their ears or their necklaces snatched from around their necks. A shopper in the midst of a transaction is particularly vulnerable to a thief who grabs her money as it leaves her wallet or her wallet as it leaves her purse. Weary folks heading home at night are also vulnerable to thieves, who stake out the bus stops and attack them as they are about to board. A seller can lose her entire day's earnings, meager though they might be, in one sudden assault, and many market vendors live in fear of such an eventuality. They also fear the loss of revenue that crime produces, both in stolen merchandise and in the loss of customers, who shun the Cancha for fear of falling victim to the delinquents. Every criminal assault contributes to the Cancha's reputation as a dangerous place, and such a reputation, as every market vendor knows, is bad for business.

There are other sources of insecurity in the market, however, besides the ubiquitous polillas and delinquents. Doña María is an abarrotera (a dry-goods dealer) in La Pampa and Don Rafo's cousin. She says that one's customers can make a seller insecure. She once had a faithful customer whom she observed slipping a tub of Fleishmann's margarine into her bag. María did not say anything at the moment, but when the customer went to pay for her other stuff, María asked her innocently, "Don't you want some Fleish-mann's?" The customer said no, she already had some. "Yes," María says she told the customer, "you have some. I saw you put it into your bag. 'Oh, I forgot,' the customer said. And this shameless woman just went right on shopping!"[24] Doña María also says that one's employees can be a source of insecurity. María's stall is quite large, and she needs at least two other women to help run it. But, she says, if she is not watching them constantly, they will steal from her, pocketing half the money they collect from custom-ers. Every month she has to fire somebody. But then she has to hire someone else, and that new person was probably just fired by another comerciante in the market, and the problem repeats itself. So, María says, there is constant uncertainty. It is very hard to find people you can trust.

Ambulantes, of course, face additional sources of what we might call insecurity—namely, the fijos themselves and the municipal officials whom the ambulantes regard as the fijos' allies. The seizure of their goods, the con-stant movement, the abusive treatment, the passing traffic—all of these serve to heighten the insecurity that ambulantes confront daily. Some ambulantes—Don Silvio, for instance, the president of the ambulantes' federation—will talk about these routine dangers and challenges as threats to their "security."

For the most part, though, ambulantes rarely characterize these experi-ences and the precarious conditions they engender as security problems.[25] In Bolivia, as in other societies, the language of security, and particularly of citizen security, tends to be used in reference to specific kinds of problems and threats. If elsewhere security is about combatting the terrorist imag-ined to be lurking behind every airport kiosk, in the Cancha "insecurity" is caused by delinquents, and "security" is produced by strategies meant to control them. The boundaries placed around this discourse and the con-sciousness that that entails limit the potential of this language to effect broader political transformations.[26]

The correlation of disorder, informality, and insecurity is not coinciden-tal but a byproduct of the urban disregulation that characterizes informal spaces such as the Cancha. It is a situation that has worsened with time as informal commerce in Cochabamba continued to expand in the late twen-tieth century and early twenty-first century.

# 17. The Informal City
## Cochabamba, 1953–2014

Cochabamba city had always served as a market for the agricultural produce of the surrounding valley farms, but the relationship of small farm families to the urban markets changed following the agrarian reform of 1953.[1] Land that had been consolidated into large estates (*latifundios*) since colonial times was divided into smaller parcels (*minifundios*) and distributed to the peasants who had long worked it. While far more equitable than the estate system that had preceded it, the small parcels of land that resulted from agrarian reform proved inadequate to support large families, especially as patterns of tenure and inheritance further subdivided the land among male siblings after their father's death. Rural people had to find ways to diversify their livelihoods, and children with no land to inherit looked to the city as a way to make a living.

In addition, as independent producers on their own minifundios, peasant farmers lost control over the value of their production due to the changing nature of the urban market. Social relations in the Cancha made it almost impossible for small farmers to sell their wares directly to urban retailers or consumers. With time, the highly profitable ferias had come under the control of commercial syndicates led by wealthy vendors, who implemented strict codes that limited who could sell what and where. Inexperienced peasants coming to the city as sellers encountered the market's "rigid defense mechanisms," which denied them access to stalls from which to sell, forcing them onto the street.[2] Informal market codes were also enforced by the state, especially the Municipal Police (the comisarios) who colluded with the syndicates to maintain control over the market. These comisarios would seize (*decomisar*) peasants' wares for lack of a license, extort payments of multiple or inflated sentajes, and otherwise harass unsophisticated rural vendors who lacked syndical affiliations. Facing these obstacles, rural producers came to rely on clientelistic relationships with brokers, who would buy up their produce and bring it to market for sale.[3] These intermediaries—including *transportistas* (owners of vehicular transport) and *comerciantes mayoristas* (large wholesalers)—became increasingly wealthy and powerful, gaining ever greater footholds in the Cancha as suppliers of the market's retail vendors and political influence among the farmers and villagers of the Cochabamba valley.[4] Some of these intermediaries were women: in the production of chicha, for example, "mestiza entrepreneurs" were instrumental in linking rural corn farmers and chicha makers with urban markets and chicherías.[5] But producers suffered in these exchanges, as the intermediaries had the power to determine prices by virtue of their relative monopoly on rural-to-urban transportation and the peasants' inability to market effectively for themselves. Like the syndicates, the intermediaries were backed by the state, which regulated the pricing structure of certain basic commodities (particularly corn) to favor the growing urban population at the expense of rural producers.[6] These policies also made it difficult for peasant farmers to get credit, limiting their ability to adopt new technology and making them more vulnerable to drought. Such factors combined to further augment producers' desperation and their dependence on intermediaries.[7]

These inequalities led to increasing rural impoverishment in the Cochabamba valley during the 1950s and 1960s. The decline in rural self-sufficiency and the pressures of demographic growth in the countryside fed an immigration boom as the sons and daughters of poor peasant families turned to the city for employment. Though unable to establish themselves as vendors of their own produce, peasants and their children could, with relative ease, set themselves up as ambulant vendors of secondary items such as prepared food, small hardware and supplies, or household goods—in effect, whatever they could get their hands on. This rural-to-urban migration was not necessarily permanent, however. Peasants moved intermittently between countryside and city, returning to work on the family farm in seasons of high labor demand but returning to the city to insert themselves into casual employment situations at other times.[8] In this way, farm families diversified their household reproduction strategies, relying on the "informal" nature of the urban market to provide temporary employment during hard times. What came to be known as *comercio hormiga* (small-scale, or "ant," commerce) was an important source of income for rural women in particular: As in earlier periods, city work allowed women a greater degree of self-sufficiency than they had known in their pueblos of origin.[9]

"Informal" employment also benefited both the state and wealthy capitalists. By providing an outlet for people facing declining rural livelihoods, the urban markets absorbed the surplus labor force of the countryside, diffusing the anger and dissatisfaction of an otherwise massive, unemployed rural population. The hope that the informal economy offered, from a Marxian perspective, was critical in this regard: the commerce of the feria, though closed to small producers, could incorporate the "army" of the self-employed as service providers, artisans, and construction workers but mostly as ambulant vendors, thereby servicing the overall economy and the political needs of the state.[10] This effect was especially important in Cochabamba, a region that lacked any significant industrial development and relied almost entirely on marketing to accomplish this incorporation. The effect for wealthy capitalists was similar: the intermediaries who bought up rural produce for urban resale enriched themselves at the expense of peasant farmers, while the responsibility for maintaining farm families was borne by the farmers themselves through their work in the informal sector. From this perspective, the ferias were sites for the transfer of value from the rural producer to the urban consumer. Prices in the ferias were kept low by the pricing policies of the state and by the extractive practices of the intermediaries, who bought up rural produce at cheap prices underwritten by the "informal" labor of ambulant vendors.[11]

The market that would come to be called "La Pampa" barely existed in the early 1970s. As recalled by many of the earliest vendors, the market then was a dry, flat, and dusty piece of ground—*pampa*, in Quechua—used mostly by traveling circuses to set up their public shows.[12] The only market there was a place called the Thanta Khatu, Quechua for a place to buy secondhand things. Vendors would go door to door in residential neighborhoods, collecting items to resell in the Thanta Khatu. This market would soon come to be called the Barrio Chino, the "Chinese Neighborhood" (although no

Chinese people actually lived in the zone and the name probably began as a reference to the cheap imported goods sold there). In the 1980s, this sector would become notorious as the place to buy and sell stolen property—a different kind of "secondhand" retailing (chapter 28). People also went to the Thanta Khatu to have keys made, a service that many vendors in the Barrio Chino continue to provide today.

One of the founders of the La Pampa market, coincidentally, was my good friend and longtime field consultant Don Miguel. A resident and leader of the barrio Loma Pampa, Don Miguel featured prominently in my previous ethnography, *Outlawed*. Long before moving to Loma Pampa, Don Miguel and his father operated a puesto from which they sold used books. Their puesto was located in the street called La Pampa de las Carreras, where the working classes enjoyed horse racing and other entertainments (see chapter 8). In 1974, Mayor Humberto Coronel Rivas decided to open up the Avenida Aroma as a major east-west thoroughfare, extending the street through what had been the horse-racing grounds and displacing about 150 comerciantes from that area, who relocated south to the open area of La Pampa. Don Miguel and his father were among them. Their puesto, like others of its kind, consisted of a sunshade built of *caña hueca* (a bamboo-like plant) over a dirt floor. He remembers the area as completely barren and devoid of buildings or infrastructure—a memory that accords with what many of the first comerciantes of La Pampa recall. It is a vision of history that supports today's political struggles in the market. As I discuss in chapter 31, comerciantes' claims to market ownership (against the privatization efforts of the municipality; chapter 23) are grounded in this insistence that the market is a product of their own work and investment, accomplished without any public or official support.

Don Miguel was also involved in the creation of the first federation of market vendors, which was established in La Pampa at that time. This federation—and the many others like it that would soon follow—emerged as a broker between comerciantes and the state, negotiating with the authorities on behalf of the market vendors. The federations played an increasingly important role as the market grew, providing not only political representation but also many basic services and infrastructure to the market and its population. But the federations and their leadership suffered under the military regimes of the 1970s and early 1980s. During the dictatorship of General Hugo Banzer Suarez (1971–78), many La Pampa comerciantes declared themselves for the ruling party, the Acción Democrática

17.1  Ambulantes selling on the street. Photograph by the author.

Nacionalista, in the hope that their labor activism would not incur reprisals from the state. But the federations were forced underground, and many of their leaders, accused of fomenting "socialism" in the market, were arrested and "disappeared." With the return of democracy in the 1980s, the federations reemerged and soon became a powerful force in municipal politics (see chapter 19).

Small-scale ambulant street vendors became an ever more frequent sight in Cochabamba during the late 1970s (figure 17.1). A census conducted in 1978 in Cochabamba found 2,334 "sites," loci of people selling in the streets surrounding the Cancha, and estimated that 85 percent of those vendors were women.[13] The market of La Pampa had grown considerably during a short period of time and now had some 12,585 puestos fijos, the largest concentration of fixed stalls in the Cancha. The survey also indicated that one in every three families in the city worked in the ferias, making "commercial activities" the largest source of urban employment. The authors of the resulting study described La Pampa as having a "heterogeneous physical structure"; the market was composed of "móviles y fijos," the presence of the former lending the market an "anarchic quality, lacking the basic conditions of order."[14] This theme would become a constant in observers' descriptions of the market.

From the 1950s through the 1970s, the major sources of migration to Cochabamba city were the towns and pueblos of the Cochabamba valley. By the 1980s, however, the majority of migrants were arriving from the Bolivian highlands (the altiplano). By the early 1990s, half of the city's population consisted of migrants from the highland departments of the country: Oruro, La Paz, and Potosí.[15] This migration, provoked largely by neoliberal political and economic reforms (described in chapter 6), affected both the physical structure and the economy of the city while following familiar patterns of work and settlement. Like generations of *cochabambinos* before them, the altiplano migrants found work in the city's informal sector, principally as ambulant vendors in and around the Cancha. The national census of 1992 found that 64 percent of adults in Cochabamba were "self-employed," meaning that they worked informally.[16] Like earlier generations, the altiplano migrants purchased land on the city's south side, often in violation of municipal law, and built homes as close as possible to their workplaces in the Cancha.[17] The barrios of the southern zone expanded exponentially as migrants settled the barren hillsides and former farmland south of town. New public transportation lines sprang up to connect these neighborhoods to the market; by the end of the twentieth century, the majority of public transportation lines ran to and through the Cancha rather than the city's Plaza Principal.

Map 17.1 shows the expansion of commercial activity in Cochabamba between 1960 and 2014. Based on data provided by the municipality's Office of Urban Planning, the map represents the official view of street commerce in Cochabamba. Curiously, according to the municipality, the Cancha now extends to include even the city's Plaza Principal—a retaking of the "modern" city center by the activities of street vendors, who had been evicted from the plaza a hundred years earlier.

The expansion of small-scale commerce at the end of the twentieth and beginning of the twenty-first century was met with an outcry from many established urban interests. Echoing sentiments expressed at other times in the city's history when change at the hands of an indigenous majority threatened to upset the status quo, voices again expressed concern that the "Indian masses" would destroy the city. Newspaper headlines such as "The City Is Becoming a Giant Indian Camp" warned of the indigenous "invasion," expressing fear that the "*informales*" were taking over the city.[18] Ambulant vendors were accused of causing crowding, congestion, and pollution and of transforming the Cancha into a shopper's nightmare. Of particular

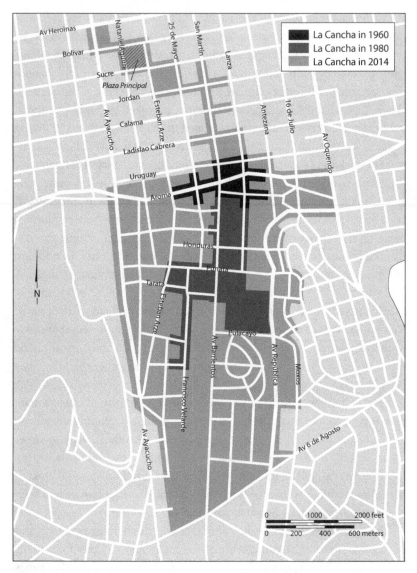

Map 17.1 The growth of the Cancha, 1960–2014. Map drawn by Bill Nelson.

concern were the "chaos," "crowding," and "disorder" that uncontrolled selling seemed to bring, and these words appeared frequently in news accounts of the time. The main streets of the city, according to one report, were becoming "an extension of the markets, with their conditions of overcrowding, lack of hygiene, and obstruction of vehicular and pedestrian traffic."[19] This expansion of informal commerce in the city's streets was seen, too, as an assault on the progress and possibilities of the city as a whole, and the ambulantes were blamed for having an antimodern effect on the urban fabric. Even in 2013, the head of the Intendencia could tell a reporter, "We can't continue like this. Cochabamba has to modernize, and part of that is to remove the comerciantes from the streets."[20] Protests of this type continue to be heard today, as informal commerce continues to expand, with no limit apparently in sight.

........................

Evo Morales was elected to the Bolivian presidency for the first time in 2006 (he was reelected in 2009 and again in 2014), hailed internationally as the region's first indigenous president. Explictly socialist and antineoliberal, Morales and the MAS (Movement Towards Socialism) administration moved quickly to rewrite the national constitution, nationalize major industries (most significantly oil and gas), increase tax rates on transnational corporations doing business in Bolivia, valorize indigenous languages and identities, and extend new benefits to the country's most vulnerable populations. But even as the gross national product rose, employment for the nation's workers remained stagnant. Small-scale marketing on the streets and sidewalks of Bolivia's cities remains the nation's largest form of employment, with as much as 80 percent of the Bolivian population working in informal commerce.[21]

Cochabamba today is Bolivia's fourth-largest city, and the majority of its populace, like that of Bolivia more generally, continues to work informally. Cochabamba's *sector informal* has become a target for Bolivia's luckless and jobless, the "receptacle for all displacements of the workforce, be they rural, mining, state, [or] agricultural."[22] In a country still suffering the consequences of colonialism and neoliberalism—which include endemic poverty, a shortage of good jobs, profound inequalities, and enduring racism and sexism—the Cancha continues to offer dreams of opportunity for the poor and the displaced. "Ant commerce," the small-scale commerce of the sidewalk, provides a safety net for those who have fallen through the cracks.

The Cancha has long defied the efforts of government to regulate and control it. Despite municipal planners' repeated calls for the creation of a *mercado central de ferias* in the city, a centralized marketplace was never formally established in Cochabamba. Instead, the space of marketing developed according to its own logic, the work of the comerciantes themselves, and the needs of buyers and sellers. As the urban population expanded, demand—for both jobs and consumables—expanded with it, and the market grew to accommodate that demand. The space of the city today called "the Cancha" is itself an entity that obeys no commandments but its own.

Nevertheless, it would be a mistake to think of the Cancha as somehow appearing and developing without the intervention or guidance of human actors, particularly, as is so often assumed about informal spaces, without the involvement of the state. As the history of the Cancha illustrates, the market resulted from determined action by municipal elites to push informal commerce and indigenous and mestizo sellers out of the city center and onto the urban periphery, where they would not interfere with the modernization of the city according to a European ideal. The market's evolution has consistently been governed by the interests of the wealthy and powerful, including state authorities; its chaotic, unorganized appearance masks deeper forms of organization that serve to regulate the market and connect it in various ways to the state (chapter 19). Although it appears to be a space of equal opportunity, the market is in fact run by strict sets of codes—products of the "free market" of Cancha capitalism— that limit who can sell there and who has access to the puestos fijos from which wealth can most productively be generated. The market's informality both permits and conceals its internal relations of power and inequality, in which the state and its municipal authorities are deeply implicated. These points are explored in the ethnographic chapters that follow.

# 18. *Convenios*

Not long after my meeting with Don Silvio at my office (chapter 9), I attend the meeting of the leaders of El Paso, the ambulantes' federation, accompanied by Nacho and another assistant, Ruth, who will take notes. The meeting is to be held at an address south of the Cancha. To get there, we walk through La Pampa, across Avenida Pulacayo, and down the narrow streets where vendors sell used clothing imported from the United States. Mountains of blue jeans sit atop folding tables, and T-shirts on wire hangers flap softly in the breeze. The Bolivian government under President Evo Morales has been threatening to outlaw the sale of used U.S. clothing, which has effectively killed the Bolivian clothing manufacturing industry. Most Americans do not realize that when they donate old clothes to a charitable organization in the United States, the agency sells their donations in bulk to middlemen who resell it in poor countries like Bolivia, where it is again resold in the street markets. This clothing sells for far less than newly manufactured apparel and in the past decade has driven the domestic Bolivian clothing industry into the ground. But the vendors of secondhand clothes are a wealthy and powerful lobby and have been fighting hard against President Morales's attempts to shut them down. They are supported in this by the average consumer, who enjoys the cheap prices and good quality of the used clothing, what they call *ropa americana*. People in the United States throw out a lot of really good stuff.

We find the address of the ambulantes' meeting near Calle Guayaramerín (named for a city in the Bolivian tropics, which I am never able to pronounce), but it appears to be a construction site. A half-finished building looms above a solid metal barrier pierced by a locked door. I use my cell phone to call Don Silvio, who soon appears at the door in the metal wall, smiling and waving us in. Nacho, Ruth, and I pass through the gate and enter the construction site, down a dark narrow hall that passes through what seems like someone's living quarters. Children are playing, and in a small adjacent kitchen an old woman stirs a metal pot on a gas stove. The hallway leads to a patio, its roof open to the sky, around which several groups of people sit at small wooden tables, drinking from clay pitchers. This is a chichería, I suddenly realize, though a well-disguised one.

Under an overhang on one side of the patio, a group of about fifteen men and women sit in a semicircle of chairs before a long wooden table. These must be the leaders of the different sindicatos that make up the El Paso federation. Don Silvio retakes his seat behind this table, alongside the dark man from the other day, and gestures that Nacho and I should join him. We sit, smiling at the ring of people frowning back at us.

A discussion is under way that apparently has to do with the Alcaldía's plans to kick the ambulantes off the streets of Cochabamba. People are furious with the Intendencia, the municipal office charged with oversight of the markets and market vendors in the city, and with its head, the intendente. The ambulantes recently had a meeting to which they had invited representatives of the Intendencia; these individuals had stayed only a few minutes, looking bored, and then announced that any complaints that the ambulantes had should be directed to their offices in writing. Then they left. The leaders of the El Paso federation view this as a sign of disrespect, for themselves as individuals and for their organization, which is still quite new and has yet to establish itself as a player in Cochabamba politics.

In addition, someone says, the intendente has been spreading rumors that Don Silvio has been illegally charging the members of his association two hundred bolivianos, a claim that Silvio angrily denies. The intendente, he says, is just trying to sow discord among the ambulantes, to divide them by fostering mistrust of their leader. "It is hard to be a leader," Don Silvio says, "because the authorities are always after you, as are the leaders of other federations. But I must have the support of my *bases*"—my people.[1]

Don Silvio asserts that the intendente at one time had promised to issue a new set of regulations for dealing with the ambulantes, but this had never happened. From his point of view, such promises are just a way to mock the ambulantes, to tease them with the suggestion of reform while continuing to treat them like criminals. "We are not protected by the Alcaldía," Don Silvio says. "We have no rights and are discriminated against because we are not included in the System." ("The System" is the term the ambulantes use for the official registry of vendors who are allowed to sell in the market [see chapter 35].) According to Silvio, the intendente himself has said that the ambulantes have no right to make demands of the government, because they pay no taxes and are on the margins of the law. Instead of including us in the System, Silvio says, referring to the Alcaldía's new Ordinance 3615, they now want to exclude the ambulantes entirely from being able to sell.

A woman in traditional indigenous attire named Doña Angela raises her hand. "La palabra," she says (literally, "the word," a way to request the right to speak in a public meeting). Doña Angela is the only woman on the federation's executive board (see chapter 27). She gets to her feet and denounces the intendente as corrupt, claiming that he has been offering money and puestos to people in her sector if they agree to break off from the El Paso federation. "Don't fall for these tricks, compañeros," Doña Angela urges. "We have to insist that they let us sell or, if they want us off the streets, that they give us a market."

"So, compañeros," Don Silvio now says, "what are we going to do about this? Do we wait and see what happens? Or do we mobilize?"

A fraught silence fills the hall. Even the drunks at the other tables seem to notice, raising their heads to look in our direction.

In the silence, the palabra returns inevitably to Don Silvio. "We must declare a state of emergency," he says, answering his own question. "We must mobilize and march on the Plaza Principal to show the Alcaldía that we are organized, that we are here, and that we must be taken into account." The assembled officers grumble affirmatively, nodding their heads. There is no vote, but it seems that a decision has been taken.

The focus now, unexpectedly, shifts to me, sitting quietly at the big table with Don Silvio. He introduces Nacho and me as the representatives of a "nongovernmental organization" who want to help the members of the El Paso federation as they struggle for a market of their own.

"Yes, well," I say, hoping to downplay the expectations this last statement has probably raised, "what we can offer you is counsel (*asesoramiento*). We can give you advice, help, and publicity."[2] I describe my plan to write a newspaper article in support of the ambulantes and my intention to write a book that describes the insecurity of life as a street vendor. This coaxes some nods and smiles from some members of the audience, although others look skeptical.

I then present the audio recorder that Don Silvio asked for the last time we met. Nacho had picked it up cheap in the Cancha. Don Silvio beams and shakes my hand, and the others applaud. Silvio then proposes that we sign a *convenio*, a written agreement between their organization and ours, specifying the nature of our relationship. This is a big step, concretizing our collaboration and establishing our mutual commitment to the project. I am surprised but agree enthusiastically.

The meeting ends, and I am being greeted by everyone in attendance, a long string of handshake-hug-handshakes. People are inviting me to visit them at what they call their "puestos"—the places on the street where they habitually sell until the police chase them away or the set of streets where they can most often be found. I assure them I will visit—most immediately, I need help figuring out what to say in my newspaper article. Don Silvio shakes my hand again as I leave, asking me to try to have something in the papers before their march on the Plaza Principal, which will take place in a few weeks.

...........................

"We should sign a convenio," Don Rafo says to me, "an agreement to formalize our relationship."

Nacho, Eric, and I have been preparing for the seminar on security and insecurity in La Pampa and are now meeting with Rafo and Melvin (the *melvin-cuentes*, as we have taken to calling them among ourselves) to discuss things. We have created a flyer to announce the event, and with Rafo's and Melvin's help, we distributed it to various people in La Pampa whom we hope will attend. One afternoon, we met Melvin at his puesto but found only a young man (his son, we later learned) at a large computer screen burning DVDs. Nacho smirked. Clearly, Melvin is involved in pirating movies. It is common in Cochabamba to find DVDs of even first-run movies for sale on the streets, although this practice is illegal under Bolivian and international copyright laws. Melvin's stall, set among others selling clothing on one of La Pampa's central passageways, seems to be used not for direct marketing but for the copying of discs and, judging from the piles of stereos, DVD players, television sets, and the like, the repair of audiovisual equipment. More than that, the puesto gives Melvin legitimacy, a foothold in the Cancha, even though he lives on one of the finer streets of suburban Cala Cala and makes a good living as a lawyer and law professor at a local university. He is not a true comerciante, although he serves an important, if vague, leadership role in their federation. When Melvin finally arrived, he took us on another round of La Pampa, distributing flyers and urging the various comerciantes we met to send representatives to the seminar. No one seemed particularly enthusiastic about meeting us or attending the event, and we began to feel discouraged.

As I relate this to Rafo and Melvin, I can see the gears turning behind Rafo's small black eyes. "For this to be successful," Rafo says, "there needs to be some concrete result to come out of it." Rafo glances at Melvin and then back at me. "There is some opposition within La Pampa to your investigation," he continues. "Some people feel that it is a political thing that will have no real benefits for the market. Some people are even accusing me of taking money from you." He laughs in disbelief. "The project needs to provide something concrete so that everyone will support the research you are trying to do."[3]

I ask Rafo whether he has anything specific in mind, surmising, correctly, that he does. "What we need is a communication system in La Pampa," Rafo says, "a system that will enable the security guards to communicate dangers to the comerciantes, with loudspeakers posted all around the market. When a child gets lost in the market, for example, we could make an announcement and help his parents find him. That would be very useful."

I am uncertain, but Nacho is nodding his head enthusiastically. Nacho, among other things, is an electronics expert, and this idea immediately appeals to him. He pulls out his cell phone and begins doing some calculations, muttering to himself about "triangulation" and "sensitivity" and "impedance." Later, when we are alone, he explains to me that the whole thing will cost us only about $200 and is technically a simple arrangement. It is a good investment, Nacho feels, one that will directly benefit the comerciantes of La Pampa by enhancing their security in the market and not just go into the pocket of the *melvin-cuentes*. But for now, he just looks at me and smiles.

"Yes," I say to Rafo, smiling now, as well. "I think that's something we can do."

# 19. Political Geography

The Cancha is big and complicated, a sprawling mess on the face of it, and this contributes to the perception that it is fundamentally chaotic. But the Cancha possesses its own, detailed forms of internal ordering and regulation.[1] This is not obvious to the casual onlooker or tourist, for whom the Cancha is a cacophony of sounds and sights but even more of smells: car exhaust, raw meat aging in the sun, the enticing aromas of cooked food, the leather of the cobblers, the sawdust of the furniture makers, the Barbasol of the hair stylists. The newcomer is easily lost, distracted by the jostling elbows, the men trying to push wheelbarrows through the densely crowded alleys, the crushed tomatoes that turn the pavement slippery underfoot. The tourist, warned about the likelihood of being robbed, clutches his backpack to his chest, eyes nervously scanning the crowd, and feels the press of humanity around him.

Even the experienced market-goer, concerned as she is with buying what she needs for the week's meals and getting back home as quickly as possible, may be unaware of the deeper levels of organization that structure the Cancha's evident disarray. Unlike the casual visitor, the Cancha shopper knows her way around. I say "she" because, historically, the prototypical Cancha shopper is a woman, the housewife (*ama de casa*) responsible for the daily reproduction of the family unit. Even in the wealthiest families, in which a domestic servant (an *empleada doméstica*) is responsible for the cooking and cleaning, the senior woman of the household often does the marketing, her empleada in tow to carry the bundles. The Cancha is the place where money gets spent, and the responsible ama de casa, rich or poor, takes that duty on herself, looking for the best buys, selecting the freshest vegetables and the choicest cuts of meat for the family table. These women know exactly where to go in the market to make their purchases—to the plataneras section to buy their bananas, to the carniceras to buy their meat, to the camoteras for their sweet potatoes, to the abarroteras for their pasta, flour, and other dry goods. They have their caseras, particular vendors to whom they will regularly return, knowing they will get the best produce and a good price. They know the passageways to walk down that are likely to be safest and least congested, and they have strategies to get in, do their shopping, and get out. Even in La Pampa, which is the most disorderly sector but has the cheapest prices, experienced shoppers carry a mental geography that allows them to navigate the market's various departments and alleys. This mental map is useful, but partial. It includes only the most basic information to permit efficient shopping with minimal distress.

...........................

Another level of organization underlies the visible, physical territory of the market, a political geography that is known mostly to vendors. The market is divided among six federations, large groupings of vendors organized to defend their collective interests, and these federations, along with their subsidiary units, do the real work of running the marketplace. Each federation is led by a powerful and wealthy individual, a market vendor who through family connections and years of savvy investments of money and allegiance has established himself or herself as a powerful source of influence, not only in the market but in the wider politics of Cochabamba city. Both ambulantes and fijos belong to the federations, but only the El Paso federation (the seventh federation in the Cancha) is exclusively for ambulantes.

Trade unions, like the market federations, have been powerful political actors in Bolivia since the national revolution of 1952. Nationally, organizations such as the Central Obrera Boliviana (Bolivian Workers Central) and the Confederación Sindical Única de Trabajadores Campesinos de Bolivia (United Federation of Peasant Workers of Bolivia) serve as umbrellas for a host of smaller syndicates in both rural and urban settings. These unions have been advocates for workers' rights in the country, often opposing (and sometimes working alongside) the various national governments that have come and gone in Bolivia over the past seventy years. Throughout the country, smaller syndicates of miners, workers, peasants, and others are important local actors, serving to organize and represent groups and individuals with common interests and give them a political voice.[2] The federations of the Cancha are part of the Confederación Sindical de Trabajadores Gremiales, Artesanos, Comerciantes Minoristas y Vivanderos de Bolivia (the United Federation of Guildsmen, Artisans, Small Merchants, and Grocers), a national trade union based in the capital, La Paz.

The Cancha is divided roughly among the six federations, with vendors of different sectors belonging to one of the six. In La Pampa, three of the six federations compete for control and argue among themselves over who has the most authority in the largest and oldest of the market's sectors. Some of the incoherence that one senses in La Pampa is due to this competition for political dominance, which leaves the sector and its loyalties always somewhat in flux.

The political organization goes deeper. Each of the federations is composed of smaller units, *sindicatos* or *asociaciones* of market vendors, grouped by the service they provide or the product they sell. The *plataneras* (banana sellers), for example, have their own sindicato, as do the *paperas* (potato sellers), the *dulceras* (candy sellers), and the *ferreteros* (hardware sellers). Some sindicatos have a distinct gender bias: the *cebolleras* (onion sellers) are mostly women (thus, they are referred to using the feminine noun ending, "-as"); the *zapateros* (cobblers) are mostly men (and so their group referent ends in the masculine "-os"). The members of a sindicato also tend to have market stalls located adjacent to one another, so some sindicatos are mixes of various trades based on proximity. This may vary, though. A zapatero who has his stall alongside the meat vendors in another part of La Pampa, for example, may find greater affinity with the zapatero sindicato and join that group instead of the sindicato closer to his location. Each sindicato has its own elected president and board of directors. In La Pampa alone, there are something like one hundred different sindicatos.

Sindicatos provide a sort of insurance to market vendors—in case of an accident or some kind of material loss, the other members of the sindicato may provide economic support to their colleague, including hospitalization and burial—although some sindicatos do this more consistently and effectively than others. Sindicatos organize fiestas to celebrate saints' days or anniversaries of the market or their sindicato, and members are expected to contribute dues to the sindicato's maintenance. They also must provide material and political support to the larger federation of which their sindicato is a unit, which may include voting for the federation's candidate of choice in a municipal election or going on strike to support a federation initiative. In some cases, the leaders of the sindicato also help their constituents acquire the land on which to build a house in the peripheral neighborhoods of Cochabamba's southern zone.

Sindicatos also control who can and who cannot sell in a particular sector of the Cancha. Not just anyone is allowed to set up a stall in the market. Years ago there might have been some open space for vendors to occupy, but today there is not an inch of room to accommodate new market stalls, and comerciantes fijos actively police their sectors to ensure that no new competitors try to squeeze in. Should a market stall become vacant, the leaders of the sindicato determine who may occupy that stall—a decision that usually depends on the potential vendor's willingness to pay large fees to the sindicato and its leaders to gain access. When conflicts arise over issues of access, occupancy, inheritance of stalls, or any other matter—as they often do—the sindicato's leaders are responsible for settling the disputes. No one wants to involve the police, the courts, or other state authorities in what are considered local, market conflicts—bringing them in would only lead to more and greater bribes having to be paid and diminish the authority of the local leaders—so everyone has the incentive to resolve the problems internally.

And La Pampa has no shortage of problems to resolve. The market is old, and much of its infrastructure is in poor condition. Roofs leak, floors are uneven. Filthy pools of water collect in the stalls and alleys after every rain storm. There is no coordinated system for delivery of utilities in La Pampa. There is no municipal trash collection inside the market, and waste piles up until the vendors themselves get around to removing it. Sales are declining, due partly to these conditions, partly to the competition posed by supermarkets in the better parts of town, and partly due to shoppers' fear of crime. All of this produces tension, which leads to conflicts among vendors and between vendors and shoppers, vendors and municipal authorities, and market vendors and street vendors.

Handling problems, managing conflicts, delivering services: elsewhere these tasks may fall to the government, but in the Cancha they all are the work of sindicatos. They provide a critical level of local administration within the market. The municipal government, the Alcaldía, is the official owner of all the space in the Cancha: the market, the land beneath it, and the puestos within it (see chapter 31). Individual comerciantes own the infrastructure—the roofs, the walls, the furnishings—but the market belongs to the state. For generations, the municipality has collected taxes from legal vendors, granting them the right to sell in the market. But many fijos complain that they have nothing to show for it. The Alcaldía has done little to maintain or improve the market or its infrastructure. Instead, every sindicato collects funds from its members and uses them to maintain the market space. Sindicatos and their members pay for the paving of walkways, public illumination, removal of trash, even policing (see chapter 29). In addition, individual comerciantes are entirely responsible for the maintenance of their own puestos, even though the state remains the owner of those puestos and the individual comerciantes are merely tenants. So even as the state retains ownership of the Cancha, it has transferred responsibility for its maintenance to the women and men who depend on it for their livelihoods. Don Rafo confirms this, telling me that "right now, we are paying an annual patente, we've been paying it for forty years, and there have been no improvements. All the improvements you see here in La Pampa are from the comerciantes' money. The Alcaldía has not involved itself in anything."[3] The market is organized through the structures that the sindicatos provide, and these sindicatos enable the market to continue operating in the absence of state investment.

Although it seems "unorganized," street vending is also a highly structured business. Given the intense competition for space in the market, not just anyone can appear on the streets and begin to sell. What may appear to be just another sidewalk or street corner is in fact somebody's turf, and there is usually a sindicato of people organized to defend that turf. As with the fijos, ambulante sindicatos are formed by vendors of a particular commodity to regulate the sale of that commodity in the market. The members of the sindicato "Bolívar," for example, sell mostly cosmetics, while the affiliates of "New Alliance" sell orange juice. Other sindicatos are composed of people who sell chiflería: odds and ends, miscellany, small items of various kinds. Each sindicato has its founding documents from the state, the legal personhood (personería jurídica) that grants it permission to function as an organization, and maintains records of its meetings and decisions. Sindicatos also symbolically identify themselves on the carts and uniforms of their affiliated vendors, adopting a particular color or logo to signify membership.

One of the sindicatos affiliated with the El Paso federation is called "New Millennium," and it consists almost entirely of vendors of quinoa juice. The ambulantes of New Millennium sell on the streets immediately surrounding the old train station. As ambulantes, of course, they are constantly kept on the move by the comisarios and comerciantes fijos of the zone. Nevertheless, New Millennium has its turf. According to Don Remberto, one of its founders, the sindicato was formed in 2001, when quinoa juice was first becoming popular in Cochabamba. On a given morning, five or six vendors with their little carts might be selling quinoa juice on the same street, stepping on one another's toes and making the entire enterprise unprofitable. So the ambulantes got together and divided the area around the station into sectors: this is your block, this is my block. In that way, they established themselves as the recognized (if illegal) vendors of quinoa juice in the city. Today, Don Remberto says, "everyone in Cochabamba knows about New Millennium. If you want to sell quinoa juice, you have to go to New Millennium."

Don Remberto is from La Paz Department, from a fishing village on the banks of Lake Titicaca. When he was younger he had hoped to become a "professional," but his older brother, who had been supporting the family, died suddenly, and Remberto had to leave school in the tenth grade. "And that's why," he says with a smile, "I ended up like this."[4] Grizzled and weary, he has sold quinoa juice on the streets of the Cancha since he arrived in Cochabamba in the late 1990s. He also has a night job, watching over the garage where ambulantes park their carts when they return home.

Because street vending is relatively uncomplicated to enter into, requiring little in the way of investment or training, people move in and out of it fairly often. Street vending can be a fallback position when other kinds of work dry up or a temporary form of employment for rural people during slack seasons. But the hard-core street vendors are there all the time and constitute the majority of the members of the El Paso association and its affiliated sindicatos. Remberto distinguishes between himself and others like him, whom he identifies as "permanent" comerciantes, and those who are just casual vendors who show up for a little while, sell on the streets, and then disappear. "There are ambulantes who are just temporary," he says, "who are there for a week, just passing through. But people like us are permanent. This is our life; this is our work, our source of daily livelihood. If we don't sell one day, we don't eat that day. So we [in the sindicato] work with those who are permanent sellers." The sindicato makes sure that these "passing" vendors do not interfere with the "permanent" vendors' ability to make a living.

The sindicatos also try to regulate the distribution of ambulantes so they do not encroach on one another's turf. The entire Cancha is divided into sectors to prevent conflicts and undue competition between members of the same sindicato. The assignment of individual ambulantes to particular sectors is done on the basis of tenure on the streets: those who have been selling the longest and who are the longest-standing members of the sindicato get first choice of sectors in which to sell.

At one time, it was relatively easy to join a sindicato and start selling on the street. But then, as Don Remberto says, "with so much immigration of people from the countryside, people didn't know what to do. The only thing they could do was to get a cart and sell and survive that way." Now it is nearly impossible to join the sindicato—people can join only if they can find a sector in which to sell that will not present problems for the other sindicato affiliates who are already there. If other vendors who are not part of the sindicato were to try to sell in the same spot, there would be violence. "Maybe one day some unknown person comes along," says Don Remberto. "We can allow that, but with the warning that he has to look for another place to sell. If he comes back the next day, he'll be kicked out; he has to go look for another place. It's better if he joins [the sindicato] so that he can be assigned a place or a sector and he can stay there."

....................................

Although they perform a range of important services for their members—from infrastructure provision to conflict resolution and social insurance—sindicatos and federations are fundamentally political institutions. In Bolivia, the state will enter into dialogue only with legally recognized collective organizations (i.e., those that hold the personería jurídica), so to express their grievances, individuals must belong to collective organizations that will negotiate on their behalf.[5] The federations serve this role, providing political representation and leadership for their members and functioning as intermediaries between Cancha vendors and the state. This is true whether the state considers those vendors legal or illegal comerciantes. The state is not interested in the legal status of the individuals who make up the organizations, or in whether their activities are informal or illegal, as long as they are officially constituted as a collective organization. Thus, a federation such as El Paso, which consists entirely of informal, illegal vendors, is itself a formally recognized organization with legal personhood in the eyes of the state. Though contradictory, it benefits both state and sindicato to keep the lines between formal and informal work blurry. Political negotiations are less complicated if the question of legality does not enter into them.[6]

Comerciantes are therefore highly dependent on their sindicatos and, barring evidence of corruption or betrayal, will remain loyal to their leadership across generations. As a result, the men and women who run the sindicatos, and especially the six federations, wield considerable power, enjoying a kind of sovereignty in the market realm (see chapter 22). Authorized as the political representatives of their constituents, federation leaders exercise broad disciplinary powers, deriving their authority not from the state or from formal democratic procedures but from the clientelistic relationships that they maintain with their constituents. Federation leaders can count on the political and economic support of their members and can use that support to run lucrative business enterprises of their own or to launch political careers outside the market. Federation leaders maintain relationships with high-ranking municipal officials and play active roles in national political parties and trade organizations. Some in the government accuse the federation leaders of using their members to advance their own interests, including promising to deliver their members' votes for political candidates. One high-ranking municipal official says that the comerciantes "have been like a ladder for [the syndical leaders] to get them where they are, so that they can sell them like prostitutes to whatever authority exists."[7]

In exchange for their support, members can call on their leaders for assistance in a variety of ways. A day spent in the salon of one of these leaders illustrates: comerciantes come before the federation president as though entering the royal court, seeking help with family issues, personal financial crises, or conflicts with the police. But more than that, membership in the sindicato provides the comerciante with a basic political identity. As the anthropologist Sian Lazar confirms, sindicato members derive their very sense of citizenship from their relationship with the sindicato; much more than from the nation or the state, it is from their sindicato and federation that comerciantes gain services and a voice in the wider political world.[8]

Sindicato membership gives comerciantes the sense of being rights-bearing subjects within the national polity.

The Cancha, then, though seemingly disordered and chaotic, is in fact a highly ordered and regulated commercial environment. Many of the regulations that govern the market are, of course, informal, in the sense that they are collectively agreed upon yet not recognized or endorsed by the municipal or national governments. Still, a description of the market's political geography illustrates the extent to which attributions of chaos are exaggerated, representing the fears and anxieties of those making the attribution more than the reality of the market itself. But it is these fears and anxieties that stoke local concerns about insecurity and that underwrite the oppressive tactics used to combat it.

# 20. Fieldwork in a Flash

With access to the comerciantes fijos and comerciantes ambulantes well established, the first phase of my fieldwork is over. Now begins a period of more intense data collection. In addition to my academic goals, I have made commitments to my collaborators that I intend to fulfill. Before my fieldwork ends, I have pledged to publish books about insecurity and how it affects the lives of fijos and ambulantes alike. In the shorter term, I have to organize a seminar for the fijos and publish a newspaper article for the ambulantes. I still do not know what to do about the problem of working with two competing groups but figure that a resolution will at some point present itself.

The Cancha is a busy place, and after the initial excitement wears off Nacho and I begin to feel frustrated by our attempts to speak with people. Often when we approach the workplace of a comerciante we have met—a fixed stall or a spot on the sidewalk—she or he will greet us in a friendly way but then be distracted by shoppers' inquiries and be unable to talk to us. We spend time observing these transactions, taking notes, sometimes taking photos, capturing details that we later write up in our fieldnotes. But eventually we start to feel awkward and worry that we might be annoying the vendor who is trying to work, so we move on.[1] We may return multiple times to the same vendor without being able to enter into deeper conversations or to explore her or his feelings on a particular issue.

20.1 Shoes for sale. Photograph by Lisa Berg.

One day, for example, Nacho is trying to speak with Carmen, a shoe vendor with a fixed stall near the train station (figure 20.1). Nacho knows Carmen from somewhere, so approaching her is easy. But this is the third time he has stopped by her puesto hoping to chat, only to find her busy and distracted. While they try to talk, six different customers stop at her stall. A man asks for the price on a pair of athletic shoes; a young couple wants to buy dress shoes for their little boy; teenagers have questions about the new styles. Carmen seems uncomfortable, not wanting to be rude to Nacho but unable to attend to her customers and talk to him at the same time.

From experiences like these, we determine that the best way to converse with working comerciantes is through brief, targeted questioning. Busy puestos and sidewalks are not conducive to long conversations or interviews, but in short visits we can ask one or two questions and realistically hope to get a response. In time we develop a network of contacts, vendors we know will be friendly and receptive to talking with us and on whom we can drop in unannounced and chat for a few minutes before moving on.

We call this technique the "flash interview" (*entrevista flash*), and it is very effective for gathering information when we cannot talk with people at length. We select a topic for the day's questioning, then pass from puesto to puesto, sidewalk to sidewalk, visiting the people who make up our network of contacts, posing to each of them the same question or questions. After we talk for a few minutes and the vendor returns to her or his business, we retreat and, while Nacho reminds me of what we discussed, I jot down notes in my pocket notebook. There is no tape recording, but since I am taking notes immediately after a very short, focused conversation, I am able to capture a lot of detail, including people's exact words. We then move on to the next person in the network and repeat the process. Each night I write up my jottings as fieldnotes. Nacho reads and comments on the fieldnotes and sometimes writes notes of his own. The more data we collect, the more fieldnotes we have to write.

Among the comerciantes of La Pampa, we develop a network of contacts who are always willing to receive us, to chat and share their thoughts. Some comerciantes fijos—such as Don Ricardo, the lunch vendor; Doña Tahlia, the dry-goods dealer; and Doña Isabel, the school supplies vendor—are usually busy but can be relied on for a brief, interesting comment. Others have more time to talk: Doña Rosa's stall always seem so quiet I often wonder how she makes enough money to survive. The flash interview overall is easier to use with comerciantes fijos than with ambulantes, who are frequently on the move and often hard to locate on the street, but we manage to include them, as well. The flash approach allows us to talk with a range of people about a different topic each time we visit. The networks reliably consist of twenty people or so, with the identities of those people changing over time. They include both fijos and ambulantes, men and women, natives of the Cochabamba valley and immigrants from other departments in Bolivia. "Network" is perhaps too formal a term for the routes we follow in our flash interviewing. Our contacts are numerous and constantly changing, as people come and go in the market. Puestos may be closed when we pass by, or a street vendor may have taken his wares to a regional market for the day. Thus, both time and space can figure into our planning. For example, on one particular morning, a page from my notebook lists our network of ambulantes like this (the remarks that follow the name refer to the streets and general locations in which we hope these individuals can be found):

- Samuel: República corner of Pulacayo
- Francisca: La Pampa, sector underwear, and on the orange juice corner
- Ramiro: in the morning near San Carlos; in the afternoon between Pulacayo and Barrientos
- Policarpio: until 8 AM, on the corner of República and Guayaramerín; in the afternoon, on the corner of República and Punata, and on Colquiri

- Salvador: Lanza and Uruguay
- Severa: in Calatayud and selling orange juice on the streets
- Prudencia: after 5 PM on the corner of San Martín and Honduras
- Néstor: after midday, at San Martín and Punata selling drinks
- Julián: Colquiri and Pulacayo, selling chiflería
- Arturo: Esteban Arze near San Antonio
- Silvio: Pulacayo and República

As we get to know people better, we begin to invite them to meet with us for more extended, "semi-structured" interviews. These are longer conversations, lasting from one to two hours. They loosely follow an interview "guide" listing the various topics we want to discuss but leaving us flexibility to explore other, unanticipated issues that arise during the conversations. These interviews take place either in the comerciante's place of business or in our office at the corner of Lanza and Honduras, in the Cancha just a block north of La Pampa. The interviews are recorded and later transcribed. Sometimes we do individual interviews; at other times, we do interviews in small groups. These interviews include details about the interviewees' personal histories, their experiences as market vendors, and their perspectives on security and insecurity in the market. My research team and I also conduct interviews with other people whose work affects the lives of the comerciantes but who are not themselves market vendors. These include Municipal Police and National Police officers, officials in the Alcaldía, private security guards, shopkeepers and residents of streets surrounding the Cancha, people from the San Antonio church, and people who work with nongovernmental organizations active in the Cancha. In the course of fieldwork, we conduct about forty interviews with comerciantes ambulantes and thirty-five more with comerciantes fijos and Cancha officials.

To my surprise, both fijos and ambulantes are very willing to take time out to meet with us and talk about their lives, their work, their problems, and their beliefs. The topic of security is obviously one that people care about, and they are hopeful that their contributions will help to improve things in the market. I do not pay people for their participation, but we serve refreshments (I drink enough Coca-Cola during this period to float an ark) and sometimes invite people to lunch following the interview.

After we have signed convenios with each group's leaders, the members of both groups become even more willing to collaborate, having been instructed by their leaders to do so. These convenios—formal written agreements with Rafo's Federación de Comerciantes de La Pampa (FCP) and Silvio's El Paso federation—stipulate that the comerciantes will give me their full cooperation in my research and that, in return, I will provide them with a written product at the end of the research period. This "book" will contain the results of the investigation, including (in the words of the convenio with the FCP) "recommendations to the organization and to the departmental and national authorities that will serve as a basis for the adoption of measures that contribute to improving the situation of insecurity in the market."[2] Although Rafo and Silvio were the ones who suggested signing convenios, I find that these documents give me confidence that I will be able to complete my research, even if they also obligate me to render my findings in a way that serves the interests of my collaborators.

It is through the "flash" conversations and a few initial semi-structured interviews that I begin to understand how ambulant vending works. I discover, for example, that while the comerciantes fijos are specialists in a particular product or type of merchandise, ambulantes have to be flexible, adapting to the needs of the local clientele. "Flexibility" is often identified as a quality that workers in the globalized neoliberal economy need to survive, and nowhere is this more the case than among the ambulantes of the Cancha.[3]

Comerciantes ambulantes, Nacho says, are the "antennae" of the Cancha. With little capital investment and low overhead, the ambulantes can quickly switch their merchandise in response to sudden changes in consumer demand. Some ambulantes will change their offerings multiple times in the same week, taking on small amounts of product and turning it over quickly, then acquiring something else in its place. Often the goods they sell are contraband, brought into Bolivia illegally from Argentina or Peru, and can be sold for prices that undercut local stores with higher overhead. Often ambulantes sell to match seasonal demand; sometimes they sell whatever is available. Says one ambulante, "Right now I am selling watches, but I have my seasons. In another season I sell brooms. . . . Ambulantes know when a particular thing is in season, when something else is in season, so we change our business."[4]

Many ambulantes begin their careers by selling small items, what they call chiflería. Starting small, an ambulante may find her way into a more permanent situation—selling juice, for instance, which requires more equipment, a more regular place on the street so clients can find you, and a more stable base of clientele. The availability of resources also determines what an ambulante sells. Starting out, Doña Prudencia sold small items that she could carry in her hand. From there she evolved to carrying things in bags, then on a burro, and finally, with a child in tow, in a wheelbarrow. "You can't just buy everything from the get go," she says. "Little by little, if you pay attention to your merchandise, it will begin to grow."[5] This careful nurturing of one's merchandise requires the comerciante to be flexible and adaptable to new situations. "To this point I have sold everything," boasts Doña Prudencia. "I change for every season. For Mother's Day, flowers. For San Juan, I'm going to sell sparklers. For Urkupiña, the same. Other things I get hold of, I get a little of everything. Right now I'm selling marshmallows."

Ethnographic work helps to debunk certain normative ideas about the informal economy. Economists define "informal" selling in part by the fact that it is supposedly easy to enter, requiring little in the way of training, skill, or capital investment. But the ambulantes tell a different story. "At first it involves a lot of suffering," says Don Fausto, a longtime seller of orange juice in Cochabamba. "We know how to suffer. When your business is going, then it's easy, no? You know how to sell, how to run things. But at first we know nothing. When I was in other businesses I was fine, but when I started here as a *juguero*—from the very start I sold juice, no?—it was strange to be out here squeezing juice. Later I learned the tricks."[6] Other sellers talk about the challenges involved in learning how to sell: knowing how to use the equipment, how to avoid getting hit by passing vehicles, how to be alert to the presence of street criminals trying to rob you, comisarios trying to fine you, or competitors looking to chase you away. Street vendors learn by experience and sometimes through the kindness of other ambulantes. Don Fausto says, "When I was first selling, other friends taught me, no? . . . So now I, too, teach other compañeras the same way."

..........................

Through these ethnographic forays I also gain enough of an understanding of the ambulantes' predicament to write the promised newspaper article. Before going to the press, I show the article to Don Silvio and some of the leaders of the El Paso federation. They are pleased with what I have written, offer a few suggestions, and thank me for the effort. The timing is good: their march on the Plaza Principal, to protest the Alcaldía's plan to remove them from the streets, is coming up soon. The ambulantes have made a formal request for an audience with the Alcaldía, but if the request is denied, they will march.

Nacho and I head to the offices of *Opinión*, one of the two major dailies in Cochabamba, where I buy space in the next day's paper to publish my article. In the end, we publish it under a pseudonym to avoid conflicts with the fijos who may read it (we call ourselves the Center for the Study of Security and Democracy [CISD]). The article appears under the heading, "Comerciantes Ambulantes: The Two Faces of (In)Visibility," and it reads, in part, this way:

> They are invisible, even though we see them every day in the streets and markets of Cochabamba. They can be seen on every corner, every sidewalk, every market in the city, merchandise in hand. But, though visible, they are at the same time invisible, without a voice, rights, or any protection in their daily struggle for work. They are the comerciantes ambulantes.
>
> They are in fact so visible that the Alcaldía has decided to deny them the right to work in the streets, erasing them from the urban fabric, with the authority of those who give orders from behind a desk. Cochabamba is a mercantile society in which, for thousands of people, selling in the streets means survival. To remove them from the city, without giving them any viable alternative to provide the basic necessities for their families, is to condemn them to misery. It is this measure that the 1,500 affiliates of the Federación Integral de Comerciantes Minoristas "El Paso" are resisting, with the threat of blockades and marches.
>
> But what do these people want? There is nothing unusual in their demands. They don't want to remain in the streets, selling from four in the morning until ten at night, returning home with 10 or 15 pesos in their pockets, only to begin again in the same streets the next day. All they ask for is a permanent place, a market of their own, where they can make a living with dignity and have a reasonable chance of improving their working conditions. This doesn't seem like a particularly radical demand. . . .
>
> It is against their imposed invisibility that the comerciantes ambulantes are protesting. They take to the streets, this time not to sell their

products but to make themselves even more visible to the citizens of Cochabamba and the authorities, in their demand for the right to make a living. In a supposedly democratic society like Bolivia, when all the institutional channels are closed off and people are denied the exercise of their rights, this is the predictable result.[7]

When the article appears in *Opinión*, Don Silvio is at a loss for words. To actually see his perspective expressed in print is startling, overwhelming. For a man unused to being heard by the authorities, this is a powerful moment.

And, as expected, the request for a meeting with the authorities is denied. The leaders of the ambulantes' federation declare a "state of emergency" and announce to their membership that they will march on the plaza on April 2.[8]

# 21. Women's Work

Nacho is in the market one Saturday morning, making his way past the fruit and vegetable stalls. Like most cochabambinos, he does his shopping on Saturday mornings, and La Pampa is crowded. He is nearing the corner of Tarata, sector carrots, when he hears a ruckus, people talking in raised voices. Nacho assumes it is a fight among drunks—a common sight on Saturday mornings in the Cancha, when the *trasnochadores* from the night before stumble out of the chicherías, blinking in the sun and quarreling with one another and with passersby. But much to Nacho's surprise, the fight is between two of his *caseras*, women from whom he regularly buys carrots.

Carrots sold in the market originate in one of two principal sites: Oruro, on the altiplano, and Parotani, in the Cochabamba valley. There is no clear consensus on which carrots are the best, and carrot vendors constantly debate the issue. On this Saturday morning, a customer is looking to buy a large quantity of carrots and finds herself caught in the middle of this perpetual disagreement. She has been talking with a vendor of Oruro carrots, who has offered her a discount of about 6 percent if she buys two *cargas* (a *carga* weighs 40–45 kilos, a little less than 100 pounds). The buyer says she needs at least four cargas, which she plans to take to El Alto of La Paz to make and sell juice. But a nearby vendor of Parotani carrots has been listening attentively to the conversation. Hearing the quantities under discussion, she jumps in. "Señora," she says in that whiny, beseeching tone people use when they really want to get their way, "you don't want Oruro carrots. Oruro carrots are no good; they're bad for your health and give you diarrhea."[1] She explains that this is because they are grown in the arid fields of Oruro, where the earth is red and the produce is contaminated. "Now, the carrots from Parotani are the best. They are from the valley where the soil is good and suited to this type of production." Parotani farmers do not use chemical fertilizers, she claims; the farming is all natural, and the carrots produced in this soil are juicy because there is abundant water, whereas Oruro is dry and bleak.

This speech produces the desired effect. The shopper says she is simply looking to buy a load of the juiciest carrots available, which would appear to be the carrots from Parotani, so she turns to that vendor's stall. But now the first vendor reacts. "Don't believe what this bitch tells you," she says to the client. "Her carrots only seem juicy because she soaks them in water all night!" The water makes them heavier, so the customer gets fewer carrots per carga. "With me you get the exact weight that you pay for!"

"Even if they were the exact weight," responds the vendor from Parotani, "those carrots are so dry you'll need to use more of them to get the same amount of juice. The carga will get used up quicker, and anyway the juice will come out tasteless, and you'll have to add sugar to it."

From there the situation only degenerates. The two women go at each other with insults and curses, disgusting both Nacho and the potential shopper, who walks off without making a purchase. The shopper says to Nacho that this arguing only makes her feel insecure. She fears being ripped off by the sellers in the market, especially because she is from out of town and came to Cochabamba just to buy better carrots at lower prices than she can find in La Paz. Nacho understands, but in the end cannot resist offering his own opinion: The soil in Oruro has a lot of copper in it, he tells her, and the produce can sometimes cause upset stomachs. For the future, he advises, go with the carrots from Parotani.

..............................

Female market vendors have been the subject of many an ethnography, especially in the Andean region of Latin America, where they historically have dominated the profession. Many classic accounts have explored the economic lives of working women in Andean cities, the gender ideologies that prevail in their households and workplaces, and the systems of family production and reproduction that characterize the domestic lives of market women.[2] Studies have examined the stereotype of the strong, aggressive, and sexually promiscuous female market vendor, exploring how such identities and perceptions are constructed within the intersection of broader ideas about race and gender in the Andes.[3] Although men are now a numerically significant presence in the market (see chapter 27), women still constitute the majority of Cancha market vendors.

As I mentioned in discussing the history of the Cancha, market vending in Cochabamba has long drawn women from the countryside to the city and provided them with new opportunities and independence. The informal nature of market vending—the ability to move in and out of it seasonally, to get started in it with minimal capital, the lack of technical training it requires—made it a form of work that rural women could enter with relative ease. Many of these women transitioned to urban life gradually—from working seasonally in agriculture they eventually shifted to full-time urban work and residence as prospects in the countryside diminished and opportunities in the city expanded. Market vending offered a path to greater self-sufficiency for women, allowing them to establish for themselves a measure of autonomy that they had not previously known, living and working under male domination—first of their fathers and then of their husbands—in the countryside. Urban marketing enabled them to move into a more liberated form of self-employment and sense of empowerment.

Market selling was once also an instrument of social mobility for young women from the countryside.[4] Some women arriving in Cochabamba from the valley first found jobs as domestics, working as housekeepers, cooks, and babysitters for wealthy families on the city's north side. But such jobs offered poor wages, often abusive conditions, and little opportunity for advancement, prompting many women to turn to street vending as a more promising alternative. The evolution of the comerciante followed a clear path, from setting up as an ambulante in the street to getting a "mobile puesto" (i.e., one that could be set up for certain specified hours during the day and then dismantled) and then having a puesto fijo in the market. Urban women with families already established in commerce could often skip these earlier steps and move more quickly toward acquiring their own puestos fijos.[5] Either way, market vending once offered a clear ladder of advancement for women, who had very limited employment opportunities in other domains of the economy. As informal selling expanded with the intensification of neoliberalism, puestos fijos became harder to get and competition grew cutthroat. Street vending today no longer offers women the same opportunities for upward mobility. Ambulantes tend to remain ambulantes throughout their working lives.

Andean ethnographers and historians have documented the ways in which working urban women, especially urban indigenous women, have long been the subjects of racial and gender discrimination and abuse.[6] Female market vendors challenge long-held stereotypes of women that prevail in male-dominated societies and by their very presence in public settings confound the categories that serve to organize machista culture. Women who work and indigenous people with money are difficult to reconcile within an ideology that locates women properly in the home rather than public space and that regards indigenous people as inherently rural, poor, and inferior to whites.[7] Having gained some personal and financial independence from men, market women have been known to display their personal wealth through their clothing and adornments and to speak to clients and market officials with a strength and self-confidence that are seen as threatening to dominant conceptions of ethnicity and "appropriate" female comportment. Many market women refuse to endure passively the slurs directed at them by shoppers, male and female alike, who are offended by their presence or relative affluence in the market. Conflicts over insults both real and perceived—like the conflict that opens this chapter—have long characterized the lives of market women and contribute to their overall sense of insecurity in the market.

Whatever some might think of it, selling provides women with a way to make a living independently from men. This is especially true for ambulantes, the least capitalized vendors in the market. Women work as ambulantes to support their families, sometimes with the financial support of their spouses, sometimes with funds sent by their former compañeros, sometimes on their own. Some women sell on the street because their husbands are alcoholics or are disabled and cannot work; others have been abandoned by their husbands or have left them or kicked them out. Some have abusive spouses at home whom they avoid whenever possible and on whom they cannot rely for financial support. Indeed, domestic abuse is widespread in Bolivia: according to a recent study, 53 percent of Bolivian women report having experienced domestic violence in their lives, the highest percentage of any country in Latin America.[8] Given the prevalence of violence at home, many women can establish a limited autonomy for themselves apart from their abusive partners by generating their own income through marketing (see also chapter 30).[9]

Female ambulantes are often the sole providers for their children, a difficult situation that some women, nevertheless, embrace (figure 21.1). "*Mejor sola que mal acompañada* [Better alone than in bad company]," says Doña Victoria, a sandwich vendor often found in the vicinity of Avenidas Uruguay and San Martín.[10] "But sometimes I don't have enough money, and I ask him [her ex-husband], 'Can you help me out a little bit.' Sometimes he sends me something . . . But not money. He sends me potatoes, not money, *chuño* [dried potatoes] he sends me." Even this paltry arrangement is unusual. Doña Victoria says that for every ten separated couples, one may receive some sort of financial support from her ex. The women could pursue legal remedies for the problem, she says, but such procedures take time and money, lawyers are crooked and cost a fortune, and most women would rather not bother. Another ambulante, a member of Doña Victoria's sindicato, says of her ex-husband, "It would be better if he were dead than being off somewhere, better if I were a widow. I say that he is dead because he doesn't think of us. People ask me, I tell them that he is dead."[11]

Friends and family provide little financial support for poor market women, though they are often the key to a woman's learning the market trade. Doña Esperanza began selling orange juice in the street when her husband left her alone with her two young children. Some friends showed her how to become an ambulante—how to work the device that peels the oranges and the device that squeezes them, how to negotiate the streets with her little cart. "But it was hard on me," she recalls. "I used to cut my hands all the time. I'd run over my own feet with the cart. It wasn't easy. . . . I used to crash into cars. I couldn't manage very well at first."[12] Doña Lola came to Cochabamba five years ago, and while her husband worked in construction, she learned how to be a market vendor. "When I got here," she says, "I didn't know the city, nothing, I didn't know how to work. I was coming from the countryside, after all. I came here, my sister was here, my brother-in-law had been an ambulante, so she lent me his cart, and later I learned to go around [*ambular*] with my wheelbarrow."[13] Lola's sister showed her how to shop at the *mercado campesino*, the wholesalers' market on the urban periphery, where she stocks up on fruit—pineapples, oranges, tangerines—that she then retails in the Cancha.

Not all women are alone, of course, or the sole providers for their families. Some women work alongside their husbands in the same business, selling

21.1 Comerciante ambulante and her child. Photograph by Lisa Berg.

the same product; others sell while their husbands work in construction, cut hair, or push wheelbarrows in the market. Many have a male partner who supports the family through his earnings, either from marketing or another line of work. Even men who do not work in marketing may help to pick up the slack during busy seasons. Doña Prudencia has a husband who works as a welder and runs his own small workshop. He has never worked independently as a market vendor, Prudencia says, but during holidays when business picks up in the market, he helps her to sell, taking some of her items to the streets on his own. In many cases, however, the same man who helps out with the work is also a violent abuser at home, and women have to struggle with the sense of vulnerability in both their work and domestic settings.

Like many Bolivians, comerciantes and their prospective spouses often live together as an alternative or prior to marriage (they call this *concubinaje*), with a formal marriage being celebrated only once a couple has established themselves economically and can afford to host a large party for their friends and relations. In the past, studies show, comerciantes fijos were more likely than comerciantes ambulantes to have "stable" families consisting of a husband, wife, and children. According to Fernando Calderón and Alberto Rivera, Bolivian sociologists who produced one of the few social-science accounts of the Cancha, acquiring a puesto fijo was a pathway to familial stability, enabling the formation of nuclear families integrated into more extended family networks. Families of ambulantes, in contrast and not surprising, given their relative poverty, were "less consolidated and more unstable," tending to dissolve in separation or divorce, with women having children with multiple fathers.[14] In both kinds of families, the woman played central roles as breadwinners and principal suppliers of domestic labor.[15] This continues to be the case today.

........................

Doña Tahlia has a puesto fijo in La Pampa; earlier I described my first encounter with her during Carnaval. When I return to visit Tahlia a few weeks later, we discuss the possibility of doing an interview, and I explain the protocol: my pledge to keep the data safe and to use pseudonyms to protect the identities of all my collaborators. "I want to be called 'Tahlia,'" she declares, laughing at her own choice of a pseudonym, which she says sounds elegant.[16]

And Doña Tahlia is an elegant woman. With black hair in a short po-nytail, pink lipstick, and matching fingernails, Tahlia looks younger than her thirty-eight years. But she is a strong, stern presence at the heart of her sector, a leader among her co-workers and a master of the sale. I watch her one morning as she sells ketchup to a shopper. "Which brand do you want," she asks the young man, "Kris or Dillmann?" "I'll take the Kris," the young man replies, but Tahlia shakes her head. "No," she says, reject-ing this decision, "take the Dillmann. It tastes better." She looks the man straight in the eye. He wavers, then agrees with a nod and hands over the money. When he is gone I ask her about this transaction, pointing out that while she is pushing the Dillmann, she is wearing a red apron with the Kris logo emblazoned on it, a gift from one of her suppliers. Tahlia smiles. "The Dillmann was almost at its expiration date," she says. "You've got to move the product."

Tahlia is a native cochabambina, born and raised in the city, the eldest daughter of a middle-class family. Her mother sold vegetables in La Pampa, and Tahlia would come to her puesto after school to help out. She went to college to study nursing but did not like it and eventually dropped out to work full time in the market. Selling vegetables had its advantages: she did not need to make a big capital investment, for one, as the turnover was quick, so she could build up savings. But she had to get up very early in the morning to take delivery of the fresh produce, and the profit margin was small, making life stressful. So gradually Tahlia used the money she had saved selling vegetables and switched over to dry goods (*abarrotes*). With her forceful personality it was not long before Tahlia emerged as a leader and became president of her sector's sindicato. Nearly all of the comerciantes in her sector are abarroteras, although some, like her friend the breakfast vendor Doña Irena, sell cooked food (*comedoras*).

Tahlia is a strong woman who fits the stereotype of the "tough" market woman, one who resists the insults and abuse of customers, state officials, and other market women. Tahlia is not indigenous. Like many women who sell from puestos fijos, she classifies herself as white (*blanca*). But tough-ness is a quality that she and other women I know embrace. Combativeness, a willingness to stand up for one's self, to push one's product—these are part of a gender ideology that many market women share. It is, they believe, what enables them to survive in the conflictive, competitive, and frenetic world of the Cancha.[17] As the principal providers for and caretakers of their children, women are responsible for household reproduction, with or without the help of men. If they are tough, women like Tahlia say, and strong, and vociferous in their demands, it is because of the burdens they bear and the need to make a living from selling, from a stall or on the street. Doña Tahlia acknowledges the difficulties that she and other market women face, both at work and at home; but, she declares with a laugh, "¡Somos machas! [We are tough women!]."[18]

As mentioned earlier, however, the qualities of toughness and combativeness that some market women idealize also run counter to dominant expectations that women be dependent and submissive.[19] As others have noted, market women do not fit comfortably within the dominant gender ideologies of Andean society. Seligmann calls market women "hybrid females, whose aggressive character traits are usually associated with men."[20] The challenges that women face are further complicated by this contradiction between what society expects of them and what they expect of themselves. Gender issues like these have become especially significant as the number of male competitors has increased in the Cancha, with those men playing increasingly important roles in the running of sindicatos and the management of the market. As men have emerged as the principal leaders of the market political organizations on which all vendors depend, women confront new challenges to their autonomy and self-sufficiency. These are topics to which I turn in chapter 27.

# 22. Sovereignty and Security

In the first chapter of this book, I described some of the effects of what I call *disregulation*—the state's arbitrary and discretionary practices of surveillance and law enforcement that produce and maintain a governable disorder in spaces of urban informality. These effects include the production of various forms of insecurity. Another effect of disregulation is the proliferation of new forms of sovereignty in these same informal, insecure spaces. From an anthropological perspective, sovereignty is not a formal but a de facto reality. It is understood as "the ability to kill, punish, and discipline with impunity wherever it is found and practiced, rather than sovereignty grounded in formal ideologies of rule and legality."[1] Even if sovereignty is more broadly understood (as it conventionally is in fields such as political science and international relations) as "a declaration of political responsibility for governing, defending, and promoting the welfare of a human community," then informal spaces such as the Cancha can be understood as rife with competing sovereigns.[2] Various entities and individuals make claims to local authority, claims that proliferate precisely because the arena in which they are made has been declared informal and illegal and, hence, beyond the control of the state.

The federations and sindicatos described in chapter 19 might be thought of in these terms, but the emergence of non-state sovereigns is most clear in the area of security making. In cities throughout Latin America, states allow individual, private, and other non-state actors to assume responsibility for providing security, historically a function of the state.[3] Often, this security making entails the use of violence or its threat. In some cases, people themselves adopt violent measures for dealing with insecurity; these include the vigilante lynching of suspected criminals in zones where official policing does not produce security.[4] In other cases, actors such as drug gangs and private companies have taken the responsibility for providing security, emerging as alternative, non-state sovereigns that compete directly with the state for control and governance in the space of informality.[5] The consequences of this sovereign proliferation in the security domain include an expanding use of violence to resolve problems, an unrelenting sense of uncertainty and fear in public spaces, and a denial of basic rights in the realm of justice making, as the state becomes just one player among many in the arena of security provision.[6]

The willingness to tolerate abuse in the interest of creating security is not an unfamiliar discourse within the contemporary global securityscape.[7] Here it points to the general yearning for a sovereign able to create security in the market. This is a long-standing desire among market vendors, who on numerous occasions have felt compelled to provide their own security in the absence of any public alternative. Don Andrés sells shampoos, hair dye, and other personal-care items from a large, well-lighted stall in the cosmetics sector of La Pampa. Andrés has his own theory about market insecurity: he sees the delinquents in the market as a deliberate construct of global capitalism, designed to destroy the Cancha by generating insecurity and discouraging customers from shopping there. He describes this as a form of "low-intensity warfare" waged by the new, modern supermarkets and the big capitalists against the small merchants of the Cancha. Years ago, Andrés recalls, the comerciantes in his sector would round up the delinquents and chain them to a post in the market. Then they would march them to the police and hand them over. But the police, he says, would always release them back onto the streets, because "they are their buddies."[8] Like many others in La Pampa, Don Andrés is an advocate of "community justice," shorthand for the lynching of criminal suspects, as a way to make security in the market.[9]

More typically, security in the Cancha is made by private, for-hire security companies. Most fijos and ambulantes agree that private security has made the market significantly safer than it used to be. Previously, comerciantes say, one could not walk in the Cancha without getting robbed. In the late 1990s, they claim, the Cancha was the site of about twenty-five robberies every day; the National Police, for their part, admit to six or seven cases daily brought to their attention. Organized bands of delinquents were said to roam the Cancha, and the newspapers began advising citizens to look elsewhere to do their shopping. The comerciantes fijos marched on the Plaza Principal to protest state neglect, demanding better police protection for market sellers and their customers. They also created their own forms of local policing while loudly and publicly denouncing the National Police for their inattention and threatening to lynch any delinquents they apprehended. Private security firms began to emerge in the Cancha at this time, as people sought alternatives to official policing, though the police refused to cooperate with these companies and sometimes arrested private security guards simply for patrolling the market.

The situation reached a head on December 12, 2001, when an altercation between the National Police and private security turned violent, with the police beating and arresting the private security personnel. In retaliation, a group of La Pampa market vendors set fire to a local police office. Both the police and the private security companies called in reinforcements, and a violent clash ensued, resulting in the death of a bystander. This event was followed by days of marches and protests, with comerciantes denouncing the police for their ineffectiveness and corruption. (One of the more popular chants heard during these marches, which occurred around the time of the Christmas holiday, was "Police! Murderers! They don't want to lose their Christmas bonus from the delinquents, so they kill the people!"). Peace was finally restored following a meeting of the market leadership and the Cochabamba Prefectura (the departmental government, under whose authority the National Police were administered), which resulted in a spatial division of official and private policing. The Prefectura guaranteed the private security firms that they could operate freely within the market, while the National Police would patrol outside the market but not come inside. In return, private security firms agreed to turn over any delinquents they apprehended to the state for prosecution under the law. Through this act, the state effectively established the Cancha as a territory within which new forms of sovereignty could emerge.

Private security firms proliferated in the Cancha following the events of December 2001, assuming sole authority for policing the market. Perhaps realizing that it had gone too far in agreeing to withdraw completely, in 2005 the National Police created the Office for the Control of Private Security to monitor the work of the private police, requiring that all private firms be licensed and registered with that office. But today firms in the Cancha continue to operate autonomously and disregard the legal requirements that the state has developed to regulate them. For example, the Cancha security firms ignore the mandates of the Office for the Control of Private Security and all but one are unlicensed and thus effectively illegal. Private police officers also routinely violate their promise to surrender criminal suspects to the police, preferring to use their own methods for punishing criminals and deterring crimes. Private police firms are frequently described as "mafias" by the police and other worried observers. They note that while private security officers are not allowed to carry firearms under current law, the firms are lobbying to have that changed.[10]

The private firms operate like independent sovereigns, able to exercise judgment in capturing, adjudicating, and disciplining criminal suspects. Although they lack official recognition, private security guards who work for firms such as the Men in Black—La Pampa's first private security firm—behave as if they are authorized to act as police surrogates. They patrol the market, individually and in groups, constantly on the alert for delinquents. Attired in quasi-military gear, the Men in Black look like Special Forces officers. They wear black leather jackets or nylon vests that mimic the riot gear worn by police, and at their hips they carry batons to club offenders. Most wear black hats and dark sunglasses, even in the shady interior of the market, their faces inscrutable, their eyes invisible as they perform their surveillance work, scanning the pedestrian traffic flowing around them. When they catch a delinquent in the act, or even notice the presence of an unwashed street kid in the market, the Men in Black detain him under their own authority and remove him from the market, often administering a beating to reinforce the message that he is unwelcome in the Cancha. Their occasional use of violence, and the more constant threat of violence indexed by their menacing physical presence as they conduct surveillance of the market, bestows on the Men in Black a sovereign authority that few in the market question (see chapter 29).

The work of the Men in Black includes more ordinary administrative functions, as well. The private firms divide the market into turfs and contract with the leaders of the sindicatos within each area to provide security to their constituents. These constituents pay the security providers directly, usually one to two bolivianos (about fifteen to thirty cents) daily. This money is collected by a uniformed guard who passes by every day to demand it, keeping records of these transactions in a pocket ledger and issuing a small receipt on colored paper to indicate payment. In their performance of this duty—the nonviolent though sometimes intimidating extraction of daily payments from their clients—private security further enacts its own sovereign authority, in this case the power to collect tribute from its "subjects." Sovereignty is reinscribed through the daily collection of payments, which effectively reauthorizes the Men in Black as sovereigns every time the exchange is enacted.[11]

This arrangement has had mixed results for the fijos and the ambulantes. Fijos and their sindicatos have long been the principal sponsors of the private security firms, contracting with them and advocating for them in conflicts with the National Police and municipal authorities. Nevertheless, some fijos in the La Pampa market complain about the Men in Black. Although robbery and other crimes significantly diminished in the years following the private security firms' takeover of the Cancha, and business improved as a result, crime is still a problem at night, when the private security goes off duty. Unlike the state, whose responsibility is presumed to be temporally unbounded, private security firms such as the Men in Black are obligated to serve only for the hours during which they are paid, and round-the-clock private security is prohibitively expensive. Many fijos regard private security as inadequate to their needs and are critical of the Men in Black, who seem more diligent about collecting their daily fee than about providing actual security. Don Dario, a sindicato leader, put it this way: "we have private security that each of us has to pay for, but is there a solution for our sector? When many of our compañeros leave home at 4 AM to be in the market, at 12 at night they go home, but at 12 at night there is no private security or any police. . . . Many of our compañeros are being stabbed, many of our people have been attacked . . . The [private] security is only physically present to collect their payments, [not] at night . . . because they don't provide twenty-four-hour coverage."[12] Such comments suggest the deep reservations market vendors have about the sovereignty of the security firms, whose explicitly transactional nature calls into question their commitment to local needs, much the same way that police corruption threatens the legitimate sovereignty of the state. They also echo local critiques of the state, which collects taxes but provides little in the way of security.

Ambulantes face additional problems in dealing with private security guards like the Men in Black. Though poorer than the fijos and more vulnerable to crime and other misery because of their marginal economic and social position, ambulantes often end up paying more than the fijos for private security. Because private security firms have their own areas of control within the market, an ambulante who moves across different turfs may have to pay multiple security firms in the course of a single day. Furthermore, as I discussed in chapter 16, the ambulantes themselves are identified in public discourse as a principal source of insecurity in the Cancha. Private security guards share this perspective and sometimes take it upon themselves to harass the ambulantes, doing the work of the police by refusing to allow the ambulantes to take up permanent spots in public spaces. Don Arturo, a quinoa juice vendor, complains about a guard named Marcelo who has no fingers on one hand and in the other carries a baton that he uses to beat ambulantes who linger on sidewalks and street corners. Guards like Marcelo, Arturo says, work in collaboration with the fijos to keep the ambulantes on the move, even as their firms collect daily payments from the same ambulantes. Just as they must be alert to the presence of comisarios, the Municipal Police who fine them and confiscate their things, ambulantes must watch out for private security and shift their spatial locations to avoid them. Recognizing the blurry lines between official and unofficial, state and non-state forms of sovereignty expressed in the behavior of the private security guards, Don Silvio comments, "They kick us out of places as if they were the municipal authorities."[13]

It is through public performances of sovereignty, both violent and nonviolent, that private security providers such as the Men in Black demonstrate and maintain their sovereign power, a sovereignty based not on voting but, like everything else in the market, on capitalist transaction. People pay for security daily in a ritual prestation that endorses private security as sovereign even as it subordinates the payee to that sovereign's rule. The Men in Black in turn provide surveillance and at times offer violent reminders of their right to police the market. At the same time, the Men in Black are rivaled by other sovereigns, other men who also charge for their services—notably, the police, men dressed in the green and blue uniforms of the national and municipal governments, demanding payments, bribes, and fines from those who fail to conform to official norms of law and order. These various actors—state and non-state, public and private—overlap and intersect in the space of the Cancha, where different forms of color-coded sovereignties work to create different kinds of order amid the "chaos" that is believed to characterize the informal urban market.[14]

# 23. Resisting Privatization

Well known are the popular protests that rocked Cochabamba in 2000, resulting in the cancelation of the Bolivian state's contract with a multinational corporation to privatize the city's water system.[1] The Water War, as it came to be known, gained international attention as a successful grassroots movement against the excesses of neoliberal reform, particularly significant for having occurred in the home of the "Bolivian Experiment" in structural adjustment.[2] But there have been other, less well known anti-neoliberal movements, in Bolivia as elsewhere in the world. One of these is the ongoing struggle by Cochabamba's market vendors to resist the privatization of the Cancha.

I learn much about the history of the market through time spent with Don Rafo and Don Melvin, sometimes in formal meetings, at other times just hanging around Rafo's banana stall. Surrounded by huge piles of bananas draped in canvas covers, we sit on small wooden stools, drinking soda pop and eating—what else?—bananas. Don Rafo often complains about the tribulations of being the president of a federation—the constant demands on his time, the gossip and backbiting, the huge investments of energy, of money, that leadership requires. "People just don't understand," he moans, and Melvin nods in sympathy.[3]

With time, Rafo and Melvin have begun to recognize me not just as a source of potential resources but as an actual person with a life and a career, even though my research remains baffling to them. They understand me through the lens of a comerciante. "People pay you to do this kind of work?" Melvin asks, genuinely intrigued. I try to explain about the academic career, about doing research and writing books. Melvin smiles, appearing to get it. "It is all part of God's plan," he pronounces. "Your work is one phenomenon in the great universe of God's creation." Rafo rolls his eyes. This is apparently an ongoing routine with them. Melvin is an evangelical Christian while Rafo is Catholic, but they maintain a close friendship—a mutual dependence, even—despite having fundamentally different beliefs. The discussion veers into what for me is unsteady terrain: religion, the afterlife, the existence of God. Rafo defends his faith in the pantheon of Catholic saints, claiming that at various times in his life they have directly intervened to help him. Melvin scoffs at this, as evangelicals do when Catholics talk of saints and other "intermediaries" between humanity and the Divine. He speaks instead of his personal relationship with the Lord Jesus Christ. Nacho now chimes in, denouncing organized religion in general as an opiate of the masses, speaking in favor of Taoism, which (as he has told me a million times, so now I am the one rolling his eyes) is not a religion but a philosophy. Rafo agrees with Nacho on this, stating that while God is real, religion is a system of social control, "nada más." Melvin is stunned. "But this is blasphemy!" he splutters and launches into a long disquisition on the nature of faith. I sit back, sighing, and eat bananas.

It is out of such encounters, believe it or not, that anthropological knowledge emerges. After much back and forth, I am eventually able to return the conversation to the question of the Cancha, its history, and the struggle against state efforts to privatize it.

..........................

Amid the neoliberal furor of the 1990s, the Alcaldía (under Mayor Manfred Reyes Villa) first decided on a plan to sell the market, transferring responsibility for its maintenance and operation (and, of course, the right to charge and collect fees) to a private corporation. The Alcaldía recognized that the market held vast wealth and hoped to find a way to liberate it from the hold of the comerciantes, liquidating that capital for the state. Other Bolivian municipalities, including Oruro and Santa Cruz, had successfully privatized some or all of their markets, and Manfred (as he is known) wanted to try it in Cochabamba. In September 1996, the Alcaldía issued Municipal Ordinance

23.1 A comerciante de puesto fijo. Photograph by Lisa Berg.

1864, which would create the Decentralized Municipal Supply Corporation "La Pampa," a public entity tasked with transferring the La Pampa market into private hands. Under this plan, individual comerciantes fijos would remain as tenants in their stalls, but the market would be run by a private company that would assume the functions of administration and taxation. This corporation in turn could choose to sell the stalls to individuals, independently setting the prices for those transactions. Comerciantes feared that the stalls they occupied would be priced too high for them to afford and that they would be displaced from the market as a result.

The comerciantes fijos quickly came together in opposition to this move by the Alcaldía (figure 23.1). They formed the Committee in Defense of the La Pampa Market, which organized marches, wrote letters, and demanded that the municipality abandon the project. One of the leaders to emerge at this time was Rafael Punto, a *ferretero* (hardware dealer) with a puesto in La Pampa, looking to make his way into politics. Don Rafo was born in Coro Coro, a mining center in La Paz Department. His father was a copper miner, and it was from him that Don Rafo first learned about union organizing and political leadership, lessons that were later reinforced during a stint in the military. Don Rafo studied accounting at an institute in La Paz before coming to Cochabamba in 1978 and establishing a hardware business in the young La Pampa market. Rafo became president of the ferreteros' sindicato, where he encountered what he calls the fundamental "disrespect" of the state toward comerciantes. Market vendors were expected to behave as political clients of the authorities while demanding none of the benefits that such clientelism should confer on them, including protection against precisely such schemes as the one being promoted by Manfred.[4] It was then that he "began to see the injustices done to the comerciantes," Rafo says. "The authorities of the Alcaldía unfortunately didn't want to give the right of free expression to the comerciantes. They treated us like animals, you know? 'You have to go to this march, [you have to] support us! And if you don't support us we will close your puesto.'"[5]

Together with other market leaders, Don Rafo organized the comerciantes fijos as the Committee in Defense of the La Pampa Market to resist the Alcaldía's privatization plan. After five months of negotiation and protest, including a march by the comerciantes to the Plaza Principal, in March 1997, the Alcaldía issued a retraction (Municipal Ordinance 1954), which nullified the previous Ordinance 1864 and promised "to respect and guarantee the establishment of the small-scale comerciantes of the La Pampa market in their workplaces."[6] The administration based its nullification of the ordinance on the fact that its decision was taken "unilaterally" and without adequate consultation with the comerciantes themselves. In the aftermath of this first conflict with the Alcaldía, the Committee in Defense of the La Pampa Market evolved into the Federation of Comerciantes of La Pampa (FCP), with Don Rafo as president and the lawyer Melvin Gutierrez on its board of directors.

A year later, the municipality issued another ordinance intended to shift the market from public to private control. In January 1998, the Consejo Municipal (City Council), under the leadership of Council President Gonzalo "Chaly" Terceros, approved Ordinance 2080, which privatized the market by direct sale of puestos to individual comerciantes. The ordinance, which would apply to both La Pampa and the neighboring Fidel Aranibar market, established the sale price at $350 per square meter. The council stated that funds raised by these sales would then be used to construct new markets in other parts of town, thereby, it is presumed, solving the ambulante problem by relieving congestion in the heart of the Cancha.

Once again, the comerciantes fijos organized to protest this action. Although very much desiring ownership of the puestos that they occupied, the comerciantes rejected the proposal that they should pay such large sums of money to purchase property that they already considered their own. In public statements, leaders of the comerciantes' organizations reminded the authorities that for decades they had been paying taxes for the use of the market but that the municipality had never reinvested those payments in the market itself. To the contrary, they noted, the comerciantes had been responsible for the installation of an electrical system, a sewer system, a flood control system, water service, pavement, and maintenance of the puestos themselves. Thus, they said, if the value of the land was really as high as $350 per square meter, it was due "fundamentally to the improvements that we ourselves have introduced."[7] The comerciantes of La Pampa also objected to the plan to use their money to construct other markets—such construction was the obligation of the municipality, they argued, and should be done using the tax monies that they had long been paying to the Alcaldía. Once again, in the face of strong opposition, the municipality backed off its privatization plan.

The municipality made its third attempt to privatize the Cancha in 2006. This time, however, the Alcaldía did not make its intentions public. Instead, Chaly Terceros, now the mayor of Cochabamba, presented a privatization plan directly to the Bolivian Cámara de Diputados, the lower branch of the National Congress.[8] This plan was nearly identical to the failed initiative of 1998, once again proposing to sell the puestos at prices set by the government. The comerciantes of La Pampa learned of the plan through press reports and once again took to the streets with marches, roadblocks, and hunger strikes, demanding that they be given title, free and clear, to the puestos that they already inhabited. Pressured by the diputados to further consider their decision, the Alcaldía for a third time retreated from its plan, although it refused to agree to the comerciantes' demand for title.

After more than a decade spent trying to privatize the market, the Alcaldía has succeeded in only one respect: it has privatized the Cancha's public restrooms.[9] These are now filthy, decrepit pits, where desperate comerciantes and shoppers can pay 1 boliviano for entry and a few stiff sheets of pink toilet paper. The bathrooms are owned and operated by a private corporation, and their condition is a powerful reminder of the dangers of unbridled privatization. Most comerciantes of La Pampa go up the hill across Avenida República to urinate rather than pay the 1 boliviano to use the dark hole of the public toilets.

But the impulse to privatize remains strong in the municipality of Cochabamba, despite its previous failures and Bolivia's generally anti-neoliberal mood, and the future of privatization initiatives is uncertain.[10] This uncertainty generates a great deal of insecurity for comerciantes fijos, who have occupied their stalls for years and invested in them and in the infrastructure of the market but are denied legal title to these spaces. Much of the anxiety that the fijos express, and that manifests in sometimes violent opposition to the ambulantes whom they perceive as threatening their businesses, stems from this fundamental insecurity about their futures in the market. It also conditions their generally hostile relationship with the municipal authorities, whom they regard as continually trying to expropriate their livelihoods. "We are not the legitimate owners [of our puestos]," says Doña Tahlia. "That is what the Alcaldía tells us. But we feel like legitimate owners. Why? Because we have been here for so many years."[11] Like many comerciantes fijos who belong to Don Rafo's FCP, Doña Tahlia and her constituents fear that the Alcaldía will again try to privatize the market and that they will lose their puestos. But, she says, "We will defend our workplaces." The question of ownership is one I again take up in chapter 31.

.............................

Doña Melva sells glassware from a puesto fijo in La Pampa, set among various other puestos selling similar items. She has sold from this puesto for thirty years and is a loyal supporter of Don Rafo and Don Melvin and of their federation, the FCP. One afternoon I pass by her stall to say hello. We talk for a while, and then Doña Isabel, a vendor of stationery and school supplies, arrives. Another faithful soldier in Rafo's army, Isabel has come to invite Doña Melva to a meeting with Rafo, Melvin, and Intendente Rodolfo Ferrufino, head of the Alcaldía's commerce division. It has long been rumored that the intendente is in league with Eulogia Imba, head of one of the largest federations of comerciantes fijos in the Cancha and a fierce competitor of Rafo and the FCP. Together, the intendente and Doña Eulogia are now said to be plotting to dispossess some of Rafo's affiliates from their puestos and replace them with affiliates of Eulogia. Rafo and his allies are on their way to meet with the intendente, says Doña Isabel, to put a stop to it. This is just another example, Doña Melva remarks, of how the Alcaldía does nothing for the market but meddle in its affairs for its own corrupt ends.

The conversation reminds Doña Isabel of an incident that occurred in the market two years before. Following major renovations in La Pampa, paid for by the comerciantes, Mayor Chaly Terceros appeared on television to take credit for the work. This enraged the comerciantes. A few days later, Chaly and the intendente went to the market to celebrate the improvements and to boast of the Alcaldía's achievements. (Isabel struts around like a turkey to illustrate the mayor's arrogance.) "We were furious," Isabel recalls, referring to the comerciantes fijos of the FCP, "and we weren't going to let those people take credit for what we had done."[12] In the candy section of La Pampa, supporters of the mayor had set up a table covered with flowers, bottles of champagne, and fluted glasses. That is where the FCP hit them first. Isabel roars with laughter remembering how she smacked an old lady, one of the mayor's supporters, in the side of the head, overturning the table she had so carefully arranged and smashing the pretty glassware. The comerciantes then went out to intercept the mayor, the intendente, and their party, who were marching toward the market down Avenida San Martín, a brass band playing accompaniment. When he saw the angry comerciantes coming to kill him, the mayor turned tail and ran, his loafers slapping the pavement and his tie flapping from side to side as he fled. The intendente also turned and ran, followed by the brass band, all of them fleeing for their lives back up San Martín.

Isabel and Melva laugh and laugh as they recount this incident. Isabel wipes away tears of delight and says to her friend, "It was beautiful, Melvi, wasn't it?"

# 24. Don Silvio

Like Don Rafo, president of the fijos' Federation of Comerciantes of La Pampa, Don Silvio, president of the ambulantes' El Paso federation, is a skilled politician who learned about leadership from his experience in Bolivia's highland mines. Unlike Don Rafo, Don Silvio has never had the stability of a fixed market stall, does not have the ear of the local press, does not have the mayor's number on his cell phone. Everything Don Silvio has accomplished in his life has been the result of extraordinary effort, perseverance, and sacrifice. Don Silvio is a born leader with a commitment to social justice, which makes him an appropriate person to head the ambulantes' struggle for rights in the Cancha.

Silvio Mamani was born in 1952, the year of the Bolivian national revolution, and lived the early years of his life in a farming village in La Paz Department, province of Murillo. "I was born to poor people," Don Silvio says, "and that's why I want to help the people here."[1] At fourteen he went to work in the mines as a day laborer, a *peón* hauling dirt and rocks and assisting the men excavating the earth's riches. He earned less than $1 a day at this work but continued for three years, until he turned seventeen and went to serve his compulsory year in the Bolivian armed forces. At eighteen, Don Silvio again found work in mining, this time in a small mine owned by the Compañia Minera del Sur S.A. (COMSUR), a major private mining corporation founded by Gonzalo Sanchez de Lozada, who would later become Bolivia's president and lead the country to neoliberal restructuring.

When Don Silvio returned to mining after his military service in 1970, the price of tin and other minerals was high, but the wages paid to miners were low. Workers in Don Silvio's mine were hired as "contractors," paid by the hundredweight for the tin, zinc, silver, and gold they extracted, and given no vacation, *aguinaldos* (annual year-end bonuses), or other benefits. The mine owner also controlled the *pulpería*, the company store from which miners were forced to buy their equipment, clothing, food, and other necessities at prices set by the company. In other mines, workers had organized to fight conditions like these, but the COMSUR mine was small and had no workers' cooperative. But some of the other miners were more experienced, having come from Huanuni, Colquiri, Siglo XX—mines where workers had already organized as cooperatives or sindicatos—and these older hands guided the younger men. Don Silvio recalls the fight to create a cooperative to defend workers' rights in the COMSUR mine, a significant event in his political education:

> [The older miners] told us, "We have to seize this opportunity, because there are aguinaldos, they have to give us work clothes, tools, there have to be vacations, too, and the price [they pay] for minerals has to improve."
>
> Well, we met one night, but in secret out in the *monte* (brush)—there was monte down below—because if the boss found out, he would kick us out of there. For three months we schemed there at night in the monte. Thirty of us organized; we came together . . . and we sent a commission to La Paz, to the Ministry of Labor.[2]
>
> The Federation of Miners [the national labor union] came from La Paz. They found out how we were working, and that is when the trouble started. When they showed up, that's when the boss found out [that we were organizing], and he wanted to kick us out of the mine. But he wasn't able to, because now we were recognized by the Federation of Miners, by the Ministry of Labor and all that. That is when the struggle began. . . . "I've worked here one year," [someone said]. Someone else [had worked there for] two years. We added [all of the years] up so they would pay us the aguinaldos. It was a good amount. But they wouldn't pay. . . .
>
> One day . . . they had to take out a shipment of minerals, something like fifty or sixty hundredweight. That night we organized to seize the

minerals. We blockaded the road; all night we met, and at five in the morning we blockaded the road so the trucks couldn't leave.

Pedro Maldonado was the owner's name. [He was] a first cousin of Sanchez de Lozada. We said to him, "Señor Pedro, you owe us these things, give them to us or the minerals stay here until you do." He refused; he got furious, arrogant: "Who do you think you are? I'm going to throw you out one by one." We grabbed dynamite to blow up the truck and gave instructions to destroy it all. . . .

We emptied out the truck but kept up the blockade for fifteen days. We let the empty truck leave. There were rumors that the military was going to get involved, police to take out [the minerals], but the leaders were strong . . . and we kept blocking the road. Fifteen days we were in the road, and from that we learned how to blockade roads and how all that is managed . . .

And we won. And we cooperativized that mine.

The mine owners agreed to pay the aguinaldos due the miners, to supply them with work clothes and tools, to reduce prices at the pulpería, and to give workers paid vacations. Don Silvio worked at the COMSUR mine for ten more years. For eight of them he served as secretary-general of the cooperative and for two years as its president. Before he went to the mine, Don Silvio says, "I didn't know there was such a thing as a sindicato. But in the mine I learned." Through the fight to create the cooperative, he discovered the power of collective action and, as he put it, he "learned social struggle."[3]

In 1980, the price of tin began to fall on the world market, and in a short period of time private mines such as COMSUR's began closing.[4] Don Silvio left the mine and returned to agriculture—not to his home (his family lacked sufficient land to support Silvio, his five brothers, and their families) but to another part of La Paz Department. There he helped to form a federation of rural producers. "Because I always have enjoyed expressing my opinion," he says, he was elected president of the federation. From there, Don Silvio got a job working in the municipal government of the region, where he served for four years, until the political winds changed direction and he was again out of work.

Taking the money he had managed to save from his time in the government, Don Silvio went to La Paz city. He bought a small stand and tried selling hamburgers and hot dogs. He married, and his wife worked at the hamburger stand—he had too much masculine pride (he says with a smile) to work as a comerciante (see chapter 27). But there was too much competition and no organization of workers. Envy and spite among business rivals was his undoing, he says. In 1993, Don Silvio sold his business, left his wife, and moved to Cochabamba, where he hoped to find a job. But there was little opportunity, and he soon realized he would have to swallow his pride and become a comerciante.

In the mines, the miners treated hangovers by drinking a beverage called a batido (a shake), beer mixed with an egg and sugar to make it seem more like breakfast. Miners might drink three or four glasses of batido in the morning to steel themselves for another day's toil underground. In Cochabamba, Don Silvio discovered Maltín, a nonalcoholic malt beverage produced locally by the Taquiña brewery, which he realized could be used to make a drink similar to the one he remembered from the mines. He whipped egg and sugar into a froth and mixed it with the Maltín to create something like an egg cream—"my own invention," he brags—which he sold from a cart for two bolivianos a glass.

Don Silvio struggled to sell cochabambinos on the batido, a drink with which they were not familiar. But after a time people began to appreciate the taste of the beverage and its energizing effects, and Don Silvio established a clientele, mostly among men. Other vendors began to make and sell batidos—a distinctly masculine alternative for comerciantes struggling with the stigma of their work[5]—and by 1996, there was enough competition on the streets that Don Silvio proposed forming a sindicato of batido sellers.

The sindicato quickly gathered strength, and the vendors of batidos did well. They approached the Taquiña distributors and negotiated reduced prices to purchase large quantities of Maltín. There were many distributors at the time, and Don Silvio was able to play them off against one another to get better prices for his primary ingredient. The distributors also donated equipment to the vendors, including carts from which to sell, umbrellas for shade, and glasses with the brewery logo to serve the product (figure 24.1). They even donated aguinaldos of money and beer to sindicato members. Negotiating these arrangements took a lot of time and energy, but it was worth it to Silvio and the other leaders of the sindicato because of the economic gains they made. Today, the batidos sindicato—named 6 de Enero (January 6) for the day on which it was founded—has sixty members in its ranks.

The newly formed 6 de Enero sindicato joined one of the six federations that dominate trade in the Cancha. But very quickly, Don Silvio realized that

24.1  Don Silvio's batido cart. Photograph by Lisa Berg.

this arrangement would not do: "what happened there was, I never spoke, only the executives spoke. I don't like that. "The leaders of these federations have been in power for decades, and what have they accomplished for their constituents," he asks. "Look at the condition of the La Pampa market. There is no lighting, there are no basic services, no meeting hall, and these leaders have been there thirty years. This market should have at least two stories; that would be something to benefit the people. But that has never happened. [The leaders] just keep enriching themselves."

Don Silvio founded the El Paso federation to be different, to work honestly for the benefit of the *bases*, the grassroots of the organization. The federation was formed in 2005 and quickly grew to include twelve affiliated sindicatos. Other ambulante groups are interested in joining, and ambulante leaders from other cities seek out Don Silvio for advice on starting their own associations. Using all his skills and experience, Don Silvio fights to improve the lives of the comerciantes on the streets, who until now have never been organized and have never been able to secure their basic rights. "There are ambulantes everywhere [in Bolivia]," Don Silvio says, but there is no national federation of ambulantes, no single organization to represent them and fight for them. With time, perhaps, El Paso can grow into that kind of association. For now, Don Silvio says, "I want to work for the rights of the impoverished class that is in the streets. I want those people to have their rights, to have a roof over their heads. That is my purpose. That is what I am fighting for."

# 25. Character

The competition for space and the inequities that correlate with access to it have produced strained relations between comerciantes fijos and comerciantes ambulantes in Cochabamba. Fijos are middle-class businesspeople, some from families that have been selling in La Pampa for generations, and they feel threatened and assaulted by the growth of informal commerce. As the number of ambulantes on the streets has risen, the fijos increasingly find it difficult to make a living. The ambulantes form a virtual ring around La Pampa so that any shopper coming to the market must first pass the "puestos" of the ambulantes. This has had a noticeable impact on the fijos' business: given their relative lack of overhead, ambulantes can offer lower prices on similar merchandise, and their location in the street makes them a more convenient option for shoppers in a hurry. The fear of crime and insecurity inside La Pampa also contributes to shoppers' reluctance to enter the market itself, so they satisfy their needs instead from ambulant vendors. The market is becoming increasingly isolated, cut off from the surrounding city by a belt of ambulantes circling it like asteroids. Fijos now have to diversify their commercial strategies to maintain their incomes, their social standing, and their sense of themselves as a particular type of comerciante—people who have what Doña Tahlia calls "character."

Comerciantes fijos and comerciantes ambulantes are direct competitors for space and clientele, so it is not surprising that tension and antagonism exist between them. But the tension plays out according to long-standing cultural oppositions. Old Andean racial distinctions continue to define social relations in Bolivia, despite the inclusive, multiculturalist rhetoric of Evo Morales and the Bolivian state.[1] The perceptions that color interactions between fijos and ambulantes are embedded in the history of Bolivia and linked to fears of indigenous "invasion" and "contamination," which date to the colonial era but were apparent in many of the struggles over urban growth and modernization of the twentieth century (see chapter 13).[2] Market vendors, many of them indigenous or mestizo Quechua- and Aymara-speaking people from the countryside, have long had to contend with racial stereotyping and discrimination from their clients, municipal officials, and others in the city who resent their presence and their prosperity.[3] The fact that many of these vendors are also women further confounds the postcolonial categories of gender, race, and class that continue to frame social relations, adding to the conflicts and tension that surround market life (chapter 21).

Ironically, many fijos today regard ambulantes in the same racializing terms long used to characterize market vendors. Fijos consider street vendors, especially street vendors from the altiplano, as less civilized, less human than vendors with fixed stalls. Some fijos, their families longtime residents of the Cochabamba valley, consider themselves racially superior mestizos or blancos (whites), as opposed to the indios brutos (uncivilized Indians) from the altiplano who are now taking up room on "their" sidewalks. Never mind that many of these fijos themselves speak indigenous languages, observe native ritual practices such as the q'owa (see chapter 15), and can trace their (very recent) ancestry to the countryside. Race, as we know, is manipulable and often correlates with income and status. Money whitens, as they say in Bolivia, and there is a lot of money in the Cancha. Comerciantes fijos maintain their racial aspirations, even if in a moment of anger a mestiza shopkeeper gives herself away (chapter 14), insulting a pesky ambulante by using a Quechua slur ("india kuru!").

Racial difference is often translated as cultural difference, and vice versa. Some fijos contrast their approach to market selling with that of the ambulantes, whom they interpret as fundamentally different from themselves and therefore lacking the essential qualities needed to succeed in business. Ambulantes, some fijos say, lack respect for the market, the pride in it that the more established comerciantes fijos have. Comerciantes fijos such as

Doña Tahlia say that they know how to treat customers, that they know how to establish and maintain relationships. They believe they have a culture and a style that is fundamentally about marketing—they know how to be good salespeople and how to have a good life in the market.

Eulogia Imba is the head of Cochabamba's largest federation of market vendors. She is a very wealthy woman with powerful connections in the municipal government and a direct competitor of Don Rafo and the Federation of Comerciantes of La Pampa. She contrasts the ambulantes—relative newcomers to commerce from the countryside or from other parts of Bolivia—with those she calls "*comerciantes tradicionales*," cochabambinas with long-standing family traditions of market selling. The ambulante does not think the same way as the fijo, Doña Eulogia says; she does not have the same aspirations. The traditional comerciante wants to invest, to grow her business, to make something of her life, while the ambulante just wants to survive day to day. "What does the ambulante have who sells deodorant from a wheelbarrow?" she asks. "A rented room with one light bulb that costs 40 pesos a month. She doesn't need anything more than that. She can live for years like that, because she only wants to make enough to eat and enjoy herself."[4] Doña Eulogia's evaluation identifies the ambulante as a particular type of person, one for whom the so-called culture of poverty seems entirely satisfying, in contrast to the fijo who wants to grow her business, improve herself, and advance the nation.[5]

The sense of one's self as a "good" comerciante is especially critical in a context of deep indebtedness. Most fijos, even the most prosperous, depend on credit to get by.[6] Fijos have a great deal of money invested in their puestos and often borrow against that investment to purchase the items that they sell in their puestos (figure 25.1). Many regard the fijos as wealthy, says Doña Irena, the breakfast seller and second in her sindicato to Doña Tahlia. However, she says, "These people owe a lot of money. Here in the market nobody works with their own money. They borrow from the bank, from the loan companies, and sometimes they go bankrupt and they're stuck. Comerciantes go to jail for the debt they have."[7] This advance capital must be repaid on a regular, often weekly, schedule, which increases the tension and insecurity that fijos experience as a result of declining sales. Doña Tahlia feels that she has a responsibility to her creditors and fears the consequences of falling behind, which threatens not only her livelihood but her social and racial status:

25.1 Comerciante fijo. Photograph by Lisa Berg.

I am responsible about what I am doing, and being responsible I can't just close up shop willy-nilly. The company will come to me and say, "Doña Tahlia, we've given you a week of credit, and you haven't complied." They can wait a day or two for me to pay, but they can't wait a long time. And besides, I would get a bad reputation . . . I don't have a great deal of capital, so I owe to the companies. I can say, "The market is empty; sales are down. I can only pay you a little bit." But then I won't be an excellent client, only a regular client. I don't want to become a bad client.[8]

The fear of owing her creditors and the loss of status that would entail motivates Doña Tahlia to work even harder. "So I don't allow myself to get sick," she says. "I can be sick for a couple of hours, but then I get back to work, because if I don't, I won't be able to fulfill my obligations."

For Doña Tahlia, these qualities can be distilled into the basic essence of a good comerciante, what she calls "character." Character means being constant and reliable and following through on commitments. "To be a comerciante," Doña Tahlia says, "the first thing you need is character. The first thing is character. Then consistency. Consistency counts for a lot, so that when people come looking for you, here in the market, you are there, on Sundays, every day, even if there is a general strike." This consistency, this character, is linked to Tahlia's determination to remain in her puesto even when she is sick, to do all she can for her clients but also for her creditors, to whom she is perpetually indebted. Failure to repay her debts will result in a loss of face and her acquiring a "bad reputation" (*mala fama*) among the other comerciantes of La Pampa. Even more than her income, Doña Tahlia feels compelled to preserve her character.

The status of a comerciante fijo is therefore precarious, dependent on her income to relieve her constant indebtedness and the threats it poses to her very identity. Tahlia can rely on only her character and her consistency—qualities that she sees street vendors as lacking. Those who are "outside," she says, "are much bolder than us. It is hard for them even to speak to us politely. Sometimes we have to put our products in one of their wheelbarrows, or with *cargadores* (men who carry things in the market), and ugh. . . . They are vulgar people that don't know how to speak politely." Tahlia dreads having to deal with such people, and unlike some fijos who seem to relish conflict, she detests the bickering and the violence that often arise. She regards these as beneath her dignity as someone with character. "There is constant fighting. It seems crazy, you know?" she says. "It is embarrassing to fight."

Many comerciantes fijos work with goods and capital lent to them by mayoristas, the large wholesalers who have long served as the suppliers of the market and provided the commercial link with rural producers (chapter 17). Mayoristas, says Don Florentino, a seller of plasticware in La Pampa,

> leave us stuff [to sell] on market day. If you pay them a small retainer, then they leave it for you. If you don't pay them when they come back, they won't leave stuff for you anymore. That's why you have to go out and do what you have to do. If you have a profession you can relax; you can rest at midday [lunch], happy with your family. Sunday, too, you can rest. But it is not like that here in the market. You have to go out on Saturdays and Sundays, and if you don't sell, you can't pay [the mayoristas] and you lose. They won't leave you stuff to sell, because [they'll say], "You don't pay me." That's why we work.

Living with this constant cycle of debt leads Don Florentino to conclude, "In this business, we are like slaves."[9]

...........................

Given their mounting economic challenges, many fijos have taken to diversifying their incomes. Some fijos go to the weekly ferias in other towns, closing up their Cancha puestos on slow days and hauling their goods to the provinces to sell. Some rent space to ambulantes, allowing them to sell on the skirts of their puesto for specific periods each day. Others hire ambulantes to sell for them, giving them a piece of the profit for each item sold. Still others have become ambulantes themselves, using their puestos as storage places for their goods and taking to the streets to sell. These are called *desdobles*, people who are in two places at once. In La Pampa there are many stalls that rarely seem to be open, their heavy metal shutters closed to the world as their owners are out making rounds. Doña Irena, for example, can no longer rely on people to come to her stall to eat and takes her wares to the streets in a little cart, ladling out hot chocolate, tea, and *mates* from a pot that she reheats over a small propane burner, returning to her puesto periodically to restock. While she sells on the streets, a hired woman runs the puesto. Other vendors continue to sell from their stalls in the market but also send out a child or younger relative to sell their goods on the street, particularly during the busiest times of the day. This, too, is a form of *desdoblamiento*, and many ambulantes consider it an unfair advantage for the fijos, who can turn themselves into ambulantes to advance economically without assuming any of the hardships or stigma that real ambulantes endure.

Mayoristas also have diversified into retail street vending. These wholesalers provision the comerciantes fijos but also maintain a small, private army of retail ambulantes, many with wheelbarrows or carts, who sell the mayoristas' fruit and vegetables in the street and return at the day's end to deliver a percentage of their earnings. This provides another form of competition for the fijos, who used to be the market's only produce vendors but now must contend with wholesalers in the streets.

While fijos fight to keep ambulantes out of their space, they also compete with one another and with the authorities to keep the space they have and to acquire more. The Alcaldía authorizes a certain amount of space for each puesto fijo, ranging from two to twenty meters in width. The work of the comisarios includes policing these puestos to make sure that they conform to the space allotted. But for the fijos, life in the market involves a daily, incremental expansion of their puestos. By only centimeters at a time, a fijo will advance her puesto farther out into the aisles of La Pampa, increasing the amount of space she occupies by an imperceptible but cumulatively significant margin. When the comisarios come around, they may force her to retreat. Some comisarios even carry tape measures to determine precisely the limits of the comerciante's puesto, and she will then have to pull her wares back into their designated position. But when the comisarios have passed, her incremental advance begins again. This process makes the aisles and passageways of the Cancha increasingly congested, not only by carratilleros pushing wheelbarrows and ambulantes moving through or sitting in those aisles but by the fijos themselves, whose puestos protrude into what is designated as shared public space. One reason that the fijos object so strenuously to ambulantes' sitting on the sidewalks is that the fijos have established their own sidewalk businesses in those very spots, unauthorized extensions of their puestos fijos.

The fijos not only *want* to expand their selling space—many feel that they *must* expand their space or that space will be occupied by someone else. In some aisles of La Pampa, for example, a new row of vendors has recently emerged, running down the center of what was previously a wide passageway and dividing it in two. These stalls began as temporary setups, vendors who paused for a while to sell in that open space between two puestos fijos. But in time the Alcaldía sold them the rights to those spaces, and now they occupy them permanently. Many fijos fear that something similar could happen in their aisles as temporary sellers colonize open spaces and subsequently purchase the right to stay in those spaces from the government. So the fijos encroach on those spaces themselves, filling them with their wares and defending them against the incursions of outsiders.

Doña Tahlia supports the mayor, the intendente, and other municipal authorities during elections, endorsing the candidates that her federation tells her to and even allowing them to display their campaign propaganda in her puesto. But she feels abused by these same authorities who, once in office, try to enforce the rules about the size of the selling space allotted to each vendor. After the elections are over, she says, when the comisarios come around, "They abuse us, they harass us, when our puestos are a little advanced, maybe ten centimeters, five centimeters extra. Fines. Closures." Meanwhile, Doña Tahlia says, in the streets people are selling all over the place, blocking traffic, making it impossible for her clients to find a place to park their cars. "All of the entrances to the streets are blocked. That is why for me, personally, it pisses me off when the agents come around here and tell me, 'Get up, get up. This is a walkway. Make way!' Why don't [they] first do something about the walkways that legally are supposed to be open?"

Like many other comerciantes fijos, Doña Tahlia blames the comerciantes ambulantes for many of the problems in the market. She perceives a relationship between the authorities and the ambulantes that privileges the street vendors over the legal vendors of the market. "They get preferential treatment," Tahlia says of the ambulantes, referring to their ability to take up room on the sidewalk while she is forced back into her puesto. "We are like the stepchildren of the Alcaldía, and the people who sell in the streets are their children."

Don Rafo perceives a similar relationship, although he recognizes that the Alcaldía is trying to perform a careful balancing act: "the municipal authorities . . . want to be with God and the devil at the same time, no? Of course, for us the ambulantes are the devil, and we are God. I mean, we are legally established." Both Doña Tahlia and Don Rafo express the sentiment, common among comerciantes fijos, that legality is a joke, something that should benefit them but in fact gives them no advantages, only costs. Don Rafo decries the practices of the Alcaldía—what I have called official disregulation—that in recent years have legalized what are sometimes called the "fijos of the street." Unable to privatize the market officially, the Alcaldía has generated funds by selling the right to establish new, permanent market stalls in public spaces, like those that blocked Avenida Pulacayo during the great fire in La Pampa (chapter 1). "This is completely illegal," Don Rafo complains. "Municipal law is very clear. It says that it is completely prohibited to use the streets [for selling]. It isn't allowed, but unfortunately in Bolivia, anything goes. I mean, we have ordinances. We have laws, but no one obeys them."[10] Don Rafo recognizes that this is how the system operates: "the authorities themselves allow it. 'OK,' [they say], 'Here in this street is a sindicato consisting of some fifty people.' So they do the relevant paperwork, the Alcaldía authorizes it, they have their party, hugs and kisses, and it is legalized. It's as easy as that. And every one of those fifty people has paid $200 to the authorities."

Competition in the streets makes life difficult for everyone who is already selling in the market and creates congestion and "chaos" that troubles the municipality, even as it authorizes the proliferation of that chaos. Of course, the comerciantes ambulantes—the devil, in Don Rafo's analogy—have their own perspective on this state of affairs. They also view legality and illegality as completely arbitrary but insist that legality benefits the fijos—including the fijos of the street—while illegality limits the ambulantes' ability to prosper. This fundamental contradiction is a key to the ambulantes' disadvantage—their exploitability—in the Cancha. It is to this exploitability that I now turn.

# 26. Exploitability

Since the nineteenth century, Cancha vendors have been required to make two kinds of payments to the state for the right to sell in the market (see chapter 8). One of these, the patente (license), is required of those with puestos fijos and must be renewed annually. In addition, fijos and ambulantes until recently had to pay a sentaje, a daily fee for the right to sell (or, literally, the right to sit, to occupy public space). The sentaje was collected by Municipal Police officers—*guardias municipales* or comisarios, as they are officially called, although comerciantes simply call them los *hambres* (the hungry ones), because they are always eating up their profits. But in 2006, the municipality changed the rules. By collecting a formal payment, the municipality was implicitly authorizing the illegal practices of street vendors. Plus, it had become all too evident that sentajes were mostly going into the pockets of the officials collecting them rather than into the coffers of the Alcaldía. So the city determined that legal vendors should pay an annual fee, called the Pago Único Municipal (PUM), which would replace the sentaje. The amount of the PUM is determined by the value of what one sells, and ranges from 45 bolivianos to 240 bolivianos a year. Comerciantes fijos also still pay the patente, the annual licensing fee. These payments give the legal vendor a great deal of security, allowing her to sell without fear of being dispossessed of her merchandise or forced to leave the market by the comisarios. The ambulantes are not required to pay anything to the state—they are, after all, informal workers, a designation whose key features include the fact that, theoretically, they do not pay taxes.

As I mentioned in chapter 13, comerciantes fijos and urban residents have complained about the presence of the ambulantes since at least the beginning of the twentieth century. Back then, one object of their irritation was the fact that the ambulantes do not pay the same taxes to the municipality that the legal vendors do. One hundred years later, the comerciantes fijos still offer these same complaints. In Doña Tahlia's opinion, the ambulantes have a good deal selling on the streets and enjoy a privileged relationship with the authorities. This is indicated, she says, both by their very presence on the streets—illegal but not prohibited, as the authorities apparently encourage them to sell in public spaces—and by the fact that they do not have to pay taxes to the municipality the way fijos do.[1] Doña Irena, the breakfast lady, feels this way, too. "These ambulantes, they go about their business, happily selling their products," she says. "They don't pay anything—no taxes—to the Alcaldía. We, on the other hand, have to pay the Alcaldía, plus the fines, and one thing or another. We don't earn very much."[2]

But the fact of the matter is that the ambulantes are denied the opportunity to pay taxes to the Alcaldía. They are not allowed to pay the PUM. They are not, in fact, allowed to pay anything formal to the state, not even a sentaje. While this might at first seem to be an advantage, it is actually one more factor contributing to the ambulantes' insecurity. Paying the PUM would mean that the state acknowledges their right to sell on the street—their right, in other words, to exist. Without it, the ambulantes are excluded from the domain of the state, leaving them vulnerable, rightless, and insecure. The state has formalized this exclusion through the PUM and its refusal to accept official money from the ambulantes. The elimination of the daily sentaje was part of this exclusion. "We are eradicating corruption," says Luis Bellot, the Alcaldía's director of municipal income, "because there are no longer sentajes. All that we collect is official."[3] Yet, says one ambulante, "We who don't have puestos, we have to suffer whatever those with puestos do to us . . . because [they say] we are blocking them. They say to us, 'You don't pay a sentaje; why don't you get out of here?'"[4] Without paying a sentaje, the ambulantes have no formal right to "sit," to occupy public space.

Exclusion from the formal realm leaves the ambulantes hyper-exploitable. Although they make no official payments to the state, they pay in a variety of other ways. Some ambulantes pay the comerciantes fijos or local shopkeepers to allot them a certain amount of space from which to sell their goods.[5] They might sit in front of a closed stall before it opens or on the edge of a larger space where they will not interfere with the work of the establishment. In exchange for the right to sit, the ambulante pays the fijo. It can be a flat rate or a commission based on how much they sell, but the terms are set by the fijo. My friend Doña Senobia (Don Miguel's wife) from Loma Pampa sells cooked sweet potatoes; she pays the owner of a takeout chicken shop to sit on his doorstep and sell her wares to people buying his chicken. Some ambulantes informally buy "puestos," paying $500–$1,000 for a regular place to sit—a street corner, a sidewalk, or a spot on the curb. This unofficial payment goes either to a fijo or to the comisario who allows the ambulante to remain and sell there. Whether they sit in a particular place or continually roam the streets, the ambulantes have to pay something to the sindicato that controls the sector in which they sell (usually a sindicato run by fijos). They also have to pay the private security guards who patrol the sector, and if they move between sectors, they have to pay multiple security firms (chapter 22).

And the ambulantes still have to pay los hambres, the hungry ones. Although the sentaje no longer exists, the comisarios continue to collect routine payments from street vendors whose goods they deem "irregular." "Decommissioning" (*descomisar*) improper wares—protecting public health and safety by removing unwholesome or illegal products from the markets and streets—is one of the comisarios' principal responsibilities. Comisarios also are supposed to make sure that vendors are not cheating their customers, which they sometimes do by using rigged scales to shortchange the client. But the comisarios use decommissioning as a way to make up for the lack of sentajes, which used to flow directly through them. They confiscate ambulantes' goods not because they are of poor quality but as a punishment for occupying public space and to sell their wares back to them at inflated prices. Comisarios even confiscate the ambulantes' carts, umbrellas, hats, and other equipment, which is not part of municipal law. But by doing so, the comisario can exact a payment from the ambulante to liberate her sequestered items.

The sentaje, then, has gone from being a formal payment to an informal one, feeding the hungry ones without granting the ambulantes the right to sell. Like the ancianita with the hunched back and the heavy burden (chapter 14), the ambulantes have no place to sit, to rest, to get out of the sun or the rain. Most ambulantes will flee at the sight of los hambres, which keeps them always on the move. The economic burden of their supposedly "tax-free" income is onerous for the already poor, far exceeding what legal vendors have to pay to the state. "The ambulantes invade the streets," says the historian Humberto Solares, "and the comisarios invade their pockets."[6]

...........................

Meanwhile, the ambulantes' ability to ambulate is restricted by the presence of the "fijos of the street," those with permanent market stalls set up in the streets and on the sidewalks that surround the Cancha (figure 26.1). The legal incursions of vendors into the public roadways leave the ambulantes little room to maneuver. People who are expected to be constantly in motion find it increasingly difficult to move as public space becomes clogged with new private stalls. The ambulantes are blamed for obstructing traffic with their carts and wares, but often it is the new puestos fijos that block the movement of vehicles and pedestrians, puestos that have been authorized by the Alcaldía. And when the puestos occupy the sidewalks, the ambulantes are pushed into the street. All of this blurs the lines between fijo and ambulante, formal and informal, legal and illegal sellers in the Cancha.

Don Beto is a giant of a man with a face like Shrek's who sells Band-Aids—not boxes of Band-Aids, but single strips, twenty centavos each or three for fifty—out of a fanny pack. He presents an odd contrast—such a large man selling such tiny items. Don Beto has no family. He is an itinerant vendor: On Wednesdays and Saturdays, he sells in the Cancha, but on Tuesdays he takes his fanny pack of Band-Aids to the weekly market in Punata; on Thursdays, to Sacaba; on Fridays, to Tiraque; and on Sundays, to Quillacollo. Don Beto is the president of his sindicato, one of those that make up the El Paso federation. He would be an adept public speaker but he slurs his words when he has been drinking. And Don Beto appears at most public functions dead drunk. This includes meetings of the executive board of the El Paso federation. His disruptive behavior visibly irritates Don Silvio, who stares at the floor, his gnarled fingers clasped tightly on the table in front of him, as Beto embarks on a lengthy and sometimes incomprehensible disquisition.

Big Don Beto finds it difficult to sell in the Cancha for lack of room. He sells from the fanny pack so he does not have to use a cart or a wheelbarrow—devices that require more space and are more likely to invite reprisals from angry shoppers and comerciantes fijos. Even so, the advance of the pues-

26.1 A "fijo of the street." Photograph by Lisa Berg.

tos is pushing him off the sidewalk. "One person has a puesto," says Don Beto, "and another puesto advances in front of it, so then the first puesto advances a little more. And here I am, on my little piece of sidewalk, and there's no space for me. They are the owners; no one is going to kick them out . . . , so one way or another, I have to look for somewhere else to go."[7] But when accidents happen, crises such as the fire in La Pampa that call public attention to the market's overcrowding, it is the ambulantes who are held accountable. Beto talks about a recent incident in which a bus ran over an elderly shopper making her way among the stalls and carts on Avenida Barrientos. "This affects the ambulantes with wheelbarrows, with little carts," he says. "The ambulantes are criticized; the ambulantes are blamed for these accidents. They don't say it was because of the puestos, because of the advances they make. It is always the ambulantes' fault that we are in the streets. They throw stones at the ambulantes."

Doña Candela has similar problems. She sells orange juice from a cart that can often be found on the corner of Barrientos and Punata. Doña Candela wears a blue-and-white-checked apron and a white, broad-brimmed hat with a plastic yellow flower stuck in the brim, her smile a ray of sunshine amid the grime of the Cancha. The juice she sells is fresh and sweet, squeezed from oranges and grapefruit brought that very morning from the tropics of the Chapare region. Candela buys about a hundred bolivianos worth of oranges each morning and on a good day can earn double that amount. The problem of crowding, says Doña Candela, is particularly bad on Wednesdays and Saturdays, market days in Cochabamba. On those days, everybody pours into the streets to sell. "People with puestos open other puestos, so there is no room for us. We have to stand between the cars and the people. . . . They put out giant tables, tables bigger even than their puestos . . . That is why it is so uncomfortable. [The fijos] make themselves the owners of everything."[8]

Some ambulantes are members of the federations controlled by the fijos, which gives them both advantages and disadvantages over ambulantes who are not. These ambulantes, says Doña Candela (who is a member of the ambulantes' El Paso federation), are like the employees of the fijos in the federation. The fijo sets up her sidewalk puesto and gathers in some of "her" ambulantes; they then go out and sell on her behalf. If they are hassled by the comisario or have their goods decommissioned, the federation can intervene to help them get it back. "They are their affiliates," says Candela, "and they provide mutual support." This is one of the big advantages of being part of one of the six federations: their leaders have political connections in the city, and an influence over the policing practices of the comisarios. In exchange, the ambulantes are expected to provide political support to the leaders of the federation to which they belong, to march when the leaders say march, to vote how the leaders say to vote. The ambulantes who belong to these federations may be treated like unloved stepchildren, but they deem it worth the sacrifice to gain the modicum of protection that such affiliation provides.

The ambulante who is not in a federation or is part of the El Paso federation has the dignity of being independent but a harder time of things in dealing with the comisarios, los hambres. El Paso is too new and lacks the political clout and the financial resources of the older federations, and its leaders work full time as market vendors. So when an ambulante's stuff is decommissioned, she is often on her own in trying to recover it. When her stuff has been seized, the ambulante has to present herself at the Intendencia to pay a fine and reclaim her belongings. This fine usually ranges between fifteen and thirty bolivianos, so if the value of the items seized is less than that, the ambulante will not bother to redeem them. Ambulantes can have their goods seized for failing to remain in motion, for selling contraband or poor-quality items, for blocking the sidewalk or the street, for mouthing off to the comisario, or for virtually any other offense that the comisario deems appropriate.

Confiscated items enter the netherworld of the Intendencia, from which they often do not reappear. The comisario offers no kind of receipt to the comerciante whose goods he confiscates, so finding out what has happened to one's stuff can be a challenge. Often the ambulante will offer the comisario something at the moment of decommission—a cash payment or, failing that, something in kind, such as a plate of cooked food or a bottle of Coca-Cola—knowing that once her goods enter the Intendencia, she may never see them again. Confiscated food will rot; items will get broken; valuables will get "lost." Even if she pays the fine, the stuff is often gone for good. Says Don Beto, "They don't give you a receipt, because that money you are paying goes directly to them. Imagine, it would be great if they gave receipts, because then you could defend yourself. Now there is no way to identify your belongings. There are so many confiscations, I would have so many receipts by now."

...........................

These competitions over space—competitions that the ambulantes inevitably seem to lose—motivate ambulantes such as Don Beto to seek a market of their own. Many ambulantes cite the lack of room on the streets, and the daily conflicts that selling in that environment produces, as sources of terrible insecurity and believe that if they had puestos fijos in a market like La Pampa they would be much better off. But if the Alcaldía refuses to accept a formal payment from the ambulantes (even as it routinely demands unofficial payments), the likelihood that it would grant them the space for a market seems remote.

Nevertheless, the leadership of the El Paso federation remains undeterred. Don Silvio and his colleagues on the board of directors continue to beat the drum for a market. The day of the big march on the Plaza Principal is fast approaching.

# 27. Market Men

Women, as I described in chapter 21, have been the focus of some of the most important ethnographic work on popular markets. Comparatively little has been written about men in marketing, largely due to the fact that, historically, few men could be found working as market vendors.[1] That is no longer the case. Although women still outnumber men in the formal and informal realms of market selling, in Cochabamba the male presence has increased significantly in recent years. This is true among comerciantes fijos and comerciantes ambulantes. Walking through La Pampa, it is quickly apparent that what was once the domain of women has to a large extent been integrated by men. Many men work in the puestos fijos, either independently or alongside their wives. In many cases, the women were there first and were joined by their husbands later, as other work opportunities diminished. The presence of men does not correlate with products sold, as is evident just from the contacts in my network in La Pampa. Don Ricardo, for example, is a cook and vendor of food; Don Florentino sells plastics and kitchenware; Don Andrés sells cosmetics and shampoo; Don Rómulo works alongside his wife, Doña Candy, selling, of all things, candy. Many ambulantes are also men, working by themselves or in collaboration with women. Don Beto the Band-Aid seller, for example, works alone, while Don Arturo has long worked in partnership with his wife, making, promoting, and marketing quinoa juice in the Cancha.

The presence of men working in the market is a relatively new phenomenon, the result of the intensification of neoliberalism and its consequences in Bolivia. Earlier studies of Andean markets could easily ignore the male presence because it was so small. The market was a "feminine space" populated and controlled almost exclusively by women.[2] But in the twenty-first century that is no longer the case. Doña Eulalia, an ambulante, observes, "In the 1980s when I was first here, there were no [men]. Of all the ambulantes, maybe five or six were men. But now, because there is no work, even the men [are selling]. In the 1980s, you didn't see any men ambulantes, the men worked at other things; the women, the girls, the young women, these were [the ambulantes]. But now there is no work, and husband and wife are working in sales, man and woman, the boys, the young men, all are working in sales."[3]

Doña Rosa concurs. Always knitting, always smiling, Doña Rosa is the seller of ceramics whom I met during Carnaval (see chapter 15). Nacho and I always have trouble finding her stall—we consistently lose our way when we go looking for it down some narrow forgotten aisle deep in the heart of La Pampa. But Rosa always welcomes us warmly when we find her and invites us into her puesto. She allows me behind the counter, into the private space of her stall, where she asks me to sit and offers me a cold drink (a refresco), as though she were welcoming me to her home (see chapter 30). Rosa seems to like me particularly because her son and I are tocayos—we have the same first name. He is a "special child," she says of her Daniel, and while her daughters have gone off and found professions and families of their own, Daniel stays by her side, helping her in his own way to tend the puesto. Rosa has been working in La Pampa since 1971, when her mother established a puesto there selling cooked food. In the mid-1990s, her mother retired, and Rosa switched over to selling ceramics. Rosa and I have long, rambling conversations that go beyond the details of the market into issues of politics, religion, and international affairs. Rosa has a definite opinion about most things, including gender and commerce. "A few years ago," she says, "it would have been the greatest humiliation for a man to be selling refrescos on the street to make a living. Now, men are selling refrescos, mates, everywhere."[4]

Men in the market wrestle with the contradictory gender ideologies to which Rosa's comment points (figure 27.1). On the one hand, a man is supposed to support his family, to work and provide for his children in whatever way he can. On the other hand, the only available work is

27.1 Comerciante ambulante and his child. Photograph by Lisa Berg.

in marketing, and marketing, historically, is women's work. For a man to work as an ambulante, therefore, can seem close to emasculating. Don Silvio reflects on how it was when he first became a comerciante. "I wasn't a businessman. I was at zero," he says. "I didn't know anything. I was getting skinnier, so little by little, I had to learn to bear it. I didn't sell because I was afraid. . . . I was ashamed to say, 'I'm a comerciante.' But finally, what am I going to do? Need obliges."[5] It can be especially difficult for some men to subordinate themselves to the abuse of the comerciantes fijos, many of whom are women, and to that of the comisarios and private security guards. Masculine pride, highly valued in a culture that emphasizes machismo and male dominance, is one casualty of working on the streets. Don Beto reflects on the need to keep one's cool and swallow one's anger in response to abuse. "If I get angry and try to stop them from making me move or from seizing my goods, they will just send others," he says. "Two or three of them will come back looking for revenge."[6] But men recognize that they must sell; that it is the only economic avenue available to them. On selling juice in the streets, Don Arturo says, "It used to be all women. Now there is no work. We [men] are forced to go out and sell."[7]

It would appear that at least some men have dealt with their shame at being comerciantes by getting involved in politics. Although they still represent a minority of the sellers on the streets and in the market, men represent the great majority of sindicato leaders. The Cancha federations—the much larger and longer-established associations of sindicatos—were originally founded by women and are still mostly headed by women, the scions of old market families who have been in business for generations, inheriting their puestos and their offices from the matriarchs who preceded them. But many of the sindicatos, the subsidiary organizations that constitute the federations' membership, are led by men, suggesting that it will not be long before men also head the federations. It is not a coincidence that the only one of the six federations currently headed by a man—Don Rafo's Federation of Comerciantes of La Pampa (FCP)—was founded in the past fifteen years, during the period in which men have become more numerous in the market business. The El Paso federation is of similarly recent vintage and is also headed by a man in Don Silvio.

As I noted in chapter 19, sindicatos have proliferated in recent years as the size of the comerciante population has grown. They have also taken on more importance as the representatives of the comerciantes and advocates for their interests in conflicts with other commercial entities and the state.

Although some sindicatos are led by women, many more are now headed by men. The FCP, for example, consists of about fifty sindicatos, of which about forty have male presidents. The El Paso federation is much smaller than the FCP, consisting of only twelve sindicatos; but of them, eleven are headed by men. Women do hold leadership positions on some of the sindicatos' executive boards, sometimes occupying the posts of secretary or treasurer, but they less often serve as president. It is somewhat startling to attend a meeting of one of these sindicatos, to see a roomful of women being presided over by a male board of directors. If men have been humiliated by the need to work in sales, they have addressed this by asserting a disproportionate control over the associations that represent the market vendors.

Why are there not more female sindicato presidents? Comerciantes fijos and ambulantes alike point to the excessive demands placed on women's time, demands that outweigh those on men. Women not only work a full day in the market; they also are expected to cook, wash clothes, care for children, and do the other household chores that daily life requires. "In Bolivia, at least," says Doña Tahlia, "the women work more than the men."[8]

Given this intense workload, women say, they rarely have time to take on the additional duties of leading a sindicato. Doña Tahlia is a middle-class woman with a domestic servant to help care for her home and family, and this is one reason she has been one of the few women to take a leadership role in her sindicato. Nevertheless, she says, even though she has an empleada (servant), something might be badly washed or need ironing. "We keep working at home. . . . I'm a wife; I'm a mother. I work, no? And my work eats up more than half my time. Sometimes I just want to be in my house." Her children nag her for doing leadership work. "They say to me, 'Mamita, what stupid things you do.' And when I explain to them [why I do it], they say, 'OK, you're right, mami, but we need you here, too.' To be a leader, we lose the entire morning, all afternoon, sometimes we lose the whole day, and nobody recognizes what we do."

Especially among the ambulantes, women are often less educated than men and feel they are poorly prepared to take on the tasks of leadership. Women from the countryside rarely receive much education beyond elementary grades, and many of them are illiterate or lack confidence in their abilities. Some ambulante women are monolingual Quechua-speakers (although there are fewer now than a generation ago), another factor that limits their leadership potential, as Spanish is the language of the public domain. The ability to speak like a leader—to master the cadences, the lexicon, the oratorical flourishes—is another critical skill for a political leader, and women often lack the experience and opportunity to develop these talents in the course of their careers. Don Rafo and Don Silvio are both masters of this language of leadership.

Perhaps most critical, many male vendors grew up in the mining centers of the Bolivian altiplano and cut their political teeth in the struggles of the 1970s and early 1980s. In their youths, these men learned how to organize workers, how to speak like leaders, how to fight with the authorities. When the mines closed in the 1980s, they went elsewhere to find work. On coming to Cochabamba and entering the market trade, they quickly moved to organize their co-workers into sindicatos like those they had known in the mines, bringing with them the modern language of citizenship and human rights to formulate their demands (see chapter 31). It is these men—men such as Don Silvio, founder of the ambulantes' El Paso federation, and Don Arturo, his second in command—who now provide leadership to the women and men of the Cancha.

..............................

Although selling on the street is a highly insecure way to make a living, for some it is a more stable option than it might appear (figure 27.2). Don Arturo can attest to that. Arturo is the vice-president of the El Paso federation, the dark, brooding man who accompanied Don Silvio to our first meeting. As I get to know him, I discover that he is not brooding at all but a warm, congenial fellow who speaks passionately about the ambulantes' situation and the need for reform. Arturo came to selling in the streets through a circuitous route, as have most of the male ambulantes I know. Arturo was born to a peasant family in La Paz Department but moved to the capital city when he was thirteen. He took classes at night but spent his days working for an aunt who made and sold clothing—mostly pants and jackets for men. Arturo never finished high school; at seventeen, he did his obligatory year of military service. Upon completion, he went back to work in his aunt's clothing business. Arturo learned how to work a sewing machine and could produce all sorts of apparel.

But aunts treat nephews badly, Arturo says, and his had him working from 5 or 6 AM until 10 or 11 PM. Business was booming, with large orders shipping almost daily to the lowlands and other parts of Bolivia. But

27.2 Comerciante ambulante. Photograph by Lisa Berg.

then, in 1985, neoliberal reforms brought "free trade" to Bolivia, and used clothing, the famous *ropa americana*, began to pour into the country from the United States. Very quickly, Arturo says in reference to Bolivian clothing manufacturers, "the ropa americana killed all of us."[9] Arturo needed to find new work.

About this time, *jugo de quinoa* (quinoa juice) was introduced in Bolivia from Peru. A hot beverage made from the boiled Andean grain (quinoa is often called the "food of the Incas," especially by promoters trying to appeal to an international market), quinoa juice caught on quickly in the frigid air of El Alto, the satellite city on the altiplano above La Paz. Arturo learned how to make and sell quinoa juice; soon he was married, and his wife joined him in the business. They did this for a number of years before deciding that the market in El Alto had become saturated with quinoa juice vendors. In 1999, they relocated to Cochabamba, where Arturo had a sister, to try to sell quinoa juice there.

Arturo describes the challenges he faced in introducing quinoa juice to the Cochabamba market:

> I went to visit my sister. I said to my wife, "I am going to Cochabamba. If there is work there I will come back and let you know." . . . I'm walking around, and I see there is no quinoa juice. I had brought a little cart. I had brought my little stove. So I rented a little room here [near the Can-

cha]. . . . From there I went out to sell quinoa juice. But I couldn't sell anything; the people didn't know about it. It was pointless. So I bought some disposable cups and started giving it away, promoting it. "Have some quinoa juice," I said. Some people said "What is this shit?" They had no idea what it was. . . . I didn't sell a single glass. After about two weeks, some of the people from Oruro who sell on Barrientos said to me, "*Juguero*, let me have some. What is this stuff?" They didn't know what it was, but they liked it. "It's quinoa juice, *caseritas*. It's good for headaches." "It's good," they said. They didn't know what it was, but they liked it. Little by little I began to sell. After about two months of free promotions, people began to buy it.

Sales were good for about two years, and Don Arturo established many *caseras* (regular customers) in the Cancha. Shortly after he began, his wife joined him from El Alto, and they both sold the juice and taught others how to make it. Soon there were many vendors of quinoa juice on the streets of Cochabamba, and today the competition is fierce. Arturo supplements his income by making pants and denim jackets, working in small home-based workshops in the city's southern zone, mostly for export to Argentina and Paraguay. The piecework pays badly—he makes five bolivianos (less than $1) per item sewn—and only does this work in warm months, when the sale of quinoa juice declines. Meanwhile, he continues to make and sell juice, going at 4 AM each day to Avenida Pulacayo to buy quinoa fresh from the fields in Oruro. "Need obliges us," he says. "How else will we make a living? We're not going to rob anyone, even though we only make two or three bolivianos at a time. We go out to sell, to make something, at least. But it is not like it used to be. You can't earn like you used to. My aunt . . . had a business, and she did well. It's not like that anymore. Things have changed so much."

It was in this context that Don Arturo, along with other men such as Don Remberto, got together to form the New Millennium sindicato (see chapter 19) and later, with Don Silvio, the El Paso federation. Only in this way, he believes, can the poor of the streets achieve a stable and secure life for themselves and their families. "We are never relaxed in the streets, because those with puestos fijos always tell us, 'Move along, move along. Go sell somewhere else.' We demand that the authorities give us a market. We say, that is where we will go. We will get that market, and we will go there. That is why we are demanding that the *señor alcalde* build a market for the ambulantes."

# 28. Webs of Illegality

Comerciantes consistently point to the criminal and the illegal as the principal sources of "insecurity" in the market. It is curious to note, therefore, just how integrated the illegal is into the legal world of La Pampa. This is most obvious in the structure of the market itself. In chapters 11 and 17, I described the Barrio Chino, a sector in the southeastern corner of the La Pampa market where people regularly buy and sell stolen goods. Not everything sold in the Barrio Chino is illegal: the locksmiths have stalls there, and women sell potatoes and other produce. But the Barrio Chino is most famous as the place to go when you have been robbed and want to buy back your stolen property. There is a lively trade, for example, in rearview mirrors swiped from parked vehicles and then resold to their owners by vendors in the Barrio Chino. These vendors are middlemen (and they are mostly men)—albertos, they are called, who buy from thieves, or from gangs of thieves, and then sell the stolen goods from their market stalls. Other vendors are thieves themselves who skip the middleman to enhance their percentage. The Barrio Chino is where you come face to face with the infamous delinquents, men and boys of all ages, faces scarred and clothes tattered, trying to interest you in a watch, a cell phone, or jewelry, all of it stolen.

The Barrio Chino was not always like this. The sector was originally called by the Quechua name Thanta Khatu, the place to buy secondhand goods, and it was the first sector of the La Pampa market to be founded. But in the mid-1980s, with the closures of highland mines and the explosion of rural-to-urban migration, the Thanta Khatu evolved into the Barrio Chino. "Secondhand" took on a new meaning, becoming a euphemism for things stolen. As crime rose in Cochabamba, the Barrio Chino assumed an important economic function, allowing for the laundering of hot commodities in a central location. It also served a social function by recycling stolen goods and enabling their owners to reclaim what they had lost, albeit for a price. Today the illegality of the Barrio Chino is a public secret.[1] Shoppers go to the Barrio Chino because they know it is where they can get the best prices on anything they need. You can even place an order for an item not in stock—a car radio, say, or a particular brand of headphones—and the alberto will get you what you want. The low prices attract shoppers from all social strata. The Barrio Chino, Don Rafo says, "is a sector with a tradition in the La Pampa market. Many people come and they say, 'Go to the Barrio Chino. You can get what was stolen from you. You'll get a good price.'"[2]

If everyone knows that vendors in the Barrio Chino sell stolen property, why doesn't anybody do anything about it? Powerful forces lie behind the Barrio Chino and benefit from the tremendous profits it generates. This is not something that people like to talk about, and it is impossible for me to study directly: the crime lords of the Barrio Chino, whoever they are, do not grant interviews. According to Don Rómulo, the candy seller, these power brokers include authorities high up in the Alcaldía and in the National Police, as well as many of the "legitimate" comerciantes and the leaders of their sindicatos.[3] Many of the market stalls selling stolen goods in the Barrio Chino are controlled by comerciantes who also have puestos that sell "legal" goods elsewhere in La Pampa. The profit margin for these vendors is much greater in the Barrio Chino, because the cost of selling stolen goods is obviously lower than for those acquired through other means, so their illegal sales can underwrite their more "legitimate" activities. The police refuse to close down the stalls selling stolen items because, they claim, these are the obvious places to begin a criminal investigation. More likely, jokes Nacho, it is because of what is referred to as "Article 20" of the Bolivian Constitution—that is, a twenty-boliviano payoff. People refer to these payoffs as "taxes" (impuestos), another ironic reference to the blurring of the legal and the illegal. According to Doña María, the dry-goods seller, the police work in concert with vendors of stolen goods. If you buy something in the Barrio Chino, the police may stop you and confiscate it on the grounds that it is stolen. But instead of returning it to its owner, the cop will return it to the vendor in the Barrio Chino, who will give him a kickback and then sell the item again to another customer.[4] And the process repeats itself.

People are afraid of the Barrio Chino—Doña María describes it as "dangerous," especially after dark[5]—and comerciantes lower their voices when they talk about it, as though they are afraid to wake a monster. "We can't do anything about it," whispers Doña Tahlia. "The best we can do is to avoid it."[6]

But the Barrio Chino is just the most obvious form of illegality in the market. Its existence distracts attention from the illegality that pervades the rest of the Cancha, intricately woven into webs of connection that join legal and illegal sellers, buyers, and products. Even legal vendors such as María and Tahlia routinely sell contraband—ordinary stuff such as canned goods, cooking oil, and condiments brought in from neighboring countries clandestinely, without paying import duties or taxes. Contraband costs less than goods produced domestically because the illegal imports are untaxed and the vendor makes more money selling them. The Barrio Chino, as the "face" of illegality in the Cancha, masks the more quotidian illegalities that characterize ordinary business practices among ostensibly legal or formal market vendors.

..........................

As I work to prepare the promised book for the comerciantes fijos—the "scientific study" of Cancha insecurity—I encounter editorial friction from Don Rafo and Don Melvin. I have given them an early draft to review, and they are concerned about how I am going to represent the Barrio Chino in the book. Rafo is reluctant to allow me to write about the illegality of the Barrio Chino for fear of angering the leaders of the sindicatos there and, possibly, bringing repercussions on him as president of the federation. Even the thieves and albertos of the Barrio Chino are organized into sindicatos, apparently, as are other kinds of vendors doing more legal kinds of work alongside them (figure 28.1). Rafo is afraid that if we publish something that speaks openly of the illegal practices in the Barrio Chino, he will get a lot of blowback from comerciantes who are angry about being exposed. He may also be concerned about revealing some of the webs that join the blatant illegality of the Barrio Chino with the more reputable commerce in the rest of La Pampa. Although he was previously willing to share information with me about the Barrio Chino, now Rafo is hesitant. He asks me to use an older idiom to refer to the activities in the Barrio Chino and just write that it

28.1 A comerciante fijo, barricaded behind a wall of toilet paper. Photograph by Lisa Berg.

is a place where *cosas de medio uso*—secondhand goods—are sold. What can I say? I agree to Rafo's terms.

The experience confirms what many comerciantes tell me during flash interviews about the Barrio Chino. Its illegality is a public secret, and its activities are linked to a variety of powerful forces in the city: the Alcaldía, the police, the leaders of the federations, and the "legitimate" comerciantes and syndical leaders of La Pampa. But these things are not openly mentioned or discussed in any detail. It is as though there is a cloak of silence surrounding these activities, which are apparent to everyone yet, by general convention, ignored. This, Nacho tells me, is *la ley del hampa*—the law of the underworld. The webs of the legal and the illegal become very entangled here, and as I try to write about them I realize I am treading on dangerous terrain.

# 29. Men in Black

You'll dress only in attire specially sanctioned by MIB Special Services. You'll conform to the identity we give you, eat where we tell you, live where we tell you. From now on, you'll have no identifying marks of any kind. You'll not stand out in any way. Your entire image is crafted to leave no lasting memory with anyone you encounter. You're a rumor, recognizable only as déjà vu and dismissed just as quickly. You don't exist. You were never even born. Anonymity is your name. Silence, your native tongue. You're no longer part of the system. You're above the system. Over it. Beyond it. We're "them." We're "they." We are the Men in Black.
—"Zed," *Men in Black*

Not all private security guards are bad guys or extortionists (see chapter 22). In fact, a more sympathetic view of the work these men (and they are almost exclusively men) perform suggests that they have at least as much in common with the ambulantes as they do with the police.

Hector is an employee of the security firm Men in Black and a body-builder. With his short, stocky frame, his black uniform, and his mirrored sunglasses, he looks the very picture of a brute. In other circumstances he might be mistaken for a former delinquent or convict, which many of the private security guards are. But, in fact, Hector is surprisingly gentle, the father of a brand new baby boy. He works seven days a week, from dawn to dusk, after which he takes classes at the university. He is studying for his

29.1 The Men in Black at morning muster. Photograph by the author.

bachelor's degree and hopes to own a security company rather than work for one. Hector's mother sells clothing in La Pampa. She owns four stalls but is heavily in debt, having borrowed $5,000 from a moneylender for each of the stalls she "purchased" (see chapter 31). She then had to turn around and lease out three of the stalls to finance Hector's sister's travel to Spain to look for work. Hector keeps this information secret from his colleagues, who would accuse him of favoritism if they knew his mother was a comerciante. Hector's familial ties to a market vendor are atypical of security guards, who generally lack that kind of intimate, personal connection to their clients. Hector keeps his relationship secret to maintain the otherwise clear demarcation between the providers of security (i.e., his employers) and the people they serve (the comerciantes).

I meet Hector one day at 7 AM to accompany him on his rounds through La Pampa. When I arrive, about a dozen Men in Black employees are lined up in the early morning mist to receive their assignments from their captain (figure 29.1). Before they disperse, the men take up a collection to help pay funeral expenses for the father of one of their colleagues, who died the previous day. The sense of fraternity among the guards is not shared by the firm, though. Hector tells me that the man whose father died was allowed just one paid day off from work. When his child was born, Hector was given a day off, but his wife had to spend two days in the hospital, so Hector took the second day off without pay.

Very little is going on as Hector and I roam through the market sector to which he has been assigned. Hector tells me that in 2002, when the private security firms began to proliferate in the market, the work was much more dangerous and exciting. Back then, he says, it was not uncommon to see delinquents wandering the market with knives carried openly in their hands, preying on whomever they encountered. There were fights almost every day. In those days, the guards really felt like characters from *Men in Black*, the movie starring Will Smith and Tommy Lee Jones. In *Men in Black*, the heroes are trackers of extraterrestrials illegally on earth; Hector says that in the beginning, the guards felt the same way, tough and intimidating in their black outfits going out to hunt delinquents.

Now, Hector says, the delinquents recognize and respect the guards and have changed their mode of operation. The thieves have gone underground, waiting until the guards leave to go on the prowl. They have also learned to avoid detection by not appearing to be stereotypical delinquents. Thieves today dress nicely, Hector says, sometimes even in coats and ties, their hair combed and their faces washed. This makes them harder to spot and requires extra attention by the guards and the vendors.

Delinquents come in a variety of shapes and sizes, and a rich taxonomy of lowlifes exists in the Cancha to which the Men in Black have to be attuned. Much as the Inuit are supposed to have twenty different words for snow, vendors have names for the different kinds of criminals who roam the market. Much of the delinquency in the Cancha is attributed to the ragged street children, the *polillas*, who perpetually haunt the market, grabbing dropped coins, loose handkerchiefs, shopping bags casually held. Not all street children are thieves, but many turn to crime to survive, and the polillas are widely despised by market vendors. A variety of other criminal types populate the market underworld, known as el hampa. Some thieves, called *descuidadores*, target the market vendors and their stalls, snatching items when a careless (*descuidado*) seller's back is turned. The descuidador might work with an accomplice, who distracts the seller by pretending to be interested in making a purchase while his partner takes off with the goods.

Other thieves prey on the customers. *Escaperos*, like descuidadores, take items and run: if you put down your bags to take out your wallet, for example, an escapero might snatch them and, as the name implies, escape. *Cuentistas* are con artists who tell stories (*cuentos*) to their marks (*pavos or jils*). One cuentista pretends to drop a wallet full of money at the feet of an unsuspecting shopper, perhaps a tourist or some other likely dupe. His accomplice, the second cuentista, expresses delight at having found this wallet and suggests to the *pavo* (turkey, fittingly) that they go somewhere quiet and divvy up the contents. Once there, however, the first cuentista reappears, and the pair take the victim for all he has. In another version (the *cuento del tio*, or devil's tale), the cuentista suggests that he and the dupe split the money in the wallet. However, the wallet usually contains a $100 bill that cannot easily be split, so the cuentista proposes that the pavo give him the cash he has in his pocket and keep what is in the wallet. Great, the pavo thinks, for fifty bolivianos I will get a hundred dollars. But as soon as the cuentista disappears with the pavo's bolivianos, the "owner" of the wallet arrives and demands his money. *Lanzeros* are pickpockets—they also use techniques of distraction to make their work easier. One lanzero will approach you and say, "Señor, there is something nasty on your coat" (which he, in fact, put there); while he pretends to help you clean it off, another thief lifts your wallet or snatches your bag. Once, walking on a densely crowded street, I suddenly sensed something wet and foul-smelling sprayed on the back of my neck. Instinctively, I reached up to wipe it off, at which point a man tried to reach inside my coat. I pushed him, and he ran.

Security guards must be aware of all of these ploys. They patrol their sectors, always on the lookout for problems. The guards rely extensively on their own menacing appearance to deter crime—just being present is often enough to discourage a would-be thief. But the Men in Black cannot stay too long in one place. Hector says it is important for him to be seen as much by the comerciantes as by potential delinquents. If they do not see him on patrol, they will be more reluctant to pay their daily fee, which he and his co-workers are responsible for collecting. So like an ambulante, Hector is in continuous movement; but whereas an ambulante tries to avoid being seen and chased away from the place he occupies, the security guard must be seen. Men in Black security guards must constantly perform their physical presence, making themselves visible to their many clients, because their legitimacy is derived from the explicit contrast they make with the notably absent National Police.

The Men in Black may look like police as they patrol the market, but when they apprehend delinquents, they have to determine for themselves what to do. No written code governs their behavior. Nor does private security collaborate with the police, despite their earlier promise to do so. Everyone knows that the police are in league with the delinquents, Hector says, so instead "we do justice among ourselves."[1] The private guards might hit a guy, especially if the crime he has committed is somewhat serious. If it is not too serious—say, somebody has stolen a CD or two—the guards might just drop him outside their turf, making him the problem of the private firm that patrols that area. Sometimes they will cut off a delinquent's hair as a way to mark him or her as a criminal. In any case, the entire process is handled privately, with the guard serving as police, prosecutor, and judge, determining the severity of the crime and administering an appropriate punishment. Such punishments, too, are best performed publicly, in plain sight of the clients, the market vendors—again, to justify the cost of private security and to make it apparent that the Men in Black are on the job. Visible evidence of "security," Hector seems to suggest, makes everybody feel more secure.

Officially, at least, tensions between private security and the police persist, despite the spatial separation of the two forces (private security in the market and National Police outside it) that emerged following the street battle of 2001 (see chapter 22). The Men in Black are themselves vulnerable to crime, including organized payback by the delinquents they punish. "We have no support if we are physically assaulted," complains another Men in Black employee. "Many of our compañeros have been knifed. What security does the state give us?"[2] Security guards are poorly paid; they receive no benefits; and they cannot rise through the ranks to positions of higher authority.

But this is not surprising. Private security is a corporate industry to which state functions have been outsourced.[3] The owners of the firms—often former military officers and now middle-class entrepreneurs who coordinate the firms' activities from offices on the edge of the market and persistently elude ethnographic inquiry[4]—are insulated from the violence of the work and expect their officers to provide a regular flow of resources from the payments they must collect daily from their clients. Insecurity, for these owners, is a pathway to personal enrichment. It is facilitated by the extensive contacts they enjoy within the police and other official institutions—their friendships within and bribes paid to the National Police ensure that the authorities will turn a blind eye to any illegal practices committed by the private security companies. The situation calls to mind Charles Tilly's conception of the state as a kind of protection racket, which monopolizes violence and extracts resources from its subjects in exchange for the safety it promises to provide to them.[5] Here the work of security making has been taken over by a private entity, though one that is very state-like, both in the ways in which it operates and the kinds of inequality it manifests. Private security guards such as Hector, in other words, should be understood as workers in the sovereignty business, the front-line men who do the dirty work in the protection racket through which local sovereign claims are established. Much like the ambulantes they sometimes harass, the Men in Black are informal workers in the underground economy of the Cancha.

# 30. At Home in the Market

Female fijos and ambulantes have to juggle the challenges of working in the insecure space of the Cancha while managing the varied responsibilities of home, often without support from men. Sometimes this results in the blurring of lines between public and domestic space, as female market vendors transform their workspace into something that resembles a home where they can combine their responsibilities to make them more manageable. These strategies also better enable women to supervise their children and keep them safe, one of their principal preoccupations amid the daily insecurity of urban life. Here again, though, the comerciantes fijos have many more resources available to them than do the comerciantes ambulantes to make themselves secure.

Market vendors spend virtually all of their waking hours in the market. For those with fixed market stalls, it is not surprising that their work space also serves as a kind of domestic space, a living space within the workplace of the Cancha.[1] The puestos fijos serve as a kind of home away from home for those who occupy them, as do the many little shops and stores that line the adjacent streets. In their puestos and shops, comerciantes fijos sleep, eat, watch television, and socialize with friends and neighbors. People cook in their puestos and feed their families. Children and grandchildren spend a lot of their free time—before and after school, on weekends and holidays—in the puesto, doing homework, playing, napping. Comerciantes with very young children and infants can basically raise them in the puesto without interrupting their work. Some Cancha puestos consist of a single rectangular area, but many have a front counter or table that divides the public space of the puesto from the private, inner space that lies deeper within. Across this counter business is transacted, and clients do not cross to the semi-darkness of the domestic area behind it.

The fact that so many Cancha vendors are women only adds to the sense of the domestic that the puestos present. The puesto is a place for nursing infants, preparing food, washing dishes, ironing clothes—a blurring of what are sometimes thought to be the separate worlds of the public and the domestic.[2] For many market women, maintaining this domestic space within the puesto is essential for the maintenance of their family life, as their work requires them to be away from home so many hours of the day, from very early in the morning until very late at night. It is also a place of retreat, a way to escape the conflicts and the craziness of life in the market, and a home apart from the familial residence, which may be occupied by an abusive man. A Cancha puesto thus might be more comfortable and home-like than a woman's actual house.

The ambulantes, of course, lack this domestic space. Without a puesto fijo, the ambulantes have no place to hunker down against the world. They are completely exposed. Their work lives constitute 95 percent of their waking lives, and home is somewhere in the background, a place that they rarely see in daylight. With no fixed location to pass the day, the ambulantes cannot accumulate the detritus of domestic life in their workplace the way the fijos can. Instead, they must take everything with them as they move through the market; it is carried on their backs, pushed in wheelbarrows, or slung off their ubiquitous blue and green pushcarts. This includes their children: babies ride on their mothers' backs, immobilized in tightly wrapped *aguayos*, or on racks beneath the carts. Older children trail along, playing in the streets and on the sidewalks, creating an additional nuisance for pedestrians and putting their lives at risk from the passing vehicular traffic. Mothers must keep one eye on their children, one eye on their customers, and, if such a thing were possible, a third eye open for any possible *delincuente* looking to make off with their stuff or for a policeman or security guard coming to chase them away or demand money.

Managing children is one of the main concerns of the ambulantes, especially of mothers who are typically assigned primary responsibility for their care.[3] Until children are old enough to go to school or to join their parents working on the streets, they need looking after, and in the absence of day care or a relative with whom to leave them, mothers are torn about what to do. Some ambulantes, such as Doña Candela, an orange juice vendor, take their youngest children with them while they work. Candela has no husband now—he was abusive, and after years of putting up with it, she finally left him—but she has six children, none of them older than twelve. The two littlest ones accompany her to the market every day. She leaves the six-year-old at home, supervised by the eight-year-old, but the two-year-old and four-year-old hang out on a rack under her cart or play on the sidewalk while their mother sells juice. Doña Prudencia used to walk the streets with her three young children, one slung across her back in an aguayo, another one strapped to her chest, the third walking beside her. "Yes, that was hard," she recalls now. "It was tiring to be in the street all day with one sleeping on my back, another on my front, dragging one along like any old thing. That's how women do it for the most part, even now, carrying their bundles, weighed down, their baby in front, the other one wanting to sleep. That is the life of the comerciantes" (figure 30.1).[4]

There are other dangers for children in the market. They can wander off, get injured, be abducted. Doña Juana says that once while selling in the market she lost track of her young son. "I never want to lose him again," she says. "He's very small. I wasn't able to stop, and he just disappeared. I wanted to die! Now I don't bring him along. He's four years old now, and I don't bring him, only sometimes if he's sick, and then only until midday."[5] There are also health risks in the street. When you take your child to work, Doña Ana says, "You have to give him food from the street, too. And you know how that food is in the street. . . . Sometimes it would give him fevers, infections from the filth. Caged up in my cart all day, he had to stay under my cart."[6]

Doña Celia sells cosmetics from a wheelbarrow and takes her two young daughters with her when she works. But their presence limits her ability to make a living. "I can't ambulate with my little girls," she says. "I can lose my girls. I can't move around much. My girls are small and can get hit by a car just crossing the street."[7] Wednesdays and Saturdays are the best days to make money, but they are also the most crowded days and the days that the comisarios are least tolerant of loitering ambulantes. So Celia cannot work on those days and takes an economic hit as a result. Instead, she sells only when she is relatively confident that she can stay in one place and will not be chased off, usually early in the mornings and late in the afternoons when

30.1 A comerciante ambulante and her child in the Cancha. Photograph by Lisa Berg.

the comisarios are less active. She also relies on a relationship she has established with a particular comerciante fijo, a woman who allows her to sell in front of her stall. "In other [sectors] they won't let us," she says. "'You're blocking me,' they say. So I only go to this one place in the afternoons."

For most ambulantes, the only alternative to bringing their children with them to work is to leave them at home unattended. This is a source of grave concern for these parents, who feel insecure about their residences and the high rates of crime that occur in their neighborhoods and are reluctant to leave their children home alone.[8] But in many cases, they have no choice. "We are forced to leave them at home," says Don Remberto, "with no one to care for them, no adult. They take care of themselves."[9] It is common for a two-year-old to be left in the charge of a four-year-old, one baby taking care of the other. Parents, of course, worry about the consequences of this lack of child care. Says Don Remberto, "Here we sell at least until 6 or 7 in the evening; we don't get home till 8 at night. At that hour the kids are already asleep. Some nights they go to sleep without any supper, and that is a bit worrisome, that the children aren't well nourished, that they get lazy with their studies."

Some parents will coordinate their schedules to try to accommodate their children. Again, the woman bears primary responsibility in this regard. Don Juvenal admits as much, saying, "The mother, more than anyone, [is responsible]. We [fathers] have to worry some about it, but it is always the mothers. . . . She stays home in the morning, makes them wash up and sends them off to school and right away heads out to sell. Meanwhile, we [men] leave very early—myself, at least, I leave at 5 AM."[10] In the afternoon, says Juvenal, both he and his wife go out selling, but sometimes he heads home early to see the kids. Some men share the responsibility with their compañeras. Doña Prudencia's husband is a locksmith and takes their oldest child with him to work every day. Doña Juana and her husband share the morning child-care duties. "Sometimes we go out at the same time. Sometimes one of us goes later, because we can't leave the children," Doña Juana says. "[One of us] leaves at 5 AM. At 6 we have to be here. By 7 we're working, and the other one is leaving at 9 [or] 10. We take turns."

As children get older, many join their parents in the market as sellers. Children as young as four and five will sell on street corners or on buses, boarding just long enough to hawk packs of gum, ice cream, or other small items. Young children also sell in the evenings, offering cigarettes and candy to adults dining or drinking at restaurants and sidewalk cafes. Boys and sometimes girls also work as shoeshiners, circulating through the market or hanging out in public parks with their small wooden boxes containing brushes and different colors of polish. Although parents worry about their children's safety, they also rely on their financial contributions to supplement the household economy.[11]

In the absence of a domestic space in the Cancha, ambulantes create homelike places or systems for maintaining their families while working. Even those who do not take their children with them to work may bring them in during lunchtime, typically the most significant meal of the day and one best shared with family. Some families prepare lunches and take them with them to the market, finding a quiet place to park their carts and have a family-style meal (figure 30.2). Others establish relationships with women who run small eateries (comedoras) from whom they regularly take their meals. "We know a lady [who] cooks well, and we always have lunch

30.2 A comerciante ambulante and her family eat lunch in the street. Photograph by Lisa Berg.

together there," says Don Juvenal. "After lunch, we send [the children] back home."

...........................

The market has provided to women and men the possibility of survival in the neoliberal economy, but most market vendors hope for better for their own children. The market life is corrupting, they say, and the conflicts and competition are damaging to the soul. "The market is hell," a market woman in Cuzco, Peru, told the anthropologist Linda Seligmann. "There are ladies in the market but they don't know how to respect each other, they fight just to fight with each other. So, I don't want my children to sell in the market."[12]

Vendors in the Cancha have similar feelings. They worry not only about the economic possibilities of life in the Cancha but also about its destructive moral effects. "The market, as they say, is hell," says Doña Ana. "It teaches you to be bad, to be a gossip, to be envious, big-mouthed, argumentative. The market teaches you; it changes your life."[13] Market vendors, fijo and ambulante, female and male, wish for better things for their children. Says

Don Remberto, "I think we are grand examples for our children. We have not studied. We are not professionals. We are not trained to work in a steady job, a job that pays well. And they see this. My sons say to me, 'Papá, I have to study so I don't end up like you.'"[14]

# 31. Owners of the Sidewalk

Who owns public space?[1] Who has the right to occupy that space—for work, for leisure, or for other purposes? In a sense, these are the key questions that surround the insecurity that both comerciantes fijos and comerciantes ambulantes experience. The sidewalks, the streets, the market itself—all of this is public space, publicly owned if not consistently or equitably supervised or regulated. What rights do those who habitually occupy these spaces possess?

Don Ricardo is a comerciante fijo, and he is passionate about the need to defend the market against state efforts to privatize it. Ricardo has been working in La Pampa since it was a *pampa*—bare, dusty, undeveloped open land at the far end of the ferias. No one, he remembers, wanted to come to this part of the market. But his mother and a few other intrepid souls set up shop and began to sell here. Ricardo's mother was an excellent cook, and she established one of La Pampa's first *comedores* (eateries, puestos with small kitchens and benches where market vendors and shoppers have breakfast and lunch). She taught Ricardo how to cook, and he inherited the business from her when she passed away. His three brothers also work in the stall, which seats about thirty people at a time—quite large for a Cancha comedor. Comedores serve a fixed menu that includes *sopa y segundo* (soup and second course), plus a dessert, or a la carte. The food is delicious, and

Ricardo serves the classic dishes: *chank'a de pollo, falso conejo, sillp'ancho, picante de lengua.*[2]

Don Ricardo, president of the sindicato representing the sector's comedores, is proud of La Pampa and the Cancha marketplace. He brags, "The Cancha is a place where you can find anything, and what you can't find, they'll draw it up and make it for you."[3] La Pampa, he says, is where you can buy the freshest, cheapest food. Comedores like his are looked down on by fancier folks, *jailones* who eat only in the "good" restaurants uptown. But in the Cancha, he does not have storage or refrigeration space. Everything he cooks has to be served and eaten that day, which means there are no leftovers. In the fancy restaurants, he says, they'll scrape the leftovers from your plate and serve them to someone else the next day.

Like Doña Tahlia, Don Ricardo is a skilled businessperson. He always gives the customer a little bit more than what he or she asks for. This little bit extra—*yapa*, it is called in Quechua—is to be expected with any purchase in the market, and if it is not offered a shopper may ask for it ("*¿Y mi yapa?*"). But Ricardo personalizes it, taking yapa one step further, trying to give the individual exactly what he or she is looking for—a particular piece of chicken, say, or extra *picante* in the soup. "You have to watch the customer, you have to be smart, because if you don't satisfy the customer, the customer won't come back. . . . You have to know how to handle the customer, because, say, if he comes for a meal with his two kids, you have to give him enough broth in his soup so they can share it. It's a simple matter so they all leave satisfied." This is how vendors such as Ricardo and Tahlia establish ongoing relationships with particular customers—their *caseras*—who can be relied on to return loyally time and time again. Treat the customer well, Don Ricardo says, and he will always return. "That is the best advertising there is. We have been here for so many years, always selling. It is an inheritance that our mother left us."

The idea of privatization scares and angers him. The Alcaldía is an interloper here. It gives the comerciantes the land on which they work, but nothing more. "We made the floor; we made the stalls; we furnished them," he says. "Obviously, the land belongs to [the Alcaldía]. We pay an annual fee, you understand. But they don't concern themselves about anything here. If you want a sewer, you have to do it yourself, as we have recently done. All of the Cancha is like that." This work—this investment of labor, time, energy, and money—is what gives the comerciantes fijos the right to work here, not the blessings of the state. "If they want to privatize or something like that," Ricardo says, "all the market will rise up. No one wants to be forced out of his workplace so someone else can come and take over all that he has made."

..............................

Although the specter of official privatization worries the comerciantes, Cancha puestos have long been privately traded among them. The market, as I have said, is formally the property of the municipality, and market stalls may not be bought and sold by individual vendors. Furthermore, municipal law establishes equity in puesto ownership, and Ordinance 192/87 explicitly prohibits any individual or family from occupying more than one puesto in the market. According to José Luis Soria, the man in charge of puestos for the Intendencia, such laws are based on a spirit of equality of opportunity and access and express the belief that Cancha puestos have a "social function."[4] Market puestos "have to benefit people who have no work, who have no capital, who have no economic resources," Soria says. "They have to benefit the mother or father with children, that don't have a source of daily income." If the puestos are allowed to be sold or accumulated by wealthy individuals, he contends, it would negate the spirit and social function of the market as a place of opportunity for all.

Given the Alcaldía's history of trying to privatize the market (see chapter 23), it is hard to reconcile such a philosophy with the behavior of the municipality. By attempting to sell the market, first to a corporate entity and, when that failed, to individual purchasers, the Alcaldía has shown a clear recognition of the value of the market and its stalls and has tried to liquidate that value through privatization, with little regard for equity or access. The reality of the market conflicts with the official ideology about the market, an ideology contained in laws that are routinely broken or ignored. In fact, it is this obvious disjuncture between legal philosophy and legal practice that makes some formal ordinances appear so ridiculous and so easy to disregard.

Comerciantes, of course, recognize the reality of where the value in the market lies, and those with resources can work around the law to advance themselves economically. Although it is legally prohibited, wealthy merchants can acquire multiple puestos, registering them in the names of adult children, aunts and uncles, sons- and daughters-in-law (technically members or heads of different families). "If they could buy them for their cat or their dog, they would," Soria says. While the Alcaldía remains the owner of the puestos and prohibits their sale among individuals, such sales occur all the time. A puesto's occupant can sell her or his right to occupy the stall to someone else—the current market value is $15,000–$20,000, depending on size and location, although people pay as much as $50,000 for a good puesto—who will then change the name on the registry to establish herself or himself as the legal occupant. Such a change can be legally accomplished: all the buyer has to do is claim that the previous occupant is no longer physically able to work.

This can lead to problems. My friend Doña Rosa's mother, who bought a puesto in La Pampa in the early 1970s, temporarily rented it to a friend, who then changed the papers and took legal possession. When she complained to the Alcaldía, Rosa's mother was told, "You know, señora, the puesto belongs to the one working there."[5] Another fijo vendor in La Pampa asked a neighbor to watch her puesto for her while she was out sick; when she returned, the vendor found that the neighbor had switched the name on the registry and was now the official occupant of the puesto. The original occupant had no avenue of recourse or appeal and eventually turned up at the office of the Cochabamba Human Rights Congress, which sympathized with her situation but was powerless to help her.[6] The congress, a Bolivian nonprofit organization, tries to pressure the state to enforce the law prohibiting these kinds of transactions, but without much success. The congress's office receives many complaints of this type, a representative says, but "we have been able to resolve very few individual cases. The majority of complaints remain unresolved because of the powerful subterranean forces [that control the market]."[7]

Most sellers of puestos leave the state out entirely, instead adopting their own quasi-legal devices to give their transactions an official flavor. They draw up contracts, issue bills of sale, and sign and notarize forms, none of which are legal, based as they are on an entirely illegal premise (i.e., the private transfer of public property), but serve symbolically to ratify the exchange of puestos. Often people hire lawyers to oversee these transactions, despite their illegality. Sindicatos and federations play a role in the transactions, as well: the market for puestos is regulated not by the state but by the leaders of a particular sector, who decide who may and may not sell in a given area. Such decisions are often influenced by cash payments made to the leaders and to the federation, which then gives its approval to the transaction. Federation leaders usually have extensive contacts within the Alcaldía, enabling them subsequently to legalize these transactions in exchange for a payment or the promise of future political favors.

Through these sales, some families have amassed a large number of Cancha stalls, which they then rent to vendors who sell from them. Others hold their stalls in *anticrético*, depositing a large sum (several thousand dollars is common) with the "owner" of the stall, who allows the depositor to use it for an indefinite time. This enables the stall "owner" to invest the capital in other business ventures and to keep the interest accrued on the deposit at the time of its return. Such transactions, like the sales, are completely against municipal law, but they are routine in the Cancha. Many of the fijos who sell in the market thus are not the "owners" of their stalls but renters or temporary occupants. Others, meanwhile, are wealthy enough to have a Cancha stall for their own use on market days, other stalls to rent out, and additional stalls in one or more of the various *ferias franjas* (weekly markets held in different neighborhoods around Cochabamba on particular days of the week). A truly prosperous market woman might sell in La Pampa on Wednesdays and Saturdays, in suburban Cala Cala on Sundays, and in the barrio San Pedro near the university on Thursdays, and take the rest of the week off to enjoy her rental income.

The sale of puestos occurs not only in the market, and not only through unofficial transactions. As I discussed in chapter 26, the Alcaldía routinely sells the legal rights to puestos fijos in the street. While it complains about urban congestion and blames the ambulantes for the overcrowding of the city's streets and sidewalks, the Alcaldía continues to issue new patentes that authorize vendors to occupy new stalls on the same congested *vías*. This is what happened in Avenida Pulacayo, where the puestos fijos that occupy both sides of the street, the sidewalks, and the median strip made it impossible for emergency vehicles to reach the fire in La Pampa (see chapter 1).

New administrations blame previous ones for the problems of today. The selling of spaces in Avenida Pulacayo, for example, was overseen by Manfred Reyes Villa, the mayor who originally tried to privatize the Cancha. He fled corruption charges in Bolivia in 2010 and now lives in the United States. Emilio Cortez, the current intendente of Cochabamba, says, "We are trying to clean up the sidewalks by removing comerciantes, signs, and merchandise, but unfortunately many of them have patentes for these puestos because other administrations gave them the permits."[8] But the practice continues through various administrations, not only because of the corruption of particular individuals, but also because that is how the system works. Unable to privatize the market, the state seeks every possible means to squeeze out additional resources, including privatizing the city's public spaces.

The sale of urban public space has created a mass of "owners" who believe they are entitled to sell in these spaces. Public voices cry out against the congestion, pollution, and hyper-commercialization of Cochabamba's public space, criticizing these "owners of the sidewalk" for their blatant disregard of the needs of others.[9] "Paying a patente does not give anybody the right to occupy prohibited spaces," says an unsigned editorial in the daily *Opinión*, "much less so to those who have simply paid somebody off. But we also must punish those who take money ('taxes') for literally selling the city."[10] Although such complaints are voiced year after year in Cochabamba's media and in conversations on its streets, these forms of semiofficial privatization persist.

...........................

The ambulantes, too, believe they have the right to sell in public space. Ambulantes frequently point to the Bolivian Constitution and its guarantee of the right to work as a justification for selling in public space. On this basis, the ambulantes stake a claim to the sidewalk, a space to which they believe they are legally entitled. The transnational language of "rights" features prominently in these complaints, particularly when uttered by experienced and worldly politicians such as Don Silvio.[11] He spells out this rights claim in precise legal terms: "[our] rights come from the Constitution of the state of Bolivia. . . . It may seem like we don't have the right to work in the streets, but we are authorized by the power of the state. . . . In Article 7, subsection D, it says very clearly: you cannot deny someone the right to work. To do so is unconstitutional, it is a crime against the right to work."[12]

For Don Silvio and other leaders of the ambulantes, the state's ongoing attempts to exclude them from public space is unjust, a failure to recognize them as citizens and to grant them their constitutional rights as Bolivians and their human rights as people. Silvio and other ambulante leaders decry the denial of their rights, saying, "They treat us like animals." In other words, the authorities do not recognize the ambulantes' basic humanity. These vendors note their low pay, their vulnerability to all forms of exploitation, and their status as "foreigners," as migrants from other parts of

Bolivia who are seen to have invaded Cochabamba. They always make us move, complains an ambulante, "as if we weren't Bolivians, as if we didn't even count. Because in the Constitution, a Bolivian can go to live wherever he wants. But meanwhile, there are people who can declare who is a native and who isn't."[13] Don Arturo, the vendor of quinoa juice, demands rights for ambulantes by observing simply, "We aren't from another country."

# 32. The Seminar

The day of the seminar on security in La Pampa has arrived. Comerciantes fijos from throughout La Pampa gather in the social hall of the San Antonio church at 10 AM. Padre Abelardo was reluctant to let the comerciantes use his space—given his past conflicts with the Christmas vendors trying to sell on the church patio, he is no fan of comerciantes—but he owes me a favor for my help with the bones found under his church floor. As people arrive, they sign in at a table we have set up at the back of the hall and receive a packet containing an agenda, a pen, and paper to take notes. Everything is newly printed and bears a unique logo that Nacho and I designed specifically for this event. Maybe 80 percent of the people present are men. About forty or fifty people are in attendance, including a few representatives of the private security company Men in Black. Nacho and Eric are also here. At 10 it is time to start, but Don Rafo has not yet arrived.[1]

> DON MELVIN: OK, we are now going to begin the seminar "Insecurity in the La Pampa Market." . . . The most important thing is, I want to emphasize the cooperation that this group of researchers is making. . . . Dr. Daniel Goldstein, who is American by nationality, has come with a purpose, with the will to work and to study the basis of the problem of insecurity that we live in the La Pampa market. . . .

There is not going to be a masterly lecture from these doctors; rather, they are going to listen to each of you, the experiences that you have every day in the La Pampa market. You are the experts in these subjects. You know it perfectly well. . . . In this way . . . we will plan to solve our problems and put a clear and definite plan before the authorities. . . . The only thing [the authorities] do is collect their salary, but they don't work [with us] as a team or come down to the level of the society, come down to where the people are complaining, shouting, screaming that they resolve so many things in society. Again, I am thankful for your presence and I am going to invite Dr. Daniel Goldstein to say a few words about the project. You have the floor, Doctor.

DANIEL: Many thanks, Don Melvin. Thanks again to all of you for coming this morning to this meeting that is so important to all of us. . . . Usually there is so much discussion about insecurity—you see it in the newspapers, in the halls of government, [from] the Alcaldía all the time—but from my point of view, almost nobody talks to the people most affected by the problem of insecurity, which is the people of the market, the people of the barrios, the people of the *bases*, no? You all. From our perspective, it is necessary to talk with the people to understand from them how they suffer from insecurity and what solutions they can propose to solve the problem. . . . So our purpose is to gather information. You are the experts in this matter, and we are here to talk with you. At the end of the study, of the research, we will be able to write a book to present to the authorities containing recommendations for how to resolve this problem. . . .

So what are we going to do this morning? . . . We will gather in three small groups. One group will talk about the causes of insecurity in the La Pampa market—you are going to talk about why there is so much insecurity in the market. What are the causes, from your point of view? The second group will discuss the effects of insecurity in the La Pampa market—that is, how does it affect you? How do you have to change your lives? What loss of merchandise is there? What has been the experience of living with insecurity in the market? The third group will talk about possible solutions to the problem of insecurity. What recommendations could you make to confront this problem? We will discuss these three topics in small groups, then we will get back together in a big plenary. . . . After, when we finish with that, we will give out tokens to each of you and we will go from here to a restaurant in La Pampa, where we will have a big lunch paid for by this project. That is all, I believe, Don Melvin.

The participants are divided into groups, mostly men but with a couple of women in each group. The groups meet separately for about forty-five minutes, then we reconvene for presentations and plenary discussion.

> DANIEL: Let's begin the plenary now. The first group, causes of insecurity, you will describe for us the general debate. Are all the groups ready? . . .
>
> DON DARÍO: Good day again, dear compañeros. . . . On the first point [the causes of insecurity], we put the lack of unity among leaders and comerciantes in the market. Why? Our leaders, compañeros, we have four, five federations, so when we want to advance, there is no unity in our sector. . . . So many emphasized this. How are we going to advance and achieve something for our sector if there is no unity? How will we . . . get these objectives that are so important, like the security of our market? Because what do our police do? The police personnel don't [do anything]. . . .
>
> Point two, the lack of security personnel. In that we mean the police [and the private security]. The [private] security is only physically present to collect their payments, [not] at night. . . .
>
> Three, migration because of unemployment. Right now it is the fashion to go to Spain, abandoning one's children. . . . Many are not grown, [they are] children, what we call polillas, they have turned to delinquency. Many say it is not easy now to identify them. Before, delinquents had their faces and arms all cut up, so you could identify them. Now many young people have cell phones, are very nicely dressed. They camouflage themselves, no? They look like customers. So we put a lot of emphasis on this unemployment as an important cause—parents abandoning children, migrating to Europe in search of security, for better days or better opportunities. . . .
>
> The presence of the police—the police are more corrupt and work with the delinquents. The big bosses work with the heads of the delinquents, the next day they let him go, eight hours after they arrest him, if there is no complaint, no definite proof. And that is why

the laws are not in [our] favor. The laws, if no one files a complaint, sometimes for fear after having been robbed, the next day I might be scared that there will be reprisals against me, they don't go [to file a complaint], or in the street they will grab me and suck out my fat or send me to the next world.[2] That's why the laws are failing, so that is why there is insecurity. . . .

DON PABLO: Just to clarify something that our group said about the causes of insecurity in the La Pampa market, the main point we discussed. . . . If a door is open, they will come in, right? So what is the solution? To close them, right? So under causes of insecurity, we talked about the infinite number of entrances [to the market]. These are the causes. The entrances [to the market] have to be coordinated so that one sector is the entrance and one sector the exit, so that when a delinquent [enters] there is communication, with a whistle or a personal security alarm, [and] you can [close up the exit so he can't get out].

DON RAÚL: But that part should be under "solutions," not "causes."

DON PABLO: No, it is "causes." I am clarifying that there are too many entrances and exits.

DON JORGE: Excuse me! Excuse me! Don't get away from the causes of insecurity in the market!

DON MELVIN: Compañeros, what the compañeros are requesting is that we stay on the theme—the causes that we have to understand. What are the causes? You all have to teach us, that's all. . . .

DON JORGE: That, compañeros, is a point to be addressed. The lack of unity, perhaps; for that [to happen] we all must be unified. In one sector there are so many associations, so many sindicatos, right? When these unite there will be much more power here to negotiate with the authorities. . . .

DON FELIPE: Those of us in the second group . . . in our report we have reached two important points [on] the effect that is produced in the La Pampa market . . . The first is an economic effect. . . . because when I am robbed because I'm distracted . . . many times we have a big heap of things and we turn around and they take something, isn't that so? There is a psychological effect, as well. We encounter insecurity in every way: the comerciantes, the shoppers, the leaders, we are all insecure. We are even scared. We see them robbing us, and no one helps us. Afterward, what happens? I mean, I lose my self-esteem. . . . My morning turns black, [and] I'm not going to work like I should. My woman comes along, and I begin to yell at her, "What time were you supposed to be here? It's your fault that I got robbed!" It affects my wallet, it affects my family, it affects my neighbors, it affects everybody around me. . . .

DON MELVIN: OK, third group please: solutions.

DON ANDRÉS: OK, I am going to speak of a general problem. I'm not going to offer solutions. First I'm going to present a problem. We know it is a delicate subject to talk about the delinquents and all that. . . . We know very well that the supermarkets are owned by the big capitalists, by the big transnationals, by people with lots of money. So what have they done? They met among themselves and said, "Let's create polillas," and since then there have been many more polillas. Once there are more polillas, their work is the following: to destroy the market. And why? So that the supermarket grows, and the customer says, "Things are more expensive in the supermarket, but I have security, I don't get robbed, I don't get ripped off, I have parking and security. But if I go to the market they rob me." So that was the problem. It was a sociopolitical problem. . . . Anyway, that is the introduction. Now, the solution, I don't know. . . .

DON OSWALDO: Excuse me, good afternoon, I don't want to get off the subject, the subject is possible solutions, possible solutions for insecurity. We in group three, the first thing we said for solutions to insecurity is, it would have to first come from the state. The state would have to pay the police a good salary. Then the state would have to recognize the [private] security along with the police. Why? So they wouldn't have this problem that was mentioned a little while ago, that the private security catches a delinquent, they take him to the police, and the police let him go. But if those two collaborated, they could work together better. . . .

DON DAVID: The thief has to be punished. The delinquent has to be punished according to his misdeeds. Because the justice [system], instead of being just, there has never been justice in Bolivia, or transparency or honesty. The justice [system] is vertical, not horizontal. Justice does not exist. The legal profession in Bolivia should just disappear. Why? Because they don't make justice, señores. There is no security because the justice [system] is corrupt. If the justice [system] punished the delinquent, the delinquent would think twice before committing his misdeeds. . . .

DON FRANKLIN: The law itself favors the delinquent, am I right? So here we have the solution. Thank you. . . .

DON MARCOS: Compañeros . . . the private security that we have does not live up to its mission of preventing crime and being effective. . . .

DON ANDRÉS: The problem as I see it is migration from the countryside to the city. The authorities have to put a stop to this migration. We are forming belts of misery around the cities. These people who migrate can't get work, because in the country they only know how to work the plow and here they don't get work and they turn to delinquency, am I right? You have to think about the insecurity of the customers. They are being scared away. Like I said before, the customers won't come to buy from us. They will go to supermarkets and other places. . . .

DON MELVIN: OK, thank you, I want to suggest, compañeros, because we are almost out of time and we have to have lunch at 1, that we enter the stage of solutions. We have heard about the causes, the effects. So let's enrich the [discussion] of possible solutions. . . .

DON JOSÉ: As far as solutions, compañeros, I say it is important that we have the private security in the La Pampa market. The people of La Pampa have no confidence in the city police. So the solution is we have to ask that the National Police form a direct relationship with the private security. . . .

DON CARLOS: OK, La palabra. What I want to know is, you are asking for a better coordination between the police and private security. But, if there is no confidence in the police, then why do we want more coordination?

Many voices are talking at once.

DON CARLOS: I'm not trying to invalidate any of these solutions, I'm just trying to add to the plenary discussion!

DON HENRY: Pardon me. I will explain the solutions. This is what I understand so far . . .

DON MELVIN: The compañero over here has the palabra. . . .

DON RAÚL: He's talking about private security.

DON FELIX: Another thing is the relationship that [private security] has with the comerciantes. Many times when we catch a delinquent they just leave us on our own. We call security and we are left, as they vulgarly say, "fucked." . . .

DON MELVIN: You have the palabra, señor. . . .

DON ALEX: Just a minute! You will give me the palabra, compañeros. . . . What I ask for are solutions. I am going to propose a solution. What we need to make a solution is an amplification system exclusively [for us], to give us a solution inside the La Pampa market.

DON MELVIN: Yes, yes.

DON PEDRO: They should put police modules in the four corners of the La Pampa market. . . .

More voices overlap. It is clear that the discussion has lost its direction. At some point, unknown to me, Don Rafo has made his appearance.

DON RAFO: OK, compañeros, good afternoon. . . . We have been to an infinite number of seminars, sponsored by the government, by different institutions, they have even taken us to the Hotel Cochabamba—good food, American breakfast—that have had no effect. For this seminar to be productive, you have to collaborate. I ask you, compañeros, to help us, because there are people who don't want us, who want the La Pampa market to disappear. . . . Our objective is pure, compañeros, it is pure because the only thing we want is that once and for all, the authorities direct their attention to the La Pampa market, that they do something about the delinquents to stop them from stealing from us . . . I want to emphasize the words of the compañero who said, "Let's be united. Let's all be united in the La Pampa market." And we will be united, because the division that exists in the market has served only the politicians . . . But there will be unity to defend our rights in the market. Compañeros, many thanks, I know we have taken half your day of work, but I think it will be a benefit to the La Pampa market. Thank you.

*Applause*

DANIEL: Thank you all, above all for the opportunity to have this seminar. The issue of solutions is obviously very important, and something that occurred to me is something that you all have mentioned here: the lack of an amplification system. This is something we have noticed on many of our visits to La Pampa, that there is no means of communication. If a señora loses her child or if there is a robbery and the people want to call security, they can't do that. Therefore our team is going to donate an amplification system.

*Applause*

DANIEL: A technician will set up the system and all that. The other thing is the tokens for lunch. Eric is going to take charge of the tokens. Right now we are going to head to the restaurant.

# 33. March of the Ambulantes

The day of the protest march has arrived, when the ambulantes will make their presence known and publicly demand a market of their own. But as so often happens in fieldwork, I am called away by other obligations and am unable to attend. My disappointment is tempered by the knowledge that Nacho and Eric will be there and will take notes and record audio of the event. That is another advantage of collaborative work: having others to fill in when I have to be elsewhere. Nacho's notes are written in his own personal style and capture the flavor of the moment:[1]

> I arrived at the San Sebastián plazuela [the starting point of the march] at 8:45 in the morning, but the comerciantes were not there yet. On the benches in the diagonal sidewalks of the plazuela one could observe small groups of people reading newspapers and others chatting; also, there were groups of people lying on the grass, these looked like delinquents and among them there were some polillas. Around the fountain near the south sidewalk of the plazuela there were five or six cholitas. Two of them had carts, one selling orange juice and the other salteñas. I supposed they were the first ambulantes that were now beginning to concentrate for the march.
>
> At 9:10 the ambulantes began to trickle in and to occupy the northeastern and southeastern parts of the plazuela. They gathered in small

groups, each one separate from the other. Some came with banners in the colors of the flag and an emblem in the center, the name of the association forming a half-moon below that with the date of [the sindicato's] founding. These letters were stitched in gold thread. I tried to find Don Silvio and some other people I know, but I was not successful.

At 9:40 one could observe a larger number of ambulantes, the majority of them cholitas, a mixture of La Paz hats and Cochabamba hats. Some were carrying their small children. There were very few men present. In the central part of the plazuela I spied a small group, and it was Don Silvio and his committee around a little chess table made of concrete that was there. Some were sitting on cement seats. I came up and greeted them, and Don Silvio told me that they would wait until exactly 10 for the arrival of more *compañeros de base*. I could tell that Don Silvio and some of his committee members were a little nervous, some seemed very anxious; anyone could see that they were inexperienced in this type of activity, Don Silvio told me that this was their first march, that if at least three hundred members didn't show up, this action wouldn't have the force or the desired effect. So I suggested that he send a commission to recruit the rest of the federation members. They had a quick meeting and decided to send a commission to La Pampa to recruit their membership. Other groups set about making placards. There was a big fuss because everybody wanted to express their ideas, so finally they decided democratically by voting for the winning phrases, which were the following: "We want freedom to sell in the markets of Cochabamba"; "Mr. Mayor respect Article 7 of the national constitution"; "The liberty and dignity of the people is inviolable, to comply with and respect them is the duty of the authorities."

At 10:15 there were more people, and the crowd had grown massively. They decided to hold a final meeting in which they discussed a variety of topics, above all explaining to the people what they were demanding and that they had to yell. One of the leaders of a sindicato said, "We know that they are not going to build us a market, compañeros, we have to stop dreaming, but at least we are going to make them stop screwing with us and let us work in peace." The crowd applauded with spirit. They then spoke about tactics, such as the women with their babies would go on the sides [to protect them from] repressions, tear gas attacks, etc.

They organized themselves in rows formed up like squadrons invading Avenida Aroma. Immediately they paralyzed the traffic and in the blink of an eye three blocks were full of people. The sindicato Simón Bolívar [a group of ambulantes who are not part of the El Paso federation] came in support, so three blocks became five. The route they followed went along Aroma to San Martín and then up to Heroínas to then enter the Plaza Principal.

While the march advanced through the streets, many other ambulantes joined in, so that the march gained force and greater presence. Don Silvio and his committee were at the head; behind them one could observe thirteen emblems—for [the El Paso federation's] twelve affiliates and the sindicato Simón Bolívar. Everybody shouted and launched rockets. What they shouted the most was the following: "¡Chaly, mamón, tu intendente es cabrón!" (Chaly, you prick, your intendente is an asshole!);[2] "What do we want? Markets!"; [and] "Chaly, your police are thieves!"

In the march up San Martín, many more ambulantes were joining in, some with their carts and others with their bags. When they arrived at Heroínas, the crowd was almost complete.

Spectators and the curious stopped to watch the march; others to protest. There were many who didn't know what was going on. Some suggested the marchers were demanding water; others that [the march] had to do with women's rights. Obviously 95 percent of [the marchers] were women; as I mentioned before, there was a mass of women as if it were a squadron divided between soldiers in white helmets (the women from Cochabamba) and soldiers with dark brown and black helmets (the women from La Paz).

The vehicular flow in Avenida Heroínas was totally congested, and many drivers complained. When we arrived at Heroínas and Esteban Arze, there was a driver of a red car who protested furiously. When I approached, I saw that it was Brother Juan from the San Antonio church, and he said to me, "What are you doing mixed up in all these *barbaridades* [barbarism, stupidity]?"

The march continued its course and finally entered the Plaza Principal through Santibañez Street.

Five or six policemen guarded the Mayor's Office in the galleries on the north side of the plaza. Don Silvio and his committee spoke with the aid of a megaphone; the journalists invaded the place in search of news. Eric and I observed the process attentively. The cholitas surrounded everything and wouldn't let anybody enter or leave [the plaza]; others shouted and insulted the Municipal Police [comisarios], especially one whom they called "Choco" (Whitey): "there is that crook Choco!" "Hey, Choco, give me back my umbrella!" another shouted at him. "Choco where is my hat?" . . .

[After a while] the crowd began to disperse, and what was at first a huge crowd now was a small cluster of ambulantes. Some of them had their carts and took advantage of the opportunity to sell their stuff.

..............................

The march, by all accounts, was a success. Don Silvio and the other sindicato leaders of the El Paso federation are still flush with excitement when I see them shortly afterward, their hopes and expectations lifted by the great turnout. Plus, the president of the City Council has called Don Silvio with an offer to meet with him to discuss the ambulantes' demands. Doing my part, I use this moment of recognition to arrange meetings between the ambulantes' leaders and some of my contacts, including Carlos Montoya, who works for the Intendencia's Office of Municipal Services, and Major Grover Zapata, the man in charge of the National Police's Office for the Control of Private Security.

But despite this success, I am beginning to notice some diversity of opinion on matters over which I previously saw unanimity. Cracks are beginning to appear in the façades of the political projects of the two men who have been my key interlocutors throughout my field research, Don Rafo and Don Silvio. In the latter case, it is beginning to appear that not everyone among the ambulantes shares Don Silvio's enthusiasm for a market. Even though hundreds of people had joined in the ambulantes' protest march, many, it turns out, were there under obligation. Sindicatos routinely demand the participation of their members at such events and impose fines on those who fail to show up without a valid excuse. Although it means a lost morning of work, the fine for nonparticipation (fifty bolivianos, or about $7.50) represents a considerable sum for an ambulante (figure 33.1). It seems as though many of the participants attended out of fear of being fined rather than out of passion for the issues at stake.

As I speak with more and more people, especially women, I begin to learn that, in fact, many ambulantes prefer selling in the street to having a market stall. Although the life is difficult and dangerous and full of hardships, in the current circumstances being mobile is critical to their ability to make a living. Doña Angela, for example, the only female sindicato

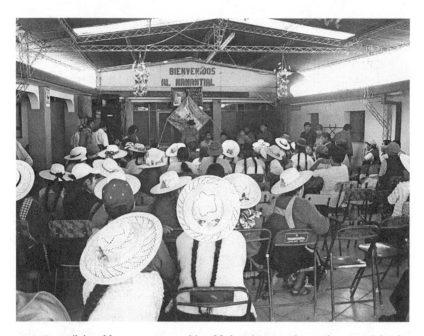

33.1 Don Silvio addresses an assembly of federation members. Photograph by the author.

leader on the El Paso federation's board of directors, says that in her case it would be very inconvenient to have a puesto fijo. She knows where to go to sell, on what days and at what times, and she has a clientele. For her, it pays to be mobile; having a fixed stall would only tie her down and limit her ability to make money. Being an ambulante gives Angela a certain amount of freedom, which she seems to enjoy.[3] Women are dubious about the proposed market's likely location, which would probably be somewhere outside the Cancha, the principal place in which to sell. And women scoff at Don Silvio's insistence on having a market with two stories. Have you ever been to such a market? they ask. No one bothers going to the second story to shop because they can get what they need on the ground floor. Why bother going upstairs? People are lazy, they say, and fear that such a market would be dead on arrival. Other women do support Silvio's desire for a market, which would give them a greater sense of security against abuse, bad weather, and so on, but I am seeing now a difference of opinion on the issue that lies at the heart of the El Paso federation's demands. There seems to be a gendered dimension to this political struggle, with male leaders pushing for a market that many of their female constituents would prefer to do without.[4]

Other signs of trouble are appearing in the El Paso federation. Although people continue to attend meetings, there is very little activism, little sense of urgency on the part of the federation members. Don Silvio and other leaders complain about a lack of engagement on the part of their affiliates, who seem more concerned about their personal incomes than about joining in collective action to bring about social change. Although the march on the plaza was a success, Silvio is worried about their ability to turn that energy into real progress. Also, Silvio is disgusted with his fellow sindicato leaders. They are short-sighted, he says, willing to negotiate with the Alcaldía, to accept some kind of an offer that would give them relief in the short term (a temporary "amnesty" for street vendors has been discussed) but would fall far short of the market that they have been demanding. Silvio is concerned about who might be able to succeed him as President of El Paso when his term is up. An election is approaching, and the board members are all urging him to accept another term. Silvio is considering it: he enjoys being a leader, and his work is not yet finished. But he also thinks that the other men on the board are fools, and he does not trust more than a handful of them to lead the federation.

The one man whom Silvio could trust is Don Arturo, the dark man, vendor of quinoa juice, who accompanied Silvio on his first visit to our office. Silvio and Arturo had seemed inseparable, friends as well as colleagues on the El Paso federation's board of directors. But somehow, over what I am not sure, they have had a falling out. Arturo, always a presence at the board meetings and federation events, is suddenly missing. Gone. He has quit the board, renounced his position as sindicato president, and vanished. Rumor has it that he grew tired of the lack of progress on the market and decided to form his own federation, apart from Don Silvio and the rest of the El Paso federation. Others say that he and Silvio fought over money. But these are just rumors. I do not know what has happened to Don Arturo. Although I look for him when I walk through the Cancha, I cannot find him and cannot find out what happened between him and Silvio. I never see him again.

..........................

Over in La Pampa, Don Rafo is having trouble of his own. The seminar revealed that, as among the ambulantes, there is a big difference of opinion among the comerciantes fijos about what to do to improve security in the market. Although there is general agreement that something needs to be done, no one can agree on what. This dissension—or lack of unity, as it was characterized in the seminar—represents a major obstacle to improving security in the market. If the leaders of the sindicatos cannot agree on a response, they will have difficulty coordinating an effort to push for reform.

There are also problems surrounding Rafo's leadership of the Federation of Comerciantes of La Pampa (FCP). Rafo, it seems, is even more of a caudillo than I had originally realized. As I get to know people better, they begin to share their grievances with me. I start to hear grumblings—that Rafo works more for his own account than for the people he represents; that he uses his political connections to enrich himself and his close associates; that his ambitions for a political career beyond the La Pampa market have compromised his judgment. People point out that in all the years he has been leader, the market has made very little progress in terms of improving its infrastructure or security, and that the FCP itself does not even have its own headquarters, being run instead out of Rafo's banana stall. Doña Rosa complains to me that Rafo has not called a meeting of the board of directors in more than a year. "The market has gone to sleep," she tells me. "We ask Rafo, 'When is the next meeting?' 'Soon, soon,' he says, but nothing happens."[5] She also claims that during the ten years Rafo has been president of the FCP, he has not called a single election, which is clearly illegal according to the bylaws of the federation and against the customs of the market. Rafo, Melvin, and their closest allies "have pushed the rest of us aside," Rosa says. Why doesn't she switch affiliations, join another sindicato, a different federation? The others are just as bad, she says, maybe worse. She and some other longtime comerciantes in her sector are conspiring, hoping to put forward a candidate to challenge Rafo and demand that he call an election.

These conflicts and ruptures, coming just as my fieldwork nears its conclusion, are troubling to me. I had thought that I was beginning to understand the nature of the relationships in these complex organizations of fijos and ambulantes. But things are shifting and changing, and once again I feel lost at sea.

That is the way things go, though, in fieldwork. We start with simple stories that get more complicated the longer we are there, the more people come to trust us and share with us the dirty details. We enter partway into people's worlds and think we have things figured out, only to discover, sometimes late in the game, that what we knew to be true is only half the story. Sometimes, in constructing our ethnographies after the fact, we paper over these cracks in our understanding, sand down the rough edges and make things appear seamless and coherent. But the reality we observe in the field is usually much more complicated than the final stories we are able to tell about it.

That does not mean, though, that all is fragmentation and incoherence. My research has identified themes, certain threads that run through the warp and weft of life's daily fabric. As my fieldwork winds down, I begin trying to pull those threads together, to weave the tapestry that will be not only my ethnography but also the books I will present to my friends and colleagues in the two federations.

# 34. Complications

Nothing is ever as simple as it seems, the previous chapter suggested. Every story has more than one side to it. Anthropological fieldwork complicates our assumptions about the world, because the more we learn, the more sides to the story we hear, the harder it becomes to live with simple answers. Every situation is more complicated than it initially appears.

The comisarios have one small office in the heart of La Pampa, where comerciantes with problems come to lodge their complaints (figure 34.1). With the end of my stay in Cochabamba approaching, I finally make the time to visit. I have been putting this off, fearing a direct encounter with the infamous market police. To my surprise, though, the head comisario, Omar Villarroel, welcomes me warmly, invites me to sit, takes time to answer all my questions. Despite all of the awful things I have heard about the Municipal Police, their captain in La Pampa seems to be an honorable man, with pride in his work and a commitment to doing things right. Like his father before him, Don Omar is a career policeman who describes his primary responsibility as "making order" in the chaos of the market.

But it is an uphill battle. Don Omar complains that while the market has 100,000 vendors, there are only fifty comisarios charged with regulating all of that commerce. This is obviously impossible. So Omar and the other comisarios do what they can to make sure the comerciantes do what the law requires. They confiscate illegal and spoiled goods and scales that have

34.1 The "chaos" of La Pampa. Photograph by the author.

been altered to deceive the consumer; they ensure that the comerciantes fijos wear their aprons and head coverings; they keep the fijos from expanding their puestos outside their allotted space. All of these small enforcements, Don Omar says, are part of the daily struggle of making order in La Pampa.

The comisarios have to deal with the ambulantes, as well. The main objective here is to keep them moving. "They have to circulate," Don Omar says. "They have to walk around. That is their obligation."[1] Omar realizes, of course, that the ambulantes' very presence in the streets violates one of the laws that he is sworn to uphold. But really, what is he supposed to do? "How else are they going to make a living?" he asks. "Better that they should sell something [than starve to death]. Because if we take a hard line [la mano dura, he says], we will create a massive social conflict . . ." He trails off. "So we let them stay. But they have to keep moving."

The law is one thing; its enforcement another. The comisarios are constrained by the limitations placed on their institution, inadequate resources being chief among them. The best of them are also constrained by a basic humanitarian impulse and by an awareness that if they really enforce the law, it will lead to worsening poverty, immiseration, and, ultimately, widespread social upheaval. There is a moral and political calculus involved here that the lawmakers might not consider but that the Municipal Police—the embodiment of the state in the space of the Cancha—must always bear in mind as they face the realities of daily market life.

Having met the comisarios in the flesh, I have more empathy for them as people and for the difficult work they face. Of course, this does not mean that the comerciantes' perspective is wrong or that the comisarios are not, in fact, capable of being exploitative, abusive, and cruel. But Don Omar's perspective does complicate the picture and makes it harder for me to put the blame entirely on the comisarios as individuals. Their abusive behavior is grounded in the bigger picture of urban disregulation, which makes their abuse possible, even desirable, as a technique of "making order" in the market.

..............................

In the days and weeks following the seminar, comerciantes fijos in La Pampa greet Nacho and me with enthusiasm when we visit their stalls. People who previously had seemed skeptical about our presence in the market, their eyes brimming with suspicion even as they greeted us with a handshake, now smile warmly when we appear, offering us the more intimate handshake-hug-handshake. One of their first questions when they greet me, though, is, when will we be installing the new amplification system that I promised them at the seminar? Soon, I tell them, soon. Nacho and I visit stores around the Cancha and price the system out at about $300—more than I had planned to spend, but given the friendly reception it seems to facilitate, well worth the expense.

Installation of the amplification system is delayed because of debate over where, exactly, to install it. Don Rafo wants the amplifier to be in his banana stall, which, since the FCP does not have its own separate headquarters, would seem to make sense. But where should the four loudspeakers be located? This is a highly politicized question. Every sector of La Pampa wants a speaker, and who gets one seems likely to depend on loyalty to Don Rafo and Don Melvin. The loudspeakers, a gift to the whole of La Pampa, has, I see, become a new instrument of power for the melvin-cuentes.

A few days after the seminar, Nacho and I meet with Rafo and Melvin to discuss plans for the public presentation of the loudspeaker system. In addition to the question of where to put the speakers—a decision with not only political but technical dimensions to consider (e.g., the optimal distribution of the loudspeakers, considering the market's layout, the ability to extend cables, and so on)—is the matter of when to schedule the presentation. Different groups within La Pampa are struggling to set the date. I am reminded of the classic ethnographic film from Papua New Guinea, in which the ability to determine the date of an event is constitutive of the power of a local "big man."[2] Something similar is at work here: like the Papuan leader, Don Rafo cannot just declare the date. He has to negotiate it with his various factions, balancing their competing needs and desires.

Finally Rafo decides on a date for the public presentation. It will be very near the end of my time in Cochabamba. Rafo suggests that for the time being we install only one speaker, in the stall of Doña María, the dry-goods seller who also happens to be his first cousin. I am fine with this—I know María quite well; she is an older woman, a longtime Cancha vendor, and generally well liked in the market. Also, her stall is centrally located within La Pampa. In any case, this will only be a temporary installation, until such time as a more permanent setup can be decided. Don Rafo expresses his hope that Nacho, a trained technician, will install the system, but Nacho politely declines. The installation will not cost much, he says, and anyway, doesn't Rafo have contacts in the Alcaldía? They could provide a técnico to do the installation for free. Rafo accepts this as the challenge Nacho intended it to be and agrees to find out.

The melvin-cuentes now enter into a discussion between the two of them, although it is obviously meant for my benefit, about an entirely different matter: the upcoming Mother's Day celebration. Their plan is to present enormous baskets filled with all kinds of household goodies (cooking oil, pasta, canned food, cleaning supplies) to some sectors of La Pampa. The sectors can then hold a raffle to choose the winner of each basket. "But who will pay for these baskets?" Rafo asks Melvin, shrugging, the two of them the very picture of innocence.[3] "They are going to cost a hundred bolivianos each." There is a long pause. No one looks in my direction. I flip through the pages of my notebook; Nacho examines his fingernails. Eventually, Melvin fills the silence. "One, two, three, four," he counts us off. "There are four of us—one hundred bolivianos each. Four baskets." I am thinking of the pending cost of the book I have promised to publish for them, not to mention the loudspeaker system and the money I gave Melvin to recharge his cell phone. But something more important than money is at stake here. I look Melvin straight in the eye. "We have already done our part," I say to him.

There is another long pause as we all regard each other. Suddenly, Rafo and Melvin burst out laughing, and Melvin slaps me on the back. Nacho and I join them, all of us laughing, about what I am not sure. But I seem to have passed some sort of test.

# 35. The Archive and the System

Cochabamba is a city without an official memory. The municipal government has no record of its past decisions, no official repository of its own history. Historical archives do, of course, exist: a collection of materials from the Cochabamba region, with a particular focus on the sixteenth century through the mid-eighteenth century, located in the Palacio de la Cultura at the corner of the Avenidas 25 de Mayo and Heroínas; a cache of old newspapers, poorly maintained, in the Hemeroteca Municipal, one flight up; a library of books and documents related to planning and urbanization at the Colegio de Arquitectos; various holdings at any number of universities and other local institutions.[1] And there are people's memories, oral histories, some of which are the sources for this book's recollections, including those of older comerciantes fijos who were present for the founding of La Pampa. But the municipal government has maintained its own official records only since 1985.[2] In the office of Planificación Urbana, where teams of city planners try to chart the course of Cochabamba's future, very little is known about the city's past. I was told that at one time there had been an archive, that the Alcaldía had relocated, that there had been a fire, that the archive had been destroyed, closed, lost: the details are fuzzy. But the upshot is that the city has no storehouse of memory—of decisions the municipality has taken in the past, of its failed plans or of those put into effect, of the management of the city even during relatively recent times. The historical resources that do exist are in private hands, held by historians or hobbyists who just happen to have taken an interest in some issue and preserved records of it. Otherwise, Cochabamba has no official past, no formal history, no institutional memory.

Not that Cochabamba has lacked for municipal decisions, for the making of laws. Efforts at urban planning and regulation have been incorporated in any number of ordinances and edicts introduced by the municipality to govern its expanding population and the spaces they inhabit. But today, even the most significant plans and proposals exist only in their residual effects on the urban landscape. For example, Carlos Montoya, a local historian who works for the municipality in the Intendencia, told me that one of the city's key master plans, the Plan Regulador of 1961, intended to govern every aspect of municipal development for the foreseeable future, has entirely disappeared. It is one of the most important documents in the history of urban Cochabamba, and no one in the Planning Office or the Mayor's Office has a copy. There had been only two copies of the document to begin with, Montoya told me, but the Alcaldía lent its copy to someone who never returned it. ¡Imagínate! Montoya himself has the last copy, and he never lets it out of his house; he refused to let me see it. To him the document is something of a sacred relic, proof of a past that otherwise might never have happened.

The history of urban markets in Cochabamba is even sketchier. A market town to its core, Cochabamba nevertheless has no official records pertaining to the Cancha, no archive of decisions taken in regard to the regulation of market space. This may be because so few of those decisions were ever officially written down—like so much else in the Cancha, the state's management of it has been done informally, sub rosa, off the books. People who know something of the city's past, such as Carlos Montoya, understand the importance of marketing, and of the Cancha, to its history. The Cancha is more than just the economic engine of Cochabamba. Montoya calls the Cancha the heart (corazón) of Cochabamba—it is of far greater significance than the colonial-era city center, which most people, politicians and academics included, refer to as the heart of the city.[3] The Cancha, Montoya insists, gives the city its identity. "Everything else," he says, "is secondary."[4] This fact makes the municipality's official ignorance of the Cancha even more suggestive.

Scholars have critiqued the archiving function of the state as a component of its ruling strategy, part of the neoliberal state's effort to "know" its population, and a fundamental tenet of its governmental approach.[5] This makes the absence of an archive in Cochabamba even more surprising and, perhaps, telling. How is a city without institutional memory governed? Does a kind of urban amnesia shape the workings of the municipality and the national state? I think it does. Unmoored from the past, the municipality and its functionaries operate in a world of ideology and imagination, free to govern without reference to the past or concern for the future. A state with no memory rules solely in response to the exigencies of the moment, content to extract what profit it can according to the dictates of a prevailing capitalist ethos that even in the "post-neoliberal" moment remains basically uninterrogated. To be ahistorical, in a sense, is to absolve oneself from responsibility. One's personal behavior—like the official edicts that are pronounced and quickly forgotten—floats into the ether like the exhaust of a passing *micro*. Forgetting the past is a critical component of what we might call the state's practice of *unknowing*, its refusal to recognize what it cannot control.[6] Rather than the "legibility" that is so important to many other projects of state rule—the rendering of a governed population "readable" and hence governable[7]—in Cochabamba we find the production of illegibility, forged through a deliberate ignorance of the past. It contributes to the manufacture of organized disorder that is fundamental to contemporary urban governance.

.............................

Although it lacks an archive, Cochabamba does have a "System."

As I discussed in earlier chapters, the Cancha, like the larger city of which it is a part, is structured in such a way as to include some and exclude others, so that the opportunities for enrichment and advancement are strictly limited and controlled. This structuring of inclusion and exclusion is an ideological and discursive complex; it is also a material fact that deploys the logic of technical regulation. With the move to replace the informal sentaje payment with the more formal Pago Único Municipal (PUM), the Alcaldía established a computerized registry for keeping track of who is legally allowed to sell and how much they have to pay to the municipality for that privilege. This form of inscription and control supposedly allows the authorities to establish rational forms of order amid the chaos of the market, to make legible and hence to "know" its subject population. In reality, it enables them to practice the politics of exclusion, of unknowing, more effectively. Rather than creating legibility among the market population to know who is there and what they are doing, the Alcaldía simply excludes those it deems undesirable by declining to recognize their existence. The ambulantes call it "the System," this computer database in which their names can never be inscribed, although the term indexes a much wider field of social and political relations from which they are similarly marginalized. By refusing to allow the ambulantes to pay the PUM or the sentaje, by refusing to enter their names in the computerized System, the authorities consign the ambulantes to the gray spaces of permanent informality.[8]

As this book has explored, the problems the ambulantes face are grounded in forms of insecurity produced by the politics of urban governance, the historically contingent relationships of countryside–city and urban center–periphery, the effects of neoliberal restructuring, and the operations of municipal and national law. But state authorities and elites justify the exclusion of the ambulantes from the System by blaming the ambulantes. Calling on very old discourses of race and class, hegemonic in Bolivia since colonial times and persistent even in the pro-indigenous era of Evo Morales,[9] elites point to what might be called the "culture" of street vendors as the principal source of their difficulties. Juan Carlos Quintana, one of the principal authorities in charge of urban commerce for the municipality, is blunt in his assessment. He attributes the problems of delinquency, disorder, and poverty in the market to the "low culture" of the people who sell there, especially the comerciantes ambulantes.[10] The market vendors "lack the values" to understand the goals of the municipality, he says, which are to establish law and order in the market, to transform it from a "Persian bazaar" into a market under municipal control. Quintana, a self-described "technical person" (técnico) who is directly responsible for the creation of the computerized System, contrasts the values of order and regulation with the cultural chaos of what he calls the comerciantes ilegales who sell in the marketplace. "In reality," he says, "we have two things in play here: the cultural and the normative. The cultural, for its part, makes the normative difficult to realize." The ambulantes' culture of informality, in other words, makes the market impossible to regulate.[11] Ambulantes, by definition, are ungovernable.

Don Silvio and the other leaders of the ambulantes reject this conclusion. For these men, their exclusion is due not to their own failings but to the unjust politics of the state, which refuses to recognize them as citizens and to grant them their constitutional rights. Don Arturo notes that "some authorities don't respect us as Bolivians. They treat us badly. The comisarios, for example, treat us badly. I think we have rights, you know?"[12] For many ambulantes, the issue is inclusion: unless they are entered in the municipality's computerized "System," they say, they have no rights as citizens. Don Fausto links the terms of inclusion to the normalizing techniques of administration. "What we want is to be allowed in," he says. "To the computer. Recognized as *comerciantes minoristas*, as ambulantes, in the System."[13] Some ambulantes even want to be allowed to pay sentajes for the security that being a taxpayer brings. "When you don't pay anything," Don Silvio notes, "there is no protection," whereas "if we pay our tribute, we will have rights. They won't be able to make us move."

This language of rights, and the idea of citizenship that it indexes, is a crucial part of the ambulantes' demands. It gives them a transnational language with which to express their desires—for inclusion, for recognition, for security, and for a place to sell without being harassed or abused.

The language of rights also gives me an idea for how to conclude the book I am writing for the ambulantes, a way to communicate their perspective to the powers that be.

# 36. Goodbyes

Anthropological fieldwork begins slowly. Getting your bearings, getting to know people, figuring out a strategy for getting your work done—all of this takes time to develop. The beginning of fieldwork can be difficult, discouraging, even painful. But the pace of work picks up as time goes along. Soon you are working almost constantly. Fieldwork has become your life, and you cannot imagine life without it. Even so, fieldwork, like everything else, does not last forever. Its exact end point is arbitrary, disconnected from the research itself. There is no particular reason for it to end when it does, except that something external brings it about: you run out of money, often, or you are needed at home. Whatever the reason, as fieldwork nears completion you feel that there are many loose ends that remain to be tied up. An experienced fieldworker recognizes this, accepts it, and anticipates the rhythms of the process. It helps to know that there is never really an endpoint to fieldwork, a moment at which you can say, "There—I'm done." There will always be more to do, more to learn, more questions to ask and answers to seek. So it is critical to use whatever time you have to collect as much information as you possibly can to feed the long months of writing that follow.

With the official presentation of the loudspeaker system in La Pampa fast approaching and my time in Bolivia nearing its end, I decide to confess to Don Silvio my ties to the comerciantes fijos. Following a meeting of the ambulantes, I pull Silvio aside and tell him that for some time I have been collaborating with Don Rafo's federation, working with its members in a manner similar to the way I have worked with Silvio and his ambulantes.[1] Seeing my discomfort, Don Silvio bursts out laughing. It turns out that he knows all about it and has for some time. Silvio, of course, has eyes and ears throughout the Cancha, and his ambulantes have been reporting back to him about my doings since my arrival. Anyway, Silvio reminds me, in signing our convenio he had never stipulated that our relationship be exclusive. Indeed, Silvio tells me, his group has been working with nongovernmental organizations that offer services similar to those that our group provides, and he sees no reason that those relationships should cause a problem for ours. He hopes, though, that I will follow through on my promise to write a book reporting the results of our study. I assure him that that is my intention.

I am relieved at Silvio's response to my confession, which has been worrying me for months. As we head out, Nacho remarks that if Silvio knows about our work with Rafo, it is certain that Rafo knows about our work with Silvio. I am again confronted by my own naïveté, and my admiration deepens for these two crafty men.

...............................

Following their march on the Plaza Principal, the ambulantes under Don Silvio and the El Paso federation have gained a certain notoriety in Cochabamba. The leaders of the federation have had meetings with the head of the Consejo Municipal, with the intendente, even with the mayor himself. More than that, they have received multiple offers of places where they can construct their market.[2] The intendente offered them a plot of land, located south of the Cancha in a region called Waka Playa. On investigation, though, it turned out that the site already had comerciantes selling in it, and the ambulantes' leaders rejected it. The Alcaldía then offered them another place, in Valle Hermoso on the far south side of town, but the spot was very small and very distant from the Cancha. After that, the subalcalde of the city's eighth district offered them a spot in Pampa Ticti, another neighborhood on the south side. But the ambulantes again deemed this too remote and unsuitable. The ambulantes are not willing to be shoved aside, relocated to some far-away corner of the city where they will struggle to make a living, just so that they can have their market. They want to be in the Cancha, recognized like other vendors as having the right to work in the heart of the city's commercial district.

As my time in Cochabamba wanes, the ambulantes gather to celebrate the anniversary of their federation's founding, just two years earlier, and to elect a new board of directors. The timing for me is good: I want a chance to say goodbye before I leave for home. I also want a public forum in which to present the ambulantes with the book that I have long been promising.

For the books are now written. Over the course of the previous several weeks, I have labored with Nacho and my other research assistants to prepare the documents—one for the ambulantes, one for the fijos—based on my work with them over the past year. After writing the text and compiling the illustrations, I contracted with a local printer to produce five hundred copies of each book. We have titled the ambulantes' book *Injustice in the Streets*. Following a contextual introduction and a discussion of methodology, the book provides a brief overview of the literature on street vendors in Latin America and explores the history of the Cancha and of the ambulantes' El Paso federation. It then goes into ethnographic detail about the experiences of the ambulantes selling in the streets. These chapters include numerous, important-looking tables and charts based on data collected through interviews, observations, and archival research. The final chapter, titled "What Do the Ambulantes Want?" expresses the various desires of the ambulantes and their leaders, focusing especially on the demand for a market of their own. The book concludes with this statement:

> The members of the El Paso federation are fighters who must battle every day to survive in the streets of Cochabamba. Although they don't enjoy any public benefits or protections, they continue to earn their living, day after day, in the city's streets. They are not going to disappear, regardless of what the law says or the official abuses that they endure. Better that the public authorities recognize them, and give them *the rights and benefits that they deserve as Bolivian citizens.*

At the ambulantes' anniversary party, I present the book publicly, distributing copies to the members of the various sindicatos that make up the federation. People are delighted with the glossy, full-color text and point out themselves or their friends in the book's many photos.[3] Don Silvio makes a speech of gratitude and appreciation. This is followed by the election of the board of directors. Silvio and his colleagues are re-elected by acclamation. "I was born for this," Don Silvio says to the crowd, "to collaborate with people who don't have any rights."[4]

In addition to the book, I have on this occasion donated fifteen cases of beer to the party, and the ambulantes have paid for a giant barrel of chicha. We drink and dance until late in the night.

....................................

The comerciantes fijos of La Pampa are also holding a public event—in their case, to celebrate the dedication of the loudspeaker system I have donated to the market. People gather at Doña María's puesto for the event, which begins at 3 PM. First Melvin speaks, then Rafo. He complains about the police, who never respond to the comerciantes' calls for help, and thanks Nacho and me for the donation of the speaker system. He says that at the seminar many people felt mistrustful, assuming that because I am a gringo I was with the CIA. People laugh. But now, he says, it is obvious that I am an honest person with a commitment to the working people of La Pampa.

I speak next, explaining that in addition to the speaker system, we have prepared a book documenting the causes, effects, and solutions to the problem of insecurity in the market. The print copies of the book are not yet ready, so I am able to present only a preliminary version, but it gives the general idea. Titled *Insecurity in the La Pampa Market: Problems and Possibilities*, the book is very similar to the one I gave to the ambulantes. Much of it is based on the data gathered at the seminar (chapter 32) and likewise contains many tables, charts, and graphs, as well as many quotes from the comerciantes themselves. And, like *Owners of the Sidewalk*, it begins with the fire in La Pampa:

> This event [the book says] awoke great public interest, calling attention to the problems of insecurity that exist in the La Pampa market. The fire was no surprise to those who know the zone, none better than the comerciantes who work there every day. The fire was due above all to the poor infrastructure, the lack of planning, and the municipal authorities' abandonment of the market, who through various administrations have shown complete inattention and neglect. That night [of the fire] was an irrefutable expression of the many kinds of insecurity that are unfortunately growing in the market and that the comerciantes must confront. This book reflects these and other forms of insecurity, some less evident, that

daily afflict the comerciante population, outlining its expressions and searching for viable alternatives to resolve it.

*Insecurity in the La Pampa Market* also describes some of the possible solutions to market insecurity that have emerged through our many conversations with comerciantes fijos. We are unable to provide a definitive answer to the question of how to solve the security problem, given the diversity of opinion that exists among market vendors themselves. So the book lists and explains the various proposals we have encountered, including encouraging collaboration between police and private security; making harsher laws that punish juveniles as adults; gating the entrances and exits to the market; paying the police higher salaries to discourage corruption; providing services and education to homeless youth; and fostering unity among comerciantes in the market. The list is long but inconclusive.

In the midst of the dedication, a young woman in traditional dress pushes to the front of the crowd. "My daughter!" she shrieks. "I have lost my daughter!" The leaders jump into action. Don Melvin seizes the microphone, calling the Men in Black over the newly installed speaker system, alerting them to search for the lost girl. The security guards immediately mobilize, combing the crowd for the missing child. Very soon one of the Men in Black strides to the head table, leading a frightened young girl by the arm. The crowd cheers. Melvin vigorously shakes my hand, and Rafo proclaims the success of the amplification system to all who will listen. It is like something out of a movie, a perfect demonstration of the speakers in action, and I can only marvel at Rafo and Melvin's timing, or luck, or dramaturgy in orchestrating such a performance.

At the end of the dedication ceremony there is a brief conflict, as Doña María begs Don Rafo to leave the speaker installed above her puesto. But Rafo insists that it be taken down until a decision about the final installation of the system can be made. María is upset, and some of her friends start to yell at supporters of Rafo, the whole scene beginning to degenerate into an argument. Taking this as our cue, Nacho and I make our exit.

The next day, Nacho and I visit Rafo and Melvin at Rafo's banana stall to say goodbye. I promise to deliver the final copies of the book before my departure, and Rafo promises to distribute them to his constituents. He is grateful for the book, but the situation with the speakers continues to trouble him. He says that people are now accusing him of having sold the speakers, because they have not been permanently installed. This is how I leave him, moaning to Melvin about the ingratitude of some people who could accuse him of putting his own interests above those of his constituents.

........................

My work in Cochabamba is finished. I have followed through on my commitments. The ambulantes and the fijos each have their book, the "scientific" study that demonstrates each group's insecurity and articulates their desires and demands for official assistance in resolving their issues. These books have been well received. I am hopeful that they might make some small difference in the comerciantes' struggles.

I make my final rounds through the market, visiting with my various friends and contacts, saying *hasta luego*. I tell everyone that I hope to return, but my funding status is uncertain, and my commitments at home are extensive. I can make no more promises in the Cancha.

My friend Doña Rosa, the seller of ceramics, invites me into her puesto, asks me to sit, pours me a *refresco*. We chat about the project, the results, the book I have written for Rafo and the comerciantes fijos of La Pampa, the system of loudspeakers that will soon be installed in the market. "Daniel, let me ask you something," Rosa says to me, for the first time in our relationship addressing me with the familiar "tu" form. "Do you really think something like this can do anything for security in the market?"[5]

I am at a loss to answer Rosa's question, so she answers it herself.

"The problem is at a much higher level. This is a poor country, a poor society. There are no jobs. It used to be that no one wanted to be a comerciante. Now everyone wants to be a comerciante. And the market just keeps growing."

# 37. Insecurity and Informality

Security and insecurity have been important themes in my analysis of Cochabamba's Cancha marketplace. One of this book's goals has been to bring the questions of insecurity and informality into dialogue by framing the challenges to security—physical, economic, "citizen," and otherwise—that comerciantes ambulantes face as a result of their informal status. Being informal is often equated with being illegal, whether one is talking about employment, housing, or just plain being, as people who live or work in informal areas themselves acquire the stigma of illegality. Ambulantes in Bolivia are regarded as "illegal," a designation that marks not just their behavior but their very existence as unruly, out of place, and threatening to the security of the greater economy and society.[1] The ambulantes—the most insecure of anyone in the Cancha—are demonized and persecuted by the state and other local sovereigns, a position that intensifies their daily insecurity.

As I have shown throughout this book, however, it is not only the ambulantes who inhabit the domain of informality, although they are the only ones who are punished for it. The comerciantes fijos, too, work in various informal ways. Like ambulantes, fijos sell contraband and illegal goods, and they occupy public space and use it for their private, commercial purposes. In addition, fijos engage in the lively trade of Cancha puestos—property of the state—which they buy and sell in a fashion that mimics the formal but which is entirely illegal. The fijos are not targeted as informal or illegal people the way the ambulantes are, but they are nevertheless rendered insecure by the state's incursions into their informal world. In particular, the wealth the fijos have produced through their marketing and their investments in Cancha infrastructure have made the market ripe for privatization, and they fear the hungry eyes of the municipality's neoliberal gaze.

The state is another actor whose practices cross the line into the shadow realm of informality, in a process I have identified as urban disregulation. As more than four hundred years of Cochabamba history shows, the state acts in ways intended to shore up its own authority, benefit its functionaries and local elites, and advance a vision of what urban life and urban society ought to be based on a model of European modernity. What it cannot reconcile with these goals and visions the state marginalizes to the gray spaces of informality, pushing unwanted people and activities to the physical, but also the social and ideological, peripheries of its fragmented yet enduring project. There, on the "margins of the state," the law operates partially and inconsistently, and the informal and the illegal are allowed to flourish.[2] These informal zones provide the poor and marginalized the ability to survive, with lives that are precarious and insecure. In these zones, too, those with resources and connections can establish powerful footholds, and we find the emergence of alternative sovereignties outside yet parallel to the state. These new sovereigns—private companies such as the Men in Black, powerful federations such as those headed by Rafael Punto and Eulogia Imba, or the murky forces behind the criminal economy of the Barrio Chino—obey no rule of law but elaborate their own systems of patronage and fear through which they maintain their rule.[3] They operate in zones that are relatively contained, "urban enclaves" that form part of the "honeycomb of jurisdictions" that constitute the modern city.[4] Even state institutions such as the Municipal Police can be understood in these terms: although their behavior is formally governed by state law, the comisarios interpret their mission and enact it through practices that they develop in response to local exigencies and their own personal objectives. All of these forms of disregulation contribute to the insecurity that is so prevalent in the informal spaces of Latin American cities such as Cochabamba.

But informal spaces can also provide room for opportunity and hope. Research on South Asian cities has recently come to identify what some are calling "subaltern urbanism," a perspective on the urban poor that sees them not as passive and defeated but as active political agents in their own lives and communities.[5] Even in the absence of organized collective resistance, we find what Asef Bayat calls "the quiet encroachment of the ordinary," the slow, silent advancement of everyday people into the spaces and property of the public, the powerful, and the wealthy as they aim to enhance their own lives and improve their conditions.[6] In contrast to models of urban social movements that have long prevailed in social-science analyses of urban Latin America,[7] quiet encroachment is largely about individual actions, interrupted by periodic collective mobilizations that tend to be poorly organized and lacking in structure and leadership.[8] But in time, Bayat says, these individual actions coalesce so that "their sheer cumulative numbers turn them into an eventual social force."[9] Quiet encroachment is characteristic of those who occupy the informal realm, because informality is marked by insecurity, and insecure people seek to improve their situations in gradual, often invisible and illegal ways. In this, quiet encroachment resembles what Partha Chatterjee has described as "political society," which includes claims to livelihood and habitation by "groups of population whose very livelihood or habitation involve violation of the law."[10] This perspective, characteristic of subaltern urbanism, "recuperates the figure of the slum dweller as a subject of history."[11]

Although an important response to the assumption that informal, marginalized urban people are powerless and passive, subaltern urbanism's focus on the "habitus of the dispossessed" tends to essentialize the urban poor.[12] The noble and resilient qualities attributed to the archetypal slum dweller or worker—"flexibility, pragmatism, negotiation, as well as constant struggle for survival and self-development"[13]—homogenize the urban poor and in extreme moments recall an older "romance of resistance" that anthropologists have struggled to discredit.[14] Subaltern urbanism, inherently progressive or even radical in its politics, also tends to emphasize the entrepreneurialism and flexibility of informal economic actors, which can lead in unexpectedly conservative directions. The depiction of informal people as bravely resisting state hegemony comes uncomfortably close to the views of commentators such as the Peruvian economist Hernando de Soto, whose influential theorizations (discussed in chapter 4) helped shape neoliberal economic policy in that country.[15] De Soto regards informality as a kind of resistance to the overly constraining requirements of legal governance, an escape by heroic entrepreneurs from the punishing effects of bureaucracy and law into the realm of autonomy and pure capitalism.[16]

Nevertheless, the idea of "quiet encroachment" offers a useful tool for understanding life in the informal world of the Cancha. It is a way of being that characterizes not only the urban poor but also the insecure middle class, the precarious bourgeoisie who inhabit the puestos fijos of the market. Quiet encroachment beautifully captures the slow, daily advances of the comerciantes fijos into the alleys and sidewalks that border their stalls, as they microscopically move to occupy more and more space, until the comisario passes by and forces them to retreat. It also describes the daily movements of the comerciantes ambulantes as they continue to sell illegally on the streets, constantly shifting their location to avoid comisarios, nasty fijos, criminal predators, and private security guards, without invading the turf of another ambulante or fellow sindicato member. Many of the informal vendors of the Cancha seek autonomy from the state (another feature of quiet encroachment) to be able to do their work without harassment or surveillance. This is true of ambulantes and fijos alike, the latter occupying both the formal and informal worlds vis-à-vis the official economy. Like Melva and Isabel chasing the mayor out of the market, many comerciantes fijos crave autonomy from the state. The state, they say, taxes and extracts and regulates while contributing nothing—no security, no infrastructure, no stability—to their lives and livelihoods. The sentiment is shared by many ambulantes, especially women, who prefer autonomy, mobility, and independence, even though this also enhances their insecurity. Like the market vendors that Daniella Gandolfo studied in Lima, "many vendors prefer to remain informal, prefer to inhabit a world that is strategically free from state regulation. . . . Vendors prefer to retain their autonomy despite the risks and costs this entails."[17]

But the desire for autonomy is not universal among the ambulantes, a fact that again cautions us against homogenizing the so-called informals or marginals. As the ethnography in this book has shown, the leadership of the ambulantes' federation does not share the desire for autonomy that some of its members express. Perhaps one might expect a man like Don Silvio to have radical political ambitions, including even a desire to overturn the entire poisoned system in which he and his people live and work.[18] But rather than launching a full-scale rebellion against exclusion, Don Silvio's politics are oriented toward inclusion and formalization. His dream of a market represents a desire to insert the ambulantes into the formal regulatory regime of the state. This dream is not a neoliberal one of a minimal state that offers little protection against uncertainty. Don Silvio and his followers do not reject the state; rather, like the street vendors that the anthropologist Jonathan Shapiro Anjaria has studied in Mumbai, the ambulantes "talk of the potential for state intervention on their behalf; their politics and collective aspirations do not index rebellion, or subversion, but desires for legitimation."[19] Don Silvio and others among the ambulantes, like informal workers elsewhere, crave "security, not anarchy."[20] A roof over their heads; protection against harassment, theft, and abuse; a reliable income—these are what the ambulantes' leadership desires. If some of them seek to escape informality, it is because they hope to subvert disregulation, insisting instead on the kinds of formal ordering that the state, ideally, provides.

Rather than homogenizing informal sellers or the urban poor, this ethnography calls attention to the diversity of political perspectives that exist in the Cancha marketplace and the different kinds of political behavior that these perspectives mobilize. Quiet encroachment and subaltern urbanism are useful heuristics, but they cannot capture the full range of political expressions that emerge in the complex domains of contemporary urban life. I follow Ananya Roy in recognizing that "at best, subaltern politics can be seen as a heterogeneous, contradictory and performative realm of political struggle,"[21] in which people do not share some essentialized habitus but exhibit a range of possible dispositions toward the insecurity of daily life. This can mean, for example, that people crave some forms of autonomy from the state but not others. As Sian Lazar has observed, although street vendors in El Alto desire informality as a relief from the tax burden that formal work imposes, these same vendors seek out other kinds of formality—namely, the right to sell on the street and in a fixed location and legal recognition of their associations—"because both may help them avoid harassment by the local authorities."[22]

In addition, while practices of quiet encroachment are important elements of Cancha politics, the spectacular, public political actions more typical of urban social movements—"loud encroachment," should we call it?—are critical forms of political behavior, as well.[23] The work of the ambulantes in the El Paso federation is a clear example: their march on the Plaza Principal gained them important, if fleeting and ultimately unproductive, recognition from the municipality that no amount of quiet encroachment was likely to bring them. Similarly, the various marches of the comerciantes fijos—against privatization, in favor of the private police, and including a full-scale riot in which they burned down a police station—were politically productive for the fijos and Don Rafo's Federation of Comerciantes of La Pampa. In Latin American cities, these forms of spectacular protest are frequent occurrences, and although they contradict the more quotidian forms of quiet encroachment practiced daily by fijos and ambulantes, they nevertheless play a critical role in the management of public political agendas. Through such actions, the invisible and the marginalized gain temporary visibility, forcing themselves, loudly and vibrantly, into the public eye.

In both spectacular and quiet forms of political behavior, it is the public spaces of the city—the streets and sidewalks of the Cancha—that are the stages of performance. Bayat calls this "street politics," calling attention to urban public space as the meeting grounds of subordinated peoples and the state.[24] In the streets, people have their daily encounters with the comisarios who are attempting to regulate their behavior and with the delinquents whose behavior they are hoping to contain. The streets and sidewalks are the sites of incursion, where ambulantes spread their wares and where fijos advance their stalls. The streets and sidewalks and parks and plazas are the locations of major gatherings, of protest marches and speech making, of assembly and debate. The streets and sidewalks are where ambulantes and fijos make their claims for rights and assert these claims through occupation. Urban public space is where people go to assert their autonomy and where they lay claim to the rights that they see as theirs. State efforts to bring "order" to these messy spaces of public life can be properly understood from this perspective as efforts to quash popular democracy as at different moments it struggles, quietly and loudly, to emerge.

# Epilogue

A year after the end of my fieldwork in the Cancha, I return to Bolivia for the summer. During the course of the intervening year I have remained in contact with Nacho and other close friends in Cochabamba. Via e-mail and Skype, Nacho has kept me updated on the doings of Don Silvio and Don Rafo and of their organizations. On my return, I hope to catch up on the events of the past year and to see what progress, if any, the fijos and the ambulantes have made toward greater security and stability in their work, their families, and their lives. I am especially eager to see whether the books I wrote and published have had any impact on those struggles.

Although my research is largely complete, I still feel a commitment to the groups with whom I worked and continue to imagine ways to remain engaged with them. To that end, I have spent the past year designing an international service learning program for undergraduates and am now leading the first group of students to "the field." They will spend the summer studying Spanish and Quechua, learning the techniques of anthropological field research, and implementing those techniques through their own research projects.[1] Most significant, the students will be engaging in community service work alongside Bolivian people. I assign most of the students to work in the barrios where I have previously conducted fieldwork, but I place one group with the ambulantes. The exact nature of their project, like those of the other groups, will be determined in collaboration with the Bolivians with whom they are working. My hope is that the program will enrich the education of North American students at the same time that it contributes something to the lives of the people with whom I have worked in Bolivia.

The ambulantes, I soon discover, are in disarray. Don Silvio is sick. An older man who spent many years working in the mines, and a bachelor with no one to look after him, Silvio has been in and out of the hospital with some sort of heart ailment. His colleagues among the ambulantes have not seen him in weeks, and without his leadership the federation has begun to unravel. People are not following through on commitments; the board of directors has not been meeting; and the campaign for a market seems to be on indefinite hold. Other leaders, strong men such as Don Remberto and Don Beto, have taken on hangdog expressions, seemingly lost without their president.

I visit Don Silvio at the Hospital Viedma, where he has been confined for nearly a month. He occupies a bed in a room that in a U.S. hospital would hold two patients, with a curtain drawn between them for privacy. Here, sixteen sick men are crowded together, coughing and wheezing and moaning, dragging themselves to the one shared bathroom at the end of the hall. Don Silvio is almost unrecognizable. A trim man to begin with, he is now bone thin and ragged, weak from illness, lack of exercise, and bad food. In his hospital gown, his black fedora stashed beneath his cot, he shows none of his habitual authority and energy. Nacho looks ready to cry as we sit by the sick man's bedside talking.

Don Silvio complains to me about the federation and his colleagues on the board of directors. In his absence, he says, no one has stepped up to lead. They are lazy, he says of his friends now, stupid, unable to take even the simplest action without his involvement. Plus, he says, while he has been in the hospital, stories have begun to circulate: that he is corrupt, that he has taken the federation's funds and skipped town, that he has cut some private deal with the intendente and is no longer running things in the federation. Perhaps the intendente himself is behind these rumors, Silvio speculates—gossip works to undermine Silvio's leadership and to weaken the bonds of unity among the ambulantes. Silvio is saddened by people's apparent willingness to believe such stories, by the sudden crumbling of everything for which he has worked.

Things are not much better with the comerciantes fijos. Nacho and I walk through La Pampa, following one of our old "flash interview" circuits to visit various friends in the market. Doña Rosa, Doña Tahlia, Don

Ricardo—everybody says that Don Rafo has failed them. The loudspeakers we donated still have not been hung, people report, the installation paralyzed by politics and indecision. The books I wrote, so highly anticipated and received with such enthusiasm, remain boxed up in Don Rafo's banana stall. Rather than distributing them freely, as we had anticipated, Rafo and Melvin have been trying to sell the books to the comerciantes. What is more, people tell me, Rafo's term as president of the Federation of Comerciantes of La Pampa was supposed to have ended this year, but Rafo never called an election and has remained in power, leading now mainly by fiat. I try calling him on his cell phone and lurking around his stall hoping to find him in, but he does not answer or appear. In six weeks our paths never cross.

At last Don Silvio is released from the hospital. Still weak, he nevertheless calls an immediate meeting of the ambulantes to dispel the rumors about his behavior and to reassure his constituents that he remains at the helm of their institution. I attend this meeting, accompanied by the group of students assigned to work on a project with the ambulantes. Silvio arranges for them to meet with various leaders of his federation, and on their own they make friends with some of the ordinary street vendors whom they encounter through their wanderings in the Cancha. Over the course of several weeks, the students learn about the needs of the ambulantes, the struggles they face, and the injustices with which they must contend. In particular, the students are moved by the challenges facing women who have nowhere to leave their young children when they go to work and decide to try and help them to establish a daycare center—something for which the women themselves have expressed a desire. The students produce a short film about the ambulantes and their lack of child care. When they return home, they plan to use the film to raise money to assist in this cause. In the meantime, with funds from the program budget, they buy a computer and donate it to the ambulantes' leadership so they can better maintain their records and correspondence. The ambulantes are still not in the computerized "System" of the Alcaldía, but now they have a computer of their own.

The ambulantes are active collaborators in the film project, and the computer is received with much joy and celebration (figure E.1). On our last night in Cochabamba, the ambulantes host a party to which all of our students are invited. We eat, drink, and dance, and ambulantes and students make long, tearful speeches of gratitude and friendship.

As I again prepare to leave Cochabamba, I meet one last time with Don Silvio. He is still sick, although he bravely continues to lead the ambulantes.

E.1 Don Beto hugs two students from the service learning program. Photograph by the author.

I give him money to help with his mounting medical bills, and he gratefully accepts. Nacho and I watch as he hobbles off and disappears into the swirling mass of humanity that is the Cancha. "I think," Nacho remarks, "that we may not see him again."

...........................

My research in Cochabamba was characterized by an approach that can be called "engaged" or "activist" anthropology. Based on a commitment to working with the subjects of our research to help them achieve their social and political goals, activist anthropology is, I believe, an important corrective to more "colonial" forms of anthropological practice that characterize the history of our discipline (chapter 10). Doing activist research, though, requires us to have realistic goals. We cannot expect to resolve all of the problems that our friends and collaborators in the field face—in some cases, nothing short of a revolution could accomplish that.[2] As Doña Rosa reminded me, systems of injustice and inequality are structural and very hard to change, even with the best of intentions and the collective will of valiant people.

But still, we can do what we can do, contribute what we can to the struggles we witness and to which we pledge our energy. Such efforts, as I have tried to show, are valuable not just for ethical or political reasons, but for ethnographic ones: activist research provides more and better access, and hence better and more complex insights into the social realities that we are attempting to document and interpret. The contributions we make as we do our research are not entirely selfless, but they can benefit the people who open their lives to us and make the research process a mutually rewarding experience for all.

In the aftermath of my research, I was initially disappointed with the inability of my work to truly alter the insecurity of the people with whom I collaborated. But the effort, on further reflection, was worthwhile. Collaborative, activist research allowed me to act in accordance with my own values and with what I consider appropriate ethics for a new century of anthropological research. Perhaps the contributions of my work and other work like it can be measured only over the long term. The same may be true of the struggles of the comerciantes themselves, of their ongoing efforts to change an unjust system. The road is a long one, and patience is required. The fijos will keep working for greater security in La Pampa, and the ambulantes will keep fighting for their market and their right to sell. Someday they may achieve their goals. In the meantime, educators will keep educating, and anthropologists will keep writing, critiquing, shining a light on the darker corners of the world where, all too often, abuses go unwitnessed and ignored. That, it seems to me, is a contribution worth making.

# Notes

### Prologue

1. Fieldnotes, March 16, 2007.

### 1. The Fire

1. The municipal government consists of two principal entities: The Consejo Municipal (City Council) and the Alcaldía (Mayor's Office). The Consejo Municipal makes laws and ordinances that the Alcaldía is responsible for enforcing; they share responsibility for the management of the city, though the Consejo Municipal holds fiduciary responsibility over the Alcaldía. For the reader's convenience, I follow local usage and conflate these two offices, referring generally to "the Alcaldía."

2. I follow J. K. Gibson-Graham in the usage "Majority World": see J. K. Gibson-Graham, "Diverse Economies: Performative Practices for 'Other Worlds,'" *Progress in Human Geography* 32, no. 5 (2008): 613–32. The term "Third World" implicitly subordinates a vast slice of land and people to the "First World," despite the fact that those so subordinated constitute the majority of the world's population.

3. International Labor Office, *Women and Men in the Informal Economy: A Statistical Picture* (Geneva: International Labor Office, 2002).

4. Karen Tranberg Hansen, Walter E. Little, and Lynne B. Milgram, *Street Economies in the Urban Global South* (Santa Fe, NM: School of Advanced Research Press, 2013).

5. David Harvey, *Rebel Cities: From the Right to the City to the Urban Revolution* (London: Verso, 2013).

6. Daniel M. Goldstein, *Outlawed: Between Security and Rights in a Bolivian City* (Durham, NC: Duke University Press, 2012). Walter Benjamin described the power of the police as a "nowhere tangible, all-pervasive, ghostly presence in the life of civilized states": Walter Benjamin, *Reflections: Essays, Aphorisms and Autobiographical Writings* (New York: Schocken, 1978), 287. See also Jacques Derrida, *Spectres of Marx: The State of the Debt, the Work of Mourning and the New International* (London: Routledge, 1994).

7. AbdouMaliq Simone, *City Life from Jakarta to Dakar: Movement at the Crossroads* (New York: Routledge, 2010).

8. Ananya Roy, "Why India Cannot Plan Its Cities: Informality, Insurgence and the Idiom of Urbanization," *Planning Theory* 8, no. 76 (2009): 80.

9. In Cochabamba, for example, high-crime neighborhoods are identified as "red zones," or *zonas rojas*. On these areas of urban disregulation, see Veena Das and Deborah Poole, eds., *Anthropology in the Margins of the State* (Santa Fe, NM: School of American Research Press, 2004); Guillermo O'Donnell, *Counterpoints: Selected Essays on Authoritarianism and Democratization* (Notre Dame, IN: University of Notre Dame Press, 1999); Oren Yiftachel, "Theoretical Notes on 'Gray Cities': The Coming of Urban Apartheid?" *Planning Theory* 8, no. 1 (2009): 88–100. See also Diane E. Davis, "Socio-Spatial Inequality and Violence in Cities of the Global South: Evidence from Latin America," in *Cities and Inequalities in a Global and Neoliberal World*, ed. Faranak Miraftab, David Wilson, and Ken Salo (London: Routledge, 2015): 75–91.

10. Katherine Boo says that 85 percent of India's workers are part of the "informal, unorganized economy": Katherine Boo, *Behind the Beautiful Forevers: Life, Death, and Hope in a Mumbai Undercity* (New York: Random House, 2012), Kindle, chapter 1.

11. On the (noncontradictory) relationship between violence and democratic governance, see Enrique Desmond Arias and Daniel M. Goldstein, eds., *Violent Democracies in Latin America* (Durham, NC: Duke University Press, 2010).

12. Daniel M. Goldstein, *The Spectacular City: Violence and Performance in Urban Bolivia* (Durham, NC: Duke University Press, 2004); Goldstein, *Outlawed*.

13. As I discuss in chapter 33, informal street vending offers people (especially women) certain advantages beyond mere survival, and some prefer it to more formal kinds of work: see Kathleen M. Millar, "The Precarious Present: Wageless Labor and Disrupted Life in Rio de Janeiro, Brazil," *Cultural Anthropology* 29, no. 1 (2014): 32–53.

## 2. Writing, Reality, Truth

1. A. L. Kroeber, "The History of the Personality of Anthropology," *American Anthropologist* 61, no. 3 (1959): 404.

2. Didier Fassin, "True Lives, Real Lives: Revisiting the Boundaries between Ethnography and Fiction," *American Ethnologist* 41, no. 1 (2014): 42.

3. Fassin, "True Lives, Real Lives," 42.

4. Fassin, "True Lives, Real Lives."

5. Michael H. Agar, *The Professional Stranger: An Informal Introduction to Ethnography* (New York: Academic Press, 1980).

### 3. Don Rafo

1. I conducted much of my research in the Cancha at the same time that I was engaged in a research project in the barrios of Ushpa Ushpa in Cochabamba's southern zone, which led to my book *Outlawed: Between Security and Rights in a Bolivian City* (Durham, NC: Duke University Press, 2012). The entire research team consisted of five individuals, most of whom (myself included) worked both in the barrios and in the Cancha. However, Nacho and I conducted the majority of the observations, and nearly all of the interviews, in the Cancha research. On those occasions when I cite from fieldnotes written by or interviews conducted by other team members, I credit them by name. Only "Nacho" is a pseudonym; given the intimacy of detail that I present about Nacho's life and activities, he and I decided that it would be best to disguise his true identity. I also use pseudonyms for all the comerciantes and other individuals mentioned in the text, and for the names of the federations of comerciantes fijos and ambulantes.

2. A *caudillo* is a Latin American political or military leader who is strong and charismatic and able to hold onto power through patronage rather than democratic approval.

3. Thomas Blom Hansen and Oskar Verkaaik describe the "charisma" of the city, and the way it infuses its "elusive spirit" in certain individuals who seem to hold the key to the city itself: Thomas Blom Hansen and Oskar Verkaaik, "Introduction—Urban Charisma: On Everyday Mythologies in the City," *Critique of Anthropology* 29, no. 1 (2009): 6.

4. Fieldnotes, February 21, 2007.

### 4. The Informal Economy

1. Fieldnotes, July 22, 2006.

2. Alejandro Portes and William Haller, "The Informal Economy," in *The Handbook of Economic Sociology*, 2d ed., ed. Neil J. Smelser and Richard Swedberg (Princeton, NJ: Princeton University Press, 2005), 403–27. The quantity of research and writing produced by social scientists, development professionals, governments, nongovernmental organizations, and others on the subject of the informal economy is truly vast and beyond the scope of this project. I do not intend my discussion here to be comprehensive or to offer a detailed bibliography on the subject of informality. For that, see, among others, Jan L. Losby et al., eds., *Informal Economy Literature Review* (Newark, DE: ISED Consulting and Aspen Institute, 2002). For some of the genealogy of the anthropology of street economies, see Florence E. Babb, "Street Economies in the Urban Global South: Where Are They Heading and Where Are We Heading," in *Street Economies in the Urban Global South*, ed. Karen Tranberg Hansen, Walter E. Little, and B. Lynne Milgram (Santa Fe, NM: School of Advanced Research Press, 2013), 201–12; Ray Bromley, "Rethinking the Public Realm: On Vending, Popular Protest, and Street Politics," in *Street Economies in the Urban Global South*, ed. Karen Tranberg Hansen, Walter E. Little, and B. Lynne Milgram (Santa Fe, NM: School of Advanced Research Press, 2013), 17–28.

3. Keith Hart, "Informal Income Opportunities and Urban Employment in Ghana," *Journal of Modern African Studies* 11, no. 1 (1973): 61–89.

4. Nezar AlSayyad, "Urban Informality as a 'New' Way of Life," in *Urban Informality: Transnational Perspectives from the Middle East, Latin America, and South Asia*, ed. Ananya Roy and Nezar AlSayyad (Lanham, MD: Lexington, 2004), 7–30. See also Cathy A. Rakowski, ed., *Contrapunto: The Informal Sector Debate in Latin America* (Albany: State University of New York Press, 1994).

5. Cited in AlSayyad, "Urban Informality as a 'New' Way of Life," 10–11. This dualistic understanding of informality appealed to policy makers as it seemed to suggest that the poor, kept to their sector, could be helped without taking any resources from the rich: see Ray Bromley, "Street Vending and Public Policy: A Global Review," *International Journal of Sociology and Social Policy* 20, nos. 1–2 (2000): 1–29.

6. Basudeb Guha-Khasnobis, Ravi Kanbur, and Elinor Ostrom, "Beyond Formality and Informality," in *Linking the Formal and Informal Economy: Concepts and Policies*, ed. Basudeb Guha-Khasnobis, Ravi Kanbur, and Elinor Ostrom (Oxford: Oxford University Press, 2006), 1–19.

7. Manuel Castells and Alejandro Portes, "World Underneath: The Origins, Dynamics, and Effects of the Informal Economy," in *The Informal Economy: Studies in Advanced and Less Developed Countries*, ed. Alejandro Portes, Manuel Castells, and Lauren A. Benton (Baltimore: Johns Hopkins University Press, 1989), 12.

8. See the critique of structural approaches to both informality and illegality in Lauren Benton, "Beyond Legal Pluralism: Towards a New Approach to Law in the Informal Sector," *Social and Legal Studies* 3 (1994): 223–42.

9. Hernando de Soto, *The Other Path: The Invisible Revolution in the Third World* (New York: Harper and Row, 1989), 11.

10. Indeed, de Soto himself assumed the role of adviser to Peru's President Alberto Fujimori in what was ultimately a frustrating and short-lived effort to implement his theories as public policy: see Cato Institute, "Hernando de Soto's Biography," n.d., http://www.cato.org/friedman-prize/hernando-desoto/biography, accessed September 12, 2013.

11. On "autoconstruction" of housing, see James Holston, "Autoconstruction in Working-Class Brazil," *Cultural Anthropology* 6, no. 4 (1991): 446–63.

12. Brodwyn Fischer, Bryan McCann, and Javier Auyero, eds., *Cities from Scratch: Poverty and Informality in Urban Latin America* (Durham, NC: Duke University Press, 2014).

13. Keith Hart, "Informal Economy," in *The New Palgrave: A Dictionary of Economics*, vol. 2, ed. John Eatwell, Murray Milgate, and Peter Newman (London: Macmillan, 1987), 845–46. See also Karen Tranberg Hansen, Walter E. Little, and B. Lynne Milgram, "Introduction," in *Street Economies in the Urban Global South*, ed. Karen Tranberg Hansen, Walter E. Little, and B. Lynne Milgram (Santa Fe, NM: School of Advanced Research Press, 2013), 3–16.

14. Sally Roever, "Street Trade in Latin America: Demographic Trends, Legal Issues and Vending Organizations in Six Cities," in *Street Vendors in the Global Urban Economy*, ed. Sharit Bhowmik (London: Routledge, 2010), 208–40.

15. Though informal workers like the street vendors I describe have long been considered a "problem" for the economies and societies in which they are found, some

economists and policy makers have recently begun to view them as valuable contributors to urban economic life: see, e.g., Kyoko Kusakabe, *Policy Issues on Street Vending: An Overview of Studies in Thailand, Cambodia, and Mongolia* (Bangkok: International Labor Office, 2006).

16. See, e.g., Alan Gilbert, "Love in the Time of Enhanced Capital Flows: Reflections on the Links between Liberalization and Informality," in *Urban Informality: Transnational Perspectives from the Middle East, Latin America, and South Asia*, ed. Ananya Roy and Nezar AlSayyad (Lanham, MD: Lexington, 2004), 33–66.

17. Larissa Lomnitz has studied the linkages between formal and informal economies in Latin America, identifying reciprocity between friends and kin as one of the "roots of informality": see Larissa Adler Lomnitz, "Informal Exchange Networks in Formal Systems: A Theoretical Model," *American Anthropologist* 90, no. 1 (1988): 442–55.

18. Mariana Cavalcanti, "Threshold Markets: The Production of Real-Estate Value between the 'Favela' and the 'Pavement,'" in *Cities from Scratch: Poverty and Informality in Urban Latin America*, ed. Brodwyn Fischer, Bryann McCann, and Javier Auyero (Durham, NC: Duke University Press, 2014), 208–37; Ayona Datta, *The Illegal City: Space, Law and Gender in a Delhi Squatter Settlement* (Surrey, U.K.: Ashgate, 2012); Edésio Fernandes and Ann Varley, eds., *Illegal Cities: Law and Urban Change in Developing Countries* (London: Zed, 1998).

19. Daniella Gandolfo, "Formless: A Day at Lima's Office of Formalization," *Cultural Anthropology* 28, no. 2 (2013): 293. In Bolivianist anthropology, Hans and Judith-Maria Buechler questioned the distinction between formal and informal as early as the 1980s: see Hans C. Buechler and Judith-Maria Buechler, *Manufacturing against the Odds: Small-Scale Producers in an Andean City* (Boulder, CO: Westview, 1992). On the distinction more generally, see Colin McFarlane, "Rethinking Informality: Politics, Crisis, and the City," *Planning Theory and Practice* 13, no. 1 (March 2012): 89–108.

20. Fijos don't pay taxes, but they do pay licensing and site-use fees (*patentes* and *sentajes*), which amount to the same thing. This is discussed in subsequent chapters.

21. Linda Seligmann remarked on this, as well: see Linda J. Seligmann, *Peruvian Street Lives: Culture, Power, and Economy among Market Women of Cuzco* (Urbana: University of Illinois Press, 2004).

22. On the La Paz *cholo* (urbanized indigenous) market and the wealth of comerciantes there, see Nico Tassi, "The Postulate of Abundance: Cholo Market and Religion in La Paz Bolivia," *Social Anthropology/Anthropologie Sociale* 18, no. 2 (2010): 191–209.

23. Daniella Gandolfo hints at this in her study of popular markets in Lima. Citing the early formulation of the idea of informality in Hart, "Informal Economy," 846, Gandolfo says, "Labeling something 'informal' is . . . merely our way of indicating that it escapes these [conventional] ways of representing reality; it is our way of contrasting it to what we have come to imagine as the formal, normative organization of our economy. While informality is assumed to be 'irregular, unpredictable, unstable, even invisible,' it does not really exist as such in any empirical way. It is that which we cannot control or comprehend from the vantage point of and with the instruments afforded by normative organization": Gandolfo, "Formless," 289.

24. Rebecca B. Galemba, "Informal and Illicit Entrepreneurs: Fighting for a Place in the Neoliberal Economic Order," *Anthropology of Work Review* 29, no. 2 (2008): 19–25; Carolyn Nordstrom, *Global Outlaws: Crime, Money, and Power in the Contemporary World* (Berkeley: University of California Press, 2007); Carlos F. Toranzo Roca, "Informal and Illicit Economies and the Role of Narcotrafficking," in *Coca, Cocaine, and the Bolivian Reality*, ed. Madeline Barbara Leóns and Harry Sanabria (Albany: State University of New York Press, 1997), 195–210.

25. Alexander S. Dent, "Piracy, Circulatory Legitimacy, and Neoliberal Subjectivity in Brazil," *Cultural Anthropology* 27, no. 1 (2012): 31.

26. Dent, "Piracy, Circulatory Legitimacy, and Neoliberal Subjectivity in Brazil," 31.

## 5. Nacho

1. I return to a consideration of collaborative ethnography and activist anthropology in chapter 10.

2. Bolivian school days are only a few hours long, and students attend morning, afternoon, or evening sessions.

3. In that project, I studied the *barrios marginales* (marginal neighborhoods) of Cochabamba's southern zone, where many people who work in the Cancha have their homes. I was interested in questions of crime and policing—or lack thereof. The marginal neighborhoods of Cochabamba, as in most cities in Latin America, are marked by extremely high levels of crime—mostly robberies, but also more violent crimes such as rape and murder. Despite the frequency of such incidents, however, poor barrios have almost no police protection, and their residents lack access to the legal system as a way to resolve problems that they encounter. During the past decade or so, people have turned to vigilante violence as a response to insecurity in their neighborhoods. My research focused on how people without access to police protection or the justice system conceptualized and made their own security and how this often conflicted with transnational conceptions of human rights. The results of that research were published in Daniel M. Goldstein, *Outlawed: Between Security and Rights in a Bolivian City* (Durham, NC: Duke University Press, 2012).

## 6. The Bolivian Experiment

1. Gracia Clark, *Traders versus the State: Anthropological Approaches to Unofficial Economies* (Boulder, CO: Westview, 1988); Sian Lazar, "A Desire to Formalize Work? Comparing Trade Union Strategies in Bolivia and Argentina," *Anthropology of Work Review* 33, no. 1 (2012): 15–24.

2. United Nations Human Settlements Program, *State of the World's Cities, 2010/2011: Bridging the Urban Divide* (Nairobi: United Nations Human Settlements Program, 2008).

3. World Bank, "Republic of Bolivia Policies for Increasing Firms' Formality and Productivity," in *Poverty Reduction and Economic Management, Bolivia, Ecuador, Peru and Ven-*

*ezuela Country Management Unit, Latin America and the Caribbean Region*, World Bank report no. 40057-BO, February 29, 2008, World Bank, Washington, DC.

4. On 2002, see Friedrich Schneider, "Size and Measurement of the Informal Economy in 110 Countries around the World," paper presented at Australian National Tax Centre workshop, Australian National University, Canberra, July 17, 2002. On 2011, see Richard Cebula and Edgar L. Feige, "America's Underground Economy: Measuring the Size, Growth and Determinants of Income Tax Evasion in the U.S.," 2011, http:// www.ssc.wisc.edu/econ/archive/wp2011–1.pdf, accessed June 8, 2013. This study measures the size of the informal economy on the basis of unreported income to the Internal Revenue Service.

5. The most that the typical North American knows about Bolivia is that the title characters in *Butch Cassidy and the Sundance Kid* died there. In the movie from 1969, directed by George Roy Hill and based on a true story, Butch and Sundance decide to give up robbing banks in the United States and try their luck in Bolivia, where, they feel, the standards of law enforcement are somewhat more lax. The pair meet their end in a gunfight with the Bolivian armed forces in 1908.

6. The economic downturn known as the Great Recession can be dated, roughly, to the collapse of the Lehman Brothers bank in September 2008; it officially ended in June 2009, when economic output began growing instead of shrinking. But the effects of the recession were presaged by a long decline in workers' wages and job security, and its effects continued to be felt long after it was declared to have ended: see Peter Coy, "The Great Recession: An 'Affair' to Remember," *Bloomberg Businessweek*, October 11, 2012, http://www .businessweek.com/articles/2012–10–11/the-great-recession-an-affair-to-remember, accessed October 1, 2014; Barbara Garson, "Before the Great Recession, There Was the Long Recession," *Mother Jones*, April 9, 2013, http://www.motherjones.com/politics/2013 /04/long-recession-before-great-recession, accessed October 1, 2014.

7. Elected to the presidency for the first time in 2006, Evo Morales adopted an explicitly socialist rhetoric in his approach to governance and implemented a number of reforms to improve the distribution of wealth and to care for the country's most vulnerable populations. However, many of his economic policies conform surprisingly to those of his neoliberal predecessors. See Jeffrey Webber, *From Rebellion to Reform in Bolivia: Class Struggle, Indigenous Liberation, and the Politics of Evo Morales* (Chicago: Haymarket Books, 2011).

8. Historical scholarship shows that Bolivian cities indeed had an indigenous presence during colonial and Republican times: see, e.g., Brooke Larson, *Colonialism and Agrarian Transformation in Bolivia: Cochabamba, 1550–1900* (Princeton, NJ: Princeton University Press, 1988).

9. Coca chewing has long been practiced by indigenous inhabitants of the Andes: to help them do hard work at high altitudes, as part of personal and community rituals, and as a basic element of everyday social interaction. Coca is not the same thing as cocaine; the latter is an addictive narcotic extracted from the former through a chemical process: see Madeline Barbara Leóns and Harry Sanabria, *Coca, Cocaine, and the Bolivian Reality* (Albany: State University of New York Press, 1997).

10. Juan Antonio Morales and Jeffrey D. Sachs, "Bolivia's Economic Crisis," in *Developing Country Debt and the World Economy*, ed. Jeffrey D. Sachs (Chicago: University of Chicago Press, 1989), 73.

11. Pitou van Dijck, "The Bolivian Experiment: Structural Adjustment and Policy Alleviation," *Cuadernos de CEDLA* no. 3 (La Paz: Centro de Estudios para el Desarrollo Laboral y Agrario, 1999).

12. Benjamin Kohl, "Stabilizing Neoliberalism in Bolivia: Popular Participation and Privatization," *Political Geography* 21 (2002): 449–72.

13. Benjamin Kohl, "Privatization Bolivian Style: A Cautionary Tale," *International Journal of Urban and Regional Research* 28, no. 4 (2004): 893–908.

14. See the discussion of Bolivian stabilization policies and their impact on agricultural prices in Ricardo Godoy and Mario De Franco, "High Inflation and Bolivian Agriculture," *Journal of Latin American Studies* 24, no. 3 (1992): 617–37.

15. Brent Z. Kaup, "In Spaces of Marginalization: Dispossession, Incorporation, and Resistance in Bolivia," *Journal of World Systems Research* 19, no. 1 (2013): 108–29.

16. Benjamin Kohl and Linda Farthing, with Félix Muruchi, *From the Mines to the Streets: A Bolivian Activist's Life* (Austin: University of Texas Press, 2011).

17. Harvey's concept builds on Marx's earlier theory of primitive accumulation; see, e.g., David Harvey, *The New Imperialism* (Oxford: Oxford University Press, 2003); David Harvey, "The Right to the City," *New Left Review* 53 (September–October 2003): 23–40.

18. John Murra, Enrique Mayer, and other anthropologists have studied the adaptation of local groups to the different ecological zones of the Andean "vertical archipelago." See the discussion in Billie Jean Isbell, *To Defend Ourselves: Ecology and Ritual in an Andean Village* (Prospect Heights, IL: Waveland, 1985). See also Thierry Saignes, "Indian Migration and Social Change in Seventeenth-Century Charcas," in *Ethnicity, Markets, and Migration in the Andes: At the Crossroads of History and Anthropology*, ed. Brooke Larson and Olivia Harris with Enrique Tandeter (Durham, NC: Duke University Press, 1995), 167–95.

19. Rolando Lazarte, "El éxodo hacia la metrópoli. Migración interna y mercado de trabajo," *Nueva Sociedad* 90 (July–August 1987): 70–86.

20. Their timing was perfect: U.S. and European demand for cocaine was reaching new heights, and international traffickers were expanding their networks like never before. Meanwhile, Bolivian governments throughout the 1980s and 1990s, under intense pressure from the United States, adopted harsh anti-coca laws that focused on curbing coca production through forced eradication of fields and lengthy prison sentences for low-level growers and transporters of coca and its byproducts. Even as the Bolivian state was adopting foreign prescriptions for structural adjustment, then, it was also fighting the U.S. drug war on Bolivian soil at a time that many Bolivian people were becoming more deeply involved in coca production: see Benjamin Kohl and Linda Farthing, "Bolivia: Sachs versus the Facts," 2013, http://upsidedownworld.org/main/bolivia-archives-31/3522-bolivia-sachs-versus-the-facts, accessed June 7, 2013.

21. The effects of neoliberalism on global patterns of urbanization are described in Alejandro Portes and Bryan R. Roberts, "The Free Market City: Latin American Ur-

banization in the Years of the Neoliberal Experiment," *Studies in Comparative International Development* 40, no. 1 (2005): 43–82.

22. Central Intelligence Agency, CIA *World Factbook*, https://www.cia.gov/library/publications/the-world-factbook/geos/bl.html, accessed June 7, 2013; John M. Reed, "International Brief, Population Trends: Bolivia," Bureau of the Census, U.S. Department of Commerce, 1998, http://www.census.gov/population/international/files/ib-9801.pdf, accessed June 7, 2013.

23. PopulationReferenceBureau, "HumanPopulation:Urbanization," n.d., http://www.prb.org/Educators/TeachersGuides/HumanPopulation/Urbanization.aspx, accessed May 6, 2013. Henry J. Kaiser Family Foundation, "Urban Population (Percent of Total Population Living in Urban Areas)," n.d., http://kff.org/global-indicator/urban-population, accessed May 6, 2013.

24. Global Sherpa, "World Cities," n.d., http://www.globalsherpa.org/cities-world-city, accessed May 8, 2013.

25. The World Bank's assessment of the motivations behind human mobility and urbanization clearly reflect a logic of "rational choice," in which people's decisions to urbanize are based primarily on their calculations of where the best rates of return on their labor lie, access to public services, and so on: see World Bank, *World Development Report 2009: Reshaping Economic Geography* (Washington, DC: World Bank, 2009).

26. Lesley Gill, *Precarious Dependencies: Gender, Class and Domestic Service in Bolivia* (New York: Columbia University Press, 1994).

27. In Latin America in the 1990s, nine out of every ten jobs created was in the "informal sector": Carlos Vilas, "The Decline of the Steady Job in Latin America," NACLA *Report on the Americas* 32, no. 4 (1999): 15–20.

28. See the essays in Mark Goodale and Nancy Postero, eds., *Neoliberalism, Interrupted: Social Change and Contested Governance in Contemporary Latin America* (Stanford, CA: Stanford University Press, 2013).

## 7. Meet the Press

1. Fieldnotes, March 11–15, 2007.

## 8. The Colonial City

1. Wendell Cox, "World Urban Areas Population and Density: A 2012 Update," May 3, 2012, http://www.newgeography.com/content/002808-world-urban-areas-population-and-density-a-2012-update, accessed July 2, 2013.

2. Instituto Nacional de Estadística, *Cochabamba*, 2014 (Cochabamba, Bolivia: Instituto Nacional de Estadística, 2014). This is an official count, and probably low. Other estimates put the population at closer to 800,000. Population counts depend on where one draws the lines around the "city" itself and whether peripheral zones are included.

3. Recent archaeological studies suggest that commercial markets have long been a feature of Andean societies, dating back even to Inca times: Kenneth Hirth and Joanne

Pillsbury, "Redistribution and Markets in Andean South America," *Current Anthropology* 54, no. 5 (2013): 642–47.

4. José Macedonio Urquidi, *El Origin de la "Noble Villa de Oropesa" (Cochabamba)* (Cochabamba, Bolivia: Imprenta Universitaria, Sección Comercial, 1949).

5. Richard L. Kagan, *Urban Images of the Hispanic World, 1493–1793* (New Haven, CT: Yale University Press, 2000).

6. Humberto Solares Serrano, *La Larga Marcha de los Cochabambinos: De la Villa de Oropesa a la Metropolitización* (Cochabamba, Bolivia: Editorial Grafisol, 2011), 30.

7. On the broader significance of the plaza in Latin America, see Setha M. Low, *On the Plaza: The Politics of Public Space and Culture* (Austin: University of Texas Press, 2000).

8. Brooke Larson, *Colonialism and Agrarian Transformation in Bolivia: Cochabamba, 1550–1900* (Princeton, NJ: Princeton University Press, 1988).

9. Solares Serrano, *La Larga Marcha de los Cochabambinos*, 31. The quote refers to several classic dishes of the Cochabamba valley: *puchero* (stew); *chicharrón* (fried chicken or pork); *mote* (corn on the cob); and *quesillo* (homemade cheese). These dishes are still commonly served today.

10. Solares Serrano, *La Larga Marcha de los Cochabambinos*, 71–72.

11. Solares Serrano, *La Larga Marcha de los Cochabambinos*, 71–72.

12. The distinction between "indigenous" and "mestizo" people is largely arbitrary, as are most racial classifications—a fact made particularly clear in the context of market exchange. By one definition, urban market vendors are essentially mestizo rather than indigenous, their ethnicity determined by the fact of their market participation. As Olivia Harris has observed, historically "the people most unambiguously classified as Indians in the high Andes are those whose economic reproduction does not depend decisively on markets": Olivia Harris, "Ethnic Identity and Market Relations: Indians and Mestizos in the Andes," in *Ethnicity, Markets and Migration in the Andes: At the Crossroads of History and Anthropology*, ed. Brooke Larson and Olivia Harris with Enrique Tandeter (Durham, NC: Duke University Press, 1995), 351.

13. *Cancha* in Spanish means playing field, or open space more generally. The same word, *kancha*, is used in Quechua, also to mean open space. The space that *kancha* refers to may also be an enclosed space, surrounded by walls, used for spectacles and performances. A *kancha* in this sense is more like a plaza (a Spanish word that is now part of the English language), a central, open space for public gatherings. In their capital city Cuzco, in Peru, the Incas worshipped the sun (*inti*) in a ritual space called the Intikancha (Temple of the Sun), or Qorikancha (Golden Courtyard), the richest and most sacred temple of the Inca empire. When the Spanish *conquistadores* arrived in Cuzco in 1534, they destroyed the Qorikancha and built a Catholic church atop the ruins, co-opting the sacred power of that place for their victorious Christian god.

14. Alcides D'Orbigny, *Viaje a la América Meridional*, vol. 3 (La Paz: Plural-Instituto Francés de Estudios Andinos, 2002).

15. Gustavo Rodríguez Ostria and Humberto Solares Serrano, *Maíz, Chicha y Modernidad: Telones y Entretelones del Desarrollo Urbano de Cochabamba (Siglos XIX y XX)* (Santa Cruz de la Sierra, Bolivia: El Pais, 2011), 28.

16. Rodríguez Ostria and Solares Serrano, *Maíz, Chicha y Modernidad*.

17. Compare with Joshua Kirschner, "Migrants and Citizens: Hygiene Panic and Urban Space in Santa Cruz," in *Remapping Bolivia: Resources, Territory, and Indigeneity in a Plurinational State*, ed. Nicole Fabricant and Bret Gustafson (Santa Fe, NM: School of Advanced Research Press, 2011), 96–115.

18. Solares Serrano, *La Larga Marcha de los Cochabambinos*, 73–74.

19. Of relevance here is Daniella Gandolfo's description of the taboo as "the complex regimen of prohibitions that human beings and societies put in place to create a sense of propriety and order by imposing a distance between themselves and the things and behaviors that they deem to be less than human, the violence and excess they associate with the dark, abyssal world of their own renounced humanity": Daniella Gandolfo, *The City at Its Limits: Taboo, Transgression, and Urban Renewal in Lima* (Chicago: University of Chicago Press, 2009), xii. Gandolfo's study of urban society in Lima, Peru, presents an interesting comparison to Cochabamba; in both cases, taboos are grounded in urban architecture and imagination, and deeply linked to racial, class, and gendered forms of social division.

20. Solares Serrano, *La Larga Marcha de los Cochabambinos*, 74. A latifundio is an agricultural estate, a basic unit of the Spanish colonial land tenure system.

21. Solares Serrano, *La Larga Marcha de los Cochabambinos*, 78.

## 9. Conflicts of Interest

1. Fieldnotes, March 16, 2007.

## 10. Decolonizing Ethnographic Research

1. On constructing a "decolonizing episteme" for the production of ethnographic knowledge, see Keisha-Khan Y. Perry and Joanne Rappaport, "Making a Case for Collaborative Research with Black and Indigenous Social Movements in Latin America," in *Otros Saberes: Collaborative Research on Indigenous and Afro-Descendant Cultural Politics*, ed. Charles R. Hale and Lynn Stephen (Santa Fe, NM: School of Advanced Research Press, 2013), 30–48.

2. Native commentators and academics have long made similar observations, among them the classic denunciation of anthropology in Vine Deloria Jr., *Custer Died for Your Sins: An Indian Manifesto* (New York: Macmillan, 1969). Some scholars suggest that not much has changed and that the research priorities of anthropologists continue to reflect "establishment" rather than native concerns: see Thomas Biolsi and Larry J. Zimmerman, ed., *Indians and Anthropologists: Vine Deloria, Jr., and the Critique of Anthropology* (Tucson: University of Arizona Press, 1997).

3. Linda Tuhiwai Smith, *Decolonizing Methodologies: Research and Indigenous Peoples* (London: Zed, 1999), 1.

4. Cholas, or more commonly cholitas, are women in traditional dress, usually speakers of an indigenous language. See the discussion of this stereotype in chapter 21.

5. The subject of the relationship between objectivity and anthropology has produced lively debate in the discipline. Useful reflections have been provided by commentators as diverse as Roy D'Andrade, "Moral Models in Anthropology," *Current Anthropology* 36, no. 3 (1995): 399–408; Johannes Fabian, "Ethnographic Objectivity: From Rigor to Vigor," in *Anthropology with an Attitude: Critical Essays* (Stanford, CA: Stanford University Press, 2001), 11–32; and Nancy Scheper-Hughes, "The Primacy of the Ethical: Propositions for a Militant Anthropology," *Current Anthropology* 36, no. 3 (1995): 409–40.

6. Shannon Speed, "At the Crossroads of Human Rights and Anthropology: Toward a Critically Engaged Activist Research," *American Anthropologist* 108, no. 1 (2006): 66–76.

7. In *Outlawed* (44), I recount the warning given me by a senior colleague, who cautioned me against "do-gooding" and advised me to keep my focus on academic research.

8. Much discussion of these issues can be found in recent writings under the heading of "engaged" or "activist" anthropology: see, e.g., Daniel M. Goldstein, "Security and the Culture Expert: Dilemmas of an Engaged Anthropology," *PoLAR* 33, no. 1 (2010): 126–42; Stuart Kirsch, "Anthropology and Advocacy: A Case Study of the Campaign against Ok Tedi Mine," *Critique of Anthropology* 22, no. 2 (2002): 175–200; Setha M. Low and Sally Engle Merry, "Engaged Anthropology: Diversity and Dilemmas." *Current Anthropology* 51, supp. 2 (2010): S203–26; Shannon Speed, "Forged in Dialogue: Towards a Critically Engaged Activist Research," in *Engaging Contradictions: Activist Scholarship in Interdisciplinary Perspective*, ed. Charles R. Hale (Berkeley: University of California Press, 2008), 213–36.

9. On collaborative research, see Luke Eric Lassiter, *The Chicago Guide to Collaborative Ethnography* (Chicago: University of Chicago Press, 2005).

10. Charles R. Hale, ed., *Engaging Contradictions: Theory, Politics, and Methods of Activist Scholarship* (Berkeley: University of California Press, 2008).

11. A decolonizing stance is particularly relevant in Bolivia, where the MAS government of Evo Morales has been deeply engaged in a process of "decolonizing" the country, though what this means in practice has been somewhat ambiguous: see Linda Farthing and Benjamin Kohl, *Evo's Bolivia: Continuity and Change* (Austin: University of Texas Press, 2014).

12. Decolonizing approaches to knowledge and scholarship are outlined in Walter D. Mignolo, *The Darker Side of Western Modernity: Global Futures, Decolonial Options* (Durham, NC: Duke University Press, 2011); Anibal Quijano, "Coloniality of Power, Eurocentrism, and Latin America," *Nepantla: Views from the South* 1, no. 3 (2000): 533–80. But see note 14, below.

13. See, e.g., the chapters in Charles R. Hale and Lynn Stephen, eds., *Otros Saberes: Collaborative Research on Indigenous and Afro-Descendant Cultural Politics* (Santa Fe, NM: School of Advanced Research Press, 2013). A project of the Latin American Studies Association, Otros Saberes fosters collaboration between intellectuals and activists across the Americas.

14. Some scholarly work represents indigenous subjects as passive objects of foreign theorizing, even as it neglects indigenous people's own work in theorizing their

condition. The Bolivian scholar Silvia Rivera Cusicanqui has criticized North American postcolonial scholarship for its uncredited appropriation of indigenous intellectual work in a way that reproduces the very coloniality it ostensibly critiques: see Silvia Rivera Cuiscanqui, "Ch'ixinakax utxiwa: A Reflection on the Practices and Discourses of Decolonization," *South Atlantic Quarterly* 111, no. 1 (2012): 95–109.

## 11. A Visit to the Cancha

1. See Michel de Certeau, *The Practice of Everyday Life*, trans. Steven F. Rendall (Berkeley: University of California Press, 2011 [1984]).

2. Various attempts have been made to resuscitate train service to and from Cochabamba, with service to the highland city of Oruro being occasionally available. None of these attempts has proved sustainable, however,

3. Herbert S. Klein, *Bolivia: The Evolution of a Multi-Ethnic Society*, 2nd ed. (Oxford: Oxford University Press, 1992).

4. Fieldnotes, February 11, 2007.

5. Official measures put La Pampa at 49,620 square meters, although it appears much bigger in real life. The figures in map 11.1 therefore may not be exactly to scale.

## 12. The Informal State

1. Invocations of "the state" often seem to suggest that the national government is their referent object. I slide between levels in my use of the term "the state," often using it to refer to the municipal government of Cochabamba. On the state, see Philip Abrams, "Notes on the Difficulty of Studying the State," *Journal of Historical Sociology* 1 (1977): 58–89; Begoña Aretxaga, "Maddening States," *Annual Review of Anthropology* 32 (2003): 393–410.

2. A useful framework for thinking about the relationship between the legal and the illegal—a distinction that parallels the relationship between formal and informal that I analyze here—is offered in Josiah McC. Heyman and Alan Smart, "States and Illegal Practices: An Overview," in *States and Illegal Practices*, ed. Josiah McC. Heyman (Oxford: Berg, 1999), 1–24.

3. Carolyn Nordstrom, *Global Outlaws: Crime, Money, and Power in the Contemporary World* (Berkeley: University of California Press, 2007), 207. Nordstrom uses the term "il/legal" to call attention to the slipperiness of a distinction that is too often taken for granted by social scientists.

4. Ananya Roy, "Why India Cannot Plan Its Cities: Informality, Insurgence and the Idiom of Urbanization," *Planning Theory* 8, no. 76 (2009): 83.

5. Ananya Roy, "Urban Informality: Toward an Epistemology of Planning," *Journal of the American Planning Association* 71, no. 2 (2005): 148. See also Ananya Roy and Nezar AlSayyad, *Urban Informality: Transnational Perspectives from the Middle East, South Asia and Latin America* (Lanham, MD: Lexington, 2004).

6. Rather than a corruption of how the state should work, as several recent studies have shown, the ambiguous and informal nature of state functioning is the very basis on which states are founded and through which they are experienced by the people whom they govern. For example, Jonathan Shapiro Anjaria examines the "unofficial arrangements" that govern informal vendors' relationships with state officials, in some cases leading to an experience of the state that is surprisingly close, even "intimate": Jonathan Shapiro Anjaria, "Ordinary States: Everyday Corruption and the Politics of Space in Mumbai," *American Ethnologist* 38, no. 1 (2011): 58–72. Similarly, Akhil Gupta writes that corruption and corruption stories are integral to the ways in which ordinary people understand the state, a multivalent set of conceptions facilitated by the very ambiguity in which the concept of corruption is itself embedded: Akhil Gupta, "Narratives of Corruption: Anthropological and Fictional Accounts of the Indian State," *Ethnography* 6, no. 1 (2012): 5–34; Akhil Gupta, *Red Tape: Bureaucracy, Structural Violence, and Poverty in India* (Durham, NC: Duke University Press, 2012). And John Cross demonstrates that the gulf between the intentions of policy makers and policy implementers (e.g., the police) leave ambiguous spaces within which organized groups of street vendors can advance their interests and improve their positions vis-à-vis state power: John C. Cross, *Informal Politics: Street Vendors and the State in Mexico City* (Stanford, CA: Stanford University Press, 1998).

7. Asher Ghertner, "Analysis of New Legal Discourse behind Delhi's Slum Demolitions," *Economic and Political Weekly*, vol. 17, May (2008), 57–66.

8. Exemptions of this sort are interpretable as part of the "states of exception" that Giorgio Agamben postulates as being at the heart of state power, a point that Roy also recognizes in her conceptions of informality: see Giorgio Agamben, *State of Exception*, trans. K. Atell (Chicago: University of Chicago Press, 2005); Roy, "Urban Informality."

9. James Holston, *Insurgent Citizenship: Disjunctions of Democracy and Modernity in Brazil* (Princeton, NJ: Princeton University Press, 2008), 19.

10. Interview with Carlos Montoya, June 13, 2007.

11. The writings of J. K. Gibson-Graham on "diverse economies" are suggestive in this regard, as well. Writing against normative assumptions about the capitalist economy, Gibson-Graham include the informal economy and street vending as domains of potentially liberatory economic and political engagement: J. K. Gibson-Graham, *A Postcapitalist Politics* (Minneapolis: University of Minnesota Press, 2006). While the street vendors of Cochabamba in some ways might be seen as performing the "new economic worlds" that Gibson-Graham envision (J. K. Gibson-Graham, "Diverse Economies: Performative Practices for 'Other Worlds,'" *Progress in Human Geography* 32, no. 5 (2008): 614), the comerciantes of the Cancha are more convincingly understood as small-scale capitalists of the first order. This interpretation is supported by other writers working in very different geographical regions, including those who have attempted to interpret street vendors in terms of the diverse economies perspective: see, e.g., Sarah Turner and Laura Schoenberger, "Street Vendor Livelihoods and Everyday Politics in Hanoi, Vietnam: The Seeds of a Diverse Economy?" *Urban Studies* 49, no. 5 (2012): 1027–44.

12. Janet Roitman describes how illegal practices can also be "licit," or normalized and acceptable—even "legitimate"—depending on a host of factors within the local context: Janet Roitman, "The Ethics of Illegality in the Chad Basin," in *Law and Disorder in the Postcolony*, ed. Jean Comaroff and John L. Comaroff (Chicago: University of Chicago Press, 2006), 247–72.

13. See Diane E. Davis, "Analytical Foundations for the Study of Informality: A Short Introduction," in *Informalidad, Incertidumbre, Metrópolis y Estado: Como Gobernar la Informalización?* ed. Felipe de Alba and Frederic Lesemann (Mexico City: Programa Universitario de Estudios sobre la Ciudad–Universidad Nacional Autónoma de México, Institut National de la Recherche Scientifique, and European Institutes for Advanced Study, Collegium de Lyon, 2012), 11–40.

14. Other authors have explored the question of what constitutes and distinguishes a "legitimate" worker or poor person from an "illegitimate" one: see, e.g., Mariano D. Perelman, "Trabajar, pedir, vender. El caso de los vendedores ambulantes en trenes de la ciudad de Buenos Aires, Argentina," *Journal of Latin American and Caribbean Anthropology* 18, no. 2 (2013): 231–50.

15. An interesting discussion of the role of circulation—of wealth, credit, and finance—in contemporary urban economies is in AbdouMaliq Simone, *City Life from Jakarta to Dakar: Movement at the Crossroads* (New York: Routledge, 2010).

16. John Cross and Marina Karides point out that Clifford Geertz's classic study of economic change in Indonesia made similar assumptions, suggesting that markets and bazaars had no place in the modern economy: see John C. Cross and Marina Karides, "Capitalism, Modernity, and the 'Appropriate' Use of Space," in *Street Entrepreneurs: People, Place and Politics in Local and Global Perspective*, ed. John Cross and Alfonso Morales (London: Routledge, 2007), 19–35; Clifford Geertz, *Peddlers and Princes: Social Development and Economic Change in Two Indonesian Towns* (Chicago: University of Chicago Press, 1968). See also Anne S. Lewinson, "Reading Modernity in Urban Space: Politics, Geography and the Informal Sector of Downtown Dar es Salaam, Tanzania," *City and Society* 10, no. 1 (1998): 205–22.

17. I have described a similar public response to the "irregular" settlement of Cochabamba's marginal barrios: Daniel M. Goldstein, *The Spectacular City: Violence and Performance in Urban Bolivia* (Durham, NC: Duke University Press, 2004).

18. Oren Yiftachel, "Theoretical Notes on 'Gray Cities': The Coming of Urban Apartheid?" *Planning Theory* 8, no. 1 (2009): 89.

19. Yiftachel, "Theoretical Notes on 'Gray Cities,'" 90.

## 13. The Modern City

1. Brodwyn Fischer, Bryan McCann and Javier Auyero, eds., *Cities from Scratch: Poverty and Informality in Urban Latin America* (Durham, NC: Duke University Press, 2014); Karen Tranberg Hansen and Mariken Vaa, eds., *Reconsidering Informality: Perspectives from Urban Africa* (Oslo: Nordiska Afrikainstitutet, 2004); Alan Smart, "Unruly Places: Urban

Governance and the Persistence of Illegality in Hong Kong's Urban Squatter Areas," *American Anthropologist* 103, no. 1 (2001): 30–44.

2. Brodwyn Fischer, "A Century in the Present Tense: Crisis, Politics, and the Intellectual History of Brazil's Informal Cities," in *Cities from Scratch: Poverty and Informality in Urban Latin America*, ed. Brodwyn Fischer, Bryan McCann, and Javier Auyero (Durham, NC: Duke University Press, 2014), 9–67.

3. Manuel Castells, *The City and the Grassroots: A Cross-Cultural Theory of Urban Social Movements* (Berkeley: University of California Press, 1985); Gracia Clark, *Onions Are My Husband: Survival and Accumulation by West African Market Women* (Chicago: University of Chicago Press, 1994).

4. Edward Murphy, "In and Out of the Margins: Urban Land Seizures and Homeownership in Santiago, Chile," in *Cities from Scratch: Poverty and Informality in Urban Latin America*, ed. Brodwyn Fischer, Bryan McCann, and Javier Auyero (Durham, NC: Duke University Press, 2014), 68–101. See also Lisa R. Peattie, "'The Concept of Marginality' as Applied to Squatter Settlements," in *Latin American Urban Research, Volume 4: Anthropological Perspectives on Latin American Urbanization*, ed. Wayne A. Cornelius and Felicity M. Trueblood (Beverly Hills, CA: Sage, 1974), 101–9; Janice E. Perlman, *The Myth of Marginality: Urban Poverty and Politics in Rio de Janeiro* (Berkeley: University of California Press, 1976).

5. Marisol de la Cadena, *Indigenous Mestizos: The Politics of Race and Culture in Cuzco, Peru, 1919–1991* (Durham, NC: Duke University Press, 2000).

6. Fischer, "A Century in the Present Tense."

7. On modernism and anthropology, see the essays in Jonathan Xavier Inda, *Anthropologies of Modernity: Foucault, Governmentality, and Life Politics* (London: Blackwell, 2005). On the relationship between modernity and coloniality, see Walter D. Mignolo, *The Darker Side of Western Modernity: Global Futures, Decolonial Options* (Durham, NC: Duke University Press, 2011).

8. Daniel M. Goldstein, *The Spectacular City: Violence and Performance in Urban Bolivia* (Durham, NC: Duke University Press, 2004). See also Asher Ghertner, "Calculating without Numbers: Aesthetic Governmentality in Delhi's Slums," *Economy and Society* 39, no. 2 (2010): 185–217.

9. Fischer, "A Century in the Present Tense," 16.

10. Diane E. Davis, "Socio-Spatial Inequality and Violence in Cities of the Global South: Evidence from Latin America," in *Cities and Inequalities in a Global and Neoliberal World*, ed. Faranak Miraftab, David Wilson, and Ken Salo (London: Routledge, 2015): 75–91.

11. Davis, "Socio-Spatial Inequality and Violence in Cities of the Global South," 78.

12. Veena Das and Deborah Poole, *Anthropology in the Margins of the State* (Santa Fe, NM: School of American Research Press, 2004).

13. Classic pieces include William Mangin, "Latin American Squatter Settlements," *Latin American Research Review* 2, no. 3 (1967): 65–98; Lisa R. Peattie, *The View from the Barrio* (Ann Arbor: University of Michigan Press, 1968); Bryan R. Roberts, *Cities of Peasants: The Political Economy of Urbanization in the Third World* (London: Edward Arnold, 1978).

14. Octavio Salamanca, El Socialismo en Bolivia—Los Indios de la Altiplanicie Boliviana (Cochabamba, Bolivia: Imprenta Roja, 1931).

15. Compare with Linda J. Seligmann, Peruvian Street Lives: Culture, Power, and Economy among Market Women of Cuzco (Urbana: University of Illinois Press, 2004).

16. Goldstein, The Spectacular City.

17. Jorge E. Hardoy, Urbanization in Latin America: Approaches and Issues (Garden City, NY: Anchor, 1975).

18. Robert Fishman, Urban Utopias in the Twentieth Century: Ebenezer Howard, Frank Lloyd Wright and Le Corbusier (Cambridge, MA: MIT Press, 1982).

19. Humberto Solares Serrano, La Larga Marcha de los Cochabambinos: De la Villa de Oropesa a la Metropolitización (Cochabamba, Bolivia: Editorial Grafisol, 2011, 104.

20. Solares Serrano, La Larga Marcha de los Cochabambinos, 102. Theories of Social Darwinism were influential in elite circles of Latin America at this time, as they were in the North.

21. Gustavo Rodríguez Ostria and Humberto Solares Serrano, Maíz, Chicha y Modernidad: Telones y Entretelones del Desarrollo Urbano de Cochabamba (Siglos XIX y XX) (Santa Cruz de la Sierra, Bolivia: El Pais, 2011), 47.

22. Rodríguez Ostria and Solares Serrano, Maíz, Chicha y Modernidad, 64–65. Diane Davis characterizes modernist urban planning as an attempt to conquer and reshape the "untamed" spaces of the city: Diane E. Davis, "Modernist Planning and the Foundation of Urban Violence in Latin America," Built Environment 40, no. 3 (2014): 377.

23. Solares Serrano, La Larga Marcha de los Cochabambinos, 107. This "dependent urbanization" is characteristic of urban development in poor capitalist countries around the world.

24. María Isabel Mena M., "La chicha ayudó al progreso," Opinion, Cochabamba, Bolivia, September 19, 2010, 5.

25. Humberto Solares Serrano, Historia, Espacio, y Sociedad: Cochabamba 1550–1950: Formación, Crisis, y Desarrollo de su Proceso Urbano (Cochabamba, Bolivia: Editorial Serrano, 1990), 242.

26. Solares Serrano, Historia, Espacio, y Sociedad, 242.

27. Jorge Urquidi Zambrana, La Urbanización de la Ciudad de Cochabamba: Sintesis del Estudio, Documentos y Antecedentes (Cochabamba, Bolivia: Editorial Universitaria, 1967).

28. Goldstein, The Spectacular City.

29. For many migrants, their children's education was an even more significant motivator of urban migration than employment: see José Blanes and Gonzalo Flores, Factores Poblacionales en el Desarrollo Regional de Cochabamba (La Paz: Ediciones CERES, 1972).

30. See Bret D. Gustafson, New Languages of the State: Indigenous Resurgence and the Politics of Knowledge in Bolivia (Durham, NC: Duke University Press, 2009).

31. Solares Serrano, La Larga Marcha de los Cochabambinos, 210.

32. Gaceta Oficial de Bolivia, Registro del Comerciante Ambulante, Decreto-Ley de 4 de abril de 1940. Leyes y Decretos Supremos que Modifican el Código Mercantil (La Paz: unknown, 1940).

## 14. Market Space, Market Time

1. Based on field notes, March 29, 2007, written by Nacho (my translation/ adaptation).

2. Michel de Certeau, *The Pratice of Everyday Life*, trans. Steven F. Rendall (Berkeley: University of California Press, 2011 [1984]), 117. Space, for de Certeau, is "practiced place"; it "occurs as the effect produced by the operations that orient it, situate it, temporalize it, and make it function in a polyvalent unity of conflictual programs or contractual proximities."

3. De Certeau, *The Pratice of Everyday Life*, 118.

4. Judith-Maria Buechler noted something similar decades ago in her study of marketing in the nation's capital. Urban markets, she concluded, "should not be studied as places fixed in space and time but as nodes in a fluid system of distribution entailing the movement of goods and persons over time. Such markets are not bounded entities, defined spatially, temporally, or in terms of social structure. They must be viewed as parts of larger systems, which evolved through time and which change in response to migration from the countryside. As such, they serve as sensitive indicators of broader social transformations and economic development, particularly rates of urbanization, mobilization, and control of the populace and patterns of class and sex-role differentiation": Judith-Maria Buechler, "The Dynamics of the Market in La Paz, Bolivia," *Urban Anthropology* 7, no. 4 (1974): 356–57.

5. For example Linda Seligmann has written extensively about spatial relations and the importance of space to Peruvian market women: see Linda J. Seligmann, *Peruvian Street Lives: Culture, Power, and Economy among Market Women of Cuzco* (Urbana: University of Illinois Press, 2004). See also Linda J. Seligmann, "Market Places, Social Spaces in Cuzco, Peru," *Urban Anthropology* 29, no. 1 (2000): 1–68; Linda J. Seligmann, "Contested Spaces: Street Vendors in the Andean Metropole of Cusco, Peru," in *Anthropology in the City: Methodology and Theory*, ed. Italo Pardo and Giuliana B. Prato (Surrey, U.K.: Ashgate, 2012), 117–34.

6. Alicia Navía Mier, "Todos Santos y el Día de Difuntos tienen características propias," *La Patria*, Oruro, Bolivia, October 30, 2011, http://lapatriaenlinea.com/?t=todos -santos-y-el-dia-de-difuntos-tienen-caracteristicas-propias&nota=87286, accessed August 1, 2013.

7. In 2014, the Morales regime ordered that the aguinaldo be increased to the equivalent of two months' salary for both public and private sector employees, a move that thrilled workers and angered employers: see "Evo decreta doble aguinaldo para el sector público y privado," *El Deber*, November 20, 2013, Santa Cruz de la Sierra, Bolivia, http://www.eldeber.com.bo/evo-decreta-doble-aguinaldo-para-el-sector-publico-y -privado/131120104222, accessed August 23, 2014.

8. Fieldnotes, March 29, 2007; written by Nacho (my translation).

## 15. Carnaval in the Cancha

1. Much has been written about the history and ethnography of Carnaval in the Andes and Latin America more generally. For starters, see Thomas A. Abercrombie, "To Be Indian, To Be Bolivian: 'Ethnic' and 'National' Discourses of Identity," in *Nation-States and Indians in Latin America*, ed. Greg Urban and Joel Sherzer (Austin: University of Texas Press, 1991), 95–130; Michelle Bigenho, "Sensing Locality in Yura: Rituals of Carnival and of the Bolivian State," *American Ethnologist* 26, no. 4 (1999): 957–80; Roberto DaMatta, *Carnivals, Rogues and Heroes: An Interpretation of the Brazilian Dilemma* (Notre Dame: University of Notre Dame Press, 1991).

2. Fieldnotes, February 21, 2007.

3. Fieldnotes, March 11–15, 2007.

4. Nacho's joke combines Melvin's name with the word *delincuente* (delinquent).


## 16. Security and Chaos

1. "Introducing Tokyo," LonelyPlanet.com, http://www.lonelyplanet.com/japan/tokyo, accessed June 21, 2013; Saskia Sassen, "La Salada, the Largest Informal Market in South America," *Forbes*, March 28, 2011, http://www.forbes.com/sites/megacities/2011/03/28/la-salada-the-largest-informal-market-in-south-america/, accessed June 21, 2013; "Merkato, Addis Ababa," *Virtual Tourist*, http://www.virtualtourist.com/travel/Africa/Ethiopia/Addis_Ababa-2025155/Things_To_Do-Addis_Ababa-Mercato-BR-1.html, accessed June 21, 2013; "Chatuchak Weekend Market Bangkok," AsiaTravelTips.com, http://www.asiatraveltips.com/ChatuchakMarketBangkok.shtml, accessed June 21, 2013; "Portobello Road Market: Traveler Reviews," TripAdvisor.com, http://www.tripadvisor.com/ShowUserReviews-g186338-d189016-r130626308-Portobello_Road_Market-London_England.html, accessed June 21, 2013.

2. In its unmappability, the Cancha presents an interesting contrast with the Tsukiji fish market of Tokyo, diagrammed and analyzed in Theodore C. Bestor, *Tsukiji: The Fish Market at the Center of the World* (Berkeley: University of California Press, 2004).

3. "Cochabamba," LonelyPlanet.com, http://www.lonelyplanet.com/bolivia/the-southwest/cochabamba/things-to-do, accessed June 21, 2013.

4. The instability of market space and the sense of chaos that big markets seem to possess are captured in the description of the Janpath market in Paolo Favero, "Phantasms in a 'Starry' Place: Space and Identification in a Central New Delhi Market," *Cultural Anthropology* 18, no. 4 (2003): 551–84.

5. Organization of American States, *Report on Citizen Security in the Americas 2012* (Washington, DC: Organization of American States, 2012).

6. Robert Albro, "Violence and the Everyday in Early Twenty-First Century Latin America," in *Religious Responses to Violence: Human Rights in Latin America Past and Present*, ed. Alexander Wilde (Notre Dame, IN: University of Notre Dame Press, forthcoming).

7. Inter-American Development Bank, *Citizen Security in Latin America and the Caribbean: IDB's Comparative Advantage* (Washington, DC: Inter-American Development Bank,

2013); United Nations Development Program, *Citizen Security with a Human Face: Evidence and Proposals for Latin America*. Regional Human Development Report 2013–14 (New York: United Nations Development Program, 2013).

8. Inter-American Commission on Human Rights, *Report on Citizen Security and Human Rights*, Washington, DC, 2009, https://www.oas.org/en/iachr/docs/pdf/Citizen Sec.pdf, accessed February 15, 2014.

9. Observatorio Nacional de Seguridad Ciudadana, *Trabajando por la seguridad ciudadana: Primera encuesta de victimización, prácticas y percepción sobre violencia y delito en La Paz, El Alto, Cochabamba y Santa Cruz. Primeros resultados* 1(1), Equipo Técnico del Observatorio Nacional de Seguridad Ciudadana, Ministerio de Gobierno, Estado Plurinacional de Bolivia, 2012.

10. Observatorio Nacional de Seguridad Ciudadana, *Trabajando por la seguridad ciudadana*.

11. Lilian Bobea, "The Emergence of the Democratic Citizen Security Policy in the Dominican Republic," *Policing and Society* 22, no. 1 (2011): 57–75; Hugo H. Frühling, "Police Reform and the Process of Democratization," in *Crime and Violence in Latin America: Citizen Security, Democracy, and the State*, ed. Hugo H. Frühling, Joseph S. Tulchin, and Heather A. Golding (Washington, DC: Woodrow Wilson Center Press, 2003), 15–44. Even in nations where the state has officially articulated a "heavy hand" (*mano dura*) approach to crime and policing, crime continues to be seen as one of the greatest threats to popular security: Daniel M. Goldstein et al., "La Mano Dura and the Violence of Civil Society in Bolivia," *Social Analysis* 51, no. 2 (2007): 43–63. Heavy-handed policing, in fact, has done little to reduce actual levels of criminal violence: see, e.g., Nicholas Phillips, "In Honduras, Going from Door to Door to Prosecutors," *New York Times*, March 4, 2014, http://www.nytimes.com/2014/03/04/world/americas/in-honduras-going-from-door-to-door-to-prosecutors.html?_r=o, accessed October 11, 2014.

12. Kairos M. Marquardt, "Participatory Security: Citizen Security, Participation, and the Inequities of Citizenship in Urban Peru," *Bulletin of Latin American Research*, 31, no. 2 (2012): 174–89.

13. David R. Mares, "The National Security State," in *A Companion to Latin American History*, ed. Thomas Holloway (London: Blackwell, 2007), 386–405.

14. Rachel Neild, "From National Security to Citizen Security: Civil Society and the Evolution of Public Order Debates." Paper written for the International Center for Human Rights and Democratic Development, Montreal, 1999, 1.

15. For example, in 2004 the U.S. Agency for International Development provided nearly $50 million to strengthen democratic institutions and improve access to justice in Bolivia: U.S. Agency for International Development, *FY 2005 Congressional Budget Justification—Bolivia* (Washington, DC: U.S. Agency for International Development, 2004).

16. Barry Buzan, Ole Waever, and Jaap de Wilde, *Security: A New Framework for Analysis* (Boulder, CO: Lynne Reiner, 1998).

17. For more on this topic, see Daniel M. Goldstein, "Citizen Security and Human Security in Latin America," in *Routledge Handbook of Latin American Security Studies*, ed. David R. Mares and Arie M. Kacowicz (London: Routledge, 2016), 138–48.

18. Observatorio Nacional de Seguridad Ciudadana, *Trabajando por la seguridad ciudadana*.

19. Diane E. Davis, "Socio-Spatial Inequality and Violence," in *Cities and Inequalities in a Global and Neoliberal World*, ed. Faranak Miraftab, David Wilson, and Ken Salo (London: Routledge, 2015): 75–91.

20. Compare with Tobias Hecht, *At Home in the Street: Street Children of Northeast Brazil* (Cambridge: Cambridge University Press, 1998).

21. The Blattman law was revised and updated in Bolivia's New Criminal Procedural Code, established in 1999. Some people continue to refer to the rights guaranteed in this code by its old name, the *ley Blattman* (named for former Justice Minister Rene Blattman, who promulgated it).

22. Daniel M. Goldstein, "Human Rights as Culprit, Human Rights as Victim: Rights and Security in the State of Exception," in *The Practice of Human Rights: Tracking Law between the Global and the Local*, ed. Mark Goodale and Sally Engle Merry (Cambridge: Cambridge University Press, 2007), 49–77.

23. Fieldnotes, April 23–24, 2007.

24. Fieldnotes, April 23–24, 2007.

25. In Spanish, "*seguridad*" can mean both "security" and "safety." The distinction is difficult to draw and tends to be conflated in ordinary usage.

26. I have written about this question elsewhere, especially in Daniel M. Goldstein, "Towards a Critical Anthropology of Security," *Current Anthropology* 51, no. 4 (2010): 487–517. See also Morten A. Pedersen and Martin Holbraad, "Introduction: Times of Security," in *Times of Security: Ethnographies of Fear, Protest and the Future*, ed. Martin Holbraad and Morten A. Pedersen (New York: Routledge, 2013), 1–27. On more local conceptualizations of security, see Nils Bubandt, "Vernacular Security: The Politics of Feeling Safe in Global, National, and Local Worlds," *Security Dialogue* 36, no. 3 (2005): 275–96; Alexandra Kent, "Reconfiguring Security: Buddhism and Moral Legitimacy in Cambodia," *Security Dialogue* 37, no. 3 (2006): 343–61.

## 17. The Informal City

1. See Jorge H. Dandler, "Campesinado y Reforma Agraria en Cochabamba (1952–1953): Dinámica de un Movimiento Campesino en Bolivia," in *Bolivia: La Fuerza Histórica del Campesinado*, ed. Fernando Calderon and Jorge Dandler (Geneva: United Nations Research Institute for Social Development and Centro de Estudios de la Realidad Económica y Social, 1984), 135–204.

2. Humberto Solares Serrano, *La Larga Marcha de los Cochabambinos: De la Villa de Oropesa a la Metropolitización* (Cochabamba, Bolivia: Editorial Grafisol, 2011), 222.

3. María L. Lagos, *Autonomy and Power: The Dynamics of Class and Culture in Rural Bolivia* (Philadelphia: University of Pennsylvania Press, 1994).

4. Augusto Guzman, *Cochabamba* (Cochabamba, Bolivia: Editorial "Los Amigos del Libro," 1972).

5. Brooke Larson, *Colonialism and Agrarian Transformation in Bolivia: Cochabamba, 1550–1900* (Princeton, NJ: Princeton University Press, 1988).

6. Juan Antonio Morales, "Structural Adjustment and Peasant Agriculture in Bolivia," *Food Policy* 16, no. 1 (1991): 58–66.

7. Carmen Ledo, *Estudio sobre las Patrones de Migración Interna e Internacional en Bolivia, Informe Nacional sobre Desarrollo Humano* (La Paz: PNUD [United Nations Development Program], 2010).

8. Jorge H. Dandler et al., *El Sistema Agroalimentario en Bolivia* (La Paz: Centro de Estudios de la Realidad Económica y Social, 1987).

9. Alberto Rivera, *La Vivienda en Economías Informales de Cochabamba* (Cochabamba, Bolivia: Centro de Estudios de la Realidad Económica y Social, 1991).

10. Solares Serrano, *La Larga Marcha de los Cochabambinos*, 222–23.

11. Fernando Calderón and Alberto Rivera, *La Cancha: Una gran feria campesina en la ciudad de Cochabamba* (Cochabamba, Bolivia: Centro de Estudios de la Realidad Económica y Social, 1984).

12. Interview with Don Miguel, June 13, 2007.

13. CONSOBOL, *Mercado Central de Ferias-Informe Final*, ms., 1978, cited in Solares Serrano, *La Larga Marcha de los Cochabambinos*.

14. Solares Serrano, *La Larga Marcha de los Cochabambinos*, 242.

15. Carmen Ledo, *Proyecciones Demográficas de la Ciudad de Cochabamba*. Ms., 1993, Cochabamba, Bolivia.

16. Instituto Nacional de Estadística, *Censo Nacional de Población y Vivienda* (Cochabamba, Bolivia: Instituto Nacional de Estadística, 1992).

17. Many if not most of the land sales in Cochabamba's southern zone were transacted between arriving migrants, ignorant of the norms of land legalization in the city, and land speculators (*loteadores*) who profited from their ignorance. Following the agrarian reform, speculators had purchased land from peasants with holdings close to the city and divided them into parcels to sell as residential lots. These lands, however, were to have remained in agriculture under the city's master plan, thus making their use for residence illegal. People who bought these lands often found themselves unable to legalize their titles, forcing them into seemingly endless legal proceedings. See the discussion in Daniel M. Goldstein, *Outlawed: Between Security and Rights in a Bolivian City* (Durham, NC: Duke University Press, 2012).

18. Solares Serrano, *La Larga Marcha de los Cochabambinos*, 288.

19. Solares Serrano, *La Larga Marcha de los Cochabambinos*, 288.

20. Jhenny B. Nava, "Más de la mitad de comerciantes en mercados y calles es informal," *Opinión*, Cochabamba, Bolivia, February 17, 2013, 4–5.

21. José Arturo Cárdenas, "Evo Morales se encamina a una nueva reelección avalado por la bonanza económica," *El Faro*, October 8, 2014, San Salvador, El Salvador, http:// www.elfaro.net/es/201410/internacionales/16051/Evo-Morales-se-encamina-a-una -nueva-reelección-avalado-por-la-bonanza-económica.htm, accessed April 23, 2015.

22. Nava, "Más de la mitad de comerciantes en mercados y calles es informal," 4–5.

## 18. Convenios

1. Fieldnotes, March 15, 2007; written by Ruth Ordoñez.
2. Fieldnotes, March 19–23, 2007.
3. Fieldnotes, March 2, 2007; written by Eric Hinojosa.

## 19. Political Geography

1. Other studies of informal markets have made the same observation: see Mitchell Duneier, Sidewalk (New York: Farrar, Straus and Giroux, 2000); Linda J. Seligmann, Peruvian Street Lives: Culture, Power, and Economy among Market Women of Cuzco (Urbana: University of Illinois Press, 2004).

2. Jorge H. Dandler, El sindicalismo campesino en Bolivia: Los cambios estructurales en Ucureña (Mexico City: Instituto Indigenista Interamericano, 1969); Juliana Ströbele-Gregor, "Ley de Participación Popular y movimiento popular en Bolivia," in Sociedad Civil en América Latina: Representación de intereses y gobernabilidad, ed. Peter Hengstenberg, Karl Kohut, and Günther Maihold (Caracas: Nueva Sociedad, 1999), 133–46.

3. Interview with Don Rafo, May 3, 2007. Eric Hinojosa assisted with this interview.

4. Interview with Remberto and Lola, April 28, 2007.

5. Sian Lazar, "A Desire to Formalize Work? Comparing Trade Union Strategies in Bolivia and Argentina," Anthropology of Work Review 33, no. 1 (2012): 15–24.

6. Lazar has observed this relationship in her work with street vendors in the Bolivian city of El Alto: Lazar, "A Desire to Formalize Work?"

7. Interview with a market administrator of the Alcaldía Municipal, April 9, 2007.

8. Sian Lazar, "Disjunctive Comparison: Citizenship and Trade Unionism in Bolivia and Argentina," Journal of the Royal Anthropological Institute 18 (2012): 349–68.

## 20. Fieldwork in a Flash

1. Gracia Clark, who has studied Ashante market women in Ghana, admits that "some weeks I spent more time nagging traders for appointments than interviewing them": Gracia Clark, African Market Women: Seven Life Stories from Ghana (Bloomington: Indiana University Press, 2010), 12.

2. Field notes, February 27, 2007.

3. Carla Freeman, "The 'Reputation' of Neoliberalism," American Ethnologist 34, no. 2 (2007): 252–67; Daniel M. Goldstein, "Flexible Justice: Neoliberal Violence and Self-Help Security in Bolivia," Critique of Anthropology 25 (2005): 389–411.

4. Group interview with ambulantes, May 12, 2007.

5. Interview with Doña Prudencia, March 15, 2007.

6. Interview with Don Fausto, June 6, 2007; interview conducted by Ruth Ordoñez.

7. Centro de Investigación: Seguridad y Democracia, "Comerciantes Ambulantes: La Doble Cara de la (In)Visibilidad." *Opinión*, Cochabamba, Bolivia, March 29, 2007, A5. Nacho Antezana and Eric Hinojosa helped to craft this statement.

8. States of emergency are usually declared by governments in moments of crisis (real or manufactured), allowing for the temporary suspension of ordinary legal and judicial operations and the superseding of individual rights in the name of state security. Similarly, a state of exception is based on the sovereign's right to suspend the rule of law in order to safeguard public interests: Giorgio Agamben, *State of Exception*, trans. K. Atell (Chicago: University of Chicago Press, 2005). It is interesting to see an association like the ambulantes' El Paso making similar claims, although here what they will be suspending is not law but the ordinary daily routine. Instead of going to work as individuals, they will gather en masse and march against state abuses.

## 21. Women's Work

1. Fieldnotes, September 16, 2006; written by Nacho.

2. On working women in Andean cities, see, e.g., Ximena Bunster and Elsa M. Chaney, *Sellers and Servants: Working Women in Lima, Peru* (New York: Praeger, 1985); Lesley Gill, *Precarious Dependencies: Gender, Class and Domestic Service in Bolivia* (New York: Columbia University Press, 1994). On gender ideologies, see Linda J. Seligmann, *Peruvian Street Lives: Culture, Power, and Economy among Market Women of Cuzco* (Urbana: University of Illinois Press, 2004). And on the domestic lives of market women, see Florence E. Babb, *Between Field and Cooking Pot: The Political Economy of Marketwomen in Peru*, rev. ed. (Austin: University of Texas Press, 1998).

3. Linda J. Seligmann, "To Be in Between: The Cholas as Market Women," *Comparative Studies in Society and History* 31 (1989): 694–721; Mary Weismantel, *Cholas and Pishtacos: Stories of Sex and Race in the Andes* (Chicago: University of Chicago Press, 2001).

4. Isabel M. Scarborough, "Two Generations of Bolivian Female Vendors," *Ethnology* 49, no. 2 (2010): 87–104.

5. Fernando Calderón and Alberto Rivera, *La Cancha: Una gran feria campesina en la ciudad de Cochabamba* (Cochabamba, Bolivia: Centro de Estudios de la Realidad Económica y Social, 1984).

6. Linda J. Seligmann, "Between Worlds of Exchange: Ethnicity among Peruvian Market Women," *Cultural Anthropology* 8, no. 2 (1993): 187–213; Laura Gotkowitz, "Trading Insults: Honor, Violence, and the Gendered Culture of Commerce in Cochabamba, Bolivia, 1870s–1950s," *Hispanic American Historical Review* 83, no. 1 (2003): 83–118.

7. Marcia Stephenson, *Gender and Modernity in Andean Bolivia* (Austin: University of Texas Press, 1999).

8. Sarah Bott et al., *Violence against Women in Latin America and the Caribbean: A Comparative Analysis of Population-Based Data from 12 Countries* (Washington, DC: Pan American Health Organization, 2012).

9. Domestic violence is a difficult issue to study, particularly for a male researcher. I was unable to elicit rich ethnographic description of how women deal with abusive partners, although its effects are clearly visible in women's accounts of their experiences. Nongovernmental organizations are active in the barrios where market women live, many of them advocating against domestic violence and offering services to counter it, although their efforts have not served to reduce the extremely high levels of violence against women in Bolivia. Authors who have discussed this phenomenon in Latin America include Lynn Stephen, *Women and Social Movements in Latin America: Power from Below* (Austin: University of Texas Press, 1997); Krista E. van Vleet, "The Intimacies of Power: Rethinking Violence and Affinity in the Bolivian Andes," *American Ethnologist* 29, no. 3 (2002): 567–601.

10. Interview with Doña Victoria, Doña Juana, and others, May 18, 2007.

11. Interview with Doña Victoria, Doña Juana, and others, May 18, 2007.

12. Interview with Doña Esperanza, July 2, 2007; interview conducted by Ruth Ordoñez.

13. Interview with Remberto and Lola, April 28, 2007.

14. Calderón and Rivera, *La Cancha*, 78.

15. Susan Vincent, "Gender Ideologies and the Informal Economy: Reproduction and the 'Grapes of Wrath' Effect in Mata Chico, Peru," *Latin American Perspectives* 25, no. 2 (1998): 120–39.

16. Interview with Doña Tahlia, April 27, 2007.

17. Victor Agadjanian describes the effects of structural adjustment on female market vendors in El Alto, arguing that neoliberal reforms have intensified competition and reduced cooperation within this group: Victor Agadjanian, "Competition and Cooperation among Working Women in the Context of Structural Adjustment: The Case of Street Vendors in La Paz-El Alto, Bolivia," *Journal of Developing Societies* 18, nos. 2–3 (2002): 259–85.

18. Interview with Doña Tahlia, April 27, 2007.

19. Seligmann, *Peruvian Street Lives*.

20. Seligmann, "Between Worlds of Exchange," 194.

## 22. Sovereignty and Security

1. Thomas Blom Hansen and Finn Stepputat, "Sovereignty Revisited," *Annual Review of Anthropology* 35 (2006): 296.

2. Michael Ross Fowler and Julie Marie Bunck, *Law, Power, and the Sovereign State: The Evolution and Application of the Concept of Sovereignty* (University Park: Penn State University Press, 1995), 12.

3. John Bailey and Lucía Dammert, "Public Security and Police Reform in the Americas," in *Public Security and Police Reform in the Americas*, ed. John Bailey and Lucía Dammert (Pittsburgh: University of Pittsburgh Press, 2006), 1–23; Mark Ungar, *Policing Democracy: Overcoming Obstacles to Citizen Security in Latin America* (Baltimore: Johns Hopkins University Press, 2011).

4. Daniel M. Goldstein, *Outlawed: Between Security and Rights in a Bolivian City* (Durham, NC: Duke University Press, 2012). See also Jennifer Burrell, "In and Out of Rights: Security, Migration, and Human Rights Talk in Guatemala," *Journal of Latin American and Caribbean Anthropology* 15, no. 1 (2010): 90–115; Angelina Snodgrass Godoy, *Popular Injustice: Violence, Community, and Law in Latin America* (Stanford, CA: Stanford University Press, 2006).

5. Rivke Jaffe, "The Hybrid State: Crime and Citizenship in Urban Jamaica," *American Ethnologist* 40, no. 4 (2013): 734–48; Ben Penglase, *Living with Insecurity in a Brazilian Favela: Urban Violence and Daily Life* (New Brunswick, NJ: Rutgers University Press, 2014).

6. See James Ferguson, *Global Shadows: Africa in the Neoliberal World Order* (Durham, NC: Duke University Press, 2006); Caroline Humphrey, "Sovereignty," in *A Companion to the Anthropology of Politics*, ed. David Nugent and Joan Vincent (Oxford: Blackwell, 2004), 418–36; Robert Latham, "Social Sovereignty," *Theory, Culture and Society* 17, no. 4 (2000): 1–18; Aihwa Ong, *Neoliberalism as Exception: Mutations in Citizenship and Sovereignty* (Durham, NC: Duke University Press, 2006).

7. Elana Zilberg, *Space of Detention: The Making of a Transnational Gang Crisis between Los Angeles and San Salvador* (Durham, NC: Duke University Press, 2011).

8. Fieldnotes, March 19–23, 2007.

9. The conflation of community justice with lynching is common in Bolivia. The new constitution, approved in 2009, authorizes the use of "traditional" forms of justice making, mostly in rural communities. This is often conflated with urban practices of vigilante violence and has been condemned by Bolivian and international human rights organizations. For more on this issue, see Goldstein, *Outlawed*.

10. Meanwhile, the police themselves have gotten into the act of private security, forming the Batallón de Seguridad Física Privada. A branch of the National Police, the Batallón contracts privately with firms interested in hiring armed and uniformed off-duty police officers. These guards can be seen outside banks, hotels, and other fine establishments throughout Cochabamba.

11. As Brenda Chalfin, drawing on Janice Thomson and Michel Foucault, has observed, sovereignty depends on "the multiplicity rather than the singularity of governing strategies, quotidian rather than extraordinary practices of rule," locating "the core of sovereign authority in the practices of administration": Brenda Chalfin (*Neoliberal Frontiers: An Ethnography of Sovereignty in West Africa* (Chicago: University of Chicago Press, 2010), Kindle edition, chapter 2. See also Michel Foucault, "Governmentality," in *The Foucault Effect: Studies in Governmentality*, ed. Graham Burchell, Colin Gordon, and Peter Miller (Chicago: University of Chicago Press, 1991), 87–104; Janice E. Thomson, "State Sovereignty in International Relations: Bridging the Gap between Theory and Empirical Research," *International Studies Quarterly* 39, no. 2 (1995): 213–33.

12. Transcription from public speech, Cochabamba, March 15, 2007.

13. Fieldnotes, June 26, 2007.

14. For more on the question of sovereignty and private policing, see Daniel M. Goldstein, "Color-Coded Sovereignty and the Men in Black," Private Security in a Bolivian Marketplace," *Conflict and Society*, forthcoming.

### 23. Resisting Privatization

1. For more on the Water War and its entailments, see Robert Albro, "'The Water Is Ours, Carajo! Deep Citizenship in Bolivia's Water War," in *Social Movements: An Anthropological Reader*, ed. June Nash (London: Basil Blackwell, 2005), 249–71; Oscar Olivera, ¡*Cochabamba! Water War in Bolivia* (Cambridge, MA: South End, 2004).

2. Jim Schultz, "Bolivians Win Anti-Privatization Battle," NACLA *Report on the Americas* 33, no. 6 (2000): 44–46.

3. Fieldnotes, March 27, 2007.

4. Ton Salman discusses the predicament of Bolivians in these sorts of clientelistic relationships, who have to strike a balance between demanding "rights" and asking for "favors": Ton Salman, "Customary Law in Search for Balance: Bolivia's Quest for a New Concept of 'Rights' and the Construction of Ethnicity," *Canadian Journal of Latin American and Caribbean Studies* 36, no. 72 (2011): 111–43.

5. Interview with Don Rafo, May 3, 2007.

6. Farid Saba V. and Hugo Salomón M., *Anteproyecto de la Transferencia a Titulo Gratuito del Mercado "La Pampa,"* Cochabamba, Bolivia, mimeograph, 2006. Cochabamba, Bolivia.

7. Asociación General de Comerciantes Minoristas, Artesanos y Vivanderos del Mercado "La Pampa," "Voto Resolutivo"; in Saba and Salomón, *Anteproyecto de la Transferencia a Titulo Gratuito del Mercado "La Pampa,"* 93.

8. In 2010, Bolivia changed from a republic to a "plurinational state" in recognition of the multiethnic composition of the country's population, and the National Congress become the Plurinational Legislative Assembly. This body consists of two houses: a thirty-six-member Senado, with four representatives from each department, and the 130 member Cámara de Diputados. For more on the Plurinational State, see Xavier Albó C. and Franz X. Barrios Suvelza, *Por una Bolivia plurinacional e intercultural con autonomías. Documento de trabajo: Informe Nacional sobre Desarrollo Humano en Bolivia* (La Paz: PNUD, 2011), and the chapters in Nicole Fabricant and Bret Gustafson, eds., *Remapping Bolivia: Resources, Territory, and Indigeneity in a Plurinational State* (Santa Fe: School of Advanced Research, 2011).

9. Compare with Brenda Chalfin, "Public Things, Excremental Politics, and the Infrastructure of Bare Life in Ghana's City of Tema," *American Ethnologist* 41, no. 1 (2014): 92–109.

10. Although Bolivia's President Evo Morales and his administration are officially and rhetorically anti-neoliberal, many of the state's practices under Morales follow lines established by earlier neoliberal governments: see Honor Brabazon and Jeffrey R. Webber, "Evo Morales and the MST in Bolivia: Continuities and Discontinuities in Agrarian Reform," *Journal of Agrarian Change* 14, no. 3 (2013): 435–65; Daniel M. Goldstein, "Decolonializing 'Actually Existing Neoliberalism,'" *Social Anthropology/Anthropologie Sociale* 20, no. 3 (2012): 304–9; Jean Grugel and Pia Riggirozzi, "Post-neoliberalism in Latin America: Rebuilding and Reclaiming the State after Crisis," *Development and Change* 43, no. 1 (2012): 1–21.

11. Interview with Doña Tahlia, April 27, 2007.

12. Fieldnotes, June 28, 2007.

## 24. Don Silvio

1. Interview with Don Silvio, April 30, 2007.

2. Juan José Torres, a socialist, was president of Bolivia during this period, and the Bolivian state looked favorably on workers' struggles like the one in the COMSUR mine. Torres was deposed in 1971 by a rightist coup led by General Hugo Banzer Suarez, and many union leaders were arrested, murdered, or forced to flee the country.

3. The mines of Bolivia are famous for producing progressive political leaders. First-person accounts of these experiences include Benjamin Kohl and Linda Farthing, with Félix Muruchi, *From the Mines to the Streets: A Bolivian Activist's Life* (Austin: University of Texas Press, 2011), and Moema Viezzer, *"Si Me Permiten Hablar": Testimonio de Domitila, una Mujer de las Minas de Bolivia* (Mexico City: Siglo Veintiuno Editores, 1978).

4. State-owned mines continued to operate until 1985, when they, too, were closed and thousands of workers were left unemployed: see Herbert Klein, *Bolivia: The Evolution of a Multi-Ethnic Society*, 2d ed. (Oxford: Oxford University Press, 1992).

5. The corporation that owns Taquiña and markets Maltín has picked up on the masculine appeal of the product: its website now promotes Maltín as "active, dynamic, a winner, entertaining, athletic" and advises consumers that drinking Maltín will help them to "meet challenges with strength, skill, and energy": see http://www.cbn.bo /nuestras-marcas/maltin, accessed August 16, 2013.

## 25. Character

1. Robert Albro, "Confounding Cultural Citizenship and Constitutional Reform in Bolivia," *Latin American Perspectives* 37, no. 3 (2010): 71–90; Andrew Canessa, "Conflict, Claim and Contradiction in the New 'Indigenous' State of Bolivia," *Critique of Anthropology* 34, no. 2 (2014): 153–73; Nancy Postero, "Morales' MAS Government Building Indigenous Popular Hegemony in Bolivia," *Latin American Perspectives* 37, no. 3 (2010): 18–34; Nancy Postero, *Now We Are Citizens: Indigenous Politics in Postmulticultural Bolivia* (Stanford, CA: Stanford University Press, 2006).

2. Andrew Canessa, *Intimate Indigeneities: Race, Sex, and History in the Small Spaces of Andean Life* (Durham, NC: Duke University Press, 2012).

3. Linda J. Seligmann, "To Be in Between: The Cholas as Market Women," *Comparative Studies in Society and History* 31 (1989): 694–721; Mary Weismantel, *Cholas and Pishtacos: Stories of Sex and Race in the Andes* (Chicago: University of Chicago Press, 2001).

4. Interview with Eulogia Imba, April 11, 2007; interview conducted by Rose Marie Achá.

5. Oscar Lewis, "Culture of Poverty," in *On Understanding Poverty: Perspectives from the Social Sciences*, ed. Daniel P. Moynihan (New York: Basic, 1969), 187–220.

6. The importance of credit to market vendors is discussed extensively in Linda J. Seligmann, *Peruvian Street Lives: Culture, Power, and Economy among Market Women of Cuzco* (Urbana: University of Illinois Press, 2004).

7. Interview with Doña Irena, April 27, 2007. Under Bolivian law, debtors can be imprisoned for defaulting on their loan payments to banks and private lending companies.

8. Interview with Doña Tahlia, April 27, 2007.

9. Interview with Don Florentino, May 20, 2007.

10. Interview with Don Rafo, May 3, 2007.

## 26. Exploitability

1. Fieldnotes, April 27, 2007.

2. Interview with Doña Irena, April 27, 2007.

3. "Pago Único Municipal ya se cobra en mercados," *Los Tiempos*, November 14, 2006, Cochabamba, Bolivia, http://www.lostiempos.com/diario/actualidad/local/20061114/pago-unico-municipal-ya-se-cobra-en-mercados_25983_25983.html, accessed October 4, 2014

4. Group interview with comerciantes ambulantes, November 18, 2006.

5. See Stephanie E. Coen, Nancy A. Ross, and Sarah Turner, "Without *Tiendas* It's a Dead Neighborhood: The Socio-economic Importance of Small Trade Stores in Cochabamba, Bolivia," *Cities* 25 (2008): 327–39.

6. Humberto Solares Serrano, *La Larga Marcha de los Cochabambinos: De la Villa de Oropesa a la Metropolización* (Cochabamba, Bolivia: Editorial Grafisol, 2011), 290.

7. Group interview with Don Beto and other ambulantes, May 12, 2007.

8. Interview with Doña Candela, November 22, 2006.

## 27. Market Men

1. Linda Seligmann, for example, admits that men take a "back seat" in her ethnography of the Cuzco market: Linda J. Seligmann, *Peruvian Street Lives: Culture, Power, and Economy among Market Women of Cuzco* (Urbana: University of Illinois Press, 2004), 15.

2. Brooke Larson and Rosario León, "Markets, Power, and the Politics of Exchange in Tapacarí, c. 1780 and 1980," in *Ethnicity, Markets, and Migration in the Andes: At the Crossroads of History and Anthropology*, ed. Brooke Larson and Olivia Harris, with Enrique Tandeter (Durham, NC: Duke University Press, 1995), 247.

3. Interview with Doña Eulalia and Doña Karmiña, June 22, 2007.

4. Fieldnotes, March 23, 2007.

5. Interview with Don Silvio, April 30, 2007.

6. Group interview with Don Beto and other ambulantes, May 12, 2007.

7. Interview with Don Arturo, April 14, 2007.

8. Interview with Doña Tahlia, April 27, 2007.

9. Interview with Don Arturo, April 14, 2007.

## 28. Webs of Illegality

1. Michael Taussig identifies the public secret as "that which is generally known, but cannot be spoken": Michael Taussig, *Defacement: Public Secrecy and the Labor of the Negative* (Stanford, CA: Stanford University Press, 1999), 50. See also Ben Penglase, "States of Insecurity: Everyday Emergencies, Public Secrets, and Drug Trafficker Power in a Brazilian Favela," *PoLAR* 32, no. 1 (2009): 47–63.

2. Interview with Don Rafo, May 3, 2007.

3. Fieldnotes, May 21, 2007.

4. Fieldnotes, May 21, 2007.

5. Fieldnotes, May 21, 2007.

6. Fieldnotes, May 21, 2007.

## 29. Men in Black

*Epigraph:* Barry Sonnenfeld, dir., *Men in Black* (film, 1997).

1. Fieldnotes, April 18, 2007.

2. Transcription from public speech, Cochabamba, March 15, 2007.

3. Lars Buur, "The Sovereign Outsourced: Local Justice and Violence in Port Elizabeth," in *Sovereign Bodies: Citizens, Migrants, and States in the Postcolonial World*, ed. Thomas Blom Hansen and Finn Stepputat (Princeton, NJ: Princeton University Press, 2005), 192–217. See also Rivke Jaffe, "The Hybrid State: Crime and Citizenship in Urban Jamaica," *American Ethnologist* 40, no. 4 (2013): 734–48.

4. Try as I might, I could not gain access to interview the heads of the Men in Black or other private security firms.

5. Charles Tilly, "War Making and State Making as Organized Crime," in *Violence: A Reader*, ed. Catherine Besteman (New York: Palgrave, 2002 [1985]), 35–60. See also Dennis Rodgers, "The State as a Gang: Conceptualizing the Governmentality of Violence in Contemporary Nicaragua," *Critique of Anthropology* 26, no. 3 (2006): 315–30.

## 30. At Home in the Market

1. Similar observations can be found in Lourdes Arizpe, *Indígenas en la Ciudad de México: El caso de las "Marías"* (Mexico City: Sep/Setentas, 1975).

2. Feminist anthropology has offered extensive treatment of the division between the public and private realms: see, e.g., Susan Gal, "A Semiotics of the Public/Private Distinction," *Differences* 13, no. 1 (2002): 77–95; Karen V. Hansen, "Feminist Conceptions of Public and Private: A Critical Analysis," *Berkeley Journal of Sociology* 32 (1987): 105–28; Sherry B. Ortner, "Is Female to Male as Nature Is to Culture?" *Feminist Studies* 1, no. 2 (1972): 5–31. Feminist anthropologists have also explored the distinction between "public" and "domestic" spheres and sometimes provided critiques of the entire formulation: see, e.g., Carole Pateman, "Feminist Critiques of the Public/Private Dichotomy," in *The Disorder of Women: Democracy, Feminism, and Political Theory*, ed. Carole

Pateman (Stanford: Stanford University Press, 1990), 118–39; Rayna Rapp, "Family and Class in Contemporary America: Notes Toward an Understanding of Ideology," *Science and Society* 42, no. 3 (1978): 278–300; Michelle Zimbalist Rosaldo and Louise Lamphere, *Women, Culture and Society* (Stanford, CA: Stanford University Press, 1974). My observations here confirm the notion that the domestic can also be a realm of work (i.e., not simply of the romanticized pleasures of the Western family), just as the public can be a realm of intimate familial practice: see Alejandro Lugo, "Destabilizing the Masculine, Refocusing 'Gender': Men and the Aura of Authority in Michelle Z. Rosaldo's Work," in *Gender Matters: Rereading Michelle Z. Rosaldo*, ed. Alejandro Lugo and Bill Maurer (Ann Arbor: University of Michigan Press, 2000), 54–89; Lynn Stephen, *Zapotec Women: Gender, Class and Ethnicity in Globalized Oaxaca* (Austin: University of Texas Press, 1991).

3. Gracia Clark, "Mothering, Work and Gender in Urban Asante Ideology and Practice," *American Anthropologist* 101, no. 4 (1999): 717–29.

4. Interview with Doña Prudencia, March 15, 2007.

5. Interview with Doña Victoria, Doña Juana, and others, May 18, 2007.

6. Interview with Doña Ana, March 5, 2007; Ruth Ordoñez assisted.

7. Interview with Doña Celia, June 27, 2007.

8. I explore the problem of residential insecurity, its causes and its consequences, in Daniel M. Goldstein, *Outlawed: Between Security and Rights in a Bolivian City* (Durham, NC: Duke University Press, 2012).

9. Interview with Remberto and Lola, April 28, 2007.

10. Interview with Juvenal and others, June 11, 2007.

11. Many of Bolivia's informal workers are children: U.S. government analysis claims that 20.2% of Bolivian children between the ages of seven and fourteen work. In 2014 the Bolivian government passed a law legalizing work for children as young as ten years old. The government explained the law as an effort to regulate child labor by legalizing it, though the law unleashed an international outcry against it: U.S. Department of Labor, Bureau of International Labor Affairs, *2012 Findings on the Worst Forms of Child Labor: Bolivia* (Washington, DC: U.S. Department of Labor, 2012); "Bolivia Makes Child Labor Legal, In an Attempt to Make It Safer," *National Public Radio*, July 30, 2014, Washington, DC, http://www.npr.org/2014/07/30/336361778/bolivia-makes-child-labor-legal-in-an-attempt-to-make-it-safer, accessed April 23, 2015.

12. Linda J. Seligmann, *Peruvian Street Lives: Culture, Power, and Economy among Market Women of Cuzco* (Urbana: University of Illinois Press, 2004), 52.

13. Interview with Doña Ana, March 5, 2007.

14. Interview with Remberto and Lola, April 28, 2007.

### 31. Owners of the Sidewalk

1. The question evokes notions of "the right to the city," on which there exists a significant body of literature. For starters, see David Harvey, "The Right to the City," *New Left Review* 53 (September–October 2003): 23–40; Peter Marcuse, "From Critical

Urban Theory to the Right to the City," *City* 13, nos. 2–3 (2009): 185–97; Saskia Sassen, "Whose City Is It? Globalization and the Formation of New Claims," *Public Culture* 8 (1996): 205–23.

2. The dishes are chicken soup; "fake rabbit" (actually a piece of beef in a rich sauce); fried meat piled high with potatoes, rice, and vegetables, topped with a fried egg; and spicy tongue.

3. Interview with Don Ricardo, May 8, 2007.

4. Interview with José Luis Soria, director of markets for the Alcaldía Municipal, March 27, 2007; interview conducted by Rose Marie Achá.

5. Interview with Doña Rosa, May 18, 2007.

6. I wrote in more detail about the Human Rights Congress in Daniel M. Goldstein, *Outlawed: Between Security and Rights in a Bolivian City* (Durham, NC: Duke University Press, 2012), chap. 6.

7. Interview with Juan Vargas, December 8, 2006; interview conducted by Rose Marie Achá.

8. María Isabel Mena M., "Comercio minorista retoma las aceras de la ciudad," *Opinión*, Cochabamba, Bolivia, February 15, 2003, http://www.opinion.com.bo/opinion/articulos/2013/0215/noticias.php?id=86254&calificacion=4, accessed July 24, 2013.

9. "Resistencia de los 'dueños' de las aceras," *Opinión*, Cochabamba, Bolivia, July 31, 2011, 9A.

10. "Resistencia de los 'dueños' de las aceras."

11. Mark Goodale has explored the introduction of transnational human rights discourse in Bolivia and its uses: see Mark Goodale, *Dilemmas of Modernity: Bolivian Encounters with Law and Liberalism* (Stanford, CA: Stanford University Press, 2008). See also Mark Goodale and Sally Engle Merry, eds., *The Practice of Human Rights: Tracking Law between the Global and the Local* (Cambridge: Cambridge University Press, 2007).

12. Even as Don Silvio spoke, the political constitution of the Bolivian state was being rewritten by the MAS government. The result, the Constitution of the Plurinational State of Bolivia, was adopted in 2009. The rights to which Silvio refers are contained in the new constitution, as well, under section III, article 47, which states, "Every person has the right to work and to dedicate oneself to commerce, industry or any licit activity, on condition that it does not harm the collective good."

13. Interview with Don Ramón, May 18, 2007.

## 32. The Seminar

1. All dialogue in this chapter is transcribed from recordings of March 15, 2007. I have shortened the remarks for readability.

2. In rural parts of the Andes, it is commonly believed that a malevolent being, called a *kharisiri* or a *pishtaco*, waylays unsuspecting people on the trail or in the fields and sucks out their fat for export to foreign industries: see Andrew Canessa, "Fear and Loathing on the *Kharisiri* Trail: Alterity and Identity in the Andes," *Journal of the Royal*

Anthropological Institute 6 (2000): 705–20; Mary Weismantel, *Cholas and Pishtacos: Stories of Sex and Race in the Andes* (Chicago: University of Chicago Press, 2001).

### 33. March of the Ambulantes

1. My translation.

2. The reference here is to Mayor Gonzalo "Chaly" Terceros of Cochabamba and Intendente Rodolfo Ferrufino, head of the market authority, the Intendencia. The word *mamón* can also mean "unweaned baby," which offers an interesting twist.

3. Fieldnotes, August 30, 2007; written by Eric Hinojosa.

4. See Kathleen M. Millar, "The Precarious Present: Wageless Labor and Disrupted Life in Rio de Janeiro, Brazil," *Cultural Anthropology* 29, no. 1 (2014): 32–53.

5. Interview with Doña Rosa, May 18, 2007.

### 34. Complications

1. Interview with Omar Villarroel, May 5, 2007.

2. Charlie Nairn, dir., "Ongka's Big Moka: The Kawelka of Papua New Guinea," *Disappearing World*, Granada Television, 1976, season 1, episode 13.

3. Fieldnotes, May 11, 2007.

### 35. The Archive and the System

1. These are some of the sources I relied on for this research, in addition to the secondary sources cited in this chapter. An official listing of the city's libraries is at http://www.archivoybibliotecanacionales.org.bo/abnb/index.php?option=com_content&view=article&id=51&Itemid=93, accessed June 22, 2013.

2. María Isabel Mena M., "Datos de las Calles," *Opinion*, Cochabamba, Bolivia, September 19, 2010, 3.

3. See, e.g., Irma Miriam Chugar Zubieta, "La preservación y revitilización del Centro Histórico como lugar de memoria urbana: El caso de la ciudad de Cochabamba, Bolivia," CONHISREMI, *Revista Universitaria de Investigación y Diálogo Académico* 5, no. 3 (2009): 1–19.

4. Fieldnotes, June 13, 2007.

5. I refer here to the literature on governmentality, which derives from Foucault, with specific reference to street vendors: see Ritajyoti Bandyopadhyay, "Politics of Archiving: Hawkers and Pavement Dwellers in Calcutta," *Dialectical Anthropology* 35 (2011): 295–316; Michel Foucault, "Governmentality," in *The Foucault Effect: Studies in Governmentality*, ed. Graham Burchell, Colin Gordon, and Peter Miller (Chicago: University of Chicago Press, 1991), 87–104.

6. Ellen Moodie writes about "unknowing" in the context of wartime and postwar violence: Ellen Moodie, *El Salvador in the Aftermath of Peace* (Philadelphia: University of Pennsylvania Press, 2010).

7. On legibility, see James C. Scott, *Seeing like a State: How Certain Schemes to Improve the Human Condition Have Failed* (New Haven, CT: Yale University Press, 1998); Michel-Rolph Trouillot, "The Anthropology of the State in the Age of Globalization: Close Encounters of the Deceptive Kind," *Current Anthropology* 42, no. 1 (2001): 125–38.

8. Oren Yiftachel, "Theoretical Notes on 'Gray Cities': The Coming of Urban Apartheid?" *Planning Theory* 8, no. 1 (2009): 88–100.

9. Nicole Fabricant, *Mobilizing Bolivia's Displaced: Indigenous Politics and the Struggle over Land* (Chapel Hill: University of North Carolina Press, 2012); Linda Farthing and Benjamin Kohl, *Evo's Bolivia: Continuity and Change* (Austin: University of Texas Press, 2014).

10. Interview with the Juan Carlos Quintana (a pseudonym), April 9, 2007.

11. Similar things are said of street vendors elsewhere. On Bogotá, Colombia, see Stacey Hunt, "Citizenship's Place: The State's Creation of Public Space and Street Vendors' Culture of Informality in Bogotá, Colombia," *Environment and Planning D: Society and Space* 27 (2009): 331–51.

12. Interview with Don Arturo, April 14, 2007.

13. Interview with Don Fausto, June 6, 2007; interview conducted by Ruth Ordoñez.


## 36. Goodbyes

1. Fieldnotes, May 31, 2007.

2. Unlike other cities in South America, Cochabamba has yet to embark on a major campaign to relocate street commerce to other parts of the city, perhaps because it was moved out of the heart of the city center in the nineteenth century and early twentieth century. On relocation plans and the responses to them in Cuzco, see Rosemary D. F. Bromley and Peter Mackie, "Displacement and the New Spaces for Informal Trade in the Latin American City Centre," *Urban Studies* 46, no. 7 (2009): 1485–506; Linda J. Seligmann, "The Politics of Urban Space among Street Vendors of Cusco, Peru," in *Street Economies in the Urban Global South*, ed. Karen Tranberg Hansen, Walter Little, and B. Lynne Milgram (Santa Fe, NM: School of American Research Press, 2013).

3. Some of the photographs in that book are also included in this book, but the text here is original. I do not reproduce the language, the tables, or the approach of those books, as they had a very different purpose and style from this one.

4. Fieldnotes, May 1, 2007.

5. Fieldnotes, March 23, 2007.


## 37. Insecurity and Informality

1. Deborah Poole, *Unruly Order: Violence, Power, and Cultural Identity in the High Provinces of Southern Peru* (Boulder, CO: Westview, 1994).

2. Veena Das and Deborah Poole, *Anthropology in the Margins of the State* (Santa Fe, NM: School of American Research Press, 2004).

3. Compare with Enrique Desmond Arias, "The Dynamics of Criminal Governance: Networks and Social Order in Rio de Janeiro." *Journal of Latin American Studies* 38, no. 2

(May 2006): 293–325. See also Jean Comaroff and John L. Comaroff, *Law and Disorder in the Postcolony* (Chicago: University of Chicago Press, 2006); Carolyn Nordstrom, "Shadows and Sovereigns," *Theory, Culture, and Society* 17, no. 4 (2000): 35–54.

4. On urban enclaves, see Nezar AlSayyad and Ananya Roy, "Medieval Modernity: On Citizenship and Urbanism in a Global Era," *Space and Polity* 10, no. 1 (2006): 3. The authors compare the contemporary city, with its division into sub-units controlled by different sovereigns, to the medieval city and its forms of rule. These are different sorts of urban enclaves from those described by such authors as Teresa Caldeira and Setha Low, who focus on elites' efforts to wall themselves off from a broader public: see Teresa P.R. Caldeira, *City of Walls: Crime, Segregation, and Citizenship in São Paulo* (Berkeley: University of California Press, 2000); Setha M. Low, "Urban Fear: Building the Fortress City," *City and Society* 9, no. 1 (1997): 53–71. See also James Holston and Arjun Appadurai, "Introduction: Cities and Citizenship," in *Cities and Citizenship*, ed. James Holston (Durham, NC: Duke University Press, 1999), 13.

5. Ananya Roy, "Slumdog Cities: Rethinking Subaltern Urbanism," *International Journal of Urban and Regional Research* 35, no. 2 (2011): 223–38.

6. Asef Bayat, *Life as Politics: How Ordinary People Change the Middle East* (Stanford, CA: Stanford University Press, 2009).

7. See, e.g., John C. Cross, *Informal Politics: Street Vendors and the State in Mexico City* (Stanford, CA: Stanford University Press, 1998); Sian Lazar, *El Alto, Rebel City: Self and Citizenship in Andean Bolivia* (Durham, NC: Duke University Press, 2008); Walter E. Little, "Getting Organized: Political and Economic Dilemmas for Maya Handicrafts Vendors," *Latin American Perspectives* 32, no. 5 (2005): 80–100.

8. Compare with Griet Steel, "Whose Paradise? Itinerant Street Vendors' Individual and Collective Practices of Political Agency in the Tourist Streets of Cusco, Peru," *International Journal of Urban and Regional Research* 36, no. 5 (2012): 1007–21.

9. Bayat, *Life as Politics*.

10. Partha Chatterjee, *The Politics of the Governed: Reflections on Popular Politics in Most of the World* (New York: Columbia University Press, 2004), 40.

11. Roy, "Slumdog Cities," 228.

12. Asef Bayat, "Radical Religion and the Habitus of the Dispossessed: Does Islamic Militancy Have an Urban Ecology?" *International Journal of Urban and Regional Research* 31, no. 3 (2007): 579–90.

13. Bayat, "Radical Religion and the Habitus of the Dispossessed," 579.

14. Lila Abu-Lughod, "The Romance of Resistance: Tracing Transformations of Power through Bedouin Women," *American Ethnologist* 17, no. 1 (1990): 41–55.

15. Roy, "Slumdog Cities."

16. Hernando de Soto, *The Other Path: The Invisible Revolution in the Third World* (New York: Harper and Row, 1989). See Ananya Roy, "Urban Informality: Toward an Epistemology of Planning," *Journal of the American Planning Association* 71, no. 2 (2005): 147–58.

17. Daniella Gandolfo, "Formless: A Day at Lima's Office of Formalization," *Cultural Anthropology* 28, no. 2 (2013): 295.

18. See the discussion in Ann Varley, "Postcolonialising Informality?" *Environment and Planning D: Society and Space* 31, no. 1 (2013): 7–8. For differing viewpoints, see Ilda Lindell, "Between Exit and Voice: Informality and the Spaces of Popular Agency," *African Studies Quarterly* 11, nos. 2–3 (2010): 1–11. Although seemingly radical, understanding informality as revolution was an important component of de Soto's analysis, as well.

19. Jonathan Shapiro Anjaria, "The Politics of Illegality: Mumbai Hawkers, Public Space and the Everyday Life of the Law," in *Street Vendors in the Global Urban Economy*, ed. Sharit Bhowmik (London: Routledge, 2010), 82.

20. Anjaria, "The Politics of Illegality."

21. Roy, "Slumdog Cities," 230.

22. Sian Lazar, "A Desire to Formalize Work? Comparing Trade Union Strategies in Bolivia and Argentina," *Anthropology of Work Review* 33, no. 1 (2012): 19. See also Sian Lazar, "Disjunctive Comparison: Citizenship and Trade Unionism in Bolivia and Argentina," *Journal of the Royal Anthropological Institute* 18 (2012): 349–68.

23. See Ritajyoti Bandyopadhyay, "Politics of Archiving: Hawkers and Pavement Dwellers in Calcutta," *Dialectical Anthropology* 35 (2011): 295–316.

24. Bayat, *Life as Politics*.

### Epilogue

1. I write about this experience in Daniel M. Goldstein, *Outlawed: Between Security and Rights in a Bolivian City* (Durham, NC: Duke University Press, 2012), chap. 2. The ISL program concluded in 2012.

2. I thank an anonymous reviewer for pointing me in this direction.

# References

Abercrombie, Thomas A. "To Be Indian, to Be Bolivian: 'Ethnic' and 'National' Discourses of Identity." In *Nation-States and Indians in Latin America*, ed. Greg Urban and Joel Sherzer, 95–130. Austin: University of Texas Press, 1991.

Abrams, Philip. "Notes on the Difficulty of Studying the State." *Journal of Historical Sociology* 1 (1977): 58–89.

Abu-Lughod, Lila. "The Romance of Resistance: Tracing Transformations of Power through Bedouin Women." *American Ethnologist* 17, no. 1 (1990): 41–55.

Agadjanian, Victor. "Competition and Cooperation among Working Women in the Context of Structural Adjustment: The Case of Street Vendors in La Paz-El Alto, Bolivia." *Journal of Developing Societies* 18, nos. 2–3 (2002): 259–85.

Agamben, Giorgio. *State of Exception*, trans. K. Atell. Chicago: University of Chicago Press, 2005.

Agar, Michael H. *The Professional Stranger: An Informal Introduction to Ethnography*. New York: Academic Press, 1980.

Albó C., Xavier, and Franz X. Barrios Suvelza. *Por una Bolivia plurinacional e intercultural con autonomías. Documento de trabajo: Informe Nacional sobre Desarrollo Humano en Bolivia*. La Paz: United Nations Development Program, 2011.

Albro, Robert. "Confounding Cultural Citizenship and Constitutional Reform in Bolivia." *Latin American Perspectives* 37, no. 3 (2010): 71–90.

———. "Violence and the Everyday in Early Twenty-First Century Latin America." In *Religious Responses to Violence: Human Rights in Latin America Past and Present*, ed. Alexander Wilde. Notre Dame, IN: University of Notre Dame Press, forthcoming.

———. "'The Water Is Ours, Carajo!' Deep Citizenship in Bolivia's Water War." In *Social Movements: An Anthropological Reader*, ed. June Nash, 249–71. London: Basil Blackwell, 2005.

AlSayyad, Nezar. "Urban Informality as a 'New' Way of Life." In *Urban Informality: Transnational Perspectives from the Middle East, Latin America, and South Asia*, ed. Ananya Roy and Nezar AlSayyad, 7–30. Lanham, MD: Lexington, 2004.

AlSayyad, Nezar, and Ananya Roy. "Medieval Modernity: On Citizenship and Urbanism in a Global Era." *Space and Polity* 10, no. 1 (2006): 1–20.

Anjaria, Jonathan Shapiro. "Ordinary States: Everyday Corruption and the Politics of Space in Mumbai." *American Ethnologist* 38, no. 1 (2011): 58–72.

———. "The Politics of Illegality: Mumbai Hawkers, Public Space and the Everyday Life of the Law." In *Street Vendors in the Global Urban Economy*, ed. Sharit Bhowmik, 69–86. London: Routledge, 2010.

Aretxaga, Begoña. "Maddening States." *Annual Review of Anthropology* 32 (2003): 393–410.

Arias, Enrique Desmond. "The Dynamics of Criminal Governance: Networks and Social Order in Rio de Janeiro." *Journal of Latin American Studies* 38, no. 2 (May 2006): 293–325.

Arias, Enrique Desmond, and Daniel M. Goldstein, eds. *Violent Democracies in Latin America*. Durham, NC: Duke University Press, 2010.

Arizpe, Lourdes. *Indígenas en la Ciudad de México: El caso de las "Marías."* Mexico City: Sep/Setentas, 1975.

Babb, Florence E. *Between Field and Cooking Pot: The Political Economy of Marketwomen in Peru*, rev. ed. Austin: University of Texas Press, 1998.

———. "Street Economies in the Urban Global South: Where Are They Heading and Where Are We Heading." In *Street Economies in the Urban Global South*, ed. Karen Tranberg Hansen, Walter E. Little, and B. Lynne Milgram, 201–12. Santa Fe, NM: School of Advanced Research Press, 2013.

Bailey, John, and Lucía Dammert. "Public Security and Police Reform in the Americas." In *Public Security and Police Reform in the Americas*, ed. John Bailey and Lucía Dammert, 1–23. Pittsburgh: University of Pittsburgh Press, 2006.

Bandyopadhyay, Ritajyoti. "Politics of Archiving: Hawkers and Pavement Dwellers in Calcutta." *Dialectical Anthropology* 35 (2011): 295–316.

Bayat, Asef. *Life as Politics: How Ordinary People Change the Middle East*. Stanford, CA: Stanford University Press, 2009.

———. "Radical Religion and the Habitus of the Dispossessed: Does Islamic Militancy Have an Urban Ecology?" *International Journal of Urban and Regional Research* 31, no. 3 (2007): 579–90.

Benjamin, Walter. *Reflections: Essays, Aphorisms and Autobiographical Writings*. New York: Schocken, 1978.

Benton, Lauren. "Beyond Legal Pluralism: Towards a New Approach to Law in the Informal Sector." *Social and Legal Studies* 3 (1994): 223–42.

Bestor, Theodore C. *Tsukiji: The Fish Market at the Center of the World*. Berkeley: University of California Press, 2004.

Bigenho, Michelle. "Sensing Locality in Yura: Rituals of Carnival and of the Bolivian State." *American Ethnologist* 26, no. 4 (1999): 957–80.

Biolsi, Thomas, and Larry J. Zimmerman, eds. *Indians and Anthropologists: Vine Deloria, Jr., and the Critique of Anthropology*. Tucson: University of Arizona Press, 1997.

Blanes, José, and Gonzalo Flores. *Factores Poblacionales en el Desarrollo Regional de Cochabamba*. La Paz: Ediciones CERES, 1972.

Bobea, Lilian. "The Emergence of the Democratic Citizen Security Policy in the Dominican Republic." *Policing and Society* 22, no. 1 (2011): 57–75.

"Bolivia Makes Child Labor Legal, In an Attempt to Make It Safer," *National Public Radio*, July 30, 2014, Washington, DC, http://www.npr.org/2014/07/30/336361778/bolivia-makes-child-labor-legal-in-an-attempt-to-make-it-safer, accessed April 23, 2015.

Boo, Katherine. *Behind the Beautiful Forevers: Life, Death, and Hope in a Mumbai Undercity*. New York: Random House, 2012. Kindle edition.

Bott, Sarah, Alessandra Guedes, Mary Goodwin, and Jennifer Adams Mendoza. *Violence against Women in Latin America and the Caribbean: A Comparative Analysis of Population-Based Data from 12 Countries*. Washington, DC: Pan American Health Organization, 2012.

Brabazon, Honor, and Jeffrey R. Webber. "Evo Morales and the MST in Bolivia: Continuities and Discontinuities in Agrarian Reform." *Journal of Agrarian Change* 14, no. 3 (2013): 435–65.

Bromley, Ray. "Rethinking the Public Realm: On Vending, Popular Protest, and Street Politics." In *Street Economies in the Urban Global South*, ed. Karen Tranberg Hansen, Walter E. Little, and B. Lynne Milgram, 17–28. Santa Fe, NM: School of Advanced Research Press, 2013.

———. "Street Vending and Public Policy: A Global Review." *International Journal of Sociology and Social Policy* 20, nos. 1–2 (2000): 1–29.

Bromley, Rosemary D. F., and Peter Mackie. "Displacement and the New Spaces for Informal Trade in the Latin American City Centre." *Urban Studies* 46, no. 7 (2009): 1485–506.

Bubandt, Nils. "Vernacular Security: The Politics of Feeling Safe in Global, National, and Local Worlds." *Security Dialogue* 36, no. 3 (2005): 275–96.

Buechler, Hans C., and Judith-Maria Buechler. *Manufacturing against the Odds: Small-Scale Producers in an Andean City*. Boulder, CO: Westview, 1992.

Buechler, Judith-Maria. "The Dynamics of the Market in La Paz, Bolivia." *Urban Anthropology* 7, no. 4 (1974): 343–59.

Bunster, Ximena, and Elsa M. Chaney. *Sellers and Servants: Working Women in Lima, Peru*. New York: Praeger, 1985.

Burrell, Jennifer. "In and Out of Rights: Security, Migration, and Human Rights Talk in Guatemala." *Journal of Latin American and Caribbean Anthropology* 15, no. 1 (2010): 90–115.

Buur, Lars. "The Sovereign Outsourced: Local Justice and Violence in Port Elizabeth." In *Sovereign Bodies: Citizens, Migrants, and States in the Postcolonial World*, ed. Thomas Blom Hansen and Finn Stepputat, 192–217. Princeton, NJ: Princeton University Press, 2005.

Buzan, Barry, Ole Waever, and Jaap de Wilde. *Security: A New Framework for Analysis*. Boulder, CO: Lynne Reiner, 1998.

Caldeira, Teresa P.R. *City of Walls: Crime, Segregation, and Citizenship in São Paulo*. Berkeley: University of California Press, 2001.

Calderón, Fernando, and Alberto Rivera. *La Cancha: Una gran feria campesina en la ciudad de Cochabamba*. Cochabamba, Bolivia: Centro de Estudios de la Realidad Económica y Social, 1984.

Canessa, Andrew. "Conflict, Claim and Contradiction in the New 'Indigenous' State of Bolivia." *Critique of Anthropology* 34, no. 2 (2014): 153–73.

———. "Fear and Loathing on the *Kharisiri* Trail: Alterity and Identity in the Andes." *Journal of the Royal Anthropological Institute* 6 (2000): 705–20.

———. *Intimate Indigeneities: Race, Sex, and History in the Small Spaces of Andean Life*. Durham, NC: Duke University Press, 2012.

Cárdenas, José Arturo. "Evo Morales se encamina a una nueva reelección avalado por la bonanza económica." *El Faro*, October 8, 2014, San Salvador, El Salvador, http://www.elfaro.net/es/201410/internacionales/16051/Evo-Morales-se-encamina-a-una-nueva-reelección-avalado-por-la-bonanza-económica.htm, accessed April 23, 2015.

Castells, Manuel. *The City and the Grassroots: A Cross-Cultural Theory of Urban Social Movements*. Berkeley: University of California Press, 1985.

Castells, Manuel, and Alejandro Portes. "World Underneath: The Origins, Dynamics, and Effects of the Informal Economy." In *The Informal Economy: Studies in Advanced and Less Developed Countries*, ed. Alejandro Portes, Manuel Castells, and Lauren A. Benton, 11–37. Baltimore: Johns Hopkins University Press, 1989.

Cato Institute. "Hernando de Soto's Biography." n.d. http://www.cato.org/friedman-prize/hernando-desoto/biography, accessed September 12, 2013.

Cavalcanti, Mariana. "Threshold Markets: The Production of Real-Estate Value between the 'Favela' and the 'Pavement.'" In *Cities from Scratch: Poverty and Informality in Urban Latin America*, ed. Brodwyn Fischer, Bryann McCann, and Javier Auyero, 208–37. Durham, NC: Duke University Press, 2014.

Cebula, Richard, and Edgar L. Feige. "America's Underground Economy: Measuring the Size, Growth and Determinants of Income Tax Evasion in the U.S.," 2011. http://www.ssc.wisc.edu/econ/archive/wp2011-1.pdf, accessed June 8, 2013.

Central Intelligence Agency. 2013. *CIA World Factbook*. https://www.cia.gov/library/publications/the-world-factbook/geos/bl.html, accessed June 7, 2013.

Centro de Investigación: Seguridad y Democracia. "Comerciantes Ambulantes: La Doble Cara de la (In)Visibilidad." *Opinión*, Cochabamba, Bolivia, March 29, 2007, A5.

Chalfin, Brenda. *Neoliberal Frontiers: An Ethnography of Sovereignty in West Africa*. Chicago: University of Chicago Press, 2010. Kindle edition.

――――. "Public Things, Excremental Politics, and the Infrastructure of Bare Life in Ghana's City of Tema." *American Ethnologist* 41, no. 1 (2014): 92–109.

Chatterjee, Partha. *The Politics of the Governed: Reflections on Popular Politics in Most of the World*. New York: Columbia University Press, 2004.

Chugar Zubieta, Irma Miriam. "La preservación y revitilización del Centro Histórico como lugar de memoria urbana: El caso de la ciudad de Cochabamba, Bolivia." *CONHISREMI, Revista Universitaria de Investigación y Diálogo Académico* 5, no. 3 (2009): 1–19.

Clark, Gracia. *African Market Women: Seven Life Stories from Ghana*. Bloomington: Indiana University Press, 2010.

――――. "Mothering, Work, and Gender in Urban Asante Ideology and Practice." *American Anthropologist* 101, no. 4 (1999): 717–29.

――――. *Onions Are My Husband: Survival and Accumulation by West African Market Women*. Chicago: University of Chicago Press, 1994.

――――. *Traders versus the State: Anthropological Approaches to Unofficial Economies*. Boulder, CO: Westview, 1988.

Coen, Stephanie E., Nancy A. Ross, and Sarah Turner. "Without *Tiendas* It's a Dead Neighborhood: The Socio-economic Importance of Small Trade Stores in Cochabamba, Bolivia." *Cities* 25 (2008): 327–39.

Comaroff, Jean, and John L. Comaroff, eds. *Law and Disorder in the Postcolony*. Chicago: University of Chicago Press, 2006.

Cox, Wendell. "World Urban Areas Population and Density: A 2012 Update," May 3, 2012. http://www.newgeography.com/content/002808-world-urban-areas-population -and-density-a-2012-update, accessed July 2, 2013.

Coy, Peter. "The Great Recession: An 'Affair' to Remember." *Bloomberg Businessweek*, October 11, 2012. http://www.businessweek.com/articles/2012–10–11/the-great -recession-an-affair-to-remember, accessed October 1, 2014.

Cross, John C. *Informal Politics: Street Vendors and the State in Mexico City*. Stanford, CA: Stanford University Press, 1998.

Cross, John C., and Marina Karides. "Capitalism, Modernity, and the 'Appropriate' Use of Space." In *Street Entrepreneurs: People, Place and Politics in Local and Global Perspective*, ed. John Cross and Alfonso Morales, 19–35. London: Routledge, 2007.

D'Andrade, Roy. "Moral Models in Anthropology." *Current Anthropology* 36, no. 3 (1995): 399–408.

D'Orbigny, Alcides. *Viaje a la América Meridional*, vol. 3. La Paz: Plural-Instituto Francés de Estudios Andinos, 2002.

DaMatta, Roberto. *Carnivals, Rogues and Heroes: An Interpretation of the Brazilian Dilemma*. Notre Dame: University of Notre Dame Press, 1991.

Dandler, Jorge H. "Campesinado y reforma agraria en Cochabamba (1952–1953): Dinámica de un movimiento campesino en Bolivia." In *Bolivia: La fuerza histórica del campesinado*, ed. Fernando Calderon and Jorge Dandler, 135–204. Geneva: United Nations Research Institute for Social Development and Centro de Estudios de la Realidad Económica y Social, 1984.

————. *El sindicalismo campesino en Bolivia: Los cambios estructurales en Ucureña*. Mexico City: Instituto Indigenista Interamericano, 1969.

Dandler, Jorge H., José Blanes, Julio Prudencio, and Jorge Muñoz. *El Sistema Agroalimentario en Bolivia*. La Paz: Centro de Estudios de la Realidad Económica y Social, 1987.

Das, Veena, and Deborah Poole, eds. *Anthropology in the Margins of the State*. Santa Fe, NM: School of American Research Press, 2004.

Datta, Ayona. *The Illegal City: Space, Law and Gender in a Delhi Squatter Settlement*. Surrey, U.K.: Ashgate, 2012.

Davis, Diane E. "Analytical Foundations for the Study of Informality: A Short Introduction." In *Informalidad, Incertidumbre, Metrópolis y Estado: Como Gobernar la Informalización?* ed. Felipe de Alba and Frederic Lesemann, 11–40. Mexico City: Programa Universitario de Estudios sobre la Ciudad–Universidad Nacional Autónoma de México, Institut National de la Recherche Scientifique, and European Institutes for Advanced Study, Collegium de Lyon, 2012.

————. "Modernist Planning and the Foundations of Urban Violence in Latin America." *Built Environment* 40, no. 3 (2014): 376–93.

————. "Socio-Spatial Inequality and Violence in Cities of the Global South: Evidence from Latin America." In *Cities and Inequalities in a Global and Neoliberal World*, ed. Faranak Miraftab, David Wilson, and Ken Salo (London: Routledge, 2015): 75–91.

de Certeau, Michel. *The Pratice of Everyday Life* (1984), trans. Steven F. Rendall. Berkeley: University of California Press, 2011.

de la Cadena, Marisol. *Indigenous Mestizos: The Politics of Race and Culture in Cuzco, Peru, 1919–1991*. Durham, NC: Duke University Press, 2000.

Deloria, Vine, Jr. *Custer Died for Your Sins: An Indian Manifesto*. New York: Macmillan, 1969.

Dent, Alexander S. "Piracy, Circulatory Legitimacy, and Neoliberal Subjectivity in Brazil." *Cultural Anthropology* 27, no. 1 (2012): 28–49.

Derrida, Jacques. *Specters of Marx: The State of the Debt, the Work of Mourning and the New International*. London: Routledge, 1994.

de Soto, Hernando. *The Other Path: The Invisible Revolution in the Third World*. New York: Harper and Row, 1989.

Duneier, Mitchell. *Sidewalk*. New York: Farrar, Straus and Giroux, 2000.

"Evo decreta doble aguinaldo para el sector público y privado." *El Deber*, November 20, 2013, Santa Cruz de la Sierra, Bolivia. http://www.eldeber.com.bo/evo-decreta-doble-aguinaldo-para-el-sector-publico-y-privado/131120104222, accessed August 23, 2014.

Fabian, Johannes. "Ethnographic Objectivity: From Rigor to Vigor." In *Anthropology with an Attitude: Critical Essays*, 11–32. Stanford, CA: Stanford University Press, 2001.

Fabricant, Nicole. *Mobilizing Bolivia's Displaced: Indigenous Politics and the Struggle over Land*. Chapel Hill: University of North Carolina Press, 2012.

Fabricant, Nicole, and Bret Gustafson, eds. *Remapping Bolivia: Resources, Territory, and Indigeneity in a Plurinational State*. Santa Fe: School of Advanced Research, 2011.

Farthing, Linda, and Benjamin Kohl. *Evo's Bolivia: Continuity and Change*. Austin: University of Texas Press, 2014.

Fassin, Didier. "True Lives, Real Lives: Revisiting the Boundaries between Ethnography and Fiction." *American Ethnologist* 41, no. 1 (2014): 40–55.

Favero, Paolo. "Phantasms in a 'Starry' Place: Space and Identification in a Central New Delhi Market." *Cultural Anthropology* 18, no. 4 (2003): 551–84.

Ferguson, James. *Global Shadows: Africa in the Neoliberal World Order.* Durham, NC: Duke University Press, 2006.

Fernandes, Edésio, and Ann Varley, eds. *Illegal Cities: Law and Urban Change in Developing Countries.* London: Zed, 1998.

Fischer, Brodwyn. "A Century in the Present Tense: Crisis, Politics, and the Intellectual History of Brazil's Informal Cities." In *Cities from Scratch: Poverty and Informality in Urban Latin America,* ed. Brodwyn Fischer, Bryan McCann, and Javier Auyero, 9–67. Durham, NC: Duke University Press, 2014.

Fischer, Brodwyn, Bryan McCann, and Javier Auyero, eds. *Cities from Scratch: Poverty and Informality in Urban Latin America.* Durham, NC: Duke University Press, 2014.

Fishman, Robert. *Urban Utopias in the Twentieth Century: Ebenezer Howard, Frank Lloyd Wright and Le Corbusier.* Cambridge, MA: MIT Press, 1982.

Foucault, Michel. "Governmentality." In *The Foucault Effect: Studies in Governmentality,* ed. Graham Burchell, Colin Gordon, and Peter Miller, 87–104. Chicago: University of Chicago Press, 1991.

Fowler, Michael Ross, and Julie Marie Bunck. *Law, Power, and the Sovereign State: The Evolution and Application of the Concept of Sovereignty.* University Park: Penn State University Press, 1995.

Freeman, Carla. "The 'Reputation' of Neoliberalism." *American Ethnologist* 34, no. 2 (2007): 252–67.

Frühling, Hugo H. "Police Reform and the Process of Democratization." In *Crime and Violence in Latin America: Citizen Security, Democracy, and the State,* ed. Hugo H. Frühling, Joseph S. Tulchin, and Heather A. Golding, 15–44. Washington, DC: Woodrow Wilson Center Press, 2003.

Gaceta Oficial de Bolivia. *Registro del Comerciante Ambulante, Decreto-Ley de 4 de abril de 1940. Leyes y Decretos Supremos que Modifican el Código Mercantil.* La Paz, 1940.

Gal, Susan. "A Semiotics of the Public/Private Distinction." *Differences* 13, no. 1 (2002): 77–95.

Galemba, Rebecca B. "Informal and Illicit Entrepreneurs: Fighting for a Place in the Neoliberal Economic Order." *Anthropology of Work Review* 29, no. 2 (2008): 19–25.

Gandolfo, Daniella. *The City at Its Limits: Taboo, Transgression, and Urban Renewal in Lima.* Chicago: University of Chicago Press, 2009.

———. "Formless: A Day at Lima's Office of Formalization." *Cultural Anthropology* 28, no. 2 (2013): 278–98.

Garson, Barbara. "Before the Great Recession, There Was the Long Recession." *Mother Jones,* April 9, 2013. http://www.motherjones.com/politics/2013/04/long-recession-before-great-recession, accessed October 1, 2014.

Geertz, Clifford. *Peddlers and Princes: Social Development and Economic Change in Two Indonesian Towns.* Chicago: University of Chicago Press, 1968.

Ghertner, Asher. "Analysis of New Legal Discourse behind Delhi's Slum Demolitions." *Economic and Political Weekly*, vol. 17, May (2008), 57–66.

———. "Calculating without Numbers: Aesthetic Governmentality in Delhi's Slums." *Economy and Society* 39, no. 2 (2010): 185–217.

Gibson-Graham, J. K. *A Postcapitalist Politics*. Minneapolis: University of Minnesota Press, 2006.

———. "Diverse Economies: Performative Practices for 'Other Worlds.'" *Progress in Human Geography* 32, no. 5 (2008): 613–32.

Gilbert, Alan. "Love in the Time of Enhanced Capital Flows: Reflections on the Links between Liberalization and Informality." In *Urban Informality: Transnational Perspectives from the Middle East, Latin America, and South Asia*, ed. Ananya Roy and Nezar AlSayyad, 33–66. Lanham, MD: Lexington, 2004.

Gill, Lesley. *Precarious Dependencies: Gender, Class and Domestic Service in Bolivia*. New York: Columbia University Press, 1994.

Global Sherpa. "World Cities," n.d. http://www.globalsherpa.org/cities-world-city, accessed May 8, 2013.

Godoy, Angelina Snodgrass. *Popular Injustice: Violence, Community, and Law in Latin America*. Stanford, CA: Stanford University Press, 2006.

Godoy, Ricardo, and Mario De Franco. "High Inflation and Bolivian Agriculture." *Journal of Latin American Studies* 24, no. 3 (1992): 617–37.

Goldstein, Daniel M. "Citizen Security and Human Security in Latin America." In *Routledge Handbook of Latin American Security Studies*, ed. David R. Mares and Arie M. Kacowicz, 138–48. London: Routledge, 2016.

———. "Color-Coded Sovereignty and the Men in Black: Private Security in a Bolivian Marketplace." *Conflict and Society*, forthcoming.

———. "Decolonializing 'Actually Existing Neoliberalism.'" *Social Anthropology/Anthropologie Sociale* 20, no. 3 (2012): 304–9.

———. "Flexible Justice: Neoliberal Violence and Self-Help Security in Bolivia." *Critique of Anthropology* 25 (2005): 389–411.

———. "Human Rights as Culprit, Human Rights as Victim: Rights and Security in the State of Exception." In *The Practice of Human Rights: Tracking Law between the Global and the Local*, ed. Mark Goodale and Sally Engle Merry, 49–77. Cambridge: Cambridge University Press, 2007.

———. *Outlawed: Between Security and Rights in a Bolivian City*. Durham, NC: Duke University Press, 2012.

———. "Security and the Culture Expert: Dilemmas of an Engaged Anthropology." *PoLAR* 33, no. 1 (2010): 126–42.

———. *The Spectacular City: Violence and Performance in Urban Bolivia*. Durham, NC: Duke University Press, 2004.

———. "Towards a Critical Anthropology of Security." *Current Anthropology* 51, no. 4 (2010): 487–517.

Goldstein, Daniel M., with Gloria Achá, Eric Hinojosa, and Theo Roncken. "La Mano Dura and the Violence of Civil Society in Bolivia." *Social Analysis* 51, no. 2 (2007): 43–63.

Goodale, Mark. *Dilemmas of Modernity: Bolivian Encounters with Law and Liberalism.* Stanford, CA: Stanford University Press, 2008.

Goodale, Mark, and Sally Engle Merry, eds. *The Practice of Human Rights: Tracking Law between the Global and the Local.* Cambridge: Cambridge University Press, 2007.

Goodale, Mark, and Nancy Postero, eds. *Neoliberalism, Interrupted: Social Change and Contested Governance in Contemporary Latin America.* Stanford, CA: Stanford University Press, 2013.

Gotkowitz, Laura. "Trading Insults: Honor, Violence, and the Gendered Culture of Commerce in Cochabamba, Bolivia, 1870s–1950s." *Hispanic American Historical Review* 83, no. 1 (2003): 83–118.

Grugel, Jean, and Pia Riggirozzi. "Post-neoliberalism in Latin America: Rebuilding and Reclaiming the State after Crisis." *Development and Change* 43, no. 1 (2012): 1–21.

Guha-Khasnobis, Basudeb, Ravi Kanbur, and Elinor Ostrom. "Beyond Formality and Informality." In *Linking the Formal and Informal Economy: Concepts and Policies,* ed. Basudeb Guha-Khasnobis, Ravi Kanbur, and Elinor Ostrom, 1–19. Oxford: Oxford University Press, 2006.

Gupta, Akhil. "Narratives of Corruption: Anthropological and Fictional Accounts of the Indian State." *Ethnography* 6, no. 1 (2012): 5–34.

———. *Red Tape: Bureaucracy, Structural Violence, and Poverty in India.* Durham, NC: Duke University Press, 2012.

Gustafson, Bret D. *New Languages of the State: Indigenous Resurgence and the Politics of Knowledge in Bolivia.* Durham, NC: Duke University Press, 2009.

Guzman, Augusto. *Cochabamba.* Cochabamba, Bolivia: Editorial "Los Amigos del Libro," 1972.

Hale, Charles R., ed. *Engaging Contradictions: Theory, Politics, and Methods of Activist Scholarship.* Berkeley: University of California Press, 2008.

Hale, Charles R., and Lynn Stephen, eds. *Otros Saberes: Collaborative Research on Indigenous and Afro-Descendant Cultural Politics.* Santa Fe, NM: School of Advanced Research Press, 2013.

Hansen, Karen Tranberg, and Mariken Vaa, eds. *Reconsidering Informality: Perspectives from Urban Africa.* Oslo: Nordiska Afrikainstitutet, 2004.

Hansen, Karen Tranberg, Walter E. Little, and B. Lynne Milgram. "Introduction." In *Street Economies in the Urban Global South,* ed. Karen Tranberg Hansen, Walter E. Little, and B. Lynne Milgram, 3–16. Santa Fe, NM: School of Advanced Research Press, 2013.

———, eds. *Street Economies in the Urban Global South.* Santa Fe, NM: School of Advanced Research Press, 2013.

Hansen, Karen V. "Feminist Conceptions of Public and Private: A Critical Analysis." *Berkeley Journal of Sociology* 32 (1987): 105–28.

Hansen, Thomas Blom, and Finn Stepputat. "Sovereignty Revisited." *Annual Review of Anthropology* 35 (2006): 295–315.

Hansen, Thomas Blom, and Oskar Verkaaik. "Introduction—Urban Charisma: On Everyday Mythologies in the City." *Critique of Anthropology* 29, no. 1 (2009): 5–26.

Hardoy, Jorge E. *Urbanization in Latin America: Approaches and Issues*. Garden City, NY: Anchor, 1975.

Harris, Olivia. "Ethnic Identity and Market Relations: Indians and Mestizos in the Andes." In *Ethnicity, Markets and Migration in the Andes: At the Crossroads of History and Anthropology*, ed. Brooke Larson and Olivia Harris with Enrique Tandeter, 351–90. Durham, NC: Duke University Press, 1995.

Hart, Keith. "Informal Economy." In *The New Palgrave: A Dictionary of Economics*, vol. 2, ed. John Eatwell, Murray Milgate, and Peter Newman, 845–46. London: Macmillan, 1987.

———. "Informal Income Opportunities and Urban Employment in Ghana." *Journal of Modern African Studies* 11, no. 1 (1973): 61–89.

Harvey, David. *The New Imperialism*. Oxford: Oxford University Press, 2003.

———. *Rebel Cities: From the Right to the City to the Urban Revolution*. London: Verso, 2013.

———. "The Right to the City." *New Left Review* 53 (September–October 2003): 23–40.

Hecht, Tobias. *At Home in the Street: Street Children of Northeast Brazil*. Cambridge: Cambridge University Press, 1998.

Henry J. Kaiser Family Foundation. "Urban Population (Percent of Total Population Living in Urban Areas)," n.d. http://kff.org/global-indicator/urban-population, accessed May 6, 2013.

Heyman, Josiah McC., and Alan Smart. "States and Illegal Practices: An Overview." In *States and Illegal Practices*, ed. Josiah McC. Heyman, 1–24. Oxford: Berg, 1999.

Hirth, Kenneth, and Joanne Pillsbury. "Redistribution and Markets in Andean South America." *Current Anthropology* 54, no. 5 (2013): 642–47.

Holston, James. "Autoconstruction in Working-Class Brazil." *Cultural Anthropology* 6, no. 4 (1991): 446–63.

———. *Insurgent Citizenship: Disjunctions of Democracy and Modernity in Brazil*. Princeton, NJ: Princeton University Press, 2008.

Holston, James, and Arjun Appadurai. "Introduction: Cities and Citizenship." In *Cities and Citizenship*, ed. James Holston, 1–18. Durham, NC: Duke University Press, 1999.

Humphrey, Caroline. "Sovereignty." In *A Companion to the Anthropology of Politics*, ed. David Nugent and Joan Vincent, 418–36. Oxford: Blackwell, 2004.

Hunt, Stacey. "Citizenship's Place: The State's Creation of Public Space and Street Vendors' Culture of Informality in Bogotá, Colombia." *Environment and Planning D: Society and Space* 27 (2009): 331–51.

Inda, Jonathan Xavier. *Anthropologies of Modernity: Foucault, Governmentality, and Life Politics*. London: Blackwell, 2005.

Instituto Nacional de Estadística. *Censo Nacional de Población y Vivienda*. Cochabamba, Bolivia: Instituto Nacional de Estadística, 1992.

———. *Cochabamba, 2014*. Cochabamba, Bolivia: Instituto Nacional de Estadística, 2014.

Inter-American Commission on Human Rights. *Report on Citizen Security and Human Rights*, Washington, DC, 2009. https://www.oas.org/en/iachr/docs/pdf/ CitizenSec .pdf, accessed February 15, 2014.

Inter-American Development Bank. *Citizen Security in Latin America and the Caribbean: IDB's Comparative Advantage*. Washington, DC: Inter-American Development Bank, 2013.

International Labor Office. *Women and Men in the Informal Economy: A Statistical Picture*. Geneva: International Labor Office, 2002.

Isbell, Billie Jean. *To Defend Ourselves: Ecology and Ritual in an Andean Village*. Prospect Heights, IL: Waveland, 1985.

Jaffe, Rivke. "The Hybrid State: Crime and Citizenship in Urban Jamaica." *American Ethnologist* 40, no. 4 (2013): 734–48.

Kagan, Richard L. *Urban Images of the Hispanic World, 1493–1793*. New Haven, CT: Yale University Press, 2000.

Kaup, Brent Z. "In Spaces of Marginalization: Dispossession, Incorporation, and Resistance in Bolivia." *Journal of World Systems Research* 19, no. 1 (2013): 108–29.

Kent, Alexandra. "Reconfiguring Security: Buddhism and Moral Legitimacy in Cambodia." *Security Dialogue* 37, no. 3 (2006): 343–61.

Kirsch, Stuart. "Anthropology and Advocacy: A Case Study of the Campaign against Ok Tedi Mine." *Critique of Anthropology* 22, no. 2 (2002): 175–200.

Kirschner, Joshua. "Migrants and Citizens: Hygiene Panic and Urban Space in Santa Cruz." In *Remapping Bolivia: Resources, Territory, and Indigeneity in a Plurinational State*, ed. Nicole Fabricant and Bret Gustafson, 96–115. Santa Fe, NM: School of Advanced Research Press, 2011.

Klein, Herbert S. *Bolivia: The Evolution of a Multi-Ethnic Society*, 2d ed. Oxford: Oxford University Press, 1992.

Kohl, Benjamin. "Privatization Bolivian Style: A Cautionary Tale." *International Journal of Urban and Regional Research* 28, no. 4 (2004): 893–908.

———. "Stabilizing Neoliberalism in Bolivia: Popular Participation and Privatization." *Political Geography* 21 (2002): 449–72.

Kohl, Benjamin, and Linda Farthing, "Bolivia: Sachs versus the Facts," 2013. http://upsidedownworld.org/main/bolivia-archives-31/3522-bolivia-sachs-versus-the-facts, accessed June 7, 2013.

Kohl, Benjamin, and Linda Farthing, with Félix Muruchi. *From the Mines to the Streets: A Bolivian Activist's Life*. Austin: University of Texas Press, 2011.

Kroeber, A. L. "The History of the Personality of Anthropology." *American Anthropologist* 61, no. 3 (1959): 398–404.

Kusakabe, Kyoko. *Policy Issues on Street Vending: An Overview of Studies in Thailand, Cambodia, and Mongolia*. Bangkok: International Labour Office, 2006.

Lagos, María L. *Autonomy and Power: The Dynamics of Class and Culture in Rural Bolivia*. Philadelphia: University of Pennsylvania Press, 1994.

Larson, Brooke. *Colonialism and Agrarian Transformation in Bolivia: Cochabamba, 1550–1900*. Princeton, NJ: Princeton University Press, 1988.

Larson, Brooke, and Rosario León. "Markets, Power, and the Politics of Exchange in Tapacarí, c. 1780 and 1980." In *Ethnicity, Markets, and Migration in the Andes: At the Crossroads of History and Anthropology*, ed. Brooke Larson and Olivia Harris, with Enrique Tandeter, 224–56. Durham, NC: Duke University Press, 1995.

Lassiter, Luke Eric. *The Chicago Guide to Collaborative Ethnography*. Chicago: University of Chicago Press, 2005.

Latham, Robert. "Social Sovereignty." *Theory, Culture and Society* 17, no. 4 (2000): 1–18.

Lazar, Sian. "A Desire to Formalize Work? Comparing Trade Union Strategies in Bolivia and Argentina." *Anthropology of Work Review* 33, no. 1 (2012): 15–24.

———. "Disjunctive Comparison: Citizenship and Trade Unionism in Bolivia and Argentina." *Journal of the Royal Anthropological Institute* 18 (2012): 349–68.

———. *El Alto, Rebel City: Self and Citizenship in Andean Bolivia*. Durham, NC: Duke University Press, 2008.

Lazarte, Rolando. "El éxodo hacia la metrópoli. Migración interna y mercado de trabajo." *Nueva Sociedad* 90 (July–August 1987): 70–86.

Ledo, Carmen. *Estudio sobre las Patrones de Migración Interna e Internacional en Bolivia, Informe Nacional sobre Desarrollo Humano*. La Paz: PNUD, 2010.

———. *Proyecciones Demográficas de la Ciudad de Cochabamba*. Ms., 1993. Cochabamba, Bolivia.

Leóns, Madeline Barbara, and Harry Sanabria, eds. *Coca, Cocaine, and the Bolivian Reality*. Albany: State University of New York Press, 1997.

Lewinson, Anne S. "Reading Modernity in Urban Space: Politics, Geography and the Informal Sector of Downtown Dar es Salaam, Tanzania." *City and Society* 10, no. 1 (1998): 205–22.

Lewis, Oscar. "Culture of Poverty." In *On Understanding Poverty: Perspectives from the Social Sciences*, ed. Daniel P. Moynihan, 187–220. New York: Basic, 1969.

Lindell, Ilda. "Between Exit and Voice: Informality and the Spaces of Popular Agency." *African Studies Quarterly* 11, nos. 2–3 (2010): 1–11.

Little, Walter E. "Getting Organized: Political and Economic Dilemmas for Maya Handicrafts Vendors." *Latin American Perspectives* 32, no. 5 (2005): 80–100.

Lomnitz, Larissa Adler. "Informal Exchange Networks in Formal Systems: A Theoretical Model." *American Anthropologist* 90, no. 1 (1988): 442–55.

Losby, Jan L., John F. Else, Marcia E. Kingslow, Elaine L. Edgcomb, Erika T. Malm, and Vivian Kao, eds. *Informal Economy Literature Review*. Newark, DE: ISED Consulting and Aspen Institute, 2002.

Low, Setha M. *On the Plaza: The Politics of Public Space and Culture*. Austin: University of Texas Press, 2000.

———. "Urban Fear: Building the Fortress City." *City and Society* 9, no. 1 (1997): 53–71

Low, Setha M., and Sally Engle Merry. "Engaged Anthropology: Diversity and Dilemmas." *Current Anthropology* 51, supp. 2 (2010): S203–26.

Lugo, Alejandro. "Destabilizing the Masculine, Refocusing 'Gender': Men and the Aura of Authority in Michelle Z. Rosaldo's Work." In *Gender Matters: Rereading Michelle Z. Rosaldo*, ed. Alejandro Lugo and Bill Maurer, 54–89. Ann Arbor: University of Michigan Press, 2000.

Mangin, William. "Latin American Squatter Settlements: A Problem and a Solution." *Latin American Research Review* 2, no. 3 (1967): 65–98.

Marcuse, Peter. "From Critical Urban Theory to the Right to the City." *City* 13, nos. 2–3 (2009): 185–97.

Mares, David R. "The National Security State." In *A Companion to Latin American History*, ed. Thomas H. Holloway, 386–405. London: Blackwell, 2007.

Marquardt, Kairos M. "Participatory Security: Citizen Security, Participation, and the Inequities of Citizenship in Urban Peru." *Bulletin of Latin American Research*, 31, no. 2 (2012): 174–89.

McFarlane, Colin. "Rethinking Informality: Politics, Crisis, and the City." *Planning Theory and Practice* 13, no. 1 (March 2012): 89–108.

Mena M., María Isabel. "Comercio minorista retoma las aceras de la ciudad." *Opinión*, Cochabamba, Bolivia, February 15, 2003. http://www.opinion.com.bo/opinion /articulos/2013/0215/noticias.php?id=86254&calificacion=4, accessed July 24, 2013.

———. "Datos de las calles." *Opinion*, Cochabamba, Bolivia, September 19, 2010, 3.

———. "La chicha ayudó al progreso." *Opinion*, Cochabamba, Bolivia, September 19, 2010, 5.

Mignolo, Walter D. *The Darker Side of Western Modernity: Global Futures, Decolonial Options*. Durham, NC: Duke University Press, 2011.

Millar, Kathleen M. "The Precarious Present: Wageless Labor and Disrupted Life in Rio de Janeiro, Brazil." *Cultural Anthropology* 29, no. 1 (2014): 32–53.

Moodie, Ellen. *El Salvador in the Aftermath of Peace*. Philadelphia: University of Pennsylvania Press, 2010.

Morales, Juan Antonio. "Structural Adjustment and Peasant Agriculture in Bolivia." *Food Policy* 16, no. 1 (1991): 58–66.

Morales, Juan Antonio, and Jeffrey D. Sachs. "Bolivia's Economic Crisis." In *Developing Country Debt and the World Economy*, ed. Jeffrey D. Sachs, 57–80. Chicago: University of Chicago Press, 1989.

Murphy, Edward. "In and Out of the Margins: Urban Land Seizures and Homeownership in Santiago, Chile." In *Cities from Scratch: Poverty and Informality in Urban Latin America*, ed. Brodwyn Fischer, Bryan McCann, and Javier Auyero, 68–101. Durham, NC: Duke University Press, 2014.

Nava, Jhenny B. "Más de la mitad de comerciantes en mercados y calles es informal." *Opinión*, Cochabamba, Bolivia, February 17, 2013, 1–15.

Navía Mier, Alicia. "Todos Santos y el Día de Difuntos tienen características propias." *La Patria*, Oruro, Bolivia, October 30, 2011. http://lapatriaenlinea.com/?t=todos -santos-y-el-dia-de-difuntos-tienen-caracteristicas-propias&nota=87286, accessed August 1, 2013.

Neild, Rachel. "From National Security to Citizen Security: Civil Society and the Evolution of Public Order Debates." Paper written for the International Center for Human Rights and Democratic Development, Montreal, 1999.

Nordstrom, Carolyn. *Global Outlaws: Crime, Money, and Power in the Contemporary World*. Berkeley: University of California Press, 2007.

———. "Shadows and Sovereigns." *Theory, Culture, and Society* 17, no. 4 (2000): 35–54.

Observatorio Nacional de Seguridad Ciudadana. *Trabajando por la seguridad ciudadana: Primera encuesta de victimización, prácticas y percepción sobre violencia y delito en La Paz, El Alto, Cochabamba y Santa Cruz. Primeros resultados* 1(1). Equipo Técnico del Observatorio Nacional de Seguridad Ciudadana, Ministerio de Gobierno, Estado Plurinacional de Bolivia, 2012.

O'Donnell, Guillermo. *Counterpoints: Selected Essays on Authoritarianism and Democratization.* Notre Dame, IN: University of Notre Dame Press, 1999.

Olivera, Oscar. ¡*Cochabamba! Water War in Bolivia.* Cambridge, MA: South End, 2004.

Ong, Aihwa. *Neoliberalism as Exception: Mutations in Citizenship and Sovereignty.* Durham, NC: Duke University Press, 2006.

Organization of American States. *Report on Citizen Security in the Americas 2012.* Washington, DC: Organization of American States, 2012.

Ortner, Sherry B. "Is Female to Male as Nature Is to Culture?" *Feminist Studies* 1, no. 2 (1972): 5–31.

"Pago Único Municipal ya se cobra en mercados." *Los Tiempos*, November 14, 2006, Cochabamba, Bolivia. http://www.lostiempos.com/diario/actualidad/local/20061114 /pago-unico-municipal-ya-se-cobra-en-mercados_25983_25983.html, accessed October 4, 2014.

Pateman, Carole. "Feminist Critiques of the Public/Private Dichotomy." *The Disorder of Women: Democracy, Feminism, and Political Theory*, ed. Carole Pateman, 118–39. Stanford: Stanford University Press, 1989.

Peattie, Lisa R. "'The Concept of Marginality' as Applied to Squatter Settlements." In *Latin American Urban Research, Volume 4: Anthropological Perspectives on Latin American Urbanization*, ed. Wayne A. Cornelius and Felicity M. Trueblood, 101–9. Beverly Hills, CA: Sage, 1974.

———. *The View from the Barrio.* Ann Arbor: University of Michigan Press, 1968.

Pedersen, Morten A., and Martin Holbraad. "Introduction: Times of Security." In *Times of Security: Ethnographies of Fear, Protest and the Future*, ed. Martin Holbraad and Morten A. Pedersen, 1–27. New York: Routledge, 2013.

Penglase, Ben. *Living with Insecurity in a Brazilian Favela: Urban Violence and Daily Life.* New Brunswick, NJ: Rutgers University Press, 2014.

———. "States of Insecurity: Everyday Emergencies, Public Secrets, and Drug Trafficker Power in a Brazilian Favela." *PoLAR* 32, no. 1 (2009): 47–63.

Perelman, Mariano D. "Trabajar, pedir, vender. El caso de los vendedores ambulantes en trenes de la ciudad de Buenos Aires, Argentina." *Journal of Latin American and Caribbean Anthropology* 18, no. 2 (2013): 231–50.

Perlman, Janice E. *The Myth of Marginality: Urban Poverty and Politics in Rio de Janeiro.* Berkeley: University of California Press, 1976.

Perry, Keisha-Khan Y., and Joanne Rappaport. "Making a Case for Collaborative Research with Black and Indigenous Social Movements in Latin America." In *Otros Saberes: Collaborative Research on Indigenous and Afro-Descendant Cultural Politics*, ed. Charles R. Hale and Lynn Stephen, 30–48. Santa Fe, NM: School of Advanced Research Press, 2013.

Phillips, Nicholas. "In Honduras, Going from Door to Door to Prosecutors." *New York Times*, March 4, 2014. http://www.nytimes.com/2014/03/04/world/americas/in-honduras-going -from-door-to-door-to-prosecutors.html?_r=0, accessed October 11, 2014.

Poole, Deborah. *Unruly Order: Violence, Power, and Cultural Identity in the High Provinces of Southern Peru* (Boulder, CO: Westview, 1994).

Population Reference Bureau. "Human Population: Urbanization," n.d. http://www .prb.org/Educators/TeachersGuides/HumanPopulation/Urbanization.aspx, accessed May 6, 2013.

Portes, Alejandro, and William Haller. "The Informal Economy." In *The Handbook of Economic Sociology*, 2d ed., ed. Neil J. Smelser and Richard Swedberg, 403–27. Princeton, NJ: Princeton University Press, 2005.

Portes, Alejandro, and Bryan R. Roberts. "The Free-Market City: Latin American Urbanization in the Years of the Neoliberal Experiment." *Studies in Comparative International Development* 40, no. 1 (2005): 43–82.

Postero, Nancy. "Morales's MAS Government: Building Indigenous Popular Hegemony in Bolivia." *Latin American Perspectives* 37, no. 3 (2010): 18–34.

———. *Now We Are Citizens: Indigenous Politics in Postmulticultural Bolivia*. Stanford, CA: Stanford University Press, 2006.

Quijano, Anibal. "Coloniality of Power, Eurocentrism, and Latin America." *Nepantla: Views from the South* 1, no. 3 (2000): 533–80.

Rakowski, Cathy A., ed. *Contrapunto: The Informal Sector Debate in Latin America*. Albany: State University of New York Press, 1994.

Rapp, Rayna. "Family and Class in Contemporary America: Notes toward an Understanding of Ideology." *Science and Society* 42, no. 3 (1978): 278–300.

Reed, John M. "International Brief, Population Trends: Bolivia." Bureau of the Census, U.S. Department of Commerce, 1998. http://www.census.gov/population /international/files/ib-9801.pdf, accessed June 7, 2013.

"Resistencia de los 'dueños' de las aceras." *Opinión*, Cochabamba, Bolivia, July 31, 2011, 9A.

Rivera, Alberto. *La Vivienda en Economías Informales de Cochabamba*. Cochabamba, Bolivia: Centro de Estudios de la Realidad Económica y Social, 1991.

Rivera Cuiscanqui, Silvia. "Ch'ixinakax Utxiwa: A Reflection on the Practices and Discourses of Decolonization." *South Atlantic Quarterly* 111, no. 1 (2012): 95–109.

Roberts, Bryan R. *Cities of Peasants: The Political Economy of Urbanization in the Third World*. London: Edward Arnold, 1978.

Rodgers, Dennis. "The State as a Gang: Conceptualizing the Governmentality of Violence in Contemporary Nicaragua." *Critique of Anthropology* 26, no. 3 (2006): 315–30.

Rodríguez Ostria, Gustavo, and Humberto Solares Serrano. *Maíz, Chicha y Modernidad: Telones y Entretelones del Desarrollo Urbano de Cochabamba (Siglos XIX y XX)*. Santa Cruz de la Sierra, Bolivia: El Pais, 2011.

Roever, Sally. "Street Trade in Latin America: Demographic Trends, Legal Issues and Vending Organizations in Six Cities." In *Street Vendors in the Global Urban Economy*, ed. Sharit Bhowmik, 208–40. London: Routledge, 2010.

Roitman, Janet. "The Ethics of Illegality in the Chad Basin." In *Law and Disorder in the Postcolony*, ed. Jean Comaroff and John L. Comaroff, 247–72. Chicago: University of Chicago Press, 2006.

Rosaldo, Michelle Zimbalist, and Louise Lamphere. *Woman, Culture, and Society*. Stanford, CA: Stanford University Press, 1974.

Roy, Ananya. "Slumdog Cities: Rethinking Subaltern Urbanism." *International Journal of Urban and Regional Research* 35, no. 2 (2011): 223–38.

———. "Urban Informality: Toward an Epistemology of Planning." *Journal of the American Planning Association* 71, no. 2 (2005): 147–58.

———. "Why India Cannot Plan Its Cities: Informality, Insurgence and the Idiom of Urbanization." *Planning Theory* 8, no. 76 (2009): 76–87.

Roy, Ananya, and Nezar AlSayyad, eds. *Urban Informality: Transnational Perspectives from the Middle East, South Asia and Latin America*. Lanham, MD: Lexington, 2004.

Saba V., Farid, and Hugo Salomón M. *Anteproyecto de la Transferencia a Titulo Gratuito del Mercado "La Pampa."* Cochabamba, Bolivia, mimeograph, 2006. Cochabamba, Bolivia.

Saignes, Thierry. "Indian Migration and Social Change in Seventeenth-Century Charcas." In *Ethnicity, Markets, and Migration in the Andes: At the Crossroads of History and Anthropology*, ed. Brooke Larson and Olivia Harris with Enrique Tandeter, 167–95. Durham, NC: Duke University Press, 1995.

Salamanca, Octavio. *El Socialismo en Bolivia—Los Indios de la Altiplanicie Boliviana*. Cochabamba, Bolivia: Imprenta Roja, 1931.

Salman, Ton. "Customary Law in Search for Balance: Bolivia's Quest for a New Concept of 'Rights' and the Construction of Ethnicity." *Canadian Journal of Latin American and Caribbean Studies* 36, no. 72 (2011): 111–43.

Sassen, Saskia. "La Salada, the Largest Informal Market in South America." *Forbes*, March 28, 2011. http://www.forbes.com/sites/megacities/2011/03/28/la-salada-the-largest-informal-market-in-south-america/, accessed June 21, 2013.

———. "Whose City Is It? Globalization and the Formation of New Claims." *Public Culture* 8 (1996): 205–23.

Scarborough, Isabel M. "Two Generations of Bolivian Female Vendors." *Ethnology* 49, no. 2 (2010): 87–104.

Scheper-Hughes, Nancy. "The Primacy of the Ethical: Propositions for a Militant Anthropology." *Current Anthropology* 36, no. 3 (1995): 409–40.

Schneider, Friedrich. "Size and Measurement of the Informal Economy in 110 Countries around the World." Paper presented at Australian National Tax Centre workshop, Australian National University, Canberra, July 17, 2002.

Schultz, Jim. "Bolivians Win Anti-Privatization Battle." NACLA *Report on the Americas* 33, no. 6 (2000): 44–46.

Scott, James C. *Seeing like a State: How Certain Schemes to Improve the Human Condition Have Failed*. New Haven, CT: Yale University Press, 1998.

Seligmann, Linda J. "Between Worlds of Exchange: Ethnicity among Peruvian Market Women." *Cultural Anthropology* 8, no. 2 (1993): 187–213.

---. "Contested Spaces: Street Vendors in the Andean Metropole of Cusco, Peru." In *Anthropology in the City: Methodology and Theory*, ed. Italo Pardo and Giuliana B. Prato, 117–34. Surrey, U.K.: Ashgate, 2012.

---. "Market Places, Social Spaces in Cuzco, Peru." *Urban Anthropology* 29, no. 1 (2000): 1–68.

---. *Peruvian Street Lives: Culture, Power, and Economy among Market Women of Cuzco*. Urbana: University of Illinois Press, 2004.

---. "The Politics of Urban Space among Street Vendors of Cusco, Peru." In *Street Economies in the Urban Global South*, ed. Karen Tranberg Hansen, Walter Little, and B. Lynne Milgram 115–36. Santa Fe, NM: School of American Research Press, 2013.

---. "To Be in Between: The Cholas as Market Women." *Comparative Studies in Society and History* 31 (1989): 694–721.

Simone, AbdouMaliq. *City Life from Jakarta to Dakar: Movement at the Crossroads*. New York: Routledge, 2010.

Smart, Alan. "Unruly Places: Urban Governance and the Persistence of Illegality in Hong Kong's Urban Squatter Areas." *American Anthropologist* 103, no. 1 (2001): 30–44.

Smith, Linda Tuhiwai. *Decolonizing Methodologies: Research and Indigenous Peoples*. London: Zed, 1999.

Solares Serrano, Humberto. *Historia, Espacio, y Sociedad: Cochabamba 1550–1950: Formación, Crisis, y Desarrollo de su Proceso Urbano*. Cochabamba, Bolivia: Editorial Serrano, 1990.

---. *La Larga Marcha de los Cochabambinos: De la Villa de Oropesa a la Metropolitización*. Cochabamba, Bolivia: Editorial Grafisol, 2011.

Speed, Shannon. "At the Crossroads of Human Rights and Anthropology: Toward a Critically Engaged Activist Research." *American Anthropologist* 108, no. 1 (2006): 66–76.

---. "Forged in Dialogue: Towards a Critically Engaged Activist Research." In *Engaging Contradictions: Activist Scholarship in Interdisciplinary Perspective*, ed. Charles R. Hale, 213–36. Berkeley: University of California Press, 2008.

Steel, Griet. "Whose Paradise? Itinerant Street Vendors' Individual and Collective Practices of Political Agency in the Tourist Streets of Cusco, Peru." *International Journal of Urban and Regional Research* 36, no. 5 (2012): 1007–21.

Stephen, Lynn. *Women and Social Movements in Latin America: Power from Below*. Austin: University of Texas Press, 1997.

---. *Zapotec Women: Gender, Class and Ethnicity in Globalized Oaxaca*. Austin: University of Texas Press, 1991.

Stephenson, Marcia. *Gender and Modernity in Andean Bolivia*. Austin: University of Texas Press, 1999.

Ströbele-Gregor, Juliana. "Ley de Participación Popular y movimiento popular en Bolivia." In *Sociedad Civil en América Latina: Representación de intereses y gobernabilidad*, ed. Peter Hengstenberg, Karl Kohut, and Günther Maihold, 133–46. Caracas: Nueva Sociedad, 1999.

Tassi, Nico. "The Postulate of Abundance: Cholo Market and Religion in La Paz Bolivia." *Social Anthropology/Anthropologie Sociale* 18, no. 2 (2010): 191–209.

Taussig, Michael. *Defacement: Public Secrecy and the Labor of the Negative.* Stanford, CA: Stanford University Press, 1999.

Thomson, Janice E. "State Sovereignty in International Relations: Bridging the Gap between Theory and Empirical Research." *International Studies Quarterly* 39, no. 2 (1995): 213–33.

Tilly, Charles. "War Making and State Making as Organized Crime" (1985). In *Violence: A Reader,* ed. Catherine Besteman, 35–60. New York: Palgrave, 2002.

Toranzo Roca, Carlos F. "Informal and Illicit Economies and the Role of Narcotrafficking." In *Coca, Cocaine, and the Bolivian Reality,* ed. Madeline Barbara Leóns and Harry Sanabria, 195–210. Albany: State University of New York Press, 1997.

Trouillot, Michel-Rolph. "The Anthropology of the State in the Age of Globalization: Close Encounters of the Deceptive Kind." *Current Anthropology* 42, no. 1 (2001): 125–38.

Turner, Sarah, and Laura Schoenberger. "Street Vendor Livelihoods and Everyday Politics in Hanoi, Vietnam: The Seeds of a Diverse Economy?" *Urban Studies* 49, no. 5 (2012): 1027–44.

Ungar, Mark. 2011. *Policing Democracy: Overcoming Obstacles to Citizen Security in Latin America.* Baltimore: Johns Hopkins University Press.

United Nations Development Program. *Citizen Security with a Human Face: Evidence and Proposals for Latin America.* Regional Human Development Report 2013–14. New York: United Nations Development Program, 2013.

United Nations Human Settlements Program. *State of the World's Cities, 2010/2011: Bridging the Urban Divide.* Nairobi: United Nations Human Settlements Program, 2008.

Urquidi Zambrana, Jorge. *La Urbanización de la Ciudad de Cochabamba: Sintesis del Estudio, Documentos y Antecedentes.* Cochabamba, Bolivia: Editorial Universitaria, 1967.

Urquidi, José Macedonio. *El Origin de la "Noble Villa de Oropesa" (Cochabamba).* Cochabamba, Bolivia: Imprenta Universitaria, Sección Comercial, 1949.

U.S. Agency for International Development. FY 2005 *Congressional Budget Justification—Bolivia.* Washington, DC: U.S. Agency for International Development, 2004. http://www.usaid.gov/policy/budget/cbj2005/lac/bo.html, accessed February 15, 2014.

U.S. Department of Labor, Bureau of International Labor Affairs, 2012 *Findings on the Worst Forms of Child Labor: Bolivia* (Washington, DC: U.S. Department of Labor, 2012).

van Dijck, Pitou. "The Bolivian Experiment: Structural Adjustment and Policy Alleviation." *Cuadernos de* CEDLA no. 3. La Paz: Centro de Estudios para el Desarrollo Laboral y Agrario, 1999.

Van Vleet, Krista E. "The Intimacies of Power: Rethinking Violence and Affinity in the Bolivian Andes." *American Ethnologist* 29, no. 3 (2002): 567–601.

Varley, Ann. "Postcolonialising Informality?" *Environment and Planning D: Society and Space* 31, no. 1 (2013): 4–22.

Viezzer, Moema. "*Si Me Permiten Hablar*": *Testimonio de Domitila, una Mujer de las Minas de Bolivia.* Mexico City: Siglo Veintiuno Editores, 1978.

Vilas, Carlos. "The Decline of the Steady Job in Latin America." NACLA Report on the Americas 32, no. 4 (1999): 15–20.

Vincent, Susan. "Gender Ideologies and the Informal Economy: Reproduction and the 'Grapes of Wrath' Effect in Mata Chico, Peru." Latin American Perspectives 25, no. 2 (1998): 120–39.

Webber, Jeffrey. From Rebellion to Reform in Bolivia: Class Struggle, Indigenous Liberation, and the Politics of Evo Morales. Chicago: Haymarket Books, 2011.

Weismantel, Mary. Cholas and Pishtacos: Stories of Sex and Race in the Andes. Chicago: University of Chicago Press, 2001.

World Bank. "Republic of Bolivia Policies for Increasing Firms' Formality and Productivity." In Poverty Reduction and Economic Management, Bolivia, Ecuador, Peru and Venezuela Country Management Unit, Latin America and the Caribbean Region, World Bank report no. 40057-BO, February 29, 2008. World Bank, Washington, DC.

———. World Development Report 2009: Reshaping Economic Geography. Washington, DC: World Bank, 2009.

Yiftachel, Oren. "Theoretical Notes on 'Gray Cities': The Coming of Urban Apartheid?" Planning Theory 8, no. 1 (2009): 88–100.

Zilberg, Elana. Space of Detention: The Making of a Transnational Gang Crisis between Los Angeles and San Salvador. Durham, NC: Duke University Press, 2011.

# Index

Note: Page numbers in *italics* indicate figures and maps.

ambulantes (continued)
associated with, 78–79; children managed by, 201–5, 203, 205; comisarios'
treatment of, 177, 180–81, 231;
competition among, 189; description
of, 21–22, 67; exclusionary system
deployed against, 237–39; exploitability of, 176–81; fijos' expansion
into territory of, 171–74, 178–79,
179; flexibility of, 135–36, 225–26;
historical records on, 84–85; increased number of, 167; informality
and insecurity's impact on, x, 55–56,
77, 105, 107, 246–51; international
service learning students placed with,
252–53, 254, 255; interstitial spaces
of, 4; interviews of people from, 134;
irregular treatment of, 7–8; march of,
119, 137, 222–25; market day sales
of, 18–19, 19; media's view of, 113,
115; men as, 182, 185–89; official fees
not collected from, 175–76; outside
municipal offices, 74, 76–77; peasant
farmers as, 109–10; photographs, 5,
19, 40, 112, 165, 184, 188; private
security paid by, 152–53; proposed
article on, published, 56, 119–20,
136–38; right to sell in public space,
212–13; semipermanent stalls of, 69;
state's regulation of, 77–79; supple-
mental income for, 189; survival
strategies of, 4–5, 40, 78; underlying
structure of selling, 126–28; unofficial
payments of, 176–78, 180–81; upward
mobility limited for, 142; voices of,
12–14; women's opportunities as,
142–43, 144, 145. See also ambulantes-
fijos conflict; El Paso federation; Silvio
Mamani
ambulantes-fijos conflict: access to space
and clientele in, 167–68, 172–74, 181;
attitudes and animosity in, 22; blame
for fire in, 2, 4–6, 22; debt and credi-

tors in, 169–71; different interests
in, 54–57; fijos' expansion into street
sales and, 171–74, 178–79, 179; privatization attempts and, 159; racial and
cultural differences in, 168–69
amplification system: never installed,
254; planned public presentation,
232–34; proposal for, 121, 220–21;
public dedication of, 243–44
Ana (ambulante), 202, 205
Andrés (fijo), 149, 182, 218, 219
Angela (ambulante), 119, 225–26
Anjaria, Jonathan Shapiro, 249–50,
270n6
Antezana, "Nacho" Ignacio (pseud.).
See "Nacho" Ignacio Antezana
anthropology. See cultural anthropology;
writing, anthropological
Arturo (ambulante): departure from El
Paso federation, 227; on exclusionary
policies, 238–39; on private security,
153; rights rhetoric of, 213; working
as ambulante, 134, 182, 185, 187–89
authority: amplification loudspeaker
locations and, 232–33; insecurity
created by new forms of, 8–9, 150–53;
people and practices underlying, 75.
See also sovereignty
autoconstruction, 20
Aymara people's beliefs, 70

Babb, Florence, 14
Banzer Suarez, Hugo, 36, 111–12,
284n2
barbecue grills, 64
Barrientos Ortuño, René, 70
Barrio Chino: fear of openly discussing,
192–93; origins of, 110–11; stolen
goods sold in, 29, 72–73, 111, 190–92
barrios: anti–domestic violence activities in, 281n9; crime and insecurity
studied in, 30, 262n3; expansion of,
113, 115; "irregular" settlement of,

Cancha (Cochabamba's outdoor market) (*continued*)

national and international context of, 33–41; night in, 91, 152; opportunities in, 8–9, 247–48; ownership of, 23, 125–26, 157–59; photograph, *vi*; private security hired by, 94, 148–53; privatization of public restrooms in, 158; purification ritual in, 95, 96; regulations and organized disorder of, 7–8, 122–23; sales mostly untracked in, 22–24; shoppers' mental map of, 122–23; size and energy of, 102–3; as space vs. place, 88–90, 274nn2, 4; state as partially but not helpfully present in, 6; state's toleration of informality and attempt to maintain control, 81–82; syndicates' control of, 108–9; system of inclusion and exclusion in, 237–39; unmappability considered, 88–90, 102–3, 275n2; wealth concealed in, 26; worries about children influenced by, 205–6. See also *ambulantes*; *fijos*; informal economy; La Pampa; *puestos*

*canchas* (spaces), 50. See also public space; space

Candela (ambulante), 178–79, 202

Candy (fijo), 182

Carlos (fijo), 219

Carmen (fijo), 132

Carnaval: celebrations described, 27, 95, 97, 100; plans to introduce author in, 17, 42–44; q'owa (purification ritual) of, 90, 95, 96; scholarship on, 275n1; special merchandise and foods for, 90, 94, 98

Castells, Manuel, 20

Catholic Church, 266n13. *See also* Carnaval; festivities; San Antonio church

*caudillo*: definition, 259n2; Rafo as exemplar of, 16, 228

Celia (ambulante), 202–3

Center for the Study of Security and Democracy (CISD), 137

Central Obrera Boliviana (Bolivian Workers Central), 123–24

Chaco War (1932–35), 85

Chalfin, Brenda, 282n11

"Chaly" Terceros, Gonzalo, 157, 158, 159–60, 224, 289n2

chaos and disorder: the Cancha viewed as, 5–6, 102–3, 122; as contestation in colonial period, 52; delinquency linked to, 104–5; exclusionary politics deployed against perceived, 237–39; origins of, 7–8; La Pampa viewed as, 230–32, 231; rhetoric on, 112–13, 115; selective law enforcement and, 78–79; state's absence blamed for, 6. *See also* insecurity; security

charisma, 259n2, 259n3

Chatterjee, Partha, 248

*chicha* (yellow corn beer): availability of, 29, 82; Carnaval traditions and, 95, 97, 98; differences in, 99; hospitality and, 96, 243; production of, 109; taxation of, 84

*chicherías* (popular bars): El Paso federation meeting in, 118; moved from city center, 50–51; rural corn producers linked to, 109; urban development funded by taxes on, 84

children: abandoned by parents, 216; ambulantes' challenges in caring for, 201–3, 203; child care needed for, 254; in domestic space of puesto fijos, 9, 200–201; left at home in daytime, 203–4; mealtimes for, 204–5, 205; parental concerns about moral influence of market on, 205–6; as polillas (street children), 105, 106, 196, 216, 218, 222; as sellers, 204, 287n11. *See also* delinquents and delinquency; schools and education cholas (*cholitas*), 26, 66, 72, 99, 222–23, 224–25, 267n4

Christians, evangelical, 97–98

Christmas vendors (*comerciantes de ferias navideñas*), 90–91

CISD (Center for the Study of Security and Democracy), 137

"citizen security," 103–5, 107. *See also* insecurity; security

city: charisma of, 259n3; defining boundaries of, 265n2; hierarchical zones of, 83–84; nature and identity contested, 48–49; "other commerce" excluded from, 84–85; "right" to, 207, 287–88n1; two ways of thinking about, 51–53; urban planning's role in, 235–36. *See also* informal city/marginal neighborhoods; urbanization

*City at Its Limits, The* (Gandolfo), 14

City Council. *See* Consejo Municipal

Clark, Gracia, 279n1

class divisions: in ambulantes-fijos conflict, 168–69; city envisioned by lower classes, 52–53; discrimination against working urban indigenous women, 142; in exclusionary politics, 238; historical context of, 80; mixing at early-morning market, 91, 93; persistent in modernist planning, 82–84; segregation by, 81. *See also* race and racial classifications; urban poor

clientelism, 109, 129, 157, 283n4

clothing and adornments: of ambulantes at march, 223; aprons and head coverings for fijos, 231; of cholas (*cholitas*), 267n4; of private security guards, 151; running inhibited by traditional, 25–26; sindicatos' logo on, 127; wealth displayed in, 142

clothing industry, 117, 187–88

coca production and use, 36, 39, 263n9, 264n20

Cochabamba (city; earlier called Villa de Oropesa): as economic and commercial center, 46–51, 265–66n3; as "garden city," 83, 83; historic downtown of, 46; as informal city, 108–16; maps, 35, 49; master plans, 85–86; modernist transformation of, 82–84; nature and identity contested, 48–49; news collection in, 43–44; official archive missing, 235–37; "other commerce" excluded from, 84–85; population, 46, 82, 265n2; taboos in, 267n19; teenager's exploration of, 29–30; two ways of thinking about, 51–53; water balloon season in, 95–96, 97, 98, 99–100. *See also* Alcaldía; Cancha; *comerciantes*; *comisarios*; economies; everyday life; laws, ordinances, and rules; markets; municipal government; Plaza Principal; privatization; transportation

Cochabamba (department): libraries of, 235, 289n1; map, 35

Colegio de Arquitectos, 235

colonial period: agricultural land in, 108; hierarchies in, maintained in modernity, 82–84; informal housing in, 80; mineral extraction under, 46–47; non-European peoples marginalized in, 81; standard social-science research reflective of, 59; urban aesthetic and commerce under, 47–52

*comerciantes*: activist (engaged), collaborative research on, x–xi, 12, 26, 31–32, 58, 60–62, 252–56; albertos as, 72, 190–91, 192; changing spaces of, 89–91; child care and hours spent selling, 200–205, 203; children as, 204, 287n11; competition among, 5, 159, 167–68, 169, 189; debt and credit issues, 169–71, 195, 285n6; decolonizing stance in approach to, 58, 62–63, 268nn11–12; evangelical Christians as, 97–98, 100, 155; gender

comerciantes (continued)
differences in education, 186–87; increased number of men as, 12–13, 82, 147, 182, 185–89; informality and insecurity's effects on, 104–7, 246–51; mayoristas and, 91, 109, 110, 171, 172; moral concerns about life in market, 205–6; private security concerns of, 149–50; quiet encroachment into public space, 248–49, 250–51; resistance to privatization of market, 154, 155–59, 207–9; types of criminals named by, 196; unofficial relations with state, 75, 270n6; whining or wheedling of, 68, 139–40; women as majority of, 82, 141, 182–83, 201, 223–25; women's opportunities and challenges as, 110, 140–43, 144, 145. See also ambulantes; ambulantes-fijos conflict; fijos; markets; puestos

comercio hormiga (small-scale commerce), 110

comisarios (Municipal Police): absence of, 94, 216; ambulantes' insults of, 224–25; ambulantes' payments to, 176–78, 180–81; Barrio Chino's protection and, 191, 193; cooperation with syndicates for market control, 109; distrust of, 61, 103, 219; function of, 6, 50, 77; insecurity due to, 105, 216–17; interviews of, 134; limitations of, 230–32; market goods decommissioned and confiscated by, 177, 180–81, 230–31; photograph, 51; policing of space allocations by, 172–73; privatization of (see Men in Black); sentaje collected by, 175; sovereignty enacted by, 247. See also policing

Committee in Defense of the La Pampa Market, 156–57

community justice, 149, 282n9

Compañia Minera del Sur S. A. (COMSUR), 161–63, 284n2

con artists (cuentistas), 106, 197

Confederación Sindical de Trabajadores Gremiales, Artesanos, Comerciantes Minoristas y Vivanderos de Bolivia (United Federation of Guildsmen, Artisans, Small Merchants, and Grocers of Bolivia), 124

Confederación Sindical Única de Trabajadores Campesinos de Bolivia (United Federation of Peasant Workers of Bolivia), 123–24

conflict. See ambulantes-fijos conflict

Consejo Municipal (City Council): El Paso federation's meeting with, 241; function of, 257n1; privatization attempt of, 157–58

convenios (agreements): with market vendors, 120–21, 134–35; with street vendors, 120, 134–35

Coronel Rivas, Humberto, 111

Coronilla heroines, 67

Cortez, Emilio, 211

criminals and crime: Barrio Chino linked to, 29, 72–73, 111, 190–91; "citizen security" and, 103–5, 107; in daily rhythm of markets, 94; homicide rates and victims, 103; informal workers linked to, 79; lynching and community justice in, 149, 282n9; at night in the Cancha, 152; parental concerns about, 203–4; pickpockets (lanzeros), 32, 67–68, 73, 106, 197; piracy as, 23–24, 120–21; private security's confrontations with, 196–98; robberies per day in the Cancha, 150; studied in barrios, 30–31, 262n3; thieves, 25–26, 196–97; underworld (el hampa) of, 29, 31, 193, 196–97. See also coca production and use; delinquents and delinquency; insecurity; justice system; violence

Cross, John, 270n6, 271n16

cuentistas (con artists), 106, 197

cultural anthropology: activist (engaged), collaborative fieldwork in, x–xi, 12, 26, 31–32, 58, 60–62, 252–56; anthropologists as professional strangers, 14; biases in, 63; complications and changes in, 228–34; concrete results vs. book writing in, 17; decolonizing stance in, 58, 62–63, 268nn11–12; denunciation of, 267n2; interviews, 132–35; objectivity in, 60, 268nn5, 7–8; official recognition of local remains and, 67; potential conflicts of interest in, 54–57, 131; reality, truth, and writing in, 10–14

Dario (fijo), 152, 216–17
David (fijo), 218–19
Davis, Diane E., 81, 273n22
Decentralized Municipal Supply Corporation "La Pampa," 156
de Certeau, Michel, 88, 89–90, 274n2
delinquents and delinquency (*delincuencia*): activities, 106–7, 150; in Barrio Chino, 190–92; discussed in seminar, 216–21; disorder and chaos viewed as fostering, 104–5; private security's confrontations with, 150–53, 196–98
Deloria, Vine, Jr., 267n2
Dent, Alexander, 23–24
deregulation. See urban disregulation areas
de Soto, Hernando, 20, 248, 260n10, 292n18
Día de los Difuntos (Day of the Dead), 90
disorder. See chaos and disorder
disregulation. See urban disregulation areas
domestic violence, 142–43, 145, 202, 281n9
drinks: api, 64; *batido*, 164, 165; beer, 97, 98, 99, 164, 243; carrot juice, 139–40; Coca-Cola, 99, 134; *gelatina de pata*

(boiled hoof), 93; *jugo de alfalfa* (alfalfa juice), 93; *jugo de quinoa* (quinoa juice), 127, 188–89; *linaza* (flax seed), 93; Maltín, 164, 165, 284n5; *mate de diente de léon* (lion's tooth tea), 93; orange juice, 25, 126, 133–34, 136, 143, 179–80, 202, 222; *refrescos* (cold drinks), 183, 245; *yerba mate*, 27, 64. See also *chicha*; foods and accompaniments

Eastern philosophies (Taoism, Zen Buddhism, New Age spirituality), 26, 27, 27, 28, 30, 155
economies: circulation in, 271n15; Cochabamba's role in, 46–51, 265–66n3; credit's role in, 169–71, 195, 285n6; diverse type of, 270n11; globalized neoliberal, 4–5, 135–36. See also formal economy; informal economy; neoliberalism
El Alto: quinoa juice sold in, 188; street vendors in, 250, 279n6; vendor's purchases for selling in, 139–40
El Paso federation of street vendors (La Federación Integral de Comerciantes Minoristas "El Paso"): author's goodbyes and book presented to, 242–43; convenio with, 120, 135, 136; divisions appearing in, 225–27, 253–54; goals and hopes for market, xi–xii, 54–56, 166, 181, 189, 225–27, 241–42; lack of political clout, 180; leadership of, ix, 185–86, 187, 189; march of, 119, 137, 222–25, 250; march's aftermath, 241–42; meetings of, 117–20, 226, 254; members of, 123, 127, 178–79; politics of members vs. leaders of, 249–50; proposed article on, published, 56, 119–20, 136–38; state of emergency declared by, 138; state's recognition of, 129. See also *ambulantes*; Silvio Mamani

employment: flexibilization of labor in, 38; job "casualization" in, 21; in rural areas, 35–36; seasonal strategies of, 38–39, 109–10, 141; urban migration for, 39–40; workers as legitimate vs. illegitimate, 271n14. *See also* agricultural produce; *comerciantes*; gender roles in market; informal/illegal workers; migrants and migration; mining industry

Eric (researcher): at ambulantes' march, 222, 224; as field researcher, 30, 42, 44; introduced to market vendors, 96–100; seminar on security/insecurity and, 120–21, 214

Esperanza (ambulante), 143

ethnographic research. *See* cultural anthropology

Eulalia (ambulante), 183

everyday life: child care and hours spent selling, 200–205, 203; economic realities of, 34; hospitality rules in, 44, 96, 243; insecurity and fear of crime in, 55–56, 103–7, 276n11; market rhythm in, 18–19, 91, 92, 93–94; poverty and struggles in, 8–9; quiet encroachment into public space in, 248–49, 250–51; quiet encroachment of people into public space, 248–49, 250–51; typical friendly greeting, 42, 43, 44, 56, 96, 120, 232. *See also* clothing and adornments; delinquents and delinquency; drinks; foods and accompaniments

familial issues: child care and hours spent selling, 200–205, 203; husband and wife as partners in selling, 143, 145; long-term links to markets, 111, 183; moral concerns about life in market, 205–6. *See also* children; domestic violence; gender roles in market; kin network

Fausto (ambulante), 136, 239

*favelas* as label, 81

Favero, Paolo, 275n4

Federación de Comerciantes de La Pampa (FCP): author's goodbyes and book for, 242, 243–44, 254; competition within, 169; convenio with, 120–21, 134–35; divisions appearing in, 225, 227–28, 244–45, 253–54; female vendors in, 159–60; leadership of, 15–16, 185–86; marches of, 250; origins of, 157, 185. *See also* "Rafo" Rafael Punto; seminar on insecurity

La Federación Integral de Comerciantes Minoristas "El Paso." *See* El Paso federation

Federation of Miners, 162

federations: benefits of, 180; competition among, 159, 169; leadership roles in, 129–30; military regimes' attacks on, 111–12; political nature of, 128–30; puesto sales and, 210–11; sindicatos in relation to, 124, 164, 166; specific market areas controlled by, 123–26; women's founding of, 185. *See also ambulantes-fijos* conflict; *sindicatos; and specific federations*

fees. *See* taxes and license fees

Felipe (fijo), 217–18

Felix (fijo), 220

*ferias. See* markets

Ferrufino, Rodolfo, 159–60, 289n2

festivities: adapting goods to, 136; Mother's Day, 233–34; sindicatos' role in, 124; special foods and goods for, 90–91, 94; Todos Santos (All Saints Day), 90. *See also* Carnaval

Fidel Aranibar market: description of, 68, 69–70; La Pampa compared with, 72; privatization of, 157

*fijos (comerciantes de puesto fijo* [market vendors]): ambulantes' payments to, 176–77; ancianita's conflict with, 87–88; aprons and head coverings required for, 231; changing spaces of, 87–88, 89–91; character of, 167–71; comedores (eateries) of, 204–5, 205, 207–9; contraband sold by, 190–92; diversification and expansion of, 171–74, 178–79, 179; familial stability linked to, 145; fire and response of, 1–2, 3, 4, 5–6; informal activities of, 23–24; informality and insecurity's effects on, 106–7, 246–51; infrastructure developed by, 2, 159–60; insurance for, 124–25; interviews of, 134; legal by virtue of official fees and recognition, 22, 175–76; licensing and site-use fees for, 22, 50, 53, 261n20; on market ownership, 111; official register of, 119; photographs, 22, 156, 170, 179, 193; private security hired by, 151–52; privatization of market resisted by, 154, 155–59, 207–9; protest of state neglect of security, 150; voices of, 12–14; wealth of, 78. See also *ambulantes-fijos* conflict; amplification system; Federación de Comerciantes de La Pampa; *puestos*; "Rafo" Rafael Punto; seminar on insecurity; taxes and license fees

fire: assumptions about state in context of, 6–8; blame for, 2, 4–6, 22; congestion's role in, 4, 76–77, 174, 211; December 2001 police conflict and, 150; description of, 1–2, 3; recounted in book for FCP, 243–44

Fischer, Brodwyn, 81

Florentino (fijo), 171, 182

foods and accompaniments: bananas, 16, 124, 154; *buñuelos* (fried dough), 66; for Carnaval and other festivities, 90–91, 94; *chicharrón* (fried chicken or pork), 48, 266n9; classic dishes served by comedores, 208, 288n2; comedores (eateries) for, 204–5, 205, 207–9; ketchup, 146; *maraquetas* (bread), 66;

market purchases for, 122–23; *mote* (corn on the cob), 48, 266n9; night sales of, 94; *puchero* (stew), 48, 98, 266n9; *quesillo* (cheese), 48, 266n9; *salteñas*, 44; *sopa y segundo* (soup and second course), 207–8; *thantha wawas* (sugary bread shaped like children), 90. *See also* drinks

formal economy: aguinaldo (holiday bonus) for workers in, 91, 274n7; blurred lines between informal and, 21–24, 74, 80, 178; exclusion from, 176–81; legality not guaranteed in, 75; order of, overstated, 7–8. See also *fijos*; taxes and license fees

Foucault, Michel, 282n11, 289n5

Francisca (ambulante), 133

Franklin (fijo), 219

Fujimori, Alberto, 260n10

Gandolfo, Daniella, 14, 21, 249, 261n23, 267n19

Geertz, Clifford, 271n16

gender roles in market: bias of sindicatos, 124; collaborators in understanding, 97; contradictory ideologies of, 183, 185; demand for ambulantes' market and, 225–27; discrimination against indigenous women, 142; female vendor's toughness and, 146–47; gender ratio changing, 182; increased number of male vendors, 12–13, 82, 147, 182, 185–89; men as comerciantes, 182–83, 184, 185–89; postcolonial categories and, 168; structural adjustment's impact on, 281n17; women as majority of comerciantes, 82, 141, 182–83, 201, 223–25; women as typical shoppers, 122–23; women's opportunities and challenges in, 110, 140–43, 144, 145; women's responsibility for children, 200–205, 203, 205

Georg (researcher), 30

urban population of, 35, 36, 47–49, 84. See also *comerciantes*; drinks; foods and accompaniments; race and racial classifications

Indonesia, economic change in, 271n16

informal city/marginal neighborhoods: absence of security in, 104–5; "citizen security" in, 103–5, 107; growth of, 85–86; housing market of, 20, 80; parental concerns about high-crime, 203–4; practices tolerated in, 81–82; "red zones" in, 258n9; segregation of, 81, 104–5, 273n22. See also barrios; urban disregulation areas

informal economy: advantages of, 258n13; blurred lines between formal and, 21–24, 74, 80, 178; Bolivia as world leader in, 33–34, 40–41; concept, x, 19–20; debates about meaning, 20–21; debunking myths of, 136; dual sectors model of, 20, 23–24, 33, 260n5; expansion of, 113, 114, 115; extent of, 18–19, 33–34; historical context of, 80; law and, 7–9; market's physical structure and, 23; as "other commerce" (el otro comercio), 84; as percentage of GNP, 33–34; political geography and structure underlying, 122–30; scholarship on, 20, 259n2; "self-employment" in, 19–20, 91, 110, 113, 141; state's interests in, x, 7–8, 52–53, 59, 79, 110, 116; use of term, 33; women's opportunities in, 110, 140–43, 144, 145. See also *ambulantes*; informal/illegal workers

informal/illegal workers: activities as survival strategies of, 4–5, 40, 78; alleged motivation of, 20; cautions against homogenization of, 248–50; children as, 204, 287n11; comisarios' view of, 231; economic contributions of, 260–61n15; exclusion of, 237–39; formal and informal jobs held by, 21;

historical context of, 80; as percentage of Latin American population, 21; taxes not collected from, 175–76; unofficial relations with state, 75, 270n6. See also *ambulantes*; *comerciantes*; private security guards

informality: of city management, 236–37; Cochabamba as city of, 108–16; criminalized vs. sanctioned, 75; dual sectors model of, 20, 23–24, 33, 260n5; insecurity linked to, x, 8–9, 13–14, 20, 102–7, 246–51; meanings of, 19–24; media's view of, 113, 115; reciprocity as, 261n17; as resistance, 248–49; as revolution, 249, 292n18; sovereign proliferation in, 148–53; of urban life, 6–9, 75

informal spaces: expansion of, 6–9, 75; potential for opportunity and hope in, 8–9, 247–48; quiet encroachment of people into public, 248–49, 250–51; state's characterization of, 5–6. See also barrios; informal city/marginal neighborhoods; markets; sidewalk and street space

*Injustice in the Streets* (Goldstein and researchers), 242–43

insecurity: approach to studying, 61–63; in barrios, 30–31, 262n3; as Bolivia's biggest problem, 103; the criminal and illegal as sources of, 190–92; difficulty in changing, 255–56; disagreement about solutions to, 227–29; disregulation underlying, 148–53; effects and solutions discussed, 216–21, 238–39; informality linked to, x, 8–9, 13–14, 20, 102–7, 246–51; new forms of authority and expansion of, 8–9, 150–53; planned publicity on, 56, 119–20; of private security guards, 198; privatization attempts as source of, 158–59; proposed meeting to discuss, 43; street vendors' understanding of,

men: as albertos (middlemen for stolen goods), 72, 190–91, 192; increased number as vendors, 12–13, 82, 147, 182–83, 184, 185–89; masculine ideals challenged, 185; product marketed to (Maltín), 284n5; stigma of comerciante work for, 163–64, 182, 183; wives as vendors, 143, 145. *See also comisarios*; gender roles in market

*Men in Black* (film), 194, 196

Men in Black (private security guards): ambulantes' payments to, 152–53; background of employees, 194–95; called via amplification system, 244; daily patrols of, 195–98; as independent sovereigns, 151–52; limited benefits of, 195–96; morning muster of, 195; patrols and function of, 195–99; as seminar participants, 214

*mestizo* people: indigenous peoples compared with, 266n12; as market vendors, 116, 168; sale of chicha to, 84; as shoppers, 49, 51; urban population of, 36, 47, 48, 84. *See also* race and racial classifications

Mexico City: population, 46

migrants and migration: land redistribution's role in, 108; motivation of, 39; origins of, 109–10, 113; post-revolution increase of, 85–86; rational choice model for, 265n25; relegated to peripheral zones, 47; rights rhetoric of, 212–13; seasonal strategies of, 38–39, 109–10, 141; seminar discussion of, 216, 219; urban housing of, 20; wage-earning tactics of, 19–20, 113, 115. *See also comerciantes*; informal/illegal workers

Miguel (fijo), 111–12

mining industry: demise of, 163, 284n4; employment in, 35–36, 187; history of, 46–47; neoliberalism's impact on, 37–38; workers emerging as leaders,

284n3; workers' struggles in (COMSUR mine), 161–63, 284n2

modernity: Cochabamba's transformation in, 82–84; comerciantes viewed as problem in, 115; Geertz on, 271n16; informal/formal persistent in, 80; marginalization in model of, 247–48; master plans tied to, 85–86; "other commerce" excluded from, 84–85; street vendors as drag on envisioned, 78–79. *See also* urban planning

money changers, 26, 67

Montoya, Carlos, 225, 236

Moodie, Ellen, 289n6

"moral disorder," surveilled, 104–5

Morales, Evo: aguinaldo (holiday bonus) increased under, 274n7; clothing industry concerns of, 117; "decolonizing" process under, 268n11; multiculturalist rhetoric of, 168; Rafo's access to, 16; reforms of, 34, 40, 115; socialist rhetoric vs. policies of, 238, 263n7, 283n10

Movement Towards Socialism (MAS), 115, 288n12. *See also* Morales, Evo

municipal government: ambulantes harassed by, 78; ambulantes outside offices of, 74, 76–77; archive absent from, 235–37; attempts to privatize the Cancha, 6, 76, 154, 155–59; attempt to privatize water system, 154; fijos officially recognized by, 22; informality tolerated in the Cancha, 81–82; informal nature of, 75–77, 270n6; infrastructural development by, 83–84; market owned by, 23, 125–26, 157–59; plan to remove ambulantes, 44–45; public space sold by, 76–77, 79; role in market, 6; street vendors regulated by, 77–79; structure of, 257n1; system of inclusion and exclusion in, 237–39. *See also Alcaldía*; Cancha; Consejo

Municipal; Intendencia; the state; taxes and license fees

municipal law. *See* laws, ordinances, and rules

Municipal Police. See *comisarios*

municipal services: attempt to privatize water system, 154; infrastructural development, 83–84; lacking in informal spaces, 6; workers of, 2, 163

Murra, John, 264n18

"Nacho" Ignacio Antezana (pseud.): on ambulantes, 135, 222–25; amplification system and, 121, 232–34, 244; author accompanied by, ix, xi, 1, 31–32, 42–43, 259n1; author's contact and return visit with, 252, 253–55; background and characteristics, ix, 17, 26–31, 155; on Barrio Chino, 191, 193; on the Cancha, 19, 87–88; Cancha visits of, 15–16, 64, 66–73, 91, 92, 93–94; collaborative fieldwork of, 26, 28, 31–32, 62, 242; on conflict of interest, 56–57, 241; El Paso federation meeting attended by, 117–20; herbal knowledge of, 26–27, 29, 66, 87; interviewing by, 131–35; as key character, 12; market vendors introduced to, 96–100, 98; meetings arranged by, 44–45; personal bias of, 63; photograph, 27; response to lawyer's request for money, 100–101; seminar on security/insecurity and, 120–21, 214; thief's encounter with, 25–26

National Police: absent from Cancha, 6, 197–98; Barrio Chino's protection and, 191, 193; distrust of, 103; insecurity due to, 105, 216–17; interviews of, 134; private security and, 150–51, 225, 282n10. *See also* policing

la Navidad (Christmas), 90–91

neighborhoods. *See* informal city/marginal neighborhoods; urban disregulation areas

neoliberalism: archiving function in, 236–37; clothing industry's demise in, 117, 187–88; consequences of, 36–41, 104–5, 141–42, 281n17; dual sectors model in, 20, 23–24, 33, 260n5; income equality in, 34–35, 37–41; job "casualization" in, 21; men's turn to comerciante work in, 183; rational choice approach and, 39, 265n25; structural adjustment in, 37, 154, 264n20, 281n17. *See also* globalized neoliberal economy; privatization

Néstor (ambulante), 134

New Economic Policy (Bolivia), 36–37

New Millennium sindicato, 127, 189

newspapers: archive of, 235; complaints about ambulantes in, 85; on delinquents in the Cancha, 150; on indigenous "invasion" and informality, 113, 115; limited coverage of the Cancha in, 58–59; planned article on street vendors for, 56, 119–20, 136–38; typical news gathering by, 43–44; uninterested in street vendors, 55

nongovernmental organizations, 134, 210, 241, 281n9

Nordstrom, Carolyn, 75, 269n3

Office for the Control of Private Security (National Police), 150–51

oil and gas industry, 38

*Opinión* (newspaper), 137–38, 212

Oruro (department): Carnaval in, 95; carrots from, 139–40; markets privatized in, 155; migrants from, 113

Oswaldo (fijo), 218

Otros Saberes project, 268n13

*Outlawed* (Goldstein), 111, 259n1, 262n3, 268n7, 278n17, 282n9, 287n8, 288n6

Pablo (fijo), 217

Pachamama (goddess of the earth), 99

Pago Único Municipal (PUM). *See* taxes and license fees

Palacio de la Cultura, 235

Pampa Grande, 50

La Pampa market: amplification system for, 121, 220–21, 232–34; attempts to privatize, 156–59, 207–9; author introduced to vendors in, 96–100; candy sellers in, 71, 182; Christmas vendors in, 90–91; comisarios' limitations in, 230–32; congestion in, 172–73; entrances/exits, 217; families' histories tied to, 111, 183; federations' and sindicatos' areas in, 124–25; fire in, 1–2, 3, 4, 5–6; focus on, 15–16; founding, 110–11, 190–91; the illegal integrated into legal, 190–92; infrastructure absent in, 125–26, 166; infrastructure developed by fijos of, 2, 159–60; interviews in, 133; making "order" of "chaos" in, 230–32, 231; map, 65; Nacho's shopping at, 139–40; private security guards of, 97, 151–53, 195–99; reputation of, 72–73; rituals of, 97, 99; security as key problem in, 16–17; seminar on security/insecurity in, 120–21, 214–21; size of, 269n5; visit to, described, 70, 72–73. *See also* amplification system; Barrio Chino; Federación de Comerciantes de La Pampa; *fijos*; gender roles in market

Pampa Ticti, 241

Paraguay, Bolivian war with, 85

Parotani (Cochabamba valley), carrots from, 139–40

*patente. See* taxes and license fees

Paz Estenssoro, Victor, 36–37

Pedro (fijo), 220

pension system, 34, 37

peripheral zones of city, 47–50. *See also* barrios; informal city/marginal neighborhoods; urban disregulation areas

Peru: market women in, 205; popular markets in, 249, 261n23; quinoa juice introduced from, 188; ritual space in, 266n13; taboos in, 267n19

*Peruvian Street Lives* (Seligmann), 14, 147, 205, 274n5, 285n1

pickpockets (*lanzeros*), 32, 67–68, 73, 106, 197

Pillsbury, Joanne, 265–66n3

piracy, 23–24, 120–21

Plan de Todos (investment strategy), 38

Planificación Urbana, 235

Plan Regulador (1961), 236

Plaza Principal: chicherías moved from, 50–51; historical meanings and uses of, 47–49; location of, 49, 67; marches and protests in, 119, 137, 138, 157, 181, 222–25, 250–51; market connected to, 93; meeting in, 42–44; as "modern commercial center," 83; retaken by vendors in recent years, 113, 114; southern zone of markets in relation to, 49–50

Plaza San Antonio, 50, 66

Plaza San Sebastián, 50

Policarpio (ambulante), 133–34

policing: as "all-pervasive, ghostly presence," 6, 258n6; in barrios marginales, 30, 262n3; of Cancha, 6; by fijos, 125; heavyhandedness in, 276n11; irregular enforcement by, 7–8; private security hired by the Cancha, 94, 149–53, 194–99; surveillance function of, 104–5, 172–73. See also *comisarios*; Men in Black; National Police; private security guards

*polillas* (street children), 105, 106, 196, 216, 218, 222. *See also* delinquents and delinquency

Quechua (language) (*continued*)
26, 27, 66; *pampa*, defined, 110; slurs
in, 168; *thanta khatu*, defined, 110;
*yapa* (little bit extra) in, 208
quiet encroachment concept, 248–49,
250–51
Quintana, Juan Carlos, 238

race and racial classifications: in
ambulantes-fijos conflict, 168–69;
central plaza's significance for, 47;
discrimination based on, 142; in exclusionary politics, 238; historical context
of, 80; income inequality linked to,
34–35; in market exchange context,
266n12; in modernist planning,
82–84; segregation by, 81. *See also* class
divisions; indigenous peoples; *mestizo*
people; white people and whiteness
"Rafo" Rafael Punto (pseud.): amplification system and, 232–34, 243,
244–45; author introduced to vendors
by, 96–100; author's concerns about,
56–57; background and characteristics, 15–16, 42–43, 156–57; on Barrio
Chino, 191, 192–93; on book draft,
192; competitor of, 169; convenio
with, 120–21, 135; interest in research
project, 16–17; as key character, 12,
42; leadership of, 94, 227–28; legality
as joke for, 174; market knowledge
of, 154–55; members' criticism of,
244–45, 254; on paying patente, 126;
research interaction as commercial
exchange for, 59, 155; at seminar
on security/insecurity, 220; Spanish
language skills of, 187; speaking with
reporters, 43–44; updates on, 252.
*See also* Federación de Comerciantes
de La Pampa
Ramiro (ambulante), 133
Raúl (fijo), 217, 219
reciprocity as informality, 261n17

"red zones," 258n9. *See also* informal
city/marginal neighborhoods; urban
disregulation areas
Registry of Ambulant Commerce, 86
Remberto (ambulante): on children,
203–4, 206; lack of leadership by, 253;
on new ambulantes, 128; on New Millennium, 127, 189
reporters. *See* newspapers
retirement, 34, 37
Reyes Villa, Manfred, 155–56, 157, 211
Ricardo (fijo): as cook and vendor,
182, 207–8; interview with, 133; on
privatization, 207, 208–9; on Rafo's
leadership, 254
rights: human rights, 105, 106, 210,
288n11; rhetoric of, 212–13, 239; sovereign's right to suspend rule of law,
280n8; to work (sell) in public space,
55, 76–77, 209–13, 223, 288n12. *See
also* human rights
ritual space, colonialized, 266n13
Rivera, Alberto, 145
Rivera Cusicanqui, Silvia, 268–69n14
Rodríguez Ostria, Gustavo, 84
Roitman, Janet, 271n12
Rómulo (fijo), 106, 182, 191
Rosa (fijo): author's friendship with,
12, 183, 245; author's introduction
to, 99; interview with, 133; on Rafo's
leadership, 228, 253–54; on systems
of injustice, 255
Rose Marie (researcher), 30
Roy, Ananya, 7, 75, 250, 270n8, 291n4
rural areas: community justice in, 282n9;
employment in, 35–36; impoverishment in, 108–10; neoliberalism's
impact on, 37–38; organizing producers in, 163; seasonal strategies of
employment in, 38–39, 109–10, 141.
*See also* agricultural produce; migrants
and migration; mining industry
Ruth (researcher), 30, 117–20

Salman, Ton, 283n4

Salvador (ambulante), 134

Samuel (ambulante), 133

San Antonio church, 66–67, 90, 134, 214

San Antonio market, described, 67–68

San Antonio prison, 64

Sanchez de Lozada, Gonzalo, 36–37, 162, 163

schools and education: gender differences in, 186–87; length of sessions, 262n2; neoliberal cuts in, 37

security (*seguridad*): approach to studying, 61–63; as key problem in La Pampa, 16–17; Latin American crisis in, 103–5; meanings of seguridad, 107, 277n25; non-state sovereignty and, 148–49; in paying official fees, 175–76; private security hired by vendors, 9, 94, 149–53, 194–99; realities of absence, 246–51; street vendors' understanding of, 55–56. *See also* chaos and disorder; insecurity; policing; seminar on insecurity

self-employment, 19–20, 91, 110, 113, 141. *See also* informal/illegal workers

Seligmann, Linda J., 14, 147, 205, 261n21, 274n5, 285n1

seminar on insecurity: book incorporating data from, 243–44; group discussions in, 215–16; introductions in, 214–15; outcome of, 221, 232–34; planning for, 120–21; plenary discussions in, 216–20

Senobia (ambulante), 177

*sentaje. See* taxes and license fees

September 11, 2001, terrorist attacks, 103–4

Severa (ambulante), 134

shoppers: fear and insecurity of, 167; response to vendors' arguing, 140; thieves' targeting of, 196–97; tourist vs. local, 122–23; yapa (little bit extra) for, 208

sidewalk and street space: ambulantes' colonizing of, 5; ambulantes' preference for selling in, 225–26; colonial ordinances on, 48–49; congestion of, 4, 76–77, 174, 211; fijo sales in, 171–72; history of commerce in, 46–49; maps, 49, 65, 114; modernist transformation of, 82–84; opportunities of, 8–9, 247–48; ownership of, 207–13, 287–88n1; politics of, 248–51; rights to sell on, 55, 76–77, 209–13, 223, 288n12; street defined as place, 88; thievery in, 25–26. *See also ambulantes*; delinquents and delinquency; Plaza Principal

Silvio Mamani (pseud.): aftermath of meeting with, 15; as ambulante, 163–64, 165, 185; at ambulantes' march, 223, 224, 225; background, 161–63, 253; convenio with, 120, 135, 136; El Paso federation meetings led by, 117, 118–20, 225–27, 226; on exclusion vs. inclusion, 238, 239; hopes of market for ambulantes, xi–xii, 181; illness of, 253–55; interests of, 54–56; interview with, 134; introduction to, 44–45; as key character, 12; leadership of, ix, 163, 164, 166, 178, 187, 242–43; political views of, x–xi; politics of members vs., 249–50; on private security, 153; research interaction as commercial exchange for, 59; response to conflict of interest confession, 240–41; response to published article, 138; rights rhetoric of, 212–13, 239; Spanish language skills of, 187; updates on, 252. *See also* El Paso federation

Simón Bolívar sindicato, 224

*sindicatos* (syndicates): ambulantes, 126–28; at ambulantes' march, 222–24; ambulantes' payments to, 177; batido sellers (6 de Enero [January 6]), 164,

urbanization (*continued*)
marginal neighborhoods; migrants
and migration
urban life: chaos vs. order in, 78–79;
indigenous presence in, 35, 263n8; informalization of, 6–9, 75. *See also* city;
everyday life; informal city/marginal
neighborhoods
urban planning: call for central market,
116; comerciantes viewed as problem
in, 113, 115; master plans in, 85–86;
modernist impulse in, 82–84; "other
commerce" excluded in, 84–85; role
in city, 235–36; segregation key to, 81;
street as place in, 88
urban poor: Carnaval celebrations of, 95;
culture of, 80; daily struggles of, 8–9;
development funded by taxes on, 84,
273n23; limited resources of women,
142–43; segregation of, 81; subaltern
urbanism concept and, 247–48, 250;
wage-earning tactics of, 19–20, 30. *See
also* informal city/marginal neighborhoods; poverty; survival strategies
U.S. Agency of International Development, 276n15

Valle Hermoso, 241
Verkaaik, Oskar, 259n3
Victoria (ambulante), 143
Villarroel, Omar, 230–32
violence: domestic, 142–43, 145,
202, 281n9; in security making,
149; vigilante type of, 149, 282n9.

*See also* criminals and crime; delinquents and delinquency; neoliberalism
Virgin Mary, 97

Waka Playa region, 241
Water War (2000), 154
white people and whiteness: idealized
city space of, 48–52; Plaza Principal
as seat of, 47; racial and cultural ideas
of, 81; wealth and cities controlled by,
34–36. *See also* class divisions; race and
racial classifications
wholesalers (*mayoristas*), 91, 109, 110,
171, 172
women: children managed by, 200–205,
203; Cochabamba defended by, 67;
on ex-husband's treatment, 143;
household duties of, 186; as leaders
in federations and sindicatos, 185;
as majority of shopperss, 122–23; as
majority of vendors, 82, 141, 182–83,
201, 223–25; market's opportunities
and challenges for, 110, 140–43, 144,
145; sales tactics of, 139–40, 146;
selling on street preferred by some,
225–26; as tough market vendors,
146–47. See also *ambulantes*; *fijos*;
gender roles in market
World Bank, 34, 36–37, 39, 265n25
writing, anthropological, 10–14

Yiftachel, Oren, 79

Zapata, Grover, 225